Erikson on Development in Adulthood

Erikson on Development in Adulthood

New Insights from the Unpublished Papers

Carol Hren Hoare

OXFORD

UNIVERSITY PRESS

2002

OXFORD
UNIVERSITY PRESS

Oxford   New York
Athens   Auckland   Bangkok   Bogotá   Buenos Aires   Cape Town
Chennai   Dar es Salaam   Delhi   Florence   Hong Kong   Istanbul   Karachi
Kolkata   Kuala Lumpur   Madrid   Melbourne   Mexico City   Mumbai   Nairobi
Paris   São Paulo   Shanghai   Singapore   Taipei   Tokyo   Toronto   Warsaw

and associated companies in
Berlin   Ibadan

Copyright © 2002 by Oxford University Press

Published by Oxford University Press, Inc.
198 Madison Avenue, New York, New York 10016

Oxford is a registered trademark of Oxford University Press.

Library of Congress Cataloging-in-Publication Data
Hoare, Carol Hren
Erikson on development in adulthood : new insights from the unpublished papers /
Carol Hren Hoare.
p.   cm.
Includes bibliographical references and index.
ISBN 0-19-513175-4
1. Adulthood—Psychological aspects. 2. Erikson, Erik H. (Erik Homburger), 1902–1994
I. Title.
BF724.5 .H59 2002
155.6—dc21   2001021918

9 8 7 6 5 4 3

Printed in the United States of America
on acid-free paper

To Ray

Étude in E

Preface

A preface permits an author to tell readers what it was that he or she had in mind from the very beginning of a book's fledgling design, the methods that led to content selection, and, perhaps, the interest that drove the book to completion.

This book began more than 12 years ago when I first visited Houghton Library at Harvard University. I wished to gain a more complete understanding of Erikson's concepts about the adult and of how he found adults to develop and change when, in fact, they do so. That first visit to the Erikson papers left me feeling surprised, deflated, and perplexed. Fully expecting to find little more than I had read in his 120 publications, I encountered a directory that listed in excess of 2,000 "items," each item containing as many as 36 file folders of material. I recall an immediate sense of the impossibility of finding my way through that great bulk of papers.

About to abandon the project, I came across a transcript of the Conference on the Adult, sponsored by the American Academy of Arts and Sciences, a manuscript proceedings that is replete with Erikson's notes, marginalia, exclamations, circlings, and question marks. His thoughtful reflections were magnetic and rather amazing to me at the time. Here was a great psychoanalyst asking over and over again what it means to be an adult and why it is that so many adults seem to settle for a restricted version of what they might yet become, whereas others always seem to create resilient, fresh renditions of themselves throughout the adult years, in effect refusing to endure halted development and its stagnation. But Erikson baffled me. Why did he question what it means to be an adult when he had first asked that question as early as 1942? Surely, in ways far beyond his adult stage permutations, he had told us what adults are like. But if I had hoped for some instant synthesis of his concepts, I was disappointed. In fact, it is only in sweeping through the great breadth of his published and unpublished thought that key concepts about the adult, what Erikson sometimes called adult "images," emerge. And it is only in placing his stage views aside that those images can come forward.

That began my quest, one that later took me to the Erikson Institute in Chicago, to the Princeton University audiotapes of Erikson's Gauss Seminars in Criticism, and to the Library of Congress Papers of Margaret Mead. I returned time and again to the Erikson Papers at Houghton Library to extend my reading, an inch at a time, through his musings, notes, annotated offprints, and letters. I interviewed persons who had known the theorist and could lend access to him as a person, and I had planned to initiate many more of these fascinating conversations. But after 12 interviews about him, I was ready to move forward. Erikson's thinking, after all, had to come from him. The late Joan Erikson, Erikson's widow, helped to put me back on track with her keen humor: "If you don't stop going around talking to people about Erik," she said, "this book is going to come out of your ears instead of your pen!"

To create boundaries for the study, I eventually confined myself to the rich composition section of the Erikson Papers at Houghton Library, to related letters found there and in the Mead Papers, to early drafts of *Young Man Luther* and *Identity: Youth and Crisis* held by the Erikson Institute, to the Princeton audiotapes of the Erikson seminar series, and to Erikson's published writings. The Papers at Houghton Library were a primary source, for those 268 items house Erikson's candid thoughts and reflections, ideas that would later become rather constricted by the processes of formalized writing, of polishing and editing for publication.

Erikson's six renditions, or "images," of the adult are the nucleus of this book. Through a process that was defined by Glaser and Strauss as "grounded theory,"[1] these renditions emerged from the data in Erikson's papers. This was a process of unearthing, examining, and clustering his various ideas into content categories, an inductive process in which the six forms of adult arose naturalistically from Erikson's writings. Two chapters that had once seemed likely to emerge failed to meet the test of substance and fell by the wayside. Approximately halfway through the project, I had anticipated that there would be one chapter on the gender-polarized adult and another on the sensing adult. Indeed, Erikson wrote about the way we live out our adult years captured by one or another gender, by gender roles, and by historically changing ideas about those roles. He spoke to the way each adult is somehow bifurcated because he or she cannot possibly exist in the other gender's skin, voice, perspective, and biases. In the end, Erikson did not elaborate or conceptualize fully enough to permit a chapter on those thoughts. His nascent ideas had not scaffolded into fully formed concepts.

The chapter on the sensing adult was to have considered Erikson's view of the now-grown person who uses and trusts only a small portion of the sensory apparatus that had once been so essential to childhood perceptions and learning. We are hearing, seeing, tasting, smelling, and touching adults, as well as limbic and rational beings. But Erikson held that we discredit much of the sensory information that comes to us as we continually discover and learn about adult life and its bounds. In the end, Erikson had said too little about these instinctual guidance systems. Here, too, his written and spoken words on the topic were in too early a stage of development. His thoughts are both tentative in nature and slim in substance.

That this project took more than a decade to complete, interrupted, of course, by teaching responsibilities, seems a rather long a period of time for one book. However, it was important to me to understand both Erikson and his thought. To do this, I had to follow Robert Coles's advice and read the thinkers Erikson had read.[2] In the end, immersion in Kierkegaard, Freud, Lao-Tse, Schopenhauer, St. Augustine, Angelus Silesius, Nietzsche, Goethe, Oswald Spengler, and New Testament verses led me to see the philosopher and spiritual thinker in Erikson. It helped me to place Erikson as a conceptualizer whose thoughts did not completely emigrate from Europe to an identity-struggling United States. The entire journey through Erikson's writings and through those of his conceptual ancestors was one of the very best learning experiences of my adult life. I can only hope that the master, Erik Erikson himself, somehow knows this.

Acknowledgments

This book would not have reached completion without the gifts of time and expertise of others. I am indebted to the superior staff of Houghton Library of Harvard University. Denison Beach helped me throughout the years, providing copies of various Erikson Papers from afar and helping me ably when I was on site at Houghton. Early on, it was Denison who saw my need for a replica of the directory to the Erikson Papers and who took the time to photocopy that directory for me. The entire staff of the Houghton Reading Room is of such a high level of competence, service, and concern that they have no peers in the care of readers and manuscripts alike.

I have treasured knowing Bonnie Salt, Cataloguer of the Erikson Papers, for her professional acumen and personal friendship. Her encyclopedic knowledge of databases and her information on ancillary Erikson sources were invaluable. I am indebted to Leslie Morris, Curator of Manuscripts at Houghton Library. Without her timely assistance, particularly in granting permission to publish excerpts from the papers, this project would have been seriously compromised.

Jane Curry, formerly Director of Communications at the Erikson Institute, provided access to early drafts of two Erikson books, to audiovisual tapes, and to related materials. I remember her kindness and generosity of spirit. At project end, the Erikson Institute's Mary Jo Lamparski, Vice President of Institutional Advancement, and Patricia Nedeau, Director of Communications, expedited permissions access.

Ann Brownell Sloane, Administrator of the Institute for Intercultural Studies, granted permission to quote from the Papers of Margaret Mead. Ben Primer, University Archivist at Princeton University, gave permission to quote from the Erikson Gauss Seminar audiotapes. Kai Erikson generously provided literary permission to quote from various Erikson sources. I recall his gracious words about my use of various Erikson excerpts.

I would not have understood Erik Erikson well enough to be secure in interpreting his ideas if it had not been for the time and remembrances supplied by those who had known Erikson and were willing to share their thoughts about him. I am indebted to the late Joan Erikson, Erik Erikson's widow, who was gracious, thoughtful, and direct. She permitted me to visit with her in her home on Cape Cod on several occasions, and we had a number of later conversations by phone. I recall her optimism, good humor, and vitality, and the way she kept her Erik alive each day. Stephen Graubard, previously editor of *Daedalus* and of the American Academy of Arts and Sciences, was a friend throughout the project. His knowledge of Erikson came through on interview and was always contextualized by a brilliant sense of history. His knowledge placed Erikson and the Conference on the Adult in perspective for me. I am grateful to Steve for pressing me to contact Joan Erikson directly. Gerard Fromm, Ess White, and Betty Oakes of the Austen Riggs Center in Stockbridge, Massachusetts, gave important insights into Erikson during his 1950s work with adolescents and young adults at Riggs. David Gutmann, who had been a teaching assistant to Erikson at Harvard in the 1960s, shared penetrating insights into Erikson's talents and insecurities. David read a portion of the manuscript at the first stage of the Oxford University Press review process and commented on the final manuscript. I treasure his incisiveness and his friendship. Clemens Kalischer, Erikson's primary photographer, was enormously helpful to me. Not only did his keen perceptions provide important insights into Erik and Joan Erikson that any number of others are likely to have missed, but he also gave of his time and trouble to locate other potential interview sources. Among others, Clemens led me to Jarvis Rockwell, son of Norman Rockwell, who had known Erikson, and to Leo Garel, a Stockbridge artist who had worked with patients at Riggs and had known both Erik and Joan Erikson professionally and personally. Through Clemens, I was able to contact Hellmut Wohl, a noted art historian and close friend of Erikson's. Hellmut made it nearly possible for me to reach out and touch Erikson's genius and style of working. I am indebted to the late Peter Heller, a student of Erikson's in the small Burlingham-Rosenfeld School in Vienna. Peter's acute mind lent access to the youthful Erik Erikson, to politics in the Freud circle, and to Joan Erikson's influence on her husband. Stephen Schlein lent essential insights into the middle-aged and older Erik Erikson. I am indebted to Steve for speaking with me at length.

I appreciate the work of Philip Laughlin, formerly an editor with Oxford University Press, who saw promise in the book and helped me through the contractual process. I sincerely thank Catharine Carlin, the Oxford editor who saw the book through to publication. My efforts were greatly aided by her competence. I appreciate the efforts of my brother-in-law, the late George P. Hoare, Jr., who provided insight into potential legal issues. George is sorely missed.

During the past 6 years, I have appreciated members of the Society for Research in Adult Development. They listened to draft portions of various chapters at annual conferences, and their thoughtful comments and questions found their way into important clarifications. Among those who read and criticized chapter drafts, I thank Martha Burns for her comments on several early chapter versions. I owe an enormous debt to my friend and faculty colleague Honey Nashman, who read every word at least twice. Her interest in the book, as well as her encouragement and good cheer, kept me as stress free as anyone could. I appreciate Vicki Sardi's careful reading of the final manuscript copy and her careful checks for meaning and redundancy.

Finally, I extend my thanks to those at The George Washington University who permitted me to take sabbatical leaves to work on this book. Without the benefits of concentrated writing time, this project would have taken much longer to complete.

CREDITS

Literary property rights granted for use of all material listed below courtesy of Professor Kai T. Erikson.

Excerpts from the correspondence sections B4 and M32 of The Mead Papers (Library of Congress number SU81-32441) published courtesy of the Institute for Intercultural Studies, Inc., New York.

Material from the original typescript of *Young Man Luther*, dated 10 July 1958, and material from items 1357 and 1358 of the Erikson Institute papers published with permission of the Erikson Institute. Copyright Erikson Institute. All rights reserved.

Material from Audiotape #1, dated 2 April 1970, of the Erik Erikson Lectures of the Gauss Seminars in Criticism (PD No. 18SS), one of the Gauss Seminars in Criticism Audio Tapes, Seeley G. Mudd Manuscript Library, Princeton University Library, published with permission of Princeton University Library.

Material from the manuscript by Peter Blos, Erik Erikson, and Stephen Jay Gould, with shelf marks, bMS Am 2031, (60), (739), (765), (811), (857), (1130), (1151), (1347), (1476), (1491), (1494), (1499), (1501), (1505), (1506), (1510), (1511), (1513), (1515), (1516), (1517), (1519), (1520), (1521), (1522), (1523), (1524), (1527), (1528), (1529), (1530), (1531), (1533), (1534), (1539), (1542), (1543), (1549), (1552), (1555), (1557), (1558), (1560), (1561), (1562), (1565), (1571), (1573), (1574), (1578), (1580), (1581), (1584), (1589), (1594), (1597), (1600), (1601), (1602), (1603), (1605), (1606), (1607), (1612), (1616), (1617), (1623), (1625), (1626), (1631), (1633), (1634), (1635), (1641), (1644), (1655), (1660), (1670), (1675), (1676), (1683), (1686), (1691), (1693), (1702), (1711), (1712), (1714), (1725), (1796), and *95M-2, is reprinted by permission of the Houghton Library, Harvard University.

Contents

Erikson on Development in Adulthood

1

Introduction

A seer must make 'em see.
—Erikson, "Notes for 80th
Birthday Party"

The theoretical views about the adult that Erik Erikson spent a great portion of his own adult life developing represent essential knowledge. In the entire twentieth century, he stands alone as the one thinker who changed our minds about what it means to live as a person who has arrived at a chronologically mature position and yet continues to grow, to change, and to develop.

Erikson was a second-stage psychoanalytic thinker, one who was trained in Freud's Vienna Institute but who quickly departed the rigidity of Freudian dogma. He then revolutionized both psychoanalytic and developmental thought. To Freud, humans were psychosexual creatures. Once genital maturity is attained, a barren desert of adult time stretches ahead. There, adults love and work. And, of course, they die. Along the way to their terminal conditions, they battle omnipresent negative, instinctual forces and deepseated rages that fight to control them. Such forces are never eliminated, not by the flow of time nor by the intervention of the adult who houses them. Enter Erikson, an artist by bent. To say that he transformed Freudian thought does not do him justice. To claim that he was a craftsman or that he was creative fail to account for his accomplishments. He was not just a tradesman, and his thought was not simply "creative," a term that sometimes implies inventiveness without originality.

No, Erikson was an originator. He was a major author of twentieth century thought, one who developed a radically new way of seeing that is a fundamental departure from Freud.[1] In the mid-1970s, he was acclaimed as

3

"the most influential living psychoanalyst" in the Freudian lineage, "the last of the psychoanalytic gurus," a "healer and an interpreter of ourselves and our times."[2] An interdisciplinary thinker of great breadth and depth, any number of scholars and reviewers of his work have held that he had "no peer," not even one "serious imitator" in his home field or in psychohistorical studies.[3]

Erikson was the first to illustrate how the social world exists in the psychological apparatus of each person, a person he saw as a biopsychosocial being who lives in the flow of one seamless, personal narrative and in one niche of total historical time. His revisions of thought to describe developmental changes in the adult were monumental. He boldly told why and how qualitative development occurs during the adult years. The ways in which one makes sense and meaning of life and the roles and commitments of one's ego-laden psychosocial energies and investments in the various adult periods necessarily differ from those of adolescence, he said. And they differ once again from each other in the various eras of adult life. Perhaps some thinkers knew this implicitly. But it was Erikson who gave this thought first form. He conceptualized content, ego investments, and needs of the adult person in what had previously been thought of as a limbo period of time, somewhere between postadolescence and death. He saw that all of the human life span holds unique, evolving content and different constellations of meaning from phase to phase. Little wonder that his Harvard students called his course "Bust to Dust."

Erikson lived in dramatic times. With a life that stretched from 1902 to 1994, his years nearly match those of the twentieth century. A sensitive person throughout his life, the century's first half was particularly traumatic to him. He lived through two world wars, the first in Germany, where, on the very day of his Bar Mitzvah, his home town was bombed. He then watched Hitler's rise to power and, later, living in the United States, saw the origin and first use of nuclear weapons. These "maldevelopments" drove him to depict ethical development in adults, to frame the meaning and universality of prejudice, and to illustrate how and when adults are insightful and wise and when they are blindly overcome by their very inventions.[4]

Erikson could sound preachy, righteous, and idealistic. But his was a driving need to lift adult consciousness, to engender ideas of possibility. Searching for sure signs of human strength, he step by step took down much of Freud's creed. Illustrating the ego's regenerative powers, he countered the irreversibility of childhood origins, giving convincing proof that origins cannot be rigidly determinative. An intellectual with great popular appeal during his lifetime, his legacy is a comprehensive and robust set of theories. He was an elegant, if sometimes diffuse, writer; reading him, one tends to feel uplifted. His is a refreshing and "edifying," as well as a "crucial," sense of what human adults can become.[5]

If, at times, Erikson seems far to the sunny side of life, too much a swing of the pendulum from the dark foreboding of a deterministic, pathology-seeking, and morbidity-minded Freud, perhaps we need to search inside ourselves for some cynical reasons, conscious or less so, that we might have for rejecting Erikson's thought. His desire was to depict mentally healthy life and health-supporting social institutions. He sometimes wrote in the style of a hopeful prophet who saw what adults, their children, and their world could yet become. This is not his "naivete," but his developmental utopia.[6] Dismissing such thought out of hand might just harbor a resistance to contemplating a better life on the globe, one that is more universally available to ourselves and to those we now hold invisible. Invisibility often accrues to those who are mentally ill, homeless, or less able than mainstream Americans, and to those who live in countries so distant that their poverty, oppression, and disease can be bracketed away from awareness.

Here was a theorist who seems always to have asked what it is that holds the adult self together, how institutions can support such ego strength and that of progeny, and how the human species can reach across its great divides to join hands. He held that the malaise of the great, privileged, middle estate could better adapt itself to new ways of seeing and caring. In the end, to him it was an ethics of adult care and responsibility for others, as well as for the self, that best reveals the strengths of healthy egos at work.

One gauge of any thinker's accomplishments lies in the influence that person has had on subsequent thought and work. By almost any measure, in terms of accolades, in terms of the fascinating anger and rejection his work inspired, or in terms of changes in thought itself, Erikson has been uniquely influential. His own publications stand at more than 120. His stage theorizing has imbued work on every attribute, from those of children to identity to wisdom. No text in human development or in psychoanalysis now ends its script with entry into adulthood. And the psychological database that held a mere 14 citations on adult development in 1950, the year that *Childhood and Society* was published, partitioned the adult into various age divisions for the first time in 1959, just 9 years after Erikson's book showed his early thought about differential content for those adult stages. In 1987, 684 references described adults and their various developmental tendencies and, by century's end in 1999, the various forms of adult development had become so numerous as to defy clustering by stage categories alone. Certainly, it is not that Erikson alone was responsible for this groundswell; however, in first saying that the adult years hold their own developmental fuel, he sponsored great interest in and gave credibility to such study.

Psychoanalytic and developmental concepts have so wound their way into the everyday understandings and parlance of contemporary persons that this book requires no additional depth. The only requirement is an interest in learning what adults are about, how each of us is shaped and motivated by conscious and unconscious forces that have molded us from childhood on, and how other contemporary influences also sway our daily thought and behavior. Readers who wish to augment this book with another source might consider selecting a book of Erikson's as a companion text. His

Young Man Luther, itself largely a psychoanalytic construction, contains his thought and his passion, his support for the adult, and his sometimes not-so-gentle chiding of institutions.[7] *Luther* was his, as well as my own, favorite among his books. But the only real need any reader will have is some interest in learning, for the first time or in greater depth, how adults are formed, how they function, and what it is that, in Erikson's mind's eye, shows their maturity and immaturity. If one great thinker could "dare to ask," then perhaps we can consider, "What, really, *is* an adult?"[8]

2

Erikson's Thought in Context

There is a tendency to look at an adult as a "grown-up"
version of what he was as a child . . . or as one who
has "reached" adult status according to tests which mark
his progress.

— Erikson, "Memorandum
on Adulthood"

Whenever Erikson considered the patients in his care or the subjects of his
psychohistorical biographies or essays, he was careful to place them in the
context of their lives and times. We owe him no less. The bulk of Erikson's
writings spans the years 1936 to 1984, nearly a half century during which
his adopted America changed significantly and Erikson himself developed
from late young adulthood to old age. That social context is important to
his thought, for it anchors his work. But his early life was an enduring influence on him as well. A sensitive, deeply reflective, and introspective man,
early sources of confusion remained with him throughout his life as a substratum of his thought and searching.

Erikson was born on June 15, 1902, in Frankfurt am Main, Germany. He
was given the surname Salomonsen, the name of Valdemar Salomonsen, to
whom his mother was married but estranged. However, it seems that Erikson was the outcome of a love liaison between his mother Karla and a Danish gentile, likely an artist. Due to her pregnancy, Karla Salomonsen fled
Denmark and gave birth to her son in Germany. In his infancy, Erikson and
his mother were alone. The two lived among his mother's artist friends, who
provided early identifications for him and on whom he "imprinted" before
having to cope with an "intruding" stepfather.[1]

7

When Erikson was 3, his mother married his pediatrician, Dr. Theodor Homburger, who adopted the child. The facts of his parentage were kept from young Erik, but he was "quietly convinced," he said, that his background was different, that he had come from other, "very kind people."[2] For although his was a stable family life, it held an "uncertainty" in which early estrangements took root.[3] In particular, throughout his life he was burdened by the fact that he had not been chosen by a father; in fact, he had been abandoned. In his studies of originators and revolutionaries—Freud, Luther, Gandhi, St. Francis, Kierkegaard—he searched for what it might have been like to have had a father. In the relationships of each of those men with their fathers he found signs of great discord. Notations about such father-son attachments and difficulties appear repeatedly in his Harvard papers.

Intensifying Erikson's sense of alienation, his Nordic features and tall, lanky frame made him stand out in the temple community and Jewish religion in which he was brought up. There he was called "goy." In the German middle class, he was disenfranchised as well, labeled "Jew" and kept at some distance.[4] Such name-calling made him "sensitive to . . . identity problems" at an early age, he said.[5] Intensifying his own isolation, in his adolescence Erikson declared himself a Dane during Denmark's World War I neutrality.[6] And, symbolizing his discomfiture with what he saw as Judaism's irrelevant ritualism, its "transparent ceremonialism," he resigned from the Jewish synagogue in which his stepfather was prominent.[7]

Growing up on the castle square in Karlsruhe, he remembered his mother as consistently "sad," a devotee of Kierkegaard, Brandes, and Emerson.[8] She was Erikson's introduction to beliefs beyond Judaism, leading her son to understand that a Jewish upbringing was not antagonistic to the "core values of Christianity."[9] Erikson wrote little about his stepfather, noting only an adolescent rebellion against him coupled with an "ambivalent identification" with him.[10]

Erikson graduated from Das Humanistisch (the humanistic) Gymnasium with a classical education but a lackluster scholastic record. He was uninterested in school and dismissed his stepfather's interest in having him attend medical school, a source of further tension. Thinking of himself as genetically similar to his artistic, biological father, he attended art school for a brief period but soon dropped out to become a wandering artist.

His period of wandering the Black Forest as an itinerant artist was his psychosocial moratorium. Hiking about with his childhood friend Peter Blos and others, he roamed Germany and Italy and read passages from works by Lao-Tse, Nietzsche, Silesius, and Schopenhauer. This was his "shiftless," neurotic period, a time of glorying in the status of a dropout and luxuriating in work aversion.[11] In a later era, Erikson believed, he would have been diagnosed a "borderline character" because he had teetered between neurosis and psychosis.[12] In late life he mourned the lost time that his extensive roaming about to find himself had occupied. Yet Erikson also found that his restless itinerant period of wandering through the Black Forest, his *Wander-*

schaft as he called it, had served a purpose, providing time to determine the kind of engaging work that would attract his idealism and his deep commitment. Searching for signs that might justify his own prolonged moratorium, he found "locomotor restlessness" and delayed identity crises in a number of innovators and revolutionaries, among them Freud, Gandhi, Kierkegaard, St. Francis, and Luther.[13]

With the help of his friend Peter Blos, Erikson eventually found his way to Vienna and the Freud circle. By then Erikson was in the middle of a "florid identity crisis" due in part to confusions about his parentage, uncertainty about his fit in society, and competing national, vocational, ethnic, and religious identity attributes.[14] He later credited his own identity confusion as that which made it possible for him to conceptualize the "identity crisis" professionally so as to cure himself and others. If his self-cure was as "grandiose" as he claimed, it also served him well in his American years in a country whose elements of national identity were as obscure and diverse as his own.[15]

In Vienna, Erikson at first tutored in the small Burlingham-Rosenfeld School that had been established for children whose parents were undergoing psychoanalysis; some of the children were patients themselves. He also sketched children's portraits for the Institute's wealthy clientele. But Anna Freud noticed his sensitivity to children and their needs and invited him to study psychoanalysis, a discipline that intrigued him. He was analyzed daily by Anna Freud, and he studied with her and with August Aichhorn, Paul Federn, and Heinz Hartmann; Helene Deutsch and Edward Bibring supervised his initial treatment of an adult. He eventually had a small coterie of his own patients. Simultaneously he studied for a Montessori diploma, uncertain perhaps about his eventual direction.

Psychoanalysis became Erikson's compelling idea. It housed a revolutionary element, an intellectual underground that appealed to the young Bohemian.[16] Further, it was congenial to his artist's eye and a conduit to a life's work. But Erikson could not remain in Freud's rigid establishment. Even before Hitler's threat was fully apparent, the young Erikson planned to leave Vienna. He had "imprinted" on Freud, a "duckling" who deeply wished to have been analyzed by Freud himself, a young man who felt an abiding affinity for the originality and artistic genius in Freud's writing.[17] Yet teaching in the Institute had become perversely conservative. He had come to feel "alienated and estranged there."[18] Anna Freud was forceful and domineering, fresh thought was discouraged, and some members of the circle were strangely bent on determining the exact location and quantity of the libido. Due in part to Aichhorn, Erikson had begun to place great importance on the social world and to move away from Freud's insistence on origins alone as causative factors in pathology. Thus, with a Montessori diploma and a diploma from Freud's Vienna Psychoanalytic Institute in hand, Erikson's only earned academic credentials for a lifetime of work, and by then married to the Canadian Joan Mowat Serson and with two young sons to support, he set out to establish the second phase of psychoanalysis:

The question remained, I felt dimly, whether an image of man reconstructed primarily on the basis of observation in the clinical laboratory
might not lack what, in man's total existence, leads *outward* from self-
centeredness to the mutuality of love and communality, *forward* from the
enslaving past to the utopian anticipation of new potentialities, and *up-
wards* from the unconscious to the enigma of consciousness.[19]

He did not know it at the time, but "outward . . . forward . . . and up-
wards" would become his hallmarks for adults in their development. Adults,
he later wrote, strive beyond themselves toward an outward connection with
others in the social world. They move forward in time and space, building
on prior resolutions and using those as stepping-stones to fresh challenges.
Their developmental movement is upward toward a conscious, ethical concern for others and a deeper sense of a spiritual self.

The Erikson family left an impoverished Vienna in 1933, planning to settle in Denmark, where Erikson hoped to reclaim his Danish citizenship.
However, long years of residence would have been required for this, a period
during which he would not be able to obtain a permit to work.[20] Thus the
family set out for the United States, where citizenship would not be an issue.
Writing to his grandson Per Bloland in 1977, Erikson remarked on his fears
and his feelings of uncertainty when arriving in New York; elsewhere, he
spoke of the resurgence of his identity confusion on the occasion. Yet he said
he felt an "energy in this country" which, along with his need to support a
young family, put him in a survivor's mode.[21] One was given the opportunity to work, he said, and "that is the main thing."[22]

Taken with the optimism and grand scale of the country, and imbued
with the upbeat, liberal tones of Franklin D. Roosevelt's politics, the family
settled first in Boston. As Boston's first child psychoanalyst, opportunities
came to Erikson readily. He was appointed a research fellow in neuropsychiatry at Harvard Medical School, held an appointment at the prestigious
Massachusetts General Hospital, and established a private practice to treat
disturbed children. He enjoyed considerable success teaching and began to
establish a research agenda by studying play constructions among Harvard
undergraduates.

In the year of Erikson's arrival in the United States, economic conditions
were considerably better than in the bleak Vienna he had left, but his
adopted country was poor as well. Deep into its Great Depression after the
stock market crash of 1929, factories had closed and soup kitchens fed the
hungry. Franklin D. Roosevelt had announced a "New Deal" for the American people on accepting the presidential nomination in 1932, a time when
the country suffered an unemployment rate of nearly 24 percent. It might
have seemed foolish in such conditions to ask how adults might be developmentally different from children. Age, size, and strength were the primary
descriptors for adults. Discrete content and stages for adults, who, after all,
struggled just to survive, were not yet considered. Among slightly more than
6,000 psychological articles published in 1933, only 4 considered the adult,

and they covered topics that were mightily peripheral to development.[23] Yet life expectancy was 59 years in 1933, a gain of 12 years from the turn of the century. A long and growing period of adulthood meant that it would not be long before scholars began to consider how that expanse of mature life might hold its own content, crises, and trajectory.

As for Erikson, his great U.S. *Wanderschaft* had begun. With the promise of greater research freedom, in 1936 Erikson left Harvard for Yale. There he would work as a research assistant in psychoanalysis, teach in the Yale Medical School, and advance his interpretive studies on children's play. In his first year there, the Yale Institute of Social Relations established a series of seminars to connect psychoanalysis and behaviorism. But Erikson found himself interested in a different connection, that of psychology and anthropology. This focus would lead him to see the extent to which the social and cultural world is internal to each person's psyche. In his studies of native Americans, he was particularly indebted to Scudder McKeel and Alfred Kroeber, anthropologists who, along with Margaret Mead and Gregory Bateson, created opportunities for him. In 1938, McKeel invited him to visit the Sioux natives of the South Dakota Pine Ridge Reservation. Learning that those natives were the very ones he had read about as a child and hoping to observe important cultural traits, Erikson eagerly departed Yale for his trip west. As he said about his anthropologist friends, "At the borderline of their studies they had been left with questions which were also on the borderline of mine."[24]

Erikson's observations led to an impressive article in 1939, "Observations on Sioux Education," and began to establish him as a thinker who ranged well beyond the Freudians.[25] After the Sioux, he visited the Yurok natives of the California coast. There he expanded his thoughts to include concepts about the many ways the external physical landscape infuses psychological content. His 1943 article, "Observations on the Yurok: Childhood and World Image," shows Erikson thinking on a different level from his earlier work.[26] He had moved afield of education and childhood alone, now considering adult meanings and mature psychological content and rituals.

Erikson's Yale tenure included his naturalization and his family's change in surname from his adoptive father's name of "Homburger" to "Erikson." Erikson never fully explained his reasons for the name change, saying only that he would do so one day, but that explanation was not forthcoming. It remained part of his incomplete writing itinerary when he died.[27] He did say that it was not unusual for immigrants to change their surnames on naturalization and that "Erikson" was a commonly chosen name among Scandinavians. Speculations on his name change and on the reasons for his choice of surname have ranged from Erikson's potential desire to separate himself from a father who was not his own to his intent to establish himself as his own person to his wish to distance himself from anti-Semitism. Although his reasons are not significant to his work on adulthood, the fact of his name change tells of Erikson's need for his own identity and points as well to his lifelong insecurity.[28]

Erikson remained at Yale for a 3-year period of time, just as he had at Harvard. In 1939, dismayed by Yale's antipsychoanalytic trend, its focus on genetics and behaviorism, its anti-Semitism, and his own lack of potential for research productivity, Erikson left the East for California and Berkeley. Residence in San Francisco permitted him to once again engage in the practice of child psychoanalysis, to explore connections between psychology and anthropology, and to participate in the longitudinal child guidance study associated with the University of California's Institute of Child Welfare. This was Erikson's first opportunity to answer his own questions about how healthy development is best nurtured. It was also his chance to advance his writing agenda.

In the United States of 1939, bleak conditions had been somewhat transformed by New Deal policies. The Social Security Act of 1935 established unemployment insurance and pensions for those over 65. Federal funds were dispersed to the states for poor children, and appropriations for health under the Social Security Administration had grown dramatically. Increasingly, the United States had come to recognize the relationship between health, including mental health, and socioeconomic status. Illness was higher in the 17 percent of families whose breadwinners were unemployed and in families on relief, in which 1 in 20 heads of household was disabled. In 1939, the maternal mortality rate for African American women was double that for white women, another ramification of class separation and social deprivation.[29]

On the international front, the isolationist United States did not enter the fray in 1939 when France and England declared war on Germany. It would take the Japanese attack on Pearl Harbor in 1941 to press the United States into war, an engagement that reduced unemployment at home and led the United States out of its Great Depression. In Berkeley at the time, Erikson diverted his attention from developmental studies and papers to contribute to the war effort. In nine important papers between 1940 and 1945, he analyzed submarine psychology, wrote on the use and ethics of psychological observations and interrogations of prisoners of war, appraised Nazi mentality and Hitler's propagandistic imagery, and considered postwar needs of mentally fragile veterans. In his writings he remained uncritical of the United States, even avoiding comment on lukewarm reactions to growing knowledge about the millions of children and adults who had been murdered in Nazi death camps. Nor did he publicly concern himself about the 120,000 Japanese Americans who were interned in U.S. camps, their rights to legal recourse fully suspended. But learning about the 100,000 civilians who were destroyed by the U.S. nuclear bombings of Hiroshima and Nagasaki in 1945 led him to speak out, even though it would take decades for him to find the voice and the psychological vehicle with which to do so. The human race had finally "overreached itself," he then wrote; the nuclear invention was a "historical maladaptation" in species evolution.[30] That development, plus knowledge that the future could harbor another Hitler, led him to write about prejudice, the pseudospecies tendency that exists in each and every human adult.

The war years were important to Erikson in one other respect. As he saw veterans return to the United States, he observed that a number of them showed fractured egos. This, he said, led him to name and to conceptualize psychosocial identity as a entity that is first built during adolescence but whose very solidity can be jeopardized during times of extraordinary stress. In such periods, egos can lose their coherence, in effect collapsing into constituent elements.

As the country pulled itself together after World War II, Erikson returned to his psychoanalytic work. The late 1940s saw him solidifying his work on childhood to publish, in 1950, *Childhood and Society*, the book that to this day is his best known and most widely read publication. Erikson's was the first effort to conceptualize the life span in its entirety as a cumulative process and as a linear development that unfolds according to specific stages, each stage harboring unique psychological dynamics and crises. But despite the fact that his 1950 book sketched the eight stages of life, he did not then describe adult development in other than skeletal form. In five pages of text, he laid out the ground plan for adult ego investments and for his eventual work on adulthood but wrote that "we cannot improve on (Freud's) formula."[31] Being adult meant *lieben und arbeiten*, as Freud had claimed; it was a time "to love and to work."[32] To conceptualize that terrain of loving and working, and to do so in greater depth, he would have to move away from cross-cultural studies and extend his thought first to preadolescence and then to adolescence, moving decidedly upward through the life span. In 1951 he made his first excursion into preadolescence, publishing an article on gender differences in preadolescents' play constructions. This placed him on the brink of conceptualizing identity as the principal crisis of adolescence, the link to adulthood.

But the suspicions of the postwar McCarthy years and Erikson's immigrant status would temporarily divert him. By 1949 Erikson had secured a full professorship in psychology at Berkeley, a prestigious position for an immigrant without full academic credentials. At the same time, cold war and anti-Communist sentiments were spreading through the country. Caving in to Senator Joseph McCarthy's panicky claims that Communists had infiltrated the government at high levels, in 1950 Congress passed the McCarran Internal Security Act. That act required pro-Communist organizations to register with the U.S. Attorney General. In educational institutions, the signing of loyalty oaths became prominent as a way of ensuring faculty and staff solidarity with the United States. The Board of Regents of the University of California was no exception, requiring each faculty member to sign a loyalty oath of nonsubversion. Erikson refused, and although his own faculty status was not eventually imperiled, he resigned his position. In his statement to the university, Erikson claimed that he was not a Communist, that he had signed a constitutional oath previously, and that he would not participate in national hysteria. The students were watching, he said. His conscience would not permit him to engage in an empty gesture designed to exorcise some imperceptible evil, in effect colluding with forces which his own field sought to cure.

Erikson's resignation resulted in a 10-year absence from university environments. In that extended sabbatical, Erikson accessed clinical material that prompted him to fully conceptualize the identity crisis. Although a number of opportunities presented themselves to him, among them a clinical position at the Menninger Clinic, Erikson decided to cross the country once again. On Robert Knight's urging, Erikson joined the teaching staff of the Austen Riggs Center in Stockbridge, Massachusetts.[33] There Erikson worked with troubled adolescents and young adults in its open, residential facility nestled in the Berkshire hills, in a setting as idyllic as the scenes Norman Rockwell painted in his studio nearby. Riggs opened the door for his "spiritual return to (his) roots," Erikson said.[34] There he began the clinical studies that led to *Young Man Luther,* his book about young adulthood through the lens of Martin Luther's difficulties with identity, intimacy, and faith. Riggs and *Luther* were Erikson's instruments for reconnecting with art, with history, with his ideas about the "curative" power of work in resolving identity difficulties, and with his own issues about belief in an Ultimate Power in the universe.[35] At Riggs he became convinced that the mental difficulties which surfaced in youth who were then on the brink of adulthood were potentially less damaging and permanent than mental illnesses which appeared later in life. He believed that the rapid physical and cognitive growth of adolescence provoked intense psychological changes. Those changes led sensitive adolescents in particular to experience severe ego crises that might be ameliorated. Such adolescents were in moratoria, he held. En route to adulthood, they had lost their psychological footing because the threat of becoming adult was too enormous to deal with as part of mentally intact reality.

Erikson's own identity travails as a wandering, failing artist helped him to understand and to empathize with traumatized adolescents who were having difficulties finding a way to express themselves in adult identities. Identity, in the years and experiences that either force-feed or blunt its development, was Erikson's permanent link to his ideas about adolescence and to all of the developmental phases of adulthood that follow along after it. To Erikson, identity was a normative crisis, a priming pump, and an ongoing life process.

At Riggs and later, Erikson was a champion of adolescents.[36] His views are best expressed in a letter he wrote to Margaret Mead during his Harvard years in the 1960s. In that letter Erikson enclosed a copy of the memorandum he had sent to the Committee on the Year 2000 in lieu of his attendance.[37] In an uncharacteristically biting tone, he wrote that he discerned, in the commission's letter to him, certain "stereotypes" about adolescents that could serve only as an "ideological mote" in any ideas about them presently or in some future "vision" of their lives.[38] This prohibited an ability to see in youth their search for "authority" that could be trusted, for "relevant experience" that honored life, and for "ethical boundaries" they could depend on:

> So now the young must experiment with what is left of the "enlightened" and "analyzed" world; but their search, I believe, is not for all-permissibility, but for new logical and ethical boundaries. . . . As for the desacrilization of life by the young, I don't believe it. We de-sacrilized life by our dogmatic rationalism, naive liberalism and pleasure in gadgets, not to speak of our denial of the infinite and of death.[39]

He always held to this view. Later he wrote: "The modern adult, being pseudo-adolescent, does not permit (the) impact of (the) adolescent."[40] Further, Erikson noted that the cycle perpetuated itself, for when society eventually did open up to youth by permitting their participation in adult work roles, employing institutions quickly co-opted youth's ideals to self-serving, bureaucratic needs. This tendency undermined higher order principles perpetually. Throughout his writing, Erikson used his identification with adolescents and his belief in their abilities, oppression, and potential power to show how much adults had to lose in their own movement through life, losses he frequently had difficulty terming *development*. In part, Erikson selected the giant identity models he wrote about to provide adolescents with heroic examples of ethical adults, believing that youth had difficulty finding an adequate supply of such models in their contemporary world.

In the 1950s, during Erikson's tenure at Riggs, the country changed dramatically. Not having experienced the ruin of war-devastated Europe and with a gross national product that grew from $285 billion in 1950 to $483 billion in 1959, the country's economy was the healthiest in the world. Overtaking agriculture, manufacturing revolutionized jobs and the business side of life; unions became prominent. Long enchanted with their cars, Americans watched movies from drive-in theaters, were enticed into long car trips by the growth in motels, were made more comfortable in their travels by the National Highway Act, and moved to the suburbs in record numbers. Shopping malls flourished, and consumerism swung into full force as the first credit cards were placed into common use. Switching almost universally from audio to video, the 20 percent of households that had television sets in 1950 would grow to nearly 90 percent by decade's end.

Socially, the desegregation of public schools with the Supreme Court's 1954 ruling on Brown v. Topeka Board of Education launched early efforts toward racial equality, but integration was slow in developing. Martin Luther King, Jr.'s, voice was heard; yet in the South violence against African Americans countered most efforts toward civil liberties. It would take another long decade for the civil rights momentum to build. Meanwhile, coexisting national anxieties erupted with the launch of Sputnik by the Union of Soviet Socialist Republics in 1957. Believing that the various U.S. educational curricula were lax and far inferior to the Soviets,' the National Science Foundation expanded, and, in the schools, educators launched a return to basics and to improved science teaching. The "space race" was on, an evolved form of the "red scare."

By decade's end in 1959, life expectancy was 69.7 years, a long enough period to declare a separate stage for old age. But the psychological literature showed little advance in its focus on adults. Of more than 8,500 articles published in 1960, a mere 13 considered adulthood. And, as before, those few were tangential to development.[41]

During the 1950s at Austen Riggs, Erikson wrote first about preadolescents, about the healthy personality, and about cross-cultural patterns in child adjustment.[42] He then turned his attention to adolescent identity issues and wrote about inner identity,[43] and identity and "totality" in youth.[44] Moving forward through the lifespan and upward from the unconscious to the conscious in his description of stages, Erikson was then on the brink of codifying adulthood proper. Thus, adolescence, identity, and Erikson's clinical years at Riggs were his bridge between concepts about children and his thinking about adults' identity quests for intimacy, generativity, and completeness.

In writing on identity at Riggs, Erikson was taking one more step toward unification theory, as Einstein had done but Freud had not. Erikson had studied Einstein's adult years and the scientist's search for unity in the physical universe of matter, energy, gravity, space, and light. Erikson too intended to work toward a "unified theory" of biopsychosocial development, first for the early period of infancy through childhood, and then forward from identity through old age.[45] He wanted to connect life in its complete design. In Erikson's Harvard notes from the mid-1950s on, one can almost hear him asking how adulthood begins and then leaps forward into its own terrain, while remaining bound to the dependent structures and identifications that continue on from childhood. It is, after all, the self-same body and psyche of old, if now in a different form. In a letter to Dorothy Burlingham written when he was in his 70s, Erikson said he had just finished writing *Toys and Reasons*[46] as "some kind of conclusion to a psychoanalytical-historical point of view which in all these decades I was almost driven to formulate."[47] He could not leave development where Freud had, upward through five stages but with a backward pull. Erikson wanted to show what drove the adult along through all of *I* time, through the one adult space each *I* is given.

As Erikson said, he wanted to be "telos (endpoint) oriented," knowing that Freud had been "origins oriented."[48] He aimed to revise Freudian thought, disputing its arbitrary fixation on beginnings and neuroses. To Erikson, its view "backward . . . downward . . . and inward" to instincts and to pathology presumably originating in infancy held an "implicit fatalism" that latter-day psychoanalysts such as he had to dislodge.[49] He wrote, "I developed some of what I learned, asking: if we know what can go wrong in each stage, can we say what should have gone and can go right?"[50] Thus with positive, healthy development in mind, Erikson moved upward and forward through childhood and into the adult years. He conceptualized identity as the work and aim of adolescence. He then continued along teleologically, asking what developmental accomplishments might lead to each adult's "self-perfectability."[51] What are the purposes and goals of biopsychosocial adulthood as a consequence of conscious and unconscious development?

Erikson also wished to understand and show the regularities of nature against the irregularities shown by different societies and cultures. He knew that an indeterminate portion of his thinking would be bound to his era because he was compelled to locate his thinking in the society, values, knowledge base, and historical times in which he wrote. However, to the greatest extent possible, he tried to avoid "era-centricity." His aim was to show timeless insights into the adult by filtering the lives of historically acclaimed adults through the lens of twentieth-century psychoanalysis and by joining ancient ideas about the adult with Western-world, postrational developmental thought. In important respects, his work on the culturally and historically relative adult began in his Riggs period, partly through his focus on Martin Luther and partly because of the connections he made between physical and cultural relativity.

Erikson interspersed his early work on identity with two papers on Freud and then wrote his influential article on "The Problem of Ego Identity."[52] After that 1956 paper went to press, Erikson presented its points in a panel presentation that was later published but is rarely referenced.[53] In it, Erikson used the word *adult* for the first time in a title (at the third meeting of the World Health Organization Study Group on the Psychobiological Development of the Child in 1955). His thoughts about the realm of adulthood that constitutes a separate developmental terrain were tentative. They were buttressed largely by his knowledge about identity diffusion in adolescents.

But it was at that panel in 1955 that Erikson officially began his itinerary on adulthood. Clearly, he had had many things to say about adults before this. His writings about ego development, his analysis of failed egos, and his articles on the Sioux and the Yurok had revealed beginning concepts about the adult. Further, his many chapters and articles about children's play and childhood development had told psychoanalysts, social workers, physicians, teachers, and parents how to care for children and adolescents so that such youth would become mentally healthy adults. These show Erikson's belief in the childhood nurturance that is fundamental to every healthy adult.[54] They show as well his firsthand knowledge of the ego sturdiness, health, and fragility that together form a common heritage for mentally intact adults and of the disturbing collective heritage all adults share, the "humiliation" of having been children.[55] As he said, "a sense of smallness forms a substratum in (the adult) mind, ineradicably."[56] To Erikson, it was this substratum that led so many adults to punish others and themselves, thereby becoming and remaining negative and nonadult, deteriorating in important respects and losing essential tendencies to become what he epitomized as a childlike, playing adult.

In the mid-1950s, Erikson's appraisals of Freud in "The Dream Specimen of Psychoanalysis" (1954), "The Origins of Psychoanalysis" (1955), and "The First Psychoanalyst" (1956) prepared him to venture into young adulthood proper through *Luther*.[57] It seems that Erikson had to first think about Freud's ego and the way the founding father had worked in self-psychoanalyzing himself as an adult before he could move forward to chart the stages and investments of his own and others' adult years. Erikson saw Freud as the genius who had built a theory, literally, out of his own dreams. He knew Freud as an empire builder as well. Erikson emulated the former, substituting the play of children for the dreams of Freud, but he built neither a school nor an empire. To Erikson, Freud's territorial, empire-driven aims were distasteful. They represented Freud's nonegalitarian, nongenerative tendencies, the aspects of Freud that were not adult.

Nonetheless, Freud was an ongoing resource to Erikson's ideas, creativity, and professional development, both at Austen Riggs and later. Throughout his many notes and annotations in the Harvard files and Erikson Institute manuscripts, one finds Erikson musing about Freud's ideas, quirks, and artistic interests. He credited Freud as the originator who helped to alter the very "image of adulthood" but believed that Freud had taken the morality of adults "for granted."[58] Considering the dawn of the nuclear age, Erikson believed that second-generation psychoanalytic thinkers such as he could not afford that luxury; neither could humanity. Erikson's agenda of personifying adults' ego investments thus held both a social science and a policy imperative. His 1942 paper provided a harbinger of this:

> I am attempting to develop a series of systematic understandings of the great contemporary cultures so that the special values of each may be orchestrated in a world built new.[59]

Thus, amorphously in the 1940s and decidedly in the Austen Riggs of the 1950s, Erikson's early agenda for portraying adults in their development and potential is in evidence: All humans had to eventually understand their need for self-development and their need for each other. This plan would continue to circumscribe his life's work.

In 1960, Erikson left Austen Riggs for a professorship in human development at Harvard. It would be his last full-time appointment, a decade-long commitment. The 1960s were Erikson's most prolific writing years, a period in which his thought once again shows movement upward through the life span. Now he worked to consider the largest span of adulthood, the middle years. Previously, he had conceptualized identity and, in Luther, had considered identity against intimacy. In his notes of the period he wrote, "The 'I'—therefore Luther-Gandhi."[60] Now, particularly in light of forces afoot in the United States, it was time to look to the responsible generativity of midlife, to show how a true adult can take a forceful stand while maintaining the position of militant nonviolence. His primary vehicle was Mahatma Gandhi.

The 1960s was among the most turbulent decades in the century, a time of civil rights riots, of the assassinations of John and Robert Kennedy and of Martin Luther King, Jr., of Vietnam war losses and protests, of escalation in nuclear arms, and of beginning knowledge about global warming. But it was a period of hope that held a sense of the future as well. Through the use of intellect, social programs, and American leadership in the world, many were optimistic that living conditions could be improved for the country's citizens and for the disenfranchised in the far reaches of the world. The Peace Corps began, Great Society programs were initiated, and Medicare and Medicaid initiatives were put in place. Due in part to technological advances, health care became the fastest growing industry in the United States. Higher education boomed, the war on poverty showed early advances, and the Civil Rights Act of 1964 and Bill of 1968 made inroads into segregation and unfair housing. The feminist movement began in earnest, ecumenism was on the rise, the first gene was isolated, and the integrated circuit launched the computer and information age.

In his writings of the period, Erikson focused on the problems of the era, building from a positive approach. The 1960s and early 1970s was the period during which his work was most closely linked to the social context and its concerns. He addressed racial understanding and relationships, advanced thought about nonviolent strategies, and conceptualized the meaning of prejudice and of a wider species identity.[61] He countered illusions about the war in Vietnam and spoke about the meaning of adult responsibility and the need for a higher level Golden Rule.[62] He was inspired by ecumenical initiatives, "bored" with his own stage content, and deeply concerned about new generational schisms.[63] He saw in youth a "mocking deviance" and drug culture and, in the parent generation, a change-resisting establishment ethos that youngsters had scant reason to honor or to emulate.[64] Erikson had long functioned as a cautious social critic. But in the 1960s he wrote with greater directness, protesting the inhumane continuance of thoughtless patterns of belief and of living. His was the voice, if not the political activism, of a leader. He ended the decade with the publication of *Gandhi's Truth* in 1969, a book that had taken him just over 7 years to write, one that won him the Pulitzer Prize and the National Book Award.[65] And with his belief in looking at the adult anew, a belief that sharply contrasted with the violent times, he spearheaded the Conference on the Adult in 1970 under the sponsorship of the American Academy of Arts and Sciences.

The 1970s saw the firm beginnings of Erikson's elder years. Retired from Harvard in 1970, he was invited back in 1972 to give the Godkin Lectures under the aegis of Harvard's John F. Kennedy School of Government. Expected to apply his thinking to some feature of "free government," and with an interest in rounding out his life's work by returning full circle to his psychoanalytic origins as an analyst observing children at play, he juxtaposed youthful play against the adult's ideas and political visions.[66] He was amazed, he wrote, by the uncanny association between the child's play and political imagination. In meeting the Godkin requirements at that moment in time, he believed he could illustrate how the ego needs and pseudo-reasons of presidents and military leaders, as well as the political games of his or any other era, can build artificial realities that blind all to the truth.

The year of his Godkin Lectures, 1972, was a troubled year in U.S. history. Erikson wrote that an "American Dream" had turned into a "nightmare" with the Vietnam War.[67] President Lyndon Johnson had declared war in the mid-1960s and, in 1969, the newly elected president Richard Nixon secretly escalated military efforts there. Erikson held that widespread government deceit had led Americans to "depersonalize" the war, to consider it a mere use of military capacity.[68] Meanwhile, we had involved ourselves in a country whose people and spirit we had radically underestimated. Then, with U.S. military frustrations and casualties soaring, American soldiers killed children in My Lai, in effect illustrating "panic" and a breaking point of the species.[69] At home, U.S. citizens were rapidly "losing their grip on reality,"[70] fed by politicians and a military command who were possessed of such "illogic" that, comparatively speaking, "our schizophrenic friends (are) sane."[71] As for Nixon, the Watergate scandal occurred just after Erikson's Godkin address of 1972, thus giving him scant opportunity to comment publicly. Nonetheless, Erikson quietly wondered whether we, the American people, understood how much the fact of Nixon as president said about us.

With the publication of *Toys and Reasons*, Erikson's text of the Godkin Lectures, his prolific writing years largely came to a close. The remainder of his writing focused on a variety of reflections on the adult years of Freud, Jung, and Einstein, on historical change, and on the relationship of adolescence to parenthood. He wrote only one major theoretical work after the Godkin, his examination of the Galilean Jesus against "a sense of 'I,'" an impressive article published in 1981.[72] Without much fanfare in those later years, he altered his thought in one important respect. "Wisdom," the vital strength he had theorized as the outcome of the last stage of life, was now far too much to ask of any senior. Credit elders for "integrality" instead, he wrote, for attaining some vital ability to keep body, psyche, wits, and soul together against the losses of aging.[73] In this change Erikson showed that it is not the social context or the resolutions posed by experts that are important. Persons must experience each age and stage subjectively, in the form of a personal context, in order to understand it. Such experiential understanding is particularly important for any theorist who would chart stages and resolutions for others.

In his later years, Erikson said he wished to be known as one who had tried to "round out" his work by considering what it means to be an adult.[74] In fact he did this; however, what he did not do was synthesize his findings in any one work. It is his unpublished and published papers and his books that one must search to find his insights about the adult. In those various sources, through one immigrant life in its American context, against the meanings and values seen through one Euro-American lens, and through our theorist's care to understand healthy human development, Erikson was explicit about what adults are, cannot avoid being, and might hope to become.

In subsequent chapters, we take up the question of what it means to be adult. In the richest, most powerful, freest, and most materialistic country in the world, Erikson believed it was incumbent on us to grapple with this question. It was time to consider the "structure and function of adulthood," particulars we were taking for granted and, in our busy, possession-oriented society, considering irrelevant.[75]

3

Erikson and Rethinking the Meaning of "Adult"

In my own field there is no definition of adulthood.

—Erikson, *Erikson on Erikson*

In 1970, Erikson ended his "all too extroverted years" of teaching, writing, and traveling.[1] He was 68 years old, had completed a lifetime of clinical work and writing, and had just retired from his professorship at Harvard. Against the backdrop of the 1960s with its various tensions, Erikson felt a resurgence of concern about humanity's direction and eventual end. He hoped in the fundamental goodness of humans but feared that the species would soon destroy itself. Since 1965, he had written about the dangers of violence in a nuclear age. He now began a period of life fully beyond institutional life. The writing years left to him would be brief, but before he disengaged completely, he inspired one last, large-scale effort, the "Conference on the Adult," sponsored by the American Academy of Arts and Sciences.[2] Through this conference, he hoped to surface new insights about undiscovered adult potentials that he held as essential in light of recent social events. Because his various audiences had largely focused on his eight-stage model of the human life cycle alone, most readers had missed his points about what it means to be developmentally mature. It was time to ask his question bluntly, "What *is* an adult?"

PLANNING THE CONFERENCE

Pressing his question on the American Academy of Arts and Sciences, Erikson explained that experts from various disciplines had explored child development to the near exclusion of studying adults. He asked the academy to sponsor a conference with the sole purpose of examining the potentials and possible difficulties that arise in the adult sui generis, that is, based on adult possibilities and requirements in and of themselves, those attributes and functions that do not redound to childhood origins.[3] In particular, he wondered how immersion in loving and caring during the prime eras we call young and middle adulthood might bring forth fresh potential for positive development, as well as fuel for pathology. Importantly, he was interested in how the word *maturity* might best be defined and in how those who are arbitrarily called "mature," frequently on the basis of age alone, might advance developmentally.[4] Might some good thinkers, reflecting together, begin to unearth latent powers in adults that had gone unnoticed? he asked. And, if such potentials could be found, would this knowledge not advance contemporary thought and serve as a springboard to later work?

Launching the conference, Erikson held that there were problems with the exploration of adult development beyond the fact that it had been barely studied. He elaborated on this point and its attendant problems in his invitational memorandum to participants and in the conference sessions themselves. There were six main difficulties, he held, in current concepts about the adult. First, Freud had conceptualized adulthood as a barren terrain for development. In the Western world, this viewpoint had taken root. Second, based on the idea that the many years of adulthood were postdevelopmental, there was a tendency to think of adults as though they are solely physically developed children. Third, and related to this problem, was an apparent inability to consider adulthood as separate from its origins in childhood. Nearly all developmental thought harkened back, in one way or another, to developmental notions based on the earlier years of life. Fourth, when development in adults *was* entertained, concepts showed their dependence on chronology and marker events within the adult years instead of on qualitative differentials in development. Fifth, concepts of adulthood depicted very limited, established parameters of adult normalcy. And sixth, developmental thinkers and the general public in the United States tended toward middle-class and ethnocentric biases. They devalued modes and expressions of adult behavior that did not fit within the American mainstream.

Taking these in turn, first Erikson held that Freud had been far too influential. Not only had Freud believed that psychosexual development ended with entry into adulthood, but he had also led thinking along a path of developmental negatives. Using Freud's thought, all one could expect of mentally healthy adults was the comparative absence of overriding childhood "guilt," "fixations," "repressions," and "infantile" drives.[5] Expectations for adult behavior were also stated in negatives, in terms of what adults "shouldn't do."[6] Erikson held that by expressing only what was or should be absent, theorists had missed examining what adults are in their development, as well as what they might yet become.

Second, although social scientists and the general public no longer saw children as miniature adults, as had been the case throughout the nineteenth century, theorists now tended to portray adults as completed or "grown up" editions of their prior selves.[7] Erikson was on target. It is as though twentieth-century thinkers had reversed prior ideas about size and distention. The previous, now abandoned, image of children as miniature adults had found new form in that of adults as blown-up children. This idea took thinking about adults regressively backward in time to circa 190 B.C., when the term *adultus* was first used to describe fully engorged and ripened children, as well as crops, seasons, animals, and all else that had "adult-ed."[8] Erikson found such thinking inadequate at best, for completed growth and physical bloating have little to do with mature development or with behavior worth emulating.

Third, adult attributes and developmental accomplishments were captured as if they existed on a continuum from childhood. Again, Freud's work had lent its hand. It was as though a giant rubber band stretched between infancy and senescence; developmental traits of adulthood were seen as fixed, albeit immaturely, at the band's beginning point. One might stretch that elastic band out, but it always snapped back, in theorists' minds, to its tight beginnings. Even in the Conference on the Adult, when reading the conference transcripts after its sessions were held, Erikson added a handwritten note to the effect that the participants could not discuss the adult without going back, time after time in their discussions, to the child and to childhood origins.

Fourth, just as there was a tendency to consider adult development on a linear continuum with childhood, studies that examined adult development separate from that of children were hampered by chronology dependence. Such studies locked the development of adults to the passing of time and to temporally ordered marker events within the adult time span. Bound to a linear notion, researchers had primarily considered adulthood's beginning and ending points and its changes in a temporal sequence. As a result, meanings, contexts, and differential abilities had been ill examined. Capturing development as a function of time meant that persons' cumulative adult years and various watershed events such as marriage and retirement had become artificial substitutes for qualitative changes in developmental complexity. Changing ways of seeing and interpreting the world and oneself and fresh adult potentials and abilities were missing. Erikson was interested in such attributes, in unearthing qualitative potentials and complexity.

Erikson knew that his own theory was lodged in infantile origins and in unfolding linear, normative development. By 1970, the telescoping stage regularities he had portrayed had found their way into established use by professionals and the general public alike. Stage crises had become an exact script against which one could establish developmental parameters and departures from them. Once built into a tight theory, not only had Erikson's stage thinking become rigidly deterministic in people's minds, but it also seemed to have assumed a self-generating life of its own. His eight-stage grid had led to the inculcation of its design in lives. Erikson's identity concept in particular had spawned fresh sightings of it everywhere, leading even its originator to say that he had become "allergic to the term identity because of its general misuse."[9] Further, the identity concept and the stages in his life span theory had been reduced to achievement and self-rating scales that he scorned.[10] At best, such standardization presented enormous obstacles to his own agenda for fresh inquiry.

Thus, by the date of the conference, Erikson may have wished that he had not been quite so influential in norming the entire life span. He recognized that he had inadvertently colluded with Freud to convey a standardized version of psychosocial, if not of psychosexual, development. But it was late. By the 1970s, the United States, a nation taken with newness and with most ideas that somehow housed thoughts of fresh opportunity, was charmed with adolescence and with the very notion of identity. Erikson's thinking had played an important role in our fascination with youth and with its principal crisis. In fact, by the date of the conference, Erikson's portrayal of the adolescent identity crisis had inspired thought about and the display of such crises. This was on a par with the way Jung's individuation concept inspired Jaques to name and Levinson to elaborate the "midlife crisis," a concept that fired up middle-agers to appear in their therapists' waiting rooms with crisis-appropriate complaints.[11] Symptoms follow concepts, as well as preceding them.

Erikson's fifth point was that a tendency exists to accept only established parameters of adult normalcy. In fact, he held that there were parallels between the way psychoanalysis traced aberrations back to infantile origins and the manner in which so many adults limited contemporary concepts of adult behavior, normalcy, and adjustment to the confines of narrow, and frequently regressive, thought. He held that those in positions of institutional power in particular tended to classify individuals who deviated from the norm—through, for instance, rioting, defecting, or exhibiting mental instability—in terms and clinical labels that often biased thought about what *normal* might entail in some more expansive definition.[12] The idea of "normal" needed greater latitude. Particularly with respect to the Vietnam War, he asked why *normal* meant compliance with killing in a distant land when everything that young adults believed and valued told them they had to resist. How healthy was adjustment to death, in service to elected, so-called leaders' inabilities to acknowledge the error of the war they had begun? With respect to civil rights, could Americans not see that preventing social inclusion of minorities meant paralysis of development for all? Adjustments had been required, but to conditions to which no one should be expected to comply.

Perhaps "normal" was too readily equated with "socially acceptable" according to the in-group's definition of normal. Erikson maintained that the caring, generative person was the developmental pinnacle for each adult, embracing in his notion the Hindu concept of those who maintain the world they are soon destined to leave. He held that many of the nation's, the legal system's, and the mental health system's core ideas, work modes, and care environments were nongenerative. In many instances, he said, mainstream standards for adult normalcy were so askew that many of the mentally ill and deviant seemed less abnormal than those who expected such social outliers to conform. He asked how a wider, more generative leeway might be possible for all adults, an "actuality" of engaged exchange and "interaction."[13] In effect, his questions were unpalatable. They required conference participants to cast aside some of the very norms, modes, and ideas that validated their central positions in institutional life.

Sixth, Erikson insisted that most individuals, by the time they are adults, prefer their own notions about what it means to be mature and to work within society. As a result, they cast aside and sometimes denigrate other equally valid adult ways of being in the world. To counter this tendency, Erikson sought the explicit "ideals" and "images" of adulthood held by the various fields of inquiry represented at the conference against other modes of adulthood.[14] Concerned about what we lose as adults, he prodded participants to consider how adults fit into the institutions that employ them, what adults give up in the process of adjusting themselves to work requirements, and why some kinds of persons are nearly always excluded from gainful work. And he pressed discussions about American adults against ideas established by the nation's founders. How, after all, had America evolved into such a consumer mentality, and why was this mentality both abhorred and emulated by those who imported it for their uses abroad? He asked why young people, on returning to America's shores after traveling to other countries, saw their own country as a place that fostered adulthood immaturity. He tied many of these questions to his concepts of prejudice. In his memorandum to conference participants and in the conference sessions themselves, he questioned how adults, as they age, might counter the tendency to become defensive and rigidly protective of their favored images and customs of adult life and work. How might they better entertain, sanction, and integrate other adult images and mores as well?

Erikson wanted participants to think in terms of adult complexity and dualism. He implicitly offered a "both/and" view of developmental consistency and irregularity. He refuted that one must accept an "either/or" premise about development and behavior, that behavior is *either* in line with genetics and with the self-same unfolding body-mind of early life and the social expectations of that period *or* that it begins afresh in the discontinuities of adulthood and its leaps of being. Erikson wanted to keep these "both/ands" intact. This is difficult enough for an imaginative thinker working alone. It is nearly impossible for a group, particularly one whose members hold differing views about the nature of knowledge.

It is likely that Erikson knew that such conceptual complexity could not be kept intact. As someone who understood adult behavior, and as an immigrant who had once been foreign to the English tongue, he knew that Western minds tend to deduce, to search down decision trees toward reduction and simplicity. Both numerically and conceptually, Americans are habituated to their preference for reduction, and their English language supports this. In English dictionaries, there are more than twice as many words containing the prefix *sub-*, meaning "below," "reduce," or "under," as there are words employing the prefix *super-*, meaning "above" or "of a higher order."[15] English-language users are thus led to think as they speak, in deductive categories that are subordinate instead of superordinate. Even the sophisticated thinkers present at the conference showed this trait.

Nonetheless, Erikson urged his agenda. Framing his principal question, he wondered why some persons seem to display a "shining newness" as adults in the "autonomy" and uniqueness of their "singular personalities," whereas others seem to stagnate and rigidify.[16] How do those adults manage to entertain a less simplified and reduced view of the world? Early in 1971, Erikson had reviewed data on the middle-aged participants he had studied in their early teens in the 1940s as part of the Child Guidance Study of the University of California. Considering his assessments of them 30 years earlier, he interviewed a select few whose radiance had sparked his interest originally. He was once again impressed with their vitality. It was not just their resistance to psychopathology that interested him but the way they seemed to have re-created themselves anew throughout the demands of adulthood. In his memorandum to those scholars who would think together at the Conference on the Adult, Erikson emphasized his concern about the absence of any substantial theory that explored adult development, potential, and behavior other than in its continuity with childhood, on the basis of linear events, or in terms of the presence or absence of pathology. The occasion of the conference thus gave him a fresh opportunity to consider adulthood, an agenda that had occupied his work since 1955.

ADULT IMAGES AND PROBLEMS

In its Conference on the Adult, the American Academy of Arts and Sciences used as its springboard Erikson's thinking about the possibility of unearthed adult potentials. Sessions were held in Cotuit, Massachusetts. They incorporated wide-ranging discussions about the various meanings of adulthood both at the time of the conference and throughout history. A variety of thoughtful experts from a range of disciplines participated.[17] However, as is clear on reading Erikson's copy of the conference transcripts, he was dissatisfied with the outcome.[18] His cryptic annotations, exclamations, underlinings, circlings, arrows, and question marks show his annoyance with the deliberations. He had expected far too much of a group of men and women who were trying to think together. A few talkative, opinionated members seemed to avoid deliberating with others at all. And some highly verbal participants had even missed the subtle point that Erikson had planted in his early memo to participants: Americans tend to talk when they might profit from listening and reflecting.

Erikson had been ill during the main conference sessions. As a result, he could not redirect a sometimes argumentative group. Thus the adult potentials he had hoped to bring to the surface in some beginning way did not come forth. The questions Erikson asked were difficult ones that proceeded from a psychoanalytic lens and an ethical intent. Further, his agenda seems to have been caught between a desire to advance developmental thought and some messianic wish to improve adults and their social institutions. Noting his wish to better society, detractors had long criticized his premises and aims as utopian. In fact, Erikson believed this about himself as well.[19]

Despite participants' efforts and the development of a number of essays that were later published, the conference transcript and its related papers show insurmountable difficulties in the work of the conference. First, the thought terrain was difficult, particularly for those who were unaccustomed to thinking from within a psychoanalytic view. Discussants tended to reduce concepts about the adult, they largely espoused standardized views about adult potentials, and their discussions were bound to mainstream ideas on normalcy. Second, a number of participants were not of Erikson's bent. They were unaccustomed to riding mental escalators—up and down, back and forth—between humans as individuals and as a collective and between earlier notions of adulthood and those of the contemporary period. Just as Erikson had feared, the elasticity of adult images at the stretched points of life's rubber band could not be maintained. Time and again the band snapped back to its childhood origins.[20]

Nonetheless, two positive outcomes resulted. These were, first, acknowledgment that there is such cultural and social class profusion in the many different ways *adult* is defined and played out that any newly developed norms would be exclusionary. Second, just as the very fact of the conference and its published papers were a mirror of the times, they were also a watershed event and a prod to later thought. Only two decades had elapsed since experts had first begun to think about adults as persons who continue to develop. Both childhood and old age were currently under scrutiny. With increased longevity, psychologists could now consider the changing ways in which those in adulthood's central scope of time outlive the investments and meaning making of one life epoch and use such resources for new and different understandings of themselves and others in later periods of life.

Before considering Erikson's ideas of adults that take us beyond the conference, in line with the way he thought, we should notice how the evolution of psychoanalysis and of developmental thought posed difficulties. In the psychologically enlightened world, by 1971 it was too late to revise thought about adults' developmental potential using a fresh psychoanalytic prism. Freud's successes and resulting psychoanalytic rigidities had taken prisoners. The field had hardened into rock as though Freud, like a latter-day Moses, had passed down a stone tablet complete with recipes and directions for gauging mental aberrations, their origins, and cures. Erikson understood psychoanalysis, its insights and methods, as work-in-progress. To him, it was not a static system but a methodology for ongoing discovery which, in every historical epoch, had to begin anew to comprehend itself, its history, and the human manifestations of the era. Otherwise, rigidities accumulate that represent group-based symptoms. Terms, classified diagnoses, and equations solidify. Beliefs build that there is a precise formula for determining mental and social difficulties instead of a fluid discovery and rediscovery against the current times that are themselves embedded in history. Erikson knew Freud as one who had altered his own ideas and methods several times in the course of a life's work. Yet, to Erikson, by 1971, his field had largely become a shorthand, recipe discipline for psychoanalysts, historians, social scientists, and the general public. To him, the ability to see things anew, unbound by stereotype and by frozen ideas of mental structures and fixations, had been lost.[21]

The occasion of the conference represents Erikson's effort to take his own thinking another step beyond his prior advances about the nature of the adult. By September 1971, when the main sessions of the conference were held, Erikson was a mature scholar. With the bulk of his writing and teaching now behind him, his ideas and questions about the developing adult, as he completed his most active years, provide a fulcrum against which one can sweep backward and forward through his time and writings to find a legacy of insights about adults. Although his hopes for the Conference on the Adult were not realized, Erikson himself provided many important insights into the adult that he had hoped others would come to from their various disciplines. These insights appear in his Harvard papers and notes, in his audiotapes and seminar sessions, and in portions of his publications as well.

In addition to his classical stage framework that illustrates the loving, caring, integrating adult, his lifetime of work lends cameolike portraits of six fresh images of what the adult is and might become. These are the *prejudiced* adult, the *moral-ethical, spiritual* adult, the *playing, childlike* adult, the *historically and culturally relative* adult, the *insightful* adult, and the *wise* adult. Portions of these images are not flattering, for they show adults at their twentieth-century point of physical, cognitive, and psychosocial evolution, complete with biases, hang-ups, and divisions. Some, like Erikson's *childlike* adult, speak more to possibility than to actual tendencies. And all are, necessarily, captured by Erikson from within his psychoanalytic lens in his adoptive America. His ideas reflect the adult he saw in the mid-to late twentieth century, as well as the ideas of "adult" he had found in ancient thought.

IDENTITY TELESCOPED TO AND THROUGH ADULTHOOD

Erikson held that identity does not end with its formation but that identity is the rare attainment and ongoing process which captures and sponsors one's investments throughout the long years of adulthood. More than anything, identity is one's own "*Motiv des Forchens*—what makes you move."[22] Thus psychosocial identity is both a normative period of late adolescence and evolving content for all of adulthood. It is capstone to youth and, as such, is both the springboard and the ongoing nutrient for the developmental terrain that follows. By *identity*, Erikson meant the partly conscious but predominantly unconscious sense of who one is as a person and as a contributor to the work of one's society. It is personal coherence or self-sameness throughout evolving time, through social change, and through altered role requirements. Identity is a deep sense of ideological commitment, of knowing what is worth one's fidelity in the expansive social world.

Erikson said he did not remember when he had first heard the term used, that it might have been in Paul Federn's seminar on the "boundaries of the ego."[23] But it was August Aichhorn who led Erikson to see the *social* in psychosocial identity, walking with him and others through the neighborhoods of Vienna and illustrating its importance. In his early 70s, Erikson said that through the "great August Aichhorn" his "eyes" were "first opened . . . to the problems of youth."[24] As a result, Erikson learned "a way of being" with adolescents, "a way of thinking about them" as well, and methods of treatment.[25]

A benchmark to the late adolescent, identity is both the gateway to and the cornerstone content of adult development. Identity is partially built from the childhood identifications each youth has with a number of different adults. These wrap into, but do not fully constitute identity. Identity's achievement is the hard work of building one's own "adult" through knowing personal talents, interests, and ideological commitments and working to mesh these into a self-image and then an ongoing process of vocational, ideological, and personal commitments. As such, "identity is not the same as identification," for identifications alone cannot forge a coherent, complete identity.[26]·Rather, as William James had claimed and Erikson concurred, such identifications constitute the self one must "murder" to move beyond.[27]

In what must be the most concise answer Erikson ever gave, the Harvard files hold a single page of questions to which Erikson responded in a filmed interview of him and his wife Joan. Two linked questions were: "Does identity express itself through intimacy and generativity (love and work)? Does it do so differently at various stages of life?" To this, Erikson simply wrote, "Yes."[28] Once into adulthood proper, one's earlier identity is not "murdered," but ego investments necessarily change. Identity is, necessarily, "a lifelong development."[29] If, as Erikson held, "a sense of 'I' . . . presides over the pronomial (pronoun) core of all languages," it is a sense of identity that presides over adulthood.[30] Identity is the "integrator" that moves one toward "wholeness."[31]

Identity is intricate and irreducible, yet Erikson feared that some would see its attainment as uncomplicated or, worse, as "common sense."[32] Speaking about himself, no doubt, he said that identity "appears as a most complex achievement to whose who have tasted its absence."[33] Aware of the criticisms addressed to the fact that he had claimed an evolution of identity throughout adulthood, and not wanting his thought to be taken lightly, he illustrated the complexity of identity through his books on Martin Luther and Mahatma Gandhi. In those psychobiographies, he illustrated how two remarkable men did not come to their identities easily or without great work and sacrifice. For both the monk and for the ascetic, identity, once attained, was an ongoing life process. Each struggled to find the compelling causes to which they could commit their entire lives. They thereby gained and solidly owned their missions, their sense of personal coherence, and, consequently, their identities.

In those biographies, Erikson also illustrated his point that identity is best seen in its absence. He showed Luther's and Gandhi's overpowering absence of a sense of self and their intense needs to shear themselves from their paths to comfortable legal careers that would only own them, offering no mission or joy. In other writings, he illustrated identity's absence in negative identities that are shown by prejudice, deviance, substance abuse, and suicide and in identity's fracturing after it had been attained.[34]

Criticisms of Erikson's stretching of the identity construct beyond adolescent and young adult parameters have some validity. In sweeping so great a terrain under the identity rubric, he abandoned the solidarity of identity as a tight construct for the crisis and normative period of adolescence alone. There is validity in Gutmann's point that in moving further and further away from identity as a circumscribed crisis, Erikson rejected identity as the fruit of his creation and thereby evinced a self-rejectivity.[35] But there is also validity to Erikson's point: Once a young person joins the issue of identity, identity is then and always an issue. Young adults' immersion in deep intimacy nearly eclipses their considerable work toward vocational identity if it is by then attained. In the middle years, once intimacy has been achieved and maintained, and as sexual vigor begins to wane, caring for others, for products, and for ideas does eclipse earlier needs and ego investments. Sponsoring and mentoring others then assumes prominence. Later, among older adults, a sense of identity transcends one physical body and world to become both a fear and a longing for a realm beyond the material. Eclipsing prior repressions of death, existential identity is, to elders, both a prescient and an actual personal reality. Thus identity is that which deeply engages the late adolescent's and then the adult's psychological energies in a social world that first accordions out and later collapses down. As Erikson said in cryptic notes about identity: "Fidelity—to go back on it, weakens; to carry it forward, strengthens".[36]

LUTHER: ADULTHOOD JOINED

Young Man Luther was Erikson's first full-fledged book to show identity issues as they were portrayed in Luther's young adult spiritual and intimacy needs. It was also his first complete book on identity proper. When writing about Luther, Erikson was past his own young adulthood and could consider that stage at some distance from intimacy's requirements. Believing that good thinking, reflective writing, and the "peace" to do these arise from "inner space," Erikson wrote most of the book away from his work environment.[37] He was on retreat from Riggs, a minisabbatical that marked several forks in his life: From then on, he saw far fewer patients, and his writing shifted thematically and methodologically. He moved from a form of writing in which he had illustrated developmental issues that were buttressed by clinical data to conceptual essays that he crafted for their ethical, historical, developmental, and teaching appeal. He took himself and his readers down a seer's pathway toward the end of adult life. The clinician was in retreat. The psychoanalytic writer with pressing historical and ethical messages increasingly took center stage. This helped him move decidedly into his own generative ethical years. Comparing his origin with his aims, he wrote:

> That a stepson's negative identity is that of a bastard need only be acknowledged here in passing . . . (but) working between the established fields can mean avoiding the disciplines necessary for any one field; and being enamored with the aesthetic order of things, one may well come to avoid their ethical and political . . . implications.[38]

By first elaborating Martin Luther's identity and then showing the power of militant, nonviolent resistance through the identity needs of a middle-aged Mahatma Gandhi, Erikson shifted permanently to "social and historical implications . . . possibly inspired by my great compatriot Kierkegaard's differentiation of the aesthetic and the ethical life."[39] *Luther* was Erikson's first effort to extend beyond his own aesthetic stage as a psychoanalytic, developmental clinician and to move into his generative period of caring more deeply about his message and about the survival of his legacy of concepts.

Beginning with *Luther*, we can see a change in Erikson's level of thinking, as well as an altered focus of thought. With this period, Erikson showed his climb up the metacognitive and historical ladder. *Childhood and Society* was "written for psychiatrists (and) social workers . . . *Gandhi's Truth* . . . (was) for people interested in history (and) . . . the emergence of nonviolence."[40] By the closing chapters of *Toys and Reasons*, Erikson had moved up cognitively yet again to "shared visions . . . shared nightmares" and worldviews.[41] In his always broader and higher metaperspective, he expanded his vista.

At the time he wrote *Luther*, Erikson was in the middle of his sixth decade of life and, as such, was increasingly considering the meaning of life. The book served many purposes for Erikson personally; thus we cannot simplify its meaning to him. Principally, its writing was his vehicle for finding his voice, for coming to grips with his upbringing, and for understanding where he stood on issues of faith.[42] With *Luther*, Erikson considered the meaning to him of eternity, of the spiritual, and of the way religious institutions required reformation. He began to consider in earnest the human's personal transcendence of the physical boundaries of life. In this fresh terrain of border thinking, Erikson showed the meaning of his own generativity as he moved toward the end of life. As others before and after him, Erikson journeyed from absorption in himself and his discipline, content, and methods to panhuman concerns—from aesthetics through ethics to spiritual introspection. Through *Luther*, Erikson fully joined the problems and issues of adulthood. In this, he believed he had had little choice. Referring here to Darwin, Erikson was autobiographical:

> It is enough to have persisted, with the naiveté of genius, in the dissolution of one of the prejudices on which the security and the familiarity of the contemporary image of man is built. But a creative man has no choice. He may come across his supreme task almost accidentally. But once the issue is joined, his task proves to be at the same time intimately related to his most personal conflicts, to his superior selective perception, and to the stubbornness of his one-way will.[43]

Thus, with *Luther*, Erikson launched a two-pronged effort that continued throughout the rest of his writing years. These were his efforts to understand and more completely portray what it means to be an adult who develops through the conflicts of one life and its times. This is the adult who, through the context and content of his or her changing adulthood, comes to a heightened, introspective self-understanding and a better understanding and care of others. In his analyses, Erikson illustrated how the society-infused adult influences one microcosm of time and space. His related aim was to broaden the reach of his perspectives on developmental ethics. In large-scale psychohistories about Luther and Gandhi, and through briefer sketches of Einstein, Freud, and Jesus, Erikson's concerns about the intermingled issues of insight, prejudice, ethics, and spirituality come through. He showed these against the border at which one adult life joins other lives responsibly and against the fringe of life at which adults face issues of nonexistence.

Erikson's *Young Man Luther* sparked near-instant interest in Freudian applications to history and led to a beginning tide of inquiry and theory that inspired the formation of psychohistorical conferences and journals. That tide has ebbed somewhat, chased back by apt criticisms of some historians' reductionistic and simplistic misuses of psychoanalytic concepts. But *Luther* led irreversibly to two major happenings.

First, historians and social scientists in this country changed their prisms to look more to the ways in which adults of different eras consistently thought, felt, and were motivated to behave, how they supported self and family, and how they adapted to the opportunities and burdens, inclusions and exclusions, of respective positions in their social structures. Persons, and the relativity of their views and needs, were now better visualized against where, when, and how history and society serendipitously lodged them. This is "historical relativity" to Erikson. To historians and social scientists alike, place, time, and the prevailing views and values of different eras came to assume new prominence. By the mid-1990s, thoughtful scholars had become wary about taking contemporary notions, knowledge, understandings, and difficulties and casting them backward through time to interpret and reconstruct history through latter-day lenses.

Second, for Erikson personally, the publication of *Young Man Luther* heralded dramatic changes. Writing *Luther*, he edged along the catwalk on which psychology and history meet but cannot be known firsthand. Although he had ventured there before, psychohistory now became his concentration, a focused way to show how adult psyches intertwine with their own history, with history proper, and with a tendency to preordain parts of the future through identity images, visions, ideas, and plans. Erikson's *Luther* and his concepts about ego identity and its problems opened a pathway to original work. It also helped him drive toward depicting the entire life span. Erikson tackled a great part of this plan by showing how unique, charismatic leaders reverberate against their own psychological needs and against the demands and deprivations of their special social and historical eras. Instead of crumbling before ego-thwarting, oppressive conditions, the young man whom Erikson found in Luther and the middle-aged man whom he uncovered in Gandhi rode their egos and identity needs to change history.

Luther, published just before Erikson brought his clinical work at Riggs to a close, gave Erikson notoriety and exposure to a different audience, that of historians and theologians. It was his favorite among the books he wrote.[44] But with the dangerous territory of psychohistory, he furthered his distance from traditional psychoanalysis and advanced his own decline in mainstream psychoanalytic circles. By stretching beyond known data, first in *Luther* and later in *Gandhi,* he opened himself to excoriating criticism. Marking his departure from contemporary clinical work in this way, Erikson furthered his marginality yet again as he had done in his youth, even as he simultaneously advanced scholarship about what some—Luther, Gandhi—had to do in order to gain their identities. More conceptually borderline now than ever, the spotlight he had once cast onto society and culture, forcing a view to these as both internal and external to the person's psyche, was now directed backward in the hopes that this light would then show the way forward. This spotlight onto the comparatively recent historical past began a fresh view of the developing adult as a biopsychosocial-historical human. It became Erikson's lens into portraying the *historically, culturally relative adult*, an image of the highly abstract, cognitively developed person who lives in history yet knows the self as residing in one era in the total flow of time. Erikson's previous triple bookkeeping of the biopsychosocial person thus evolved into a quadruple ledger. He included the adult self in historical time and context, as well as within his or her very contemporary psyche, soma, and culture.

A number of points about Erikson's images of the adult bear mentioning before I move to the chapters that consider them separately. These points have to do with Erikson's aims, with his images and spatial tendencies, with his word connections and writing style, and with his cosmic sense of things. I take these in turn.

First there is the question of Erikson's aims. Writing notes for his *Daedalus* article on Dr. Isak Borg (the main character in Ingmar Bergman's film *Wild Strawberries*), an Erikson then in his early to mid-70s wrote how "inspiring" it was to find his ground plan laid out so well in Bergman's film. In handwriting, he first said "emerging image," but substituted the word "concept."[45] In this and other notations, Erikson revealed his intention of bringing forward psychosocial concepts about adulthood portrayed in a *Vorstellung,* in images or figural impressions.[46] These images are Erikson's loving, caring, and integrated adult, as well as his images of the prejudiced, childlike and playing, moral-ethical and spiritual, historically and culturally relative, wise, and insightful adult. The images are sometimes hazy, somewhat like a pointillist painting seen too close. They overlap and fuse considerably. A psychoanalyst and an artist was at work. The net effect of his visual imagery is a montage, one image overlaid on the next with significant blurring, crossover, and contradictions.

Typically, Erikson's images are positive, but this is not always the case. Often the qualities Erikson described as polarities result in ambiguity. For example, a playing, childlike adult is disinclined to reside within a prejudiced adult; however, the necessity of growing up in one family, in one religious or areligious view, and in one culture or society, lead even a prejudice-disinclined adult to favor one way of being and one way of life, norms, and mores over others. Such ambiguities are thus not of Erikson's making. They are the facts of a complex human. They are artifacts, as well, of both one theorist's complex thought and his disinclination to represent concepts more simply than they actually are. The reader's need for pinpoint clarity and distillation is often matched by Erikson's need to avoid these.

Clearly, one of Erikson's major aims was to provoke insight so that readers would learn new ways of thinking and seeing. Another aim was to lift adult behavior to higher ethical positions. Some see this as psychology's fallacy, for it turns the field into one of "shoulds" instead of mirroring back what humans are in their era and how disturbances come about. Yet Erikson was convinced that the fully developed adult is, of necessity, a generative, integrated, and ethical adult, the endpoint to which we all "ought to" aim.

This leads into another of Erikson's purposes and then into his manner of working. For his own purposes, Erikson wanted to understand phenomena as they became apparent to him. He understood the power of expressions, found in the use of his pen, heard in his mental voice, or arising from his unconscious. These were his prods to current and subsequent thought and understanding. He captured verbal content and ideas visually; he thought spatially instead of linearly. Hellmut Wohl often watched his friend organize his thoughts on paper that he displayed in front of him horizontally instead of vertically.[47] This was Erikson's way to avoid linear, time-ordered thinking. Moving his ideas about in "circles or in spirals . . . things would expand around the central thought and often in a way that came to him as he was writing . . . (and) . . . thinking."[48] Indeed, in the Harvard papers, horizontal notes and jottings appear on great sheets of artists' paper. His nonlinear thinking appears in his publications as well, for one finds Erikson darting first here and then there in his writing. This tendency makes him a difficult, sometimes disorienting, read, as one tries to follow the main threads of his thought.

In his writing, Erikson's nonnative use of the English tongue was a difficulty. The burden of writing in a language in which he did not originally learn to speak and think led to his habituation to the dictionary. Throughout his Harvard notes and papers, one finds him chasing back to his *Websters* to look up words and ponder their etymology. But his dictionary dependence was also useful to him, for with it he connected concepts and ideas. He went historically back to origins, traveled laterally across words in different languages (Latin to English, German to Latin, English to German, Greek to German), and crossed from one concept to another. When he wrote, for instance, about adults who maintain their continuity with childhood's radiant newness as they leap into cognitive, and then move into role-responsible, adult behaviors, he joined the word "adult" with *Wirklichkeit*, meaning reality.[49] He then connected *adult* and *reality* with *Erwachen*, meaning *awake* or *wake up,* and wondered how the youth "wakes up" in his or her own mental apparatus and in collective reality.[50] Then he connected *adult* with *child* and pondered how the awakened adult keeps alive a childlike sense of wonder and joy in the immediate moment.

Due to his Germanic language and his classical gymnasium education, Erikson's writing is dense and sometimes cumbersome. As Margaret Mead told him in the early years of their association, it is content "packed."[51] Writing to Erikson about the difficulty of reading his work, she said it was "almost as if you had conformed in style to the tight abstraction of the material you are presenting."[52] In the same letter Mead said: "I think it needs some editing, it is . . . full of not quite authentic English words—that is words which you have derived straight from Latin and Greek roots without worrying about idiom."[53] Mead urged him to write more loosely: "the more packed and compact the material, the more lucid and flowing a presentation is needed," she said.[54] Writing an autobiographical memoir at age 75, Erikson said he was displeased with his ability to bring this about. He was disappointed, he said, that many reviewers were not interested in his full range of content. He had somehow been unable to engage their "empathy" for his mission.[55] Instead they honed in on concepts of his that were applicable only to "*their* ethnic or professional kind" or to their interests in his identity failings, his stepson status, and reasons for his name change.[56] This is an important point, for Erikson wanted audiences to entertain his complete thinking, to suspend intellectual criticism long enough to hear and to identify with his points.

At times, Erikson played with words to spark his imagination. He compared the roots of different words, looking, for instance, for associations between *adult* and *adultery, monk* and *monkery*. Sometimes such linkages became his alliterative free association in print. Notice of word origins, of meanings in different languages, and of his play on words shows the way he put his thoughts and writings together. It also illustrates his insight that, due to their distillation, words artificially reduce complex phenomena. They further the human tendency to think restrictively and deductively. In various places Erikson said that, although the English language is profuse in words and meanings, he frequently found that no term adequately expressed an idea he wished to convey. Thus, for a variety of reasons, Erikson jogged through words and meanings, sometimes playfully, sometimes intending to show the limitations of language, and sometimes to take readers in a direction of thought they might not otherwise have entertained. Frequently this tendency makes his writing come alive. At other times, it obscures the complex basis of his thought and his primary points.

When he could, Erikson wrote while overlooking nature. As he scanned the marsh and woodlands from his Alpine-like home on the outskirts of Stockbridge, Massachusetts, in 1950, overlooked the tiny fishing village of Lake Chapala, Mexico, in 1956, or looked out to the sea from his Cotuit, Massachusetts, study in the 1960s,[57] he reflected. He scanned history and disciplines. His wish to avoid the narrow lock of any one discipline found him pulling concepts from one content base and source and then from another. Hellmut Wohl, in the wing of whose Stockbridge home the Eriksons lived for several blustery months in the mid-1960s, recalled the thinking of his friend. Erikson kept alive the "far eastern mysticism" of his youth, a "sort of cosmic sense."[58] Erikson's notes back up Wohl's sense of him. Planning a presentation to Harvard alumni in 1977, Erikson said he had found the "Hindu world view the oldest and most comprehensive view of the whole life cycle."[59] Particularly when writing about the generative adult, he turned to the thought of the "6th–3rd century B.C."[60] This tendency lends a "universality" to his work and connects him as well to Jung, whom Erikson saw as Freud's "crucial complement."[61]

Scuttling Western rationalism and linear thought required that Erikson depart his psychoanalytic discipline alone, for it would have inculcated a linear, time-bound pull to origins and restricted him to concepts of the unconscious that came to the fore in the era of rational enlightenment. So he turned to Eastern thought, to history, to religion, and to philosophy, to any domain that served his conceptual need. With these in hand, he used the comparatively new prism of psychoanalytic knowledge and its methodology to portray his concepts about the adult. In a sense he filtered both the historically known adult and latter-day knowledge about developmental tendencies in the adult through his awareness of mental structures and constraints. He blended these with knowledge about species' evolution. In this way, he tried to update adults as they unfold within the species and within known historical time and against ideas of what he held as important for adults to ethically become.

ERIKSON'S BIASES AND OUR BLINDERS

Throughout his imagery of adults, there are two integrated biases of Erikson's that permeate his thought. These are his placement of humans decidedly within the animal kingdom and his disinclination to believe that highly cerebral, tool-driven humans are developmentally more advanced than less industrially or technologically progressive humans, either in the contemporary world or historically. At times these biases are explicit. At other times they are soft undercurrents in his thought. From 1965 on, they became more prominent in his work.

Looking to these biases, it is a fact of the twentieth century that humans understand their species as part of the animal kingdom, typically placing Homo sapiens at the upper rung of evolution. Further, many people tend to believe that later, more progressive and "civilized" humans are more rational, and thus are better, than earlier or more primitive humans. Erikson disputed such notions. He accepted that the development of grey matter, upright posture, linguistics, and tool use places humans on top of the evolutionary ladder and gives them dominance. However, he found that humans are far less dependable and trustworthy than lower-form creatures. To Erikson, at least nonlinguistic beasts have predictable reliable instincts as behavioral guidance systems, whereas most human adults were a different case. Highly cerebral animals, human adults frequently behave in de-cerebrate ways, even after long eras of evolution and extended human childhoods of teaching and nurturing. Further, he held that human adults' rational, order-prone, de-emotionalized thinking obscures their limbic powers to feel and "to see" with feeling. To him, the intellect of the evolved human adult sits on top of, and obliterates, senses, sense, and insight. Rational intellect evaluates from its power center in some icy cold region of the cerebrum where "thinking" adults calculate how one or another option might lead to greater personal gain or good. Such "reason" necessarily mixes with variable doses of infantile rage. This is a rage-reason blend that exists in every adult. But in some persons and situations, its blend is volatile. Detached reason and aggressive rage can obliterate feeling, leading to the destruction of others and of the self. Watching along as Erikson thought and wrote, readers find him wondering how the evolved, tool-making, manipulating, intellectualized adult might be intentionally reversed down the evolutionary tree to a person who feels and cares deeply.

Erikson's related bias was that humans are contained within the animal kingdom in perpetuity. He found that many adults tend to deny the biological forces and controls that life places on all animals, just as he found mid-to late-twentieth-century adults in particular tending to deny the reality of death. In his Harvard papers and audiotapes, we find Erikson musing about the sounds of bird chirpings, about the rhythmic beat of the songwriting Beatles of the 1960s, about the pull and sway of native American and African drums, and about the lyrical symmetry of elders' reveries in songs and poems. Softly planted in Erikson's images is his sense of humans as creatures of the wild, now domesticated perhaps, but only arbitrarily wrenched from a more natural ecological niche. He held that human preferences to see the species as separate from these natural abodes and as both separate from and better than lower creatures creates difficulties that most adults themselves cannot see.

The images that follow in the next chapters do not specify stages or the specific contents of adult love, care, and completeness. Erikson's psychosocial stage energies, investments, and sequencing are integral to his writing. They are implicit in the chapters and content that follow. However, when singled out, they obscure the images Erikson conveyed in which such content necessarily finds its form. In fact, Erikson's stage content blinds readers to seeing his images in published works. This is partly because Erikson intended other primary messages and partly because readers will find what has been memorialized in more than 60 years of Erikson's work in print. Adults always find what they expect to see. Erikson wished to teach lessons to his public, those of stage-unfolding potentials and requirements and that of the integration of the unconscious in a partly conscious, connected, potentially ethical and developing, biopsychosocial, and historically embedded human. Had he emphasized from the outset the insights and images that are built so carefully into his telescoping stage concepts about the adult, those would by now define his thought. Instead, he took another path and left behind the work of unearthing the images he and development portray.

4

Prejudiced Adult

Prejudice: Offensive Projection of Id on Enemy.
                    — Erikson, "Jefferson Lectures"

On many occasions in his life, Erikson walked through the stone arch of the gate in which the following message is chiseled: "Enter to grow in wisdom. Depart to serve better your country and your kind."[1] Erected in 1901, in an era of mass immigration, the gate leads onto the grounds of a major American university. The closing words of its message convey the insular thinking that characterized a nation at the turn of the century, conveying a form of prejudice which Erikson studied and countered throughout his life. Who, he repeatedly asked, *is* one's "kind?"

One's *kind*, Erikson said, is the entire human species, something its full membership did not yet appreciate. As a psychoanalyst and a student of cultural anthropology, history, and the species' origin and evolution, Erikson understood the irrational proclivities that shape personal values and behavior. This led him to explain biases through his image of the *prejudiced adult*. This is Erikson's most powerful identity image. Its power derives from its removal of blame and guilt, and therefore of personal defensiveness, from the prejudice equation and due to Erikson's illustration of the developmental relationship between each child's imprinting and tool learning and that child's later adult biases and behavioral mind-set. To Erikson, these characteristics explain adult resistance to insight about personal prejudice. He held that when persons understand the reasons for their unconsciously accumulated biases, they are more likely to use such knowledge and, hopefully, an accompanying empathy for others to move beyond narrowness. Prejudice evolves from natural, partly irrational phenomena, but adults can and must transcend such inclinations in order to express more mature, inclusive iden-

41

tities. We live in an era of vastly diverse ethnic, racial, national, religious, and sexual expression and mores, one in which adults can profit from understanding their own absolutist, moralizing judgments about how other people "should" live in this world. Knowledge and understanding tend to counter narrow judgmentalism. Thus this image of Erikson's is conceptually and practically tied to one of the most pressing problems of the times. At the group and species levels, his vision that nuclear annihilation is likely unless exclusion of others is consciously and collectively abandoned raises the stakes. Yet, in the Western world, and in the individualistic United States in particular, autonomous, egocentric identity development augurs against movement to higher, more relational forms of adult identity.

HUMAN GROUPINGS IN EVOLUTION

Erikson's overarching concept of prejudice is that individuals always hold membership in one or another group, such as families, nations, and clans, and that all such groups espouse certain cohesive views and inculcate identifications among their members. This group membership houses preferences, biases, and prejudices. As well, there are national, cultural, and racial human groups whose particular prejudices, ill known and unappreciated by them and others, divide the species into potentially warring units. In conceptualizing the prejudiced adult, Erikson found a coherent way to understand and explain the exclusionary, anti-Semitic cultures of his youth and young adulthood and then to explain the heightened danger to all that first arrived with the invention of the atomic bomb. He revealed the "human propensity" in every person, traceable to the tribe-based beginnings of humans' first groupings, to lift personal confidence in identity, personal centrality, and competence by branding, "prejudging," and excluding entire groups of other humans.[2] Erikson understood human tendencies to feel guilt, to project fears, blame, ego deficits, and negative inclinations on others, and to deflect these backward onto the self. Showing the substantial complexity that characterizes his writing, he conceptualized the dilemma of prejudice and showed a way beyond some of it. He accomplished this by giving adults a vehicle for casting blame retrospectively onto evolution and the group-based origin of the species. He variously illustrated what he saw as an early evolutionary and ongoing need to believe that all who are not members of their tribe or clan must be a "freakish and gratuitous invention of some irrelevant deity."[3] This makes members of the "out" group minimally useful as a "screen" onto which the "in" tribe can project its negative identity elements and antipathies.[4] The negative identity is none other than one's id, "one's personal devil."[5] Thus projection is useful and important. It is always better to position the devil, evil, and the id among the possessions of others instead of within the self.

The tribe of distant eras was discrete content for Erikson. It was also a metaphor through which he led contemporary adults to understand why and how everyone harbors prejudice. This was Erikson's teaching ground for visualizing current problems and solutions minus the threat and defensiveness each person feels when seeing him- or herself as one who excludes and devalues others. On recognizing behavioral evidence of prejudice and reflecting on its origins and partial necessity, adults might join affect with reason and, in so doing, cast such inclinations aside. As Erikson believed in 1929 and held to throughout his life, rational explanations alone are insufficient: "Anything the affect has taken into its possession, it will yield only under the impact of a stronger, vital experience; but not under the impact of intellectual arguments."[6] Expressed differently by Rokeach, it is only when an adult acutely perceives, with his or her entire awareness, that the real self is prejudiced and, as such, is very much inferior to the ideal, nonprejudiced self that he or she had thought embodied his or her personal thought and behavior all along that values and actions have a prayer of shifting toward the ideal.[7]

From his first publication in 1930 onward, each of Erikson's books and nearly every paper houses his efforts to understand, explain, and teach about prejudice. Clinical notes from 1929, on which basis Erikson wrote his 1930 paper, "Psychoanalysis and the Future of Enlightenment," illustrate how an anxious fear of otherness can be turned back against the self.[8] However, he said that the phenomenon of groups' acting as though they were, in fact, a deity-glorified species was first apparent to him on visiting the Yurok and the Sioux and observing suspicions between those tribes. In the same context, he also saw group-based anxieties and prejudices between native Americans and whites: "'The whites *teach* their children to cry,' and 'the Indians *teach* their children to masturbate,' contains a differentiation which creates or rationalizes hate between groups: It implies that foreign customs are based on bad intentions."[9] If different child-rearing views can be maligned as harmful or deviant, he wrote, one's neighbor can then be readily labeled as a monster, as someone, and as a representative of some others, who took a giant detour from the self-image known clearly as the incarnate of God. Other tribes, many of whose early names meant "'*the* people,' the only mankind," can then be thought so nonhuman that they, just as clearly, are believed to be "in league with the id as well as the Devil."[10] To Erikson, "castes, classes, and cliques . . . (are) the strongest causes of true panic, namely the (often anachronistic) fear of extinction."[11] Writing in the late 1930s, Erikson hoped that "cultural enlightenment" would come from "learning to grasp the correspondence between prejudices and group virtues."[12]

The World War II years of 1940 to 1942 intensified Erikson's efforts to understand prejudice. But it was not until the mid-1960s that world events pressed him to find exact words to express his concept, the hyphenated term *pseudo-species*. This was the "most polite" term he could find, he said.[13] Based on Konrad Lorenz's use of the German words *schein*, meaning "mock" or "pretense," and *gattung*, meaning "kind," "sort," or "species," Erikson imported the term for his own use.[14] He first explored this concept at the Royal Society of London in 1966. Later, on August 6, 1968, he elaborated it in a formal address to faculty and students of the University of Cape Town, South Africa.[15]

The date of Erikson's Cape Town lecture was the 23rd anniversary of the bombing of Hiroshima. In the 1968 of Erikson's lecture, a number of world events led him to fear that the final nuclear holocaust might be at hand. Troubling events saw a species increasingly divided against itself. There was a risk that such division and aggression would be diverted into nuclear weapons and outer space. Using the frames of psychoanalytic and social evolutionary thought, he defined prejudice both as a "natural" fact of life and as the principal species crisis of twentieth-century adulthood.[16] He described adults as prisoners of group mentalities that held their version of humanity as the best or only kind of humanity:

> The term denotes the fact that while man is obviously one species, he appears and continues on the scene split up into groups (from tribe to nations, from castes to classes, from religions to ideologies) which provide their members with a firm sense of distinct and superior identity—and immortality. This demands, however, that each group must invent for itself a place and a moment in the very centre of the universe where and when an especially provident deity caused it to be created superior to all others, the mere mortals.[17]

Thus, from its historical beginnings forward, Erikson saw the species as needing both individual identities and pseudo-, group-based identities. The development of individual ego identities had been good, normal, and conducive of survival, he wrote. The species had survived because of the active engagement of its members in the mainstream of the sponsoring collective. At that collective level, pseudo-speciation had propelled survival because of the illusion it afforded each group of being chosen and, therefore, capable of survival. However, group identities had taken cohesiveness to the extremes of exclusivity and superiority over all other groups. Such exclusionary groups had inculcated and focused the ever-present human rage; this had heightened aggression.

MANIFESTATIONS, EXPLANATIONS, AND ERIKSON'S FEARS

Erikson scanned nations, societies, and smaller groups of adults and found the prejudice phenomenon everywhere, in professions, associations, clans, clubs, neighborhoods, races, ethnic groupings, families, ideologies, religions, political factions, and nations. Manifestations of this false belief in a group's specialness could be seen in early legends and mythology, in early and later roles, taboos, rules, tools, weaponry, credentials, and ceremonials. These "bind" each group into an amalgam, he wrote, and bless it with such "super-individual significance" that it can "inspire loyalty, heroism—and poetry."[18] This is the best of its lifeblood and effects. He saw its negatives in compulsive ritualisms, in tendencies to call others names such as "pigs . . . rats . . . snakes," and in "forbidding boundaries" against those who must be kept out.[19] Language and cerebral development would seem to have distinguished humans from the other animals, but it did not. Adults might not spray the periphery of their properties with excretions to show where others had better not step, but they do so with fences, tools, laws, customs, and words instead.[20] For the psyche and in human language, those who are "outside" too easily become "nameless," then "unmeaningful," then "strange," and finally "*wrong.*"[21]

Erikson also wrote that some parents treat their children as if they were pseudo others, using them for self-serving purposes. In particular, he held that fathers "mark and brand" their sons with "circumcisions, puberty rites, 'confirmations' and graduations of many kinds . . . preparing (them) for being sacrificed in 'holy' wars."[22] In such a way, "adolescing man is enjoined for the first time to become a full member of his pseudo-species, and often of a special *elite* within it."[23] The rites by which adolescents are confirmed as worthy to fight their fathers' wars link the rituals of the youngster's infancy and childhood with "an ideological world-image, provide a convincing coherence of ideas and ideals, and give the youth the feeling of active participation in the preservation or renewal of society."[24] Rarely did Erikson sound so sure of his thought as when he wrote:

> This is terribly important because I'm absolutely sure that the repression of the Laius' complex has a lot to do with war, with the father generations always sending the young ones out to fight their battles, fight for their territories, to fight for ideals.[25]

Evidence is not found in mythology.However, contrary to some critics' claims, Erikson had data. In the case of pseudo-species tendencies, he had accumulated clinical findings to build and support his conclusions. It was a compilation of

> studying, in case after case, the way in which a patient's integrative forces are inactivated by fragments of the past which remains highly actual and yet refuses to be transformed into future: undigested memories, unsatisfied drives, unallayed fears, unconsummated relationships, unappeasable demands of conscience, unused capacities, incomplete patterns of identity, suppressed spiritual needs.[26]

He then lifted his aggregate of clinical findings and cases to the grand social scale of contemporary and historical eras. Erikson did not support his findings with what has become known as hard, objective data. In fact, he bristled that the era had consecrated and deified objectivity, along with its built-in reductionism, beyond all reason. Humans are subjects, Erikson wrote. As much more than objects, they cannot be understood other than as complex persons in the subjective and in the intersubjective. The intersubjective is the space and dynamic between and among persons. Erikson refused to "reify" that intersubjective, but he gave great validity to the power that persons have on others through human abilities to connect with one another in order to validate thought and behavior, as well as to sway thought.[27]

Other researchers have agreed with Erikson's premises of group mentalities and have supported his case. Johnson, for example, analyzed the prejudice phenomena in a number of twentieth-century religions. Examining ideology and group identity as a solidarity that leads to mechanisms of exclusion, there is, he found, a fascinating similarity between headhunters and a number of modern religious groupings. Each would agree, he argued, that "you ought *not* to hunt heads within your own tribe. . . . Such trophies are to be garnered from outside the in-group."[28] To Erikson, the extreme belief that one group, nation, culture, or ideology alone possesses a manifest destiny places all other identities in danger, for fellowship or brotherly love can then be defined in the most exclusive terms: "You are not *my kind* of person."

Erikson's concerns were that prejudice in a time of high technology permits mass incarceration, dislocation, banishment, and even elimination of so-called "dangerous groups." He wrote of the violence to Native Americans and African Americans in the United States and, in Germany, of the technology of Hitler's anti-Semitic methods that eliminated whole segments of groups believed dangerous to the in-group. He had visited the holding-tank reservations in which Native American tribes were contained; by then they had been uprooted and robbed of their buffalo, their spirit, and their future. He had watched the World War II captivity of Japanese American citizens, enclosed in fences on their own home ground. And he had seen that many millions of Chinese were held invisible beyond "a bamboo curtain."[29] He understood these phenomena as extensions of the ways in which the human mind separates and walls things off, thereby making its self and its own world clearer, more real, better, and more understandable. When others are visually removed, they can then be readily bracketed away from consciousness as though they do not exist. This permits adults to justify as extinguishable those who are invisible.

Erikson explained the prejudice tendency in other ways as well. One of these was in terms of the potential malignancy of a person's and group's identity deprivation. In Hitler, he had seen an absence of identity achievement mingled with such anxious fear of nonbeing that the führer was able to inflate many Germans' individual identity fears and their collective fears about their country's and culture's potential demise into a grand hysterical balloon. Such extremes of malevolent fear and prejudice signified that such persons and their in-groups had threateningly incomplete identities. This was manifest in the need to gain some measure of identity by forcing others to relinquish theirs. It was, of course, self-ruinous, of which Hitler was a prime example: His pathology led him to extinguish others first and himself finally.[30]

When Erikson connected the human propensity toward pseudo-speciation with human territoriality and with his studies of identity deprivation, two particularly destructive threats concerned him most. Placing these in the priority order he gave them, these are, first, the tendency of a dominated "minor" group to incorporate negative or "derisive opinions" of the majority into its own self-assessment, and second, the potential for nuclear annihilation of the entire species.[31] For the first of these concerns, the terms "minor" and "minority" are negative terms that reference a shared, "negative identity"of certain people in society.[32] A group that is forced to "accept minority status . . . is apt to make an adjustment to such status by colluding with it—unconsciously, of course."[33] Further, being held down leads to a rage that is expressed in harmful ways: It is directed inward as depression, self-hate, and personal destruction and outward as dependency first and vented aggression later. Rage, and its incorporated guilt, prevent authentic development of those in the "minor" and in the "major" group, for violence against one's opponents is inseparable from self-inflicted violence.[34] Holding others down prohibits self-development to higher levels of ethical behavior and personal authenticity and the expression of these in a mature identity. And rejection of others also leads, inexorably through the passing years, to rejection of all humans, including oneself.

The second threat is a continued species divisiveness in which one group will eventually destroy all others and itself in the "dubious glory" of nuclear annihilation.[35] This second-order threat is a natural consequence of the first. It is also a consequence of tool development and industrialization. Early on, primitive humans had directed some of their aggression into making tools by hand. Eventually tool and missile making were accomplished by machines. Thus sophisticated tools and missiles had become mindless aggression vents that can be used for the rage of those held down or for the needs of those seeking to keep their dominion intact.

Childhood: Imprinting, Superego Development, and Tool Learning

Erikson was the first to show the enigma, dimensions, and social anchoring of identity; it was thus his privilege to explain the negative identity, prejudice. A theorist with a hammer, with his identity-pseudo-species link in hand, he hoped to banish the worst of prejudice; however, he knew that he could not completely oust it from the human condition. Prejudice is built into the ground plan of evolution and is solidified by the lengthy years of human childhood.

In a largely unpublished manuscript that was delivered to Houghton Library after his death, Erikson had written his ideas about the linkage between the life span and community, virtues, qualities of the human spirit, and ethical guidelines for clinicians. "Ethics says," he wrote, "that the worst crime is the crushing of the human spirit." This unfinished book shows that Erikson had planned to elaborate ways in which the human spirit and ethics unfold throughout the life stages. What "animates the human?" Which attributes of that evolving spirit might be "most vulnerable" in different life epochs? "Spirit," he wrote, is "interchangeable" with "virtue," known previously as "soul."[36]

In that manuscript, Erikson had difficulty making a coherent case, but he said as much there as elsewhere about children's outer, and the later adult's inner, suppression by forces that keep them small, dispirited, and developmentally thwarted. At best, he said, children move through developmental time under the care of loving parents and community. At worst, Erikson saw children, historically and today, treated like some foreign pseudo-species: "as soil to be ploughed and implanted; animals to be whipped and tamed; property to be disposed of; cheap labor to be exploited."[37] Between these two versions resides the great gray terrain in which harsh or more gentle imprinting and judicious or restrictive superegos grow.

Erikson never published most of those passages. But he had set in motion a conceptual engine that he had intended to drive beyond the ego and identity itself. Leave ego to itself and to the ages, he wrote. Ego is "organ (and organizer) of active mastery," of mental life and reality, the "creation of the personal mind itself." Ego is person in his or her own unique centrality and originality; "ego is society, and society ego." Ego is strong, enduring, and, in persons and groups, brandishes great power.[38]

Humans are always entranced by their "awe and . . . wish to master" that which is larger than the self and cannot be apprehended by "immediate consciousness."[39] The larger-than-life, awe-inspiring mechanism that remained for Erikson himself to understand and bring under control was superego, a far greater challenge than ego. For superego is the weapon of the self against self and others. It is the rigidity-indoctrinating controller of morality and the implementor of judgment, an agent, in person and group, that is developed and bolstered by the highly important family and the great world of religions. The latter were themselves now rigidified into pseudo-species variants.[40] Thus, superego now had to be understood as the "both/and" minister of necessary, conscious and unconscious, childhood grooming and of disproportionate control. Morality itself begged to be controlled and transcended. In the history of development, for each individual and for the collective history of the species, Erikson insisted that superego had to be considered a most temporary, stopgap apparatus.[41]

Erikson saw superego as an arbiter of good and evil, an institutor of morality and moralism, that had been developed and guarded throughout long centuries of the childhood of the species. In individuals, he saw its development in childhoods that seemed to grow longer and longer. Superego seemed to have become a weapon that counters the lifeblood of vital, animating adults and their children. This made it an imminent danger to the species, for it breeds lethal prejudice. Amidst the numerous relativities of different ideological systems' competing values, individual and group superegos had to be transcended. Shortly after Erikson had first conceptualized ego identity as a self-in-ideology and vocational crisis of adolescence, he had written that movement to a more mature identity requires adults to transcend egocentric, individualistic identities that are construed as self in autonomy and work alone. Due to the nuclear crises of the times, particularly from the mid-1960s on, he felt compelled to write the next part of the script. In this script, a species-wide supraego and a superordinate ethics would define adult development. Individuals' and groups' separate egos and moralities had to be taken beyond their absolutist, prejudicial, identity territories. Only in this way might all humans visualize, develop, consecrate, integrate, and act on an international ethics built on a mutual assent to agreed-on human values.

Freud had insisted that the "strengthening of the super-ego is a most precious cultural asset," for the superego was developed and deployed by persons who were great "vehicles" of civilization.[42] Erikson disagreed. To him it was the watchdog superego that had made the human its slave and the species-wide ego that required strengthening.[43] He hoped to illustrate this, for individual and aggregate superegos had to be prevented from developing increasingly harsh coercions against self and others. This was the only way that diverse persons and nations could advance together developmentally. The person and group had historically denied "the status of reciprocal ethics to those outside," he said, but perhaps he could find a way to breach that divide and turn things around.[44] Clearly, Erikson never accomplished his aim.

Yet Erikson fulfilled part of his agenda by alerting his reading public to the realities of prejudice. In part, he did this by changing the Golden Rule. As he saw it, the Rule had led adults to consider as highly adequate a guide that offers an immature, legalistic level of operational morality. As a principle for behavioral guidance, using the Rule, persons see themselves as bound only by a quid pro quo reciprocity in which one can feel justified in "do(ing) unto others as you would have others do unto you."[45] The Rule alternates between "exhortation" ("*Do* as you would be done by") and "warning" ("Do not to others what if done to you would cause you pain")[46] The admonition "does not presuppose much more than the mental level of the small child who desists from pinching when he gets pinched in return."[47] Erikson's rule advanced the principle to the higher level of ethical adulthood:

> I would propose that we consider moral rules of conduct to be based on a fear of threats to be forestalled—outer threats of abandonment, punishment, public exposure; or a threatening inner sense of guilt, shame, or isolation. In contrast, I would consider ethical rules to be based on a love of ideals to be striven for—ideals that hold up to us some highest good, some definition of perfection, and some promise of self-realization.[48]

Take consciousness and ethics to the next step, he wrote. Eschew reciprocal vengeance. Instead, affirm and augment growth in others and in oneself. To bring this about, Erikson described mature adult identities, those in which self-centered autonomous identity was only identity's youthful first growth. Both self-central ego identity and the narrow superego had to be superseded for those who could be considered true adults.

Immersed in the subject as a subject, Erikson tried to illustrate both the necessity of moral and superego development in childhood and the equal necessity of transcending such attainments. As the trans-Freudian who had created the concept of ideologically grounded ego identity, he had to demonstrate its ongoing validity as the mechanism that can lead to an inclusive identity. But he also had to show how one can move beyond autonomous identity without destroying its importance or the validity of his construct. The lifeblood of identity and his own credibility had to be kept intact.

To show how autonomous identity can evolve into a mature identity form and to create a dual concept of the superordinate ego-in-ethics, Erikson's case was partially in hand. He had shown early on that it was human to have long childhoods and progressive to have ever longer ones. He had illustrated how childhood modeling brought about strong moral development and prejudicial difficulties. Between 1937 and 1965, he had shown how the family and the social unit (ethnic group, tribe, race, and nation) imprint moral development and values on the child and how the child incorporates these into a conscience that eventually replaces external parental requirements. As had Freud, he portrayed the superego as that which is built on the model of the parental superego. Going beyond Freud to the social sphere, Erikson held that a number of attributes are eminent in the superego's propriety, and, therefore, its prejudicial mainstay. These are family and group variations in the meaning and demonstration of important ideas such as cleanliness, efficiency, initiative, deference to others, listening and speaking, and sense of the Almighty.[49] Through these values and the daily rituals in which they are verbalized and modeled for the child, ideas of good and bad encode the child's psyche. This first occurs in ritual experiences with the mother, for all humans experience both an infantile near-autistic lock with the mother and some form of separating from her. This "numinous" mother, initially joined with, and then severed from, the infant's universe, overcomes the infant's rudimentary but very real experience of separation, aloneness, and abandonment by behaviors that first begin rituals through cycles of feeding, holding, touching, cleaning, singing, and sleeping.[50] This begins the route through which rituals, incorporating values, are behaviorally begun and reinforced, leading inexorably to moral behavior and its concepts. The infant, watched and guarded, eventually becomes a child who "is trained to 'watch him (or her) self.'"[51] This is the "ontogenetic source of the 'negative identity,' . . . " containing all that "one is not supposed to be or show— and what one yet potentially is."[52] For one must "learn to imagine" negative "potential traits . . . in order to be able to avoid them."[53]

Learned first behaviorally through experiences such as smiles given and withheld, caregiver "yeses" and warning "nos," such sanctions find their way into a rule-driven morality, frequently born of quid pro quo reciprocity. In adolescence, on the brink of adulthood, ideological thinking captures earlier, moral reasoning, but the sanctions of childhood are never completely transcended. As a result, humans move past but are forever bound to the nursery within. This moral nursery, and subsequent childhood conditioning, become integral to mind, psyche, and soul, interminable compatriots and intermingled zealots. More than a stratum (implying early layer) of mind-psyche, the ritual-encoded moral crib of infancy and the internalized parental warnings and judgments of childhood exist in the present of each adult's psyche and life. Sometimes this seed bed is transformed to meet current needs and an altered social scheme. At other times social expectations are adjusted to meet internalized needs. But throughout all of adult life, this moral-ritual bedrock is indisputably contemporaneous. As Erikson said, absorbed parental judgments remain with us forever. Their warnings and exhortations are always ready to label us good or bad.[54]

As each child moves forward to an ego identity that is uniquely his or hers, cherished ways of being in the world cannot be cast aside, even in the most singular identity that seems markedly autonomous from the nuclear family. In childhood, said Erikson, youth become "specialized."[55] Throughout a long childhood of habituation to, and then preference for, the familiarity of oft-repeated daily rituals, these become satisfying in their expectancy and daily experience. In such a way, the value-honed, moral-ritual encryption indoctrinates. Prisms are built through which persons see and interpret, producing habits of perspective and of blindness. Each young person who has been brought up grows in his or her habituation to a deeply ingrained value system and to its related inner controls. "Every conscience," Erikson wrote, "whether in an individual or a group, has not only specific contents but also its own peculiar logic which safeguards its coherence."[56] Thus exclusion of inimical foreign values seems natural and appropriate and is, in fact, self-protective.

This was the ground plan from which Erikson built. Learning positives and negatives, what one can and cannot do and be, imprinting positive and negative notions for *clean, good, correct, industrious, trustworthy*, and a coterie of other values, these are, by adulthood, the mind's eye and the psyche's flank guard. "Self-idealization" is thus developed, family and cultural traditions are passed along, and symbols representing group mores and values, some linguistically represented, are preserved.[57] Erikson repeatedly wrote about the prolonged human childhood in which children are ritually "speciated" by their experience of family.[58] They are familiarized by human rituals within a unique form of family existence to develop "a distinct sense of corporate identity," one that builds and accumulates to preferences and prejudices of various forms.[59] Further, "to have steady values at all," Erikson said, "humans must absolutize them."[60] Absolute values for the self are projected as absolute value requirements for others. Further, "moral self-discrimination is sharpened by an indoctrination against evil others, on whom the small child can project what he must negate in himself, and against whom he can later turn that moralistic and sadistic prejudice which has become the greatest danger of the species man."[61] Knowing this, it was his difficult task to somehow de-absolutize values by demonstrating how a supreme good to one person and group can be reprehensible to others. He undertook the high challenge of demonstrating both the necessity of the individual superego and ego and the reasons for undermining portions of those mental structures in the problematical conditions of a racially diverse and nuclear-powered era.

To build his case, Erikson found it essential to include the problems implicit in mechanized tools and in the skill building that is first learned in childhood. By learning to use tools that become more and more advanced, he held, humans had become mechanistic. Intellect was now readily, icily detached from awareness. Adults could be seen everywhere so highly machine- and tool-dependent that there was scant time, awareness, or energy to think about and plan how tools might best be used. Declarative knowledge ("I know and can tell *about* something") had too easily slid down that conscious-to-less-conscious slope into a predominance of procedural knowledge ("I can *do* something—and can do that something without having to think about it or about why I am doing it."). As Erikson saw it, the inorganic world of metal, money, machines, and computers had gained control of the organic realm, including those procedural humans who had devised the subsidiary world of mechanized artifacts.

An interest in functional tools and the ability to use them skillfully and nonconsciously begins in the school age. The extended human childhood was made even longer by the era of advanced mechanization and by the adult's "worship of 'what works.'"[62] To Erikson, along with human prejudices and the way these are nurtured through the rule- and value-driven rituals and habits of childhood, adding tools to the mix had led to the brink of disaster: Weapons could be used as the tools of highly cerebral, reasoning adults against humans of other *kinds* and against all of humankind. Erikson's vision was a great, fearsome prophecy in which he clearly believed that humans' interest in mechanization and their tool immersion were tendencies that took them backward, downward to a prior stage of collective development. The best he could hope for was that this station would be but a temporary regression in service to eventual species evolution.

Adulthood Habituation and Identity Relativity

For adulthood, Erikson described the routinized performance of procedures and tasks that free the mind from having to think about every move of body and limb. Once at their jobs, adults might realize that they drove cars there, but all the while they had been mindless about the mechanics of using the steering wheel, brake, gearshift, and radio or even of the routes they followed. Adults move through aisles of a familiar grocery store, becoming instantly annoyed when the store's interior is redesigned and they must think anew about the location of essential supplies. They eat, bathe, and retire to bed in accustomed ways, most of these rituals having their own preset order in which some things are habitually done first, others second, and some third. In a psychoanalytic frame, Erikson described behavior that learning theorists later defined somewhat differently: The habitual and repetitive release the mind to work on other problems, a shift having occurred from more conscious, *declarative knowledge* to routinized, *procedural behavior*. The daily and habitual are also highly satisfying. When routine patterns are disrupted, adults are at a loss to explain their resulting discomfort. Depending on the meaning and extent of the rupture, it might take minutes or years to return to a sense of equanimity and of satisfaction in the newly habitual and familiar.

In this same way, Erikson explained, values, modes of thinking, and prejudices, first instituted in infancy and childhood by rituals and habits, are routinized below the surface of adult thought. They become satisfying, familiar patterns that resist conscious encounter and challenge. Seen through his psychoanalytic lens, such insights led Erikson to recognize that generic mindlessness, in relationships and weaponry, was something that had to be overcome. Adults had to be jolted out of their unconscious, procedural behaviors so they could develop insight into prejudice.

During his Harvard tenure in the 1960s, Erikson had hoped that the college students and young adults who worked to advance civil rights and to oppose America's involvement in Vietnam would become the vehicles of change toward equality and peace. Far earlier, Erikson had written about the ways in which youth is nearly always the medium of value and tempo change in society. But he soon saw that the high-minded ideological reasoning of young adults readily becomes enmeshed in the norms, routines, and standardization of their jobs. This is due to their need for jobs and to a behavioral adaptation to work life, both of which are augmented by a deeper patterning in their own rituals and routines of daily life.

Erikson wrote that although routine habits, roles, and beliefs provide clarity and a firm border to the dimensions of the adult self, a tightly bounded, vocationally driven, autonomous identity also leads to "territorial defensiveness."[63] Adults "stake out" their identities in the "eternal security" of work protections.[64] This, he found, is particularly so among those who vest their very identities in the safety of work roles in organizational life instead of in their ideological commitments. "Most adults submit to so-called reality, that is, a consolidation of established facts, of acquired methods, of defined roles, and of overweening values."[65] In many persons, work-role patterning and adherence to institutional norms, routines, and standards produce narrowness. Such behaviors lead to a deep habituation to institutional life. Combined with personal habits and patterns, the adult's mind is then no longer free, vital, and animated. Potentials of adulthood are limited, and tendencies toward biases and prejudice increase.

In making his points about the deadening, rigidity-inducing effects on adults of standardization and institutionalized habits, Erikson did not say he was straying over the boundary at which psychoanalysis meets explicit behaviorism, but that is what he did. His description of the adult clearly depicts a chameleon effect in which persons put on the skin and lens of their institutions, or, at minimum, of the organizational or professional roles in which they hold membership. This is the hefty basis on which their adulthoods are, in large part, established and sanctioned. As Erikson aptly demonstrated in the case of the elderly physician protagonist in his elaboration of Ingmar Bergman's film *Wild Strawberries,* what adults do is what they are.[66] And what they do and are establishes and patterns what they continue to be and to become.

Adults' Rigidity and Institutionalized Religions

To Erikson, biases are inculcated in childhood through long years of grooming; however, his prejudice image is a decidedly adult concept. The biases and habits of childhood wrap into the high ideology and group cohesion of adolescence. Each searching adolescent, with all of childhood now behind and within the self, now "stands tall" with like-minded persons to create the world anew. Identity grounds each new generation of prejudiced adult, a cohort that will differ according to the era and its changing values and inventions.

Into adulthood proper, deep patterning in work and in the habituations of everyday life is solidified by adherence to religious tenets. Erikson did not explicitly connect the habituating effect of work and jobs with the narrowing tendencies of adherence to religious forms and practices. He also did not speak of the catalytic effects that religions and work necessarily have on each other. In fact, for the most part he was careful to write about these two areas of life separately, showing each to induce deterioration into greater rigidity. He believed that each of these separate domains does its part to close the adult mind to alternate ways of seeing and being in the world. Combined with childhood values, both abet bias, opinionation, and prejudice of one form or another. Their effects on the person are more than additive.

Addressing institutionalized religion, Erikson's writing shows him in conflict. He tried to avoid detracting from religion, its symbols, imagery, and rites. In fact, he wrote that he found peace in occasional church attendance, loved the richness of Catholic ceremony, and enjoyed seeing the living use of religious forms. He also wrote of the blame that psychiatry must some day accept as its burden because of the way it had distanced itself from religion. Erikson did not wish to discredit the faith homes of so many adults, for he saw that religions serve good, ultimate aims. Psychiatry might well connect with but could not replace religious belief.

In religion, as is true for many other areas of his work, Erikson and his concepts are of a piece, a theory he developed and lived. Some interpreters of Erikson have linked Erikson's ideas directly to religion, marking him as a pseudo-religious theorist.[67] But Erikson remained at a distance from institutional religion in his writing and in his life. This is on a par with the way he eschewed his own captivity by any one discipline. Yet he was deeply concerned about the various ways religious practices focus on rite and form, seemingly for the sake of those artifacts alone. Once institutionalized and ingrained, he said, these readily lead to habituated routines and to tendencies toward narrowly patterned behavior, thought, and prejudice. In this way, live rituals, once they are institutionalized, deteriorate into what he called the *isms*: ritualism, moralism, ceremonialism, legalism, perfectionism, authoritarianism, absolutism, and dogmatism.[68] He argued against *isms* because of their stunting effect on child and adult development and because of their role in thwarting the likelihood of peaceful coexistence with many diverse others on the globe.

Erikson further believed that ritualisms are actually dangerous to faith. They make one captive of those who had devised such forms and lead readily to great feelings of guilt and to associated judgments of self and others. The bowed head, wrinkled brow, and downcast eye of guilt and blame are internalized and then projected. This prohibits vitality, a joyous active faith, and fellowship. Coercions from outside and coercions from within are of the same cloth, he held. The former readily turn into the latter, given each human's inborn and carefully developed proclivity for assimilating guilt and shame.[69] This can result in malignant prejudice that follows from an espoused morality that has lost its adult sight:

> The "lowest" in man thus is apt to reappear in the guise of the "highest": irrational and prerational combinations of goodness, doubt, and rage can re-emerge in the adult in those malignant forms of righteousness and prejudice which we may call moralism. In the name of high moral principles it can employ all the vindictiveness of derision, of torture, and of mass-extinction.[70]

In 1981, writing about the societal conditions in Jesus' era, Erikson subtly drew parallels between Galilee in first-century A.D. Judaism and the cultural diaspora of a late twentieth-century America and world. Whether due to hellenization or to human diversity on a shrinking, nuclear-armed planet, adults experience the "loss of cultural consistency" as extraordinary danger. "Under such conditions," he wrote, "live rituals can give place to a super-conscientious preoccupation with ritualistic details dominated by a compulsive scrupulosity apt to deaden the renewal and rejuvenation which is the essence of an inventive ritual life."[71]

Some will see few similarities between Galilee then and life today, considering the intervening 2,000 years of change. Difficulties in drawing comparisons are heightened by attempting to draw parallels between humans living in one tiny corner of the earth and all humans on today's globe and by the monumental problem of moving from an oral tradition in one culture to the world's multilingual, partially literate, heteroculture. But his point is well taken. Looking only to America, many adults currently subscribe to rituals and processes in which they seek "confirmation of the word as contained in the scriptures and a scrupulous search for their correct interpretation."[72] This is an example of the ritualism that Erikson saw manifest as habituation to detail. To him, it missed the New Testament conversion to a living, active, caring-of-others faith.

Clearly, Erikson's was a voice against restrictive, detail-driven behavior. Such behavior leads to diminished consciousness about what we believe and do. It results in a disinclination to engage the brain in thought. Worst of all, it leads to patterned, repetitive prejudices against those who see the world differently. The vital lifeblood of belief and of engaged concern for the human then readily serve form for the sake of form, ritual, and symbols instead of the other way around. Erikson showed his outrage when institutions used such form and practice to self-servingly survive. But as he well knew, bureaucracies, even religious ones, are the unique invention of humans, and humans tend to sustain the inventions they have had a hand in originating.

In Erikson's thought, identity is positive. Rejection is negative.[73] As for all else in adult life, adult identity had to be an ongoing petri dish of healthy growth. Repudiation of those who are different must be seen as it is, the negative identity, one's "personal devil," cast on others.[74] Prejudice is the "self-negating part of the human conscience."[75] In negating and rejecting others and oneself, it is prejudice itself that prejudices development, for it stunts the adult. Erikson had moved forward and upward from his earliest years in Vienna when he first asked what it is that brings the human upward in consciousness and forward in mentally healthy development.

ERIKSON'S SEARCH FOR ORIGINS AND CORRECTIVES:
GENETICS AND ANIMAL BEHAVIOR

The habits and biases of childhood and the identity of youth turn into the ego needs of adulthood. The adult ego, Erikson wrote, needs to feel active, central, in control, and not "tossed around" on the fringe of life or the distant outskirts of some other ego's or group's scheme of things.[76] The ego needs to know itself as original, as an actively engaged insider in the vocational-social domain, a self who is a committed, needed, and group-identified player. This is the largely unconscious need of every adolescent who seeks a life and work that are worth his or her commitment.

Extending individual ego identity to tribal, ethnic, racial, and preferential lifestyle, Erikson wrote of the person's experience of self-in-identified-group as similar to groups' anthropological origins: Each tribe or roving band saw itself as central to the group-ordained mind's eye of the smiling creator, for one's in-group was the only exact version of what the divine had "in mind" from the very beginning. At best, others could be excused as errors.

During the 1960s at Harvard, Erikson considered the possibility that human prejudice might have a genetic basis. He also tried to find behavioral symmetry between lower animals and humans, hoping that he could show how one might import the pacific tendencies he saw in beasts. Unfortunately, neither avenue of thought rewarded his efforts.

In reviewing Erikson's pseudo-species concept, the biologist Stephen Gould annoyed Erikson. To Gould, humans were no more descendants of some "killer ape" than they were biologically prepossessed of a goodness that might fit some "mushy claim of liberal sentimentality."[77] Gould held that genetic unity had been the case throughout long centuries of evolution. Biological differences between the races were so minimal as to be "trivial." Because there was but one gene pool, reasons for prejudice would not be located in biological design or in evolution. Absence of a genetic error that resulted in prejudice also meant zero possibility of finding some inborn pacific traits. This was inadequate to Erikson. To him, Nazi Germany was far too replicable. Reasons for prejudice might yet be isolated.

Erikson found a way to take advantage of Gould's point. Because genetic unity is the case, in that there is more genetic variance within racial and ethnic groups than between them, the "capacity for cross-breeding" might someday mean that humans would act on this capacity. In that case they would see all others in each other and in themselves.[78] A species-wide identity would then be more likely. In his terms:

A truly wider identity . . . includes not only the capacity for empathic identification with other people at first perceived as incomprehensibly "other"—but also the willingness to understand the otherness as well as the all-too-familiar in ourselves. For to ourselves we are always the example of humanity closest at hand.[79]

Erikson extended his search to the animal kingdom. There he looked for the behavioral correlates of rage, hostile aggression, and pacifism. Geese, wolves, lions, stags, and penguins yielded to his appraisal.[80] In them he held that he saw peaceful tendencies that had no human equal. "Lucky wolves: know their species. We don't," he wrote.[81] "A hungry lion when ready for the kill . . . shows no sign of anger or rage; he is doing his job.[82] Mutual extermination is not in nature's book."[83] He insisted that we had to learn how animals can live so well with different, neighboring creatures, whereas humans do this so poorly.[84]

Erikson recognized that humans do not possess the primal instincts of animals or the "pacific" instincts he believed he saw in wolves. But rituals were important to Erikson. He repeatedly wrote about the way human ritualization begins "with the way we welcome a newborn," a ritual that is repeated on a daily basis when the mother and baby greet each other smilingly, face-to-face, and welcoming, eye-to-eye.[85] Such early human interchange and sustenance was, to him, a kind of pacifism, traits that some humans will maintain and others will jettison.

Finding few similarities in aggression between animals and humans, Erikson nonetheless remained convinced that animals were more mild-mannered than man. In this Erikson showed his anti-Freudian bent. He countered Freud's Darwinian belief that the human "owes what is potentially brutish and over-sexed in him to his membership in the 'animal kingdom'":[86]

> We have since learned from the ethologists that there is more instinctive and, in fact, pacific discipline in the higher animals than man has ever dreamed of. As to the old naturalistic excuse of human viciousness, namely, *homo hominis lupus*, it seems that even the wolves have instinctive ways of preventing murder among themselves. Far from deserving disdain as our ancestors, then, animals could well take exception to their "descendants." No, with his sins, man stands alone among all creatures.[87]

Citing Freud's "Why War?" letter to Einstein, Erikson disputed Freud's claim that humans' inability to extricate themselves from the animal kingdom meant that human conflicts were destined to be settled violently.[88] The beasts, he said, "may justifiably beg exclusion from the human kingdom."[89] Further, humans might learn peace and sublimated aggression from animals.

In addition to their peaceful, predictable nature, Erikson found admirable in animals that which, by its absence, was reprehensible in humans: Honest in action, animals do not lie. Even in groups, Erikson found animals to regularly and "honestly" adhere to the instincts they were given. Not so for the human, "the biggest liar in the universe."[90] The lying tendency of humans placed lower order animals on a higher plane than the humans who controlled them. Erikson had witnessed lies in adults that ran the spectrum from those serving "transitory conviction" to ones housing flagrant motives to deceive and self-deceive.[91] There was fabrication in individuals' normal and abnormal mental states and pretense in masses and mobs in which lying might be intentional or foolishly unconscious. His word *pseudo*, which, he said, could mean "anything from 'illusory' to 'counterfeit,'" was a deliberate choice.[92] Although Erikson saw humanity's split into groups as a "most 'honest' division of mankind into different 'kinds,'" he used the prefix *pseudo* as it exists in the term *pseudology*, meaning *false word* or *lying*.[93]

To Erikson, the pseudo-species phenomenon was "systematic and often unconscious" but could be manifest in conscious, "murderous mass pseudologia," as in Nazi Germany.[94] Its evolution and its escalation of destructiveness revealed a collective dishonesty that kept humans from moving toward what they are, one species in a universal humankind. In the clinical realm as well, his observations found the damage that the "untruthfulness" of prejudice wields. A "violence" against others, it becomes a violence to the self as well.[95] Weapons directed outward always boomerang back to maim the source.

The human ascent to tool use, intellectual and rationalized thought, self-consciousness, ego-invested roles and boundaries, and moralisms had built a deadly blend. Adults showed an ill-fated "*territoriality of identity*" which, in their varied "progressive" groupings, combined advanced technology with group-specific beliefs.[96] Each group-belief system espoused its own version of ideology and morality, which it held to with self-justifying inerrancy. This had led to

> lethal weaponry, moral hypocrisy, and identity panic (which) is not only apt to lose all sense of species, but also to turn on another subgroup with a ferocity generally alien to the "social" animal world . . . just when . . . a more universal, more inclusive human identity seems forcefully suggested by the very need for survival.[97]

Erikson elaborated humans' behavioral asymmetry with animals to debunk belief in the universality of mass human aggression and, therefore, Freud's too readily accepted dictum that periodic wars are encoded in the species and should be expected. By his early 60s, Erikson had acquired a substantial following and felt deeply his responsibility to attenuate Freud's thought. As he wrote, he *had* to "review and amend his [Freud's] theories."[98] Wars could not be considered inevitable, for the stage on which they were set had expanded exponentially, and adults seemed to have learned so little from the two prior world cataclysms. Now, hyperrational humans had produced tools and methods that, if trends continued, would end in complete destruction. A moment of unchecked panic or irrational rage on the part of one or another key actor, acting seemingly rationally, could end all.

Believing that he might be able to help the technologically advanced and, to his mind, more dangerous portion of the tool-toting species come to insights that would cure them and spare humanity, Erikson tried to work on a planetary scale. He wanted to lift mass enlightenment to a higher consciousness about behavior. Perhaps, he said, such insights would lead to care-filled responsibility. If not this, how useful after all, were his ideas about the potentials of the caring, generative adult?

In bringing about such insight, if he could show how animals and their markings and behavior had wound their way into the human psyche and inspired early pseudo-species behavior, he felt that he could paint a useful picture. Early on, Erikson said, the human, the nonstriped, nonspotted, least colorful animal and the "most naked" of all, decorated the self and members of the in-tribe with "feathers, pelts and paints" to distinguish their kind from other kinds.[99] Later, such adornments turned into costumes and "resplendent uniforms topped with animal plumage."[100] The adornments of the technological human eventually became those of sophisticated tools and weapons. There, Erikson painted a clear picture: Adults' early jewelry, harmless in and of itself, had turned into missiles that would kill *by* themselves.

Erikson then took animals to the next step. If he could confirm the "pacific rituals of animals," he might be able to facilitate transfer of such behaviors to humans so that adults might understand and model those strengths for their species.[101] He believed there are "resources for peace even in our 'animal nature' if we will only learn to nurture nature, as well as to master her."[102] Hence his studies of animals and then of nonviolent strategies in men, the most important of whom was Gandhi. Erikson connected animals' pacific traits with Gandhi's provocative and peace-filled nonviolent resistance and then, in classic Erikson style, looked to the Mahatma's faith. Besides Gandhi's faith in the Almighty, Erikson noted the revolutionary's faith in the dignity of his opponents and in their tendencies to avoid "harming others beyond a certain point."[103] He wrote, "Here I am claiming something hopelessly complex and yet as simple as all the best things in life for, indeed, only faith gives back to man the dignity of nature."[104]

Ethology, if not genetics, helped Erikson's points along somewhat. He illustrated reasons to understand that residual animal heredity cannot be blamed for human prejudice or for resulting intergroup violence. Yet, although the ages may honor his worthy efforts, Erikson came very close to anthropomorphizing animals and also to implying that one can reason analogically from their behavior to the human case, a weak form of reasoning. Here, Erikson's Achilles heel appears. In deference to what he knew clinically about human normalcy and pathology and to that which he observed and conceptualized about the ways animals have penetrated and inspired the psyche (including his), such flaws are best seen as useful elements in his teaching scheme. Using animals to build part of his case was a useful, provocative detour to terrain that is less charged with human emotion. It was a fresh content base that adults could visualize before looking back at themselves. Then adults might understand prejudice and vengeful rage, manifest only in humans, as a deterioration from lower form, noncerebral animals. As such, his search for an equivalence in humans of the "pacifism" seen in animals, although thin in itself, is useful.

Considering Erikson's powerful intellect and range, it is likely that he knew very well what he was doing in constructing a parallel, comparable track of animal to human. Around 1960 he wrote:

> if we want to project what we are into animals, are we not apt to stress the Id-Super-Ego dichotomy . . . ? We compare our ravenousness with the eating style of dogs, or our rage with that of (attacked or hungry) tigers, and whole "bestiaries" attribute to animals the lowest vices of man. A most recent calendar relates a medieval view according to which a lion never overeats, adding, "and when he feels he might overeat, he puts his paw in his mouth to prevent himself." So here, too, man ascribes to the lion a conscious process by which he becomes aware of an elicit wish and actively prevents himself from "giving in," even as our conscience struggles with our desires.[105]

Eventually, Erikson knew that the purported pacifism of animals was not useful to his case except as a teaching tool. In an unpublished manuscript, he said that he "had begun to doubt the feasibility of deriving an understanding of human life from an ever more intricate reconstruction of its ontogenetic beginnings—such as . . . imprinting in ethology."[106]

Insofar as he thought and wrote on a metascale, and because he variously tried to demonstrate a "cogwheeled" interdependence first between the generations and later between different groups, cultures, and nations, it is a minimal stretch to see Erikson's use of animals as a step beyond facilitating the imprinting of humans on them. He wished to facilitate positive transference and countertransference between children and their parents and grandparents, and, in the grand scheme of intergroups, between the species as well. To the end of his writing years, Erikson never separated the infant's, child's, or adult's needs from interdependence with others or from the ethos and needs of the community. Because Erikson was a naturalist who believed that all living resources interdepend on one another, animals had to fit into the equation.

WHY PREJUDICE?
FUZZY SETS, CAUSES, AND CORRELATES

It cannot escape notice that, just as Freud had built an "originology" of instincts, Erikson, with his pseudo-species concept relying so heavily on evolution, climbed to a higher level to build an "originology" of the species as it first grouped itself. He seems to have believed that the best way to facilitate development, consciously and collectively, was to go all the way back to species' origins. If he was to facilitate human development to a higher plane among all who could grasp his concepts and employ them to the species' advantage, then hurt, hate, prejudice, and rage had to be brought up to the conscious surface and then set aside deliberately. Every adult, and every collection of adults, would have to see prejudice as a brand that marked all human animals. It was the only way forward.

In the entire body of his considerable writings on the pseudo-species tendency, Erikson was diffuse in describing the underpinnings and manifestations of prejudice. He variously painted prejudice as prerational, nonrational, irrational, and rational. It is normal self-idealization, it is required, and it represents identity immaturity. Prejudice shows impoverished adult development and overadjustment to roles. It feeds on the self's negative identity elements and on the autocracies of a rigidly built superego. It reveals both paranoid tendencies and universal traits. Each of these insights has merit in explaining human inclinations in all adults and remarkable narrowness in some adults. Further, Erikson's varied interpretations aptly portray the irreducible psyche and its distortions in the complex organism that is the human adult. Yet readers may mightily wish that Erikson had buttressed his points with illustrations, case examples, and repeated, consistent interpretations instead of painting so broad a canvas without specific, uniform detail. His image is sometimes strikingly clear, and at other times it hazes markedly. But Erikson was a seer with a psychoanalytic hammer, and readers do well to take him at the bell-clear ring that sounds as a mental alarm when his imagery occasionally carries sufficient detail. When, for instance, Erikson expressed annoyance that the "blonde, blue-eyed, well-fed, and immaculately groomed" children pictured in *The New York Times* seemed to all the world to represent what he meant about children, a picture of privilege, exclusion, and explicit prejudice is instantly clear.[107]

There is no mistaking it, this and other prejudice images and inclinations represented negative adult developmental tendencies and species devolution to Erikson. Yet, as he said, one cannot get to adulthood without prejudice, and neither can one live a mentally healthy adult life without some of it. Hence complexity must be kept intact in considering Erikson's varied points.

STEPPING STONES:
FREUD, SPENGLER, AND ZIMMER

Sigmund Freud, Oswald Spengler, and Heinrich Zimmer supplied grist for the mill of Erikson's notions of prejudice. Freud had connected prejudice with identity and with several elements of masses, crowds, and cultural groups. Spengler wrote about cultural groups as pseudomorphs, that is, as variants of cultural groups. And Zimmer described caste and class divisions in India. None of these thinkers went to the lengths Erikson did to conceptualize, work through, and advance understandings about the reasons for and perils of prejudice. Nonetheless, Freud's and Spengler's ideas, in particular, were critical to Erikson's thought. Zimmer's ideas likely came into play later, in Erikson's Gandhi period.

According to Erikson, Freud had spoken about identity on only one occasion. This was in a letter to the B'nai B'rith in 1926.[108] The context was Freud's attempt to explain his bond with Judaism as an "'inner identity' which was not based on race or religion, but on a common freedom from prejudices which narrow the use of the intellect."[109] Freud's statement is of interest because of the link he made between two key concepts of Erikson's, identity and prejudice. Erikson did not remark on Freud's intentional linkage, nor did he consider Freud's use of the term "identitaet" as the precursor to his own identity construct. But in conceptualizing prejudice as an absence of openness to others, Freud anticipated Erikson: Prejudice stunts adult development. Freud believed that a psyche-intellect equation was at the core of prejudice: It is intellectual narrowness that leads to prejudice. Erikson disagreed. To him, a psyche-empathy-nonrational equation defines the issue:

An inability or disinclination to engage the affect and mind so that it can reside within the social perspective and view of another leads to prejudice.

To Freud, the ability to remain intellectually open to differences in persons functions as a preventive; it forestalls closing down the world to that which exists between one's shoulders. Freud considered individual and group ideals and mentalities because, as he saw it, the latter hold overarching ideas that bond a community together and keep outsiders apart. He spoke to the ways in which religious institutions welcome and enfold their own members even while they cast aside those who will not or should not belong. Further, Freud recognized group prejudice as that which occurs on the basis of ideal prototypes within each particular culture. This permits exterior, other-group ideals to be degraded as inferior in attributes, achievement, and aspirations. To Freud, the reasons for this are found in narcissism:

> the ideal [satisfies] . . . participants in the culture [and] is thus of a narcissistic nature; it rests on their pride in what has already been successfully achieved. To make this satisfaction complete calls for a comparison with other cultures which have aimed at different achievements and have developed different ideals. On the strength of these differences every culture claims the right to look down on the rest. In this way cultural ideals become a source of discord and enmity between different cultural units.[110]

Freud did not fully elaborate such concepts, but he did fuel Erikson's ideas. It was not a far stretch between Freud's notion of group ideals, pride, and aspirations and Erikson's idea that any and all outsiders can be considered so far below the in-group's standards that they are thought of as unnecessary elements in the universe.

Oswald Spengler, a German philosopher of history, was another major influence on Erikson's ideas. Spengler's two-volume *Decline of the West* elaborated his study of civilizations according to a number of attributes.[111]Spengler studied cultural groups' ideas about the cosmos, creation, the soul, animals and plants, and overarching ideas about society. He looked as well to human relationships between cultures and to the ways in which differences in laws, music, landscapes, cities, and numerical concepts evolve to reflect distinct corporate ideas. Among his conclusions was the finding that an elemental, and very different, shared spiritual form is deeply embedded in the individual and in the collective psyche of members of each unique cultural entity. Spengler demonstrated the existence of distinct, noncomparable civilizations and countered the once prevalent view that history can be seen as a linear progression of the individual or of cultures. Because there is no world history in any linear, progressive, or ideational way, and because various peoples experience their symbols, ideas, and cultural forms differently, the many civilizations of the world are, in Spengler's thought, noncomparable.

Erikson referenced Spengler as having hinted that "antisemitism was largely a matter of projection . . . [for] . . . people see overclearly in Jews what they wish not to recognize in themselves."[112] But Spengler had also written about historical variants of cultural forms; he had borrowed the word "pseudomorphosis" from mineralogy and applied it to culture. He used the term "historical pseudomorphosis" to illustrate how an older, now "alien" culture can be so pervasive and weighty that it suffocates a younger culture. Born in the selfsame land, the "young Culture . . . cannot get its breath."[113] Instead of rising up in its own youthful juices and form, it finds expression only in the older "cultural mould" and rigidifies by acceding to it.[114] As a result, youthful ideas and creativity cannot develop any living expression. Finding no animated forms or unique consciousness of its own, its youthful vitality expresses itself in rage-filled torrents of hate against the oppressors, although the oppressors themselves are ideas, symbols, and icons that are long since dead.

In these notions, Spengler largely referenced the Arabian culture; however, he also described pseudomorphs in the classical era's "Magian" (magical) world of spatial ideas, fantasy, and belief. The group's own god was the first order "principle of good"; other people's gods were considered "impotent or evil," and, by extension, out-groups were seen as children of the inferior, impoverished, or lesser god.[115] In the mystical, Magian world of the classical era, the state, people, fairies, and god made up one integrated "spiritual unit."[116] Other cultural nation-states, when known about, were necessarily seen as beyond the pale of insiders' notions of civility, beneficence, and propriety. Truth was seen as actual substance in material form. It revealed itself in one spiritually interwebbed set of notions that the cultural group held to consensually. Consequently, such truth was not conceptual or abstract but real, concrete, and highly dependable. Those outside the group lived beyond the truth zone.

Magians were but one kind of magical pseudoform, a variety Spengler found in the likes of the "anti-Pauline Pseudo-Clementines."[117] Spengler found other varieties in the caste divisions of Augustus and in the Roman Church. Describing pseudomorphs, he did not speak directly of the prejudice phenomenon as it is known in the contemporary era. However, what he did reveal, and likely revealed to Erikson, was the way the world and human consciousness have been experienced variously and differently from place to place and from culture to culture. In that Spengler showed how each culture is embedded in its own pervading, exclusive notions of spirit, nature, substance, ideas, and ideals, and because he illustrated that such concepts form an awareness that is variously expressed in the conscious and unconscious terms and references of different cultures, he likely influenced Erikson considerably. Further, Spengler's use of the term *cultural moulds* is an exact replica of Erikson's use of those words in his early years of working with Margaret Mead. In her letter to Erikson on May 23, 1939, Mead wrote that she had read Erikson's paper, "Observations on Sioux Education" with "deep interest":

The points that interested me most were: your discussion of the way in which one culture's ideal tends to be another culture's most abhorred type and the various implications of this for inter-racial contact, and second, your statement of the way in which a disappearing custom may have left its imprint in the moulds of cultural conscience.[118]

It would be difficult to make a case for how much conscious awareness Erikson had of his use of Spengler's ideas. Spengler's history of the presumed decline of western civilization was widely read in the late-second-decade Germany of Erikson's youth. It was reviewed publicly at great length and was variously acclaimed and castigated. Because Erikson referenced Spengler, albeit minimally, insofar as there is a close relationship between *pseudomorphs* and *pseudo-species* in terminology and meaning, and because both writers used the term *cultural moulds*, the association cannot be considered accidental.

With respect to the influence on Erikson of Heimrich Zimmer's thought, in 1962 Erikson visited India for several months at the beginning of his studies that led to *Gandhi's Truth*. Then or later, Erikson read at least parts of Zimmer's 1956 book, *Philosophies of India*.[119] Writing in *Gandhi's Truth* about Indian laws (*dharma*), caste (*varna*), and life stage (*asrama*), Erikson quoted Zimmer: "One is not free to choose; one belongs to a species—a family, guild, and craft, a group, a denomination."[120] Thus, Zimmer too noted that there was a sub- or pseudo-species that guides behavior, in this case in India: "the real ideal of one's present natural character, one's concern as a judging and acting entity must be only to meet every life problem in a manner befitting the role one plays."[121]

It seems that Erikson did more than import the "polite" term *pseudo-species*. Erikson's word is but a small alteration of Spengler's term. And Erikson's concept of the prejudice that exists in incomplete identities borrows from Freud. Zimmer seems to have supported what Erikson knew about identity variants due to class and caste immersion.

THE POWER OF THE IMAGE, ERIKSON'S CHANGED MIND, AND SEVERAL DIFFICULTIES

By the time events led him in that direction, it was too late in Erikson's life for him to do much about the weaponry that superego wields. The best he could do was to make some beginning points that would be available for later study. But the body of Erikson's work on the psychodevelopmental reasons for prejudice is impressive. He made a substantial case for his image of the *prejudiced adult* and for its "both/and" dilemma. The image is a constellation of necessary values, habits, and lenses of thought and shows childhood learning, identity, and group immersion as the breeding grounds for repudiation of dissimilar others. To Erikson, each adult must retain the core essence and values that have created his or her uniqueness, *and* each mature identity must grow beyond an ingrained mind-set that excludes others. In this way, he held, adults would represent that which "the best" in them "lives by."[122] This means that every adult has to see his or her youth-inspired, tightly wrapped, self-central, and autonomous identity as a temporary vehicle to the adult life that stretches beyond. Ego-primary identity must be known as essential to development in the life span but as only an interregnum between egocentrality and a more selfless, mature identity. Further, highly ego central identities must be seen as relative to equally valid, differently constituted adult selves in the world. "From the social boundness of identity," Erikson wrote, "we have come to envisage its own transcendence." "Pseudo" identities are a center that do not hold.[123] "Immature" at heart, they "shirk" the responsibility each adult has of caring for others."[124] Further, pseudo-identities are self-defeating: "You cannot be truly yourself if your identity depends on somebody's else's identity loss, a potentially vicious symbiosis in the sense that each lives—and dies—off the other."[125]

However, Erikson had backed himself into a corner that was of his and his adopted country's making. By claiming cross-cultural universality for self-central ego identity, Erikson had projected a Western-centric concept on the many peoples of the world. His ideas for the construct of autonomous identity had been based on his own identity confusion in Germany, his resurgent identity difficulties when he immigrated to America, and the fact that he noticed identity crises in American youths who were embedded in a nation that was struggling through its own identity difficulties. Erikson himself demonstrated that the concept of *self* is culturally relative.[126] Different languages, social systems, values, rituals, and taboos shape the self differently in different ethnic, cultural, and national groups. But if *self* is not a uniform psychological entity, it would seem that personal identity is nonuniform as well, both in its construction and in its meaning. Erikson had to have seen this by the mid-1960s, for by then he had studied Gandhi's life in India, a country in which the idea of autonomous self would have then seemed radical. In 1968, in the *Insight and Freedom* address that was based on his Gandhi studies, he nodded toward softening the self-centrality of ego identity and, there as elsewhere, made it more inclusive for those he could call *adult*.

Erikson did not rewrite the developmental script or the ego identity crisis of adolescence, nor did he illustrate cultural variability in any of the life-stage grids he published, even those in his later editions. For many in the Western world, the construct does aptly describe the primary needs, issues, and difficulties of adolescents and young adults as they search for an ideological and work-engaged place in their societies. But it seems clear that the Western world's notion of autonomous identity is only one mode of self-definition that Erikson projected as the gold standard for all.

One should hasten to add that, to this day, cross-cultural human data remain incomplete. Research findings may yet demonstrate certain standard psychosocial tendencies that come into play due to the universals of puberty development in youth. Findings may then validate at least one of Erikson's identity attributes: that the conceptualizing of the self in the abstract future of the self in the social system can be considered a uniform developmental occurrence.

It is of more than passing interest that Margaret Mead suggested in a letter to Erikson in 1954 that his life-stage grid was too much of a "closed system." It would profit, she said, by opening the "edges" to include historical, geographical, and cultural variations. It needed to be a "three dimensional system with open edges."[127] Had Erikson taken Mead's suggestions to heart, he might have seen the importance of varying his identity construct so as to allow for variations in the way culturally, geographically, and historically unique psyches are fed identity ideas that vary considerably, one to another.

Although Erikson never changed his construct of the identity crisis, he did alter some of its resolutions for the adult development that begins with adolescent identity and ends in old age. On August 9, 1976, Erikson wrote to colleagues in lieu of attending a conference that was to be held in Aspen, Colorado. He could not attend, he wrote, for medical reasons. In his letter, Erikson said that he was then working on the Freud-Jung letters. In so doing, he said, "my own concepts are changing":

> You have noted . . . that I have spoken of an adult stage of *Generativity vs. Self absorption* or Stagnation. I would now say that the *antithesis* of *generativity* is *rejectivity*. Out of this antithesis there either emerges the virtue (in the sense of *strength*) of Care, or to the extent that Care, for whatever combination of reasons, can not become fully operative, a sense and a state of self-absorption and stagnation will result. For the preceding stages, I would likewise assume a somewhat different antithesis: thus the antithesis of *Intimacy* would be *Exclusivity*, the evolving strength Love, and the threatening asociality Isolation. One step further back, the antithesis of adolescence Identity would be *Cynicism*, the strength Fidelity, and the weakness Identity Confusion.[128]

In this revision, Erikson placed asocial rejectivity at the core of the greatest span of adulthood, in the generative middle years of caring. He then fanned rejection out to encompass the entire identity-unfolding years. Revisions of the two prior stages and of the final stage of life show prejudicial rejectivity in the adolescent cynicism toward others (and thereby toward the self), in the young adult exclusion of others (and therefore of self), and in the old person's rejection-based disgust with a world and self that are closing down and are, slowly or more quickly, rejecting the elder. He reminded his readers that reciprocal exclusions exist in all prejudicial narrowness, whether these are between the generations, between groups, or between individuals.[129] In a separate source he claimed that cynicism includes "self-exclusion" as a "core disturbance."[130]

Erikson's changed mind implies that the experience of receiving and handing out rejection, and therefore prejudice, increases with advancing age.

His letter to colleagues reveals his own experience at 74 years of age. It is a fascinating revision. In their middle years, adults nurture and mentor family intimates and others who need that middle-ager's care. In the same middle-aged period, work roles engage one's contributions and give such adults a sense of worth, inclusion, and ego validation. Denial of society's eventual exclusion of the person and denial of death can be kept comparatively intact. These keep rejection at bay, if only temporarily. It is far easier to avoid rejecting others when one is treasured at some level in home life, at work, and in community and is not prejudicially restricted from such inclusion. In his Aspen letter Erikson hinted that in older age, even in one's family, prejudice heightens: "enmity . . . can exist within one's family, or be turned against one's own children, and this especially where conflicting generative concerns make them suddenly appear as outsiders or worse."[131]

In those late-life thoughts, it seems that Erikson hinted that he himself was experiencing the rejection that life eventually hands out to all who live to experience it, at least in adults' postretirement years in an ageist United States. Rejection by loved ones matches society's rejection. Ultimately, rejection by one's own body occurs, amounting to a kind of prejudice against the self.[132] One can only hope, he wrote, that the Ultimate does not possess a similar rejectivity.[133]

Elsewhere, a slightly younger Erikson had written about his surprise when, in his anthropological ventures, he had come upon elderly persons who chronicled proper behavior in their own culture "with a sense of moral and aesthetic rightness unquestionably sanctioned by the universe."[134] All "rejectivity," a rejection he inferred as escalating with advancing age, is the "negative identity" afresh; one senses who one "does not care to be like or care to care for."[135]

Erikson's great effort to illustrate *prejudiced adult* as a reality that no one can escape points to understandings worth the attention of all. It is unattractive to have to accept the adult self as one who is habituated to bias, even if it is in the nature of the currently evolved human to be this way. In the jargon of the times, it is insensitive and "politically incorrect" to say so. But if a large enough number of adults can contemplate this highly complex image of prejudice without reducing it simplistically or rejecting it, its purpose will be well served. Seeing every person as biased, and learning reasons for this, adults might feel released from self-blame and guilt and thereby become capable of consciously developing beyond the violence that prejudice does to others and to the self.

There are some dilemmas. The consideration of Erikson's ideas requires the ability to take qualities that are largely nonrational and to move them and personal thinking up the cognitive-consciousness ladder to look at bias rationally and with insight and empathy. Some can do this but not all. In the United States alone, only a modest percentage of adults are cognitively capable of functioning at the upper levels of abstraction. Further, due to tendencies toward fragmentation and distillation of knowledge and to a largely deductive and reduction-inculcating society and American education system, the question of what such characteristics may have done to cognitive abilities is a great unknown. At a minimum, it is likely that many more adults are now better deductive, reductive thinkers than inductive, complexity-including thinkers. Reductionism, knowledge fragmentation, a deduction-inducing English language, and tendencies to avoid thinking about complex things *complexly*, as it were, have taken their toll.

Personal changes in attitudes can occur in the absence of highly abstract cognitive abilities. But there is no doubt that the countering of judgmental, moralistic attitudes requires intellectual openness. Both Freud and Erikson were correct: Intellectual and prejudicial narrowness intercorrelate—and both insight and the ability to empathically experience the strange other as though he or she were the self are preludes to behavioral change. There are no tools adequate to the task of estimating the percentage of adults who possess these attributes and who also have the time, mental space, and inclination to deploy them.

If an engaged consciousness that results in turning away from rabid prejudice clearly requires intellectual openness, insight, and ethical, empathic concern for others, it is also clear, and Erikson's truism, that prejudice serves no one. Erikson knew that inclusion and "greater leeway" for all require more than an absence of bias. They mean giving something up. In an unpublished letter written in 1962, Erikson was not optimistic about the likelihood that humans are willing to relinquish that which they own. Referencing Fromm, he said that "people and peoples would rather die than change."[136] And, he added, "they would also rather murder than take chances with their identity."[137]

Late in his life, Erikson saw some positive changes. He wrote about the movement he saw toward inclusiveness. He foresaw *enstehungsakt*, an "evolving all-human adulthood" developing in the species.[138] To his credit, he noted that advances in communications and transportation had united persons.[139] He might also have applauded the satellites that permit us to peer down as from outer space to see a small interconnected world and one species' niche. But he did not. The nuclear age had wrought dangers that he could not reconcile. In periods of rapid change, he found the pseudo-species tendency particularly dangerous. In his final publication about the pseudo-species tendency, he wrote of his hopes that threats of a "nuclear winter" and "species-wide destruction" would be reversed.[140] Humans had gotten themselves into a "pervasive 'craziness,'" he said, one that led them to become "adjusted" to an unthinkable specter.[141] If anything, *this* was maladjustment. The Erikson who had seen the Renaissance as a large-scale "ego revolution *par excellence*" wanted another revolution, that of finding within and between each person, family, race, culture, and nation the common bond of a human childhood.[142] Particularly, he pressed prejudiced adults, and that meant all adults, to set aside their harsh superegos in order to locate and to protect what he hoped was still a childhood of the species.

5

Moral-Ethical, Spiritual Adult

Freud forgot to include himself, "the observer, the
moral man," in the model of human he created.
— Erikson, "Miscellanous
Papers and Notes"

One of Erikson's major concerns about adults was that the mature years of
life harbor far too many internal restrictive covenants that are used against
the self and others. Adults are "such moral creatures," he wrote, "that we
invariably react to any generalization regarding *human* behavior . . . with
questions of immediate applicability to conduct."[1] Judging others quickly,
adults neglect to ask what human needs they might understand if, on wit-
nessing others' behavior, they would first try to understand the meaning of
such behavior. Instead, they draw conclusions, assign blame, and prescribe
remedies. By middle age in particular, superego development has taken its
adult as prisoner, leading adults to fear that in their expected-to-be-perfect
state, they are far from being as good as they should be, as far as childhood
is now distant from the self. As Erikson had illustrated in his prejudice imagery, this leads to self-judgment, to the magnifying of others' quirks, and to
the defensive projection of real or feared flaws onto others. Observed flaws
are one's negative identity; they come from and are deflected backward onto
the accusing self.

This is the moral adult, a rule-driven, judging, right-versus-wrong, reciprocity, quid pro quo person. To Erikson, nearly all adults are moral. Some
are also ethical. Ethical adults are principled. They build on their own and
others' strengths, give of themselves without expecting a return of favors in
kind, and avoid judging and controlling others. Erikson found that many
highly moral but ethically undeveloped adults are harshly critical and causti-

cally judgmental; they injure others and themselves. Others are downright unethical *and* immoral, at times even in the name of high-sounding principles and ideas. Erikson said little about the latter other than in vast generalities or when illustrating ethical deviations in those who were generally principled. In effect, he walled off the immoral, declining to script evil for his readers.

Instead, in his image of the moral-ethical adult, Erikson illustrated the moral strengths and difficulties that arrive with adulthood in every person and the higher reaches of ethical and spiritual development that are attained by some. Principled behavior defines advanced adult identity in Erikson's view. To him, ethical adults are those who, in most instances, affirm judiciously instead of negating arbitrarily. Ethical adults hold positive, life-affirming values. They involve themselves actively in the work of their world, honor their commitments, and eschew moralizing and blaming. They also have faith, without which "wholeness" is impossible.[2] Throughout his lifetime of writing, Erikson maintained that primal hope and faith are healthy outcomes of infancy, the first stage of life. But by his mid-life, he gave those strengths preeminence as the best-case resolution of the last stage of life as well.

ETHICAL ADULT: BECOMING AND ACTING PRINCIPLED

The idea of the absorption and partial displacement of childhood morality drove Erikson's notions about the potentially moral-ethical adult. The rule-driven, superego-bound orientation of childhood cannot be replaced, he said. Rather, the moralistic psyche is absorbed into, and is partially replaced by, the high ideology and future orientation of adolescence. In the best of development, ethical adulthood then follows. As for ideology against morality, ethics cannot fully replace either morality or ideology; rather ethics absorbs and partially converts the moral, ideological attainments of childlike morality and adolescent ideology. Erikson found the harbingers of ethics in youths' search for an identity that is worthy of sustained effort and commitment. But the first bloom of ethics proper appears in the identity-intimacy stage of loving and caring about others. Later, in the identity-generativity stage of loving and caring for persons, products, and ideas that are not abandoned but are nourished and sustained, ethics reaches its most complete form.

A Structural, Moral-Ethical Adult

For the evolution of the earlier moral child into the moral and ethical adult who assumes intimate, work, and caring roles, Erikson eventually used the term "structural adult."[3] By this he meant that one functions in the time and space, work and love zone which we call maturity. This forces the definition of who an adult is structurally. Erikson included four attributes in the structural. These are the *moral*, the *contextual*, the *memorial*, and the *prospective*. He labeled *moral* and *contextual* as such, and he defined and described but did not name the other attributes.

With his first attribute, the *moral* structural, Erikson meant superego continuity. As a result of childhood grooming, imprinting, and superego development, most adults are, at minimum, moral persons. He illustrated this in his image of the *prejudiced adult*. By moral, Erikson meant that one of three planes is attained. The first of these planes, the moralistic, is the childhood station from which some adults do not progress. The second plane is the moral-ideological level, the adolescent platform in which an ideology of commanding ideas and an ethical sense take hold. Adults who remain at this level are both moral and ideological; they may, then or later, permanently retreat back to the moralistic. In this way, Erikson wrote, "man's way stations to maturity can become fixed, can become premature end stations, or stations for future regression."[4] Erikson's highest plane is the moral-ethical. At that level, adults retain essential attributes of their childhood moral selves but incorporate such morality, and the ideology of their adolescence, into the ethical commitments of their adult years.

Erikson illustrated two problems in the highest level, the moral-ethical adult. First, as he had said about each prejudiced adult, there is always the difficulty of having grown up with imprinting and moral-code learning that cannot be relinquished. Thus one pole of adulthood is always the negative, moral pole whereas the other, for those who attain it, is the positive, ethical pole. Hence the moral-ethical adult lives in the "both/and" world of the moral, lawyerly child and of the ethical, principled adult, not in the "either/or" disjunction of one or the other. We are always in a juggling act, trying to balance the negative and the positive. But "morals," he wrote, "tell us what to say 'no' to, ethics expresses what we say 'yes' to."[5] Affirming, saying yes, means knowing what it is that humans owe others in order to foster the best developmental potential for each person. Yet it is the case that the adult can be mightily unaware of his or her moralistic side and of unconscious motives for keeping it alive. "Our most ethical and most moralistic sides tend to make deals with each other," Erikson said, just as the "superego [is the site for] making deals with the id to develop sadism through morality."[6] We then engender or allow the worst conditions for people, sometimes under the guise of high standards.

The second problem with the moral-ethical level is that by some point in middle life the adult's moral core tends to reassume prominence. This is partly due to adults' perceptions of a trend toward a general, societal erosion in the core values which they and their generational cohort had valued since youth. Different values, brought along by the change-inspired adolescents and young adults of the day, begin to replace elders' values. This leads middle-aged adults to regressively pull back to their moral code and to fight to preserve it. Attempts to conserve earlier values result in rigidity. In Erikson's words, "Step by step they go together: moralism with moral obedience, fanaticism with ideological devotion, and rigid conservatism with adult ethics."[7] Rigid modes of thought are based on fear, on the "superstitions and irrational inner mechanisms" that "undermine the ethical fiber."[8] The moral is useful, for it has made the adult "dependable," but it "can demean him as it guides him and permit him to be mean under the guise of morality."[9] What many soon-to-be replaced middle-agers do not see is that the very youths who are replacing older standards with their own youthful values will retreat and rigidify one day as well. For "what is driven out by young rebellion is always reinstated by the dogmatism of middle age."[10]

The adult is also *contextual*, Erikson's second structural attribute. This is the understanding that varied roles, environments, relationships, and skills fuel development. The adult develops "contextual mastery," in the process of which he or she creates a unique conscious and subliminal reality through a variety of home, work, civic, and personal roles.[11] As such, adults are substantially altered due to the way the psyche embeds itself in and is itself expressed through the requirements of adult life. The net effect shows who each adult is, the meanings he or she attaches to the personal self, and the principles and ideas that mirror that self. The contextual adult, whether moralistic, moral-ideological, or moral-ethical, is one who is defined by choices, by behavior, and by articulated principles.

The context of adult life provides content for reflection and, through lengthening time, permits a longitudinal retrospective to develop. In an expanding distance from the earlier self, a *memorial* moral self takes shape, Erikson's third attribute of the structural adult. By moving through developmental time, by weathering personal and social changes, and by seeing backward over a variety of cumulative and altered roles, requirements, contexts, and commitments, each person develops a sense of moral continuity. At best, this is a complex, intranarrative knowledge of a moral, ideological, and then ethical being in space and time, a self—and knowledge of that self—who has grown through intimate love, through sponsoring the next generation, and through working responsibly. Thus, for each person, there is a sense that "What I am in space, changes in time; what I was is now in me; and what I become is more than the sum of all that I have been."[12] A past of choices and experiences meets the present and a projected, envisioned future. Past, present, and future, in an experienced continuity, are fed by the adult's evolving identity and by notions of what that person believes he or she was, is, needs to be, and should continue to become. Such notions are the "adult ego-ideal," one that arises from met and envisioned commitments.[13]

Erikson split adulthood proper into two developmental periods of care. In young adulthood, he subscribed to an "ethical sense," whereas for the middle years he wrote of ethical action.[14] This is Kierkegaardian and Hindu thought updated, filtered through psychoanalysis and the values of the twentieth century Western world. In part, the care of children brings the young adult up into full ethics, which is that of adhering to the committed care of children. Prior to attaining such generativity, adults can sense but not achieve ethical care, because such care, like all else in life, is learned by doing, by immersing the self *in* the context. Throughout Erikson's writing, children and species survival were the basis for his ideas about the dovetailed fit of individual, generational, and societal strengths and linkage and of the cogwheeled way the generations move one another, and therefore the species, along. Referring to himself, he described how the ethical care of youth leads to adult learning and how this strength meshes with the larger social system:

> any adult who has managed to train a child's will must admit that he has learned much about himself and about will that he never knew before, something that cannot be learned in any other way. Thus each growing individual's strength "dovetails" with the strengths of an increasing number of persons arranged around him in the social orders of family, school, community, and society.[15]

Electing ethical adulthood as his primary vehicle, Erikson associated its development with the caritas of Christianity, agreeing with St. Paul that the behaviors of love define the highest level. Ethics requires choice and action. It means doing something, not just talking about doing it. In various writings, Erikson illustrated that insight is worthless unless it leads to responsible action. Principles must function behaviorally in order to meet the ethical test. It is only in moving beyond young adulthood and its prime period for early vocational immersion and for sexual intimacy that insight can ripen into the conscious obligations of generatively caring for others. Principled behavior, doing that which helps both others and the self to grow, leads individuals to the height of identity development, the apex of Erikson's developmental adult. Further, the ethics of care finds its proof positive at the enduring, collective level: "From generation to generation the test of what you produce is in the care it inspires."[16]

Writing about the *prospective* moral adult, the fourth attribute of the structural adult, Erikson primarily described middle-aged and older adults. He positioned this adult against eternity. Here he once again gave power to the future-scanning, visioning, planning brain that originates in adolescence. However, in the full development of insight-accomplished middle age, visioning adults know there is little liveable time and space ahead. Awareness of the coming reality of personal death creeps closer to the surface of consciousness and leads adults to contemplate and work toward a spiritual home. In this period, just as the adult cannot completely outgrow the moralistic superego of childhood or fully replace the ideology of adolescence, spirituality now becomes unavoidable. The spiritual either enters the consciousness of adult ideation for the first time or deepens, but from this point forward in life, it is a permanent part of the adult self. To Erikson, each person is an organic, integrated whole who cannot be shorn from previous development, from prior content and resolutions, or from a future sense of self. From middle age on, the moral-ethical and spiritual in the adult is an unavoidable composite. Erikson's notes show that he had contemplated this composite in terms of the late-life musings from the Analects (conversations) of Confucius.[17] The full rendition shows the link between midlife ethical and spiritual changes, of experiencing the "biddings of heaven," as well as some developmental antecedents and subsequent accomplishments:

> The Master said, At fifteen I set my heart upon learning. At thirty, I had planted my feet firm upon the ground. At forty, I no longer suffered from perplexities. At fifty, I knew what were the biddings of Heaven. At sixty, I heard them with docile ear. At seventy, I could follow the dictates of my own heart; for what I desired no longer overstepped the boundaries of right.[18]

Principled Doing and Learning

Erikson said he knew that his image of the ethical person might be incongruent with other definitions but held that it reflected human development and the test of his observations.[19] Therefore, he posed the generative adult as the sine qua non of adult identity. Ethical adults treat others as worthy, equal beings. They subscribe to the Hippocratic injunction of never intentionally harming another, defining harm as physical, mental, or economic deprivation, as any behavior or omission that decreases another's dignity, power, potential, or self-esteem.[20] Such adults "maintain the world" positively, holding it in trust for future generations, caring deeply and responsibly for children, for their own in an engaged, nurturing way, and for all others by their civic actions.[21] This requires attention to how their adult generational cohort instills and passes its strengths along. In families, transferring such strengths requires particular attention to how adults affirm strengths and positive values in infants and children so as to root them carefully in life, in health, in positive consciences, and in faith. Erikson's rhetorical question sums this up: "Should they not, also, be given a chance to reach their 'ultimate concern' unmarred by neurotic rootlessness?"[22]

Lest Erikson seem misrepresented, I point out here that, beginning with his 1963 edition of *Childhood and Society*, he softened his prior position that one must have children in order to be generative and thus ethical. In part, this change was his response to critics, particularly to an increasingly vocal group of feminists. Thus from 1963 on, he quietly omitted procreation as an essential requirement for achieving generativity and wisdom, two of the three strengths of his version of adulthood in the 1950s and early 1960s. By his late-life "Jefferson Lectures," Erikson said directly that being generative "does not necessarily mean that one must produce children."[23] But his ethical hook remained intact even then: "The right (or the obligation) to have fewer children (or none) can only be a liberated one if it means a greater personal and communal responsibility for all those born."[24] It is doubtful that Erikson was fully invested in his revision. Adversities aside, being adult meant having, loving, caring for, and launching one's own children.

Simply having children is, of course, inadequate. Ethical functioning requires that one will bring children along positively, will reinforce their loving, good, joyful tendencies, and will avoid harping on the negatives that make them "rot inside."[25] Caring adults engage children in the adult world and, when possible, join children in theirs. They avoid punishing, do not threaten children with a withdrawal of affection, and avoid shaming them.[26] By avoiding oppressive prohibitions, ultimatums, and vendettas, and by training the child's will in an affirming manner, they raise children who are willing emulators, pleased to align their behavior with loving, trusted parents who, after all, they dearly wish to pattern.

Ethical adults act on principles of *actuality* and *mutuality*, Erikson's words for engaging, activating, and including youths, coworkers, and key others within the life radius. Adults lose consciousness of and about themselves as they work and care responsibly in jobs and in their personal lives, not as impulsive or self-gratifying ids or as self-centered egos, but as those who find joy in engaged effort and in the gift of themselves to others. Erikson rarely wrote about happiness, but to him it meant just that gift: "to increase, by whatever is yours to give, the good will and the higher order in your sector of the world."[27] If this seems demanding, he also wrote about limiting what one can manage to care for in various life areas. Each adult needs a realistic reference point from which to neither retreat nor to grasp for more than can be cared for responsibly.

The authority of the adult Erikson described comes from consistently principled behavior and from a life that is based on higher order standards of what is good, fair, and just. In everyday life, such persons show deep, sustaining convictions, have the courage to talk about those convictions, are truthful, do what they say they will do, and provide reciprocal support for those who are also striving to act ethically. *Striving* is a key word here for "we are almost never totally and maturely ethical," he wrote, "we are only trying to be."[28] Thus the moral-ethical person is the authentic adult, one not given to pretense, arrogance, or haughtiness or to elevating the self above others. Neither cynical nor petulant, such persons act freely and behave autonomously. Their autonomy is not the freedom of "wanton license," for such license is only the Western world's "carricature [sic] of freedom."[29] Rather, theirs is an adult freedom from the illusion that they are better than others. They are free as well from the imposed opinions, norms, and behavioral requirements of those who try to sabotage their principles. This is Erikson's idea of integrity, qualities that make such adults informal leaders in any setting.

Ethical adults are models for youth as well. Erikson wrote again and again that youth, in particular, need adults who inspire both their loyalty and their need to repudiate, if only temporarily, the standards of such seniors. Loyalty and repudiation lend strength to youths' values and bind them in solidarity with their own cohort. In this way, youth will emulate enduring principles while refuting decaying modes for expressing them. This insight is Erikson's reason for saying that only those in the brief 20 to 30 years after young adulthood can ably serve as world leaders in contemporary times. The international system he envisioned could be "led only by men and women who are neither ideological youths nor moralistic old men."[30] That is, it must be led by those who are far enough along in their own development to renounce both the zealous, ideological revolutions that a nuclear-powered world cannot afford and the withered structures of older, archaic thought that would only retreat backward to a prior notion of partitioned, and therefore factioned, peoples of the world. Erikson was concerned that youth are too easily swayed by the sounds of ideologies that seem right but are incautious and intemperate, whereas older persons are regressive and change-resistant in their thinking. The generative years and generative leadership stand between the two adult poles of passionate intimacy and declining integrality, modulating each.

Primarily, Erikson wrote at the conceptual level, avoiding a litany of concrete stipulations. He showed instead his image of the ethical adult in an open-systems view. He wrote: "Now I know as well as the next person that individual and collective ethics vary according to specific laws of relativity which must be understood historically as well as psychologically."[31] Hence his psychobiographical portraits of Martin Luther and Mahatma Gandhi, men who lived four centuries apart. Erikson was searching for "religious genius" that exemplified a unified basis for adult ethics, an ethics that is open both to cross-cultural diversity and to era centrality. Such an ethics would avoid moral absolutes and, paradoxically, would pose truth as that which would be validated by all observers irrespective of their positions or movement.[32] This is a difficult set of "both/ands." In searching for principles and hoping to advance an international system of ethics, Erikson avoided promulgating a new version of dictates. He aimed to sponsor ethical concepts that would "re-consecrate and hold sacred all life on earth" and which would stipulate ideals held in common that express "some highest good, some definition of perfection, and some promise of self-realization."[33] In this, he prodded readers to appreciate a relativity that many missed, for his notions of cross-cultural relativity did not seem to fit with his prescriptive stance, with his claims for the cultural invariance of the identity construct, or with his hierarchical, invariant, and apparently static eight-stage model.

Erikson ultimately posed a discovery system rather than a system of ethics. He held that the uncovering of ethics is unending. Here he took readers to the Torah, which he held as showing a better understanding of ethics, human behavior, and higher principles than the later elementary and self-protective Golden Rule. "The Talmud," he wrote, "does not say: 'Here is the rule; go, and act accordingly.' It says: 'Go, and learn it.'"[34] Adults must learn ethics anew everyday in every encounter.

SPIRITUAL ADULT

In his various searches through the lives and minds of men, Erikson's notes show him finding evidence that every adult senses God, irrespective of how God is labeled and whether that divinity is seen as singular or several. Further, he found that many adults sense that they are spiritual creatures. To some, spirituality is separate from religion, whereas, to others, a sense of a spiritual self is associated with religious belonging and its premises. Erikson held that the sense of self as a spiritual being is, necessarily, a concomitant of the ethical. If, throughout life, the ego holds the self together, in middle and later adulthood the spiritual and ethical have together become the core of the ego that holds the "I" together. Erikson did not say that spirituality is precluded among those who were developmentally arrested at either the moralistic or the moral-ideological level. However, his writings imply that spirituality at those stations is but an incomplete experience.

In Erikson's thought, spiritual adults sense God in a number of ways, some of which overlap. God might be numen, a presiding divinity and great light. To some, the divine might be one creator alone, the "hidden God," one "lurking on the periphery of space and time," a pure light that is bright and beckoning, dreaded and feared, strange, familiar, and, sometimes, magnetizing.[35] God might be "pure nothing," as in the Eastern world mysticism of Angelus Silesius.[36] To others, God is a presence, a Spirit that is beyond this world's limitations of space and time, but one that is a radiant core within them as well; Spirit is a force that moves them. To others, Great Spirit is a palpable presence within them, within others, and within the dynamic of one's encounter with others. This gives an immediacy and present tense to God, an existence in which the "nearness of God confronts man with his neighbor," Erikson wrote.[37] Such persons believe that they must extend themselves to others. Many live like Taoists, viewing their "neighbor's gain . . . or loss" as their own.[38] Others, like the late-life Erikson himself, also see God's hand in their one, entire human life span as in a revelation metaphor. In this, at some point beyond middle age, the revealed life and a creation image come together. By old age, Erikson said, hope is an "attitude" that represents the revelation of creation in one life now nearly complete, a simple sense that the created life "is good," as in "'and he saw that it was good.'"[39]

Erikson discovered the idea of the numinous (divine) light in Scripture, in great writings throughout recorded time, and in every reasonably healthy person he studied. When he came across adults who were deadened by mental illness or evil, Erikson noticed that their glow of spirit was also dimmed or extinguished. In his later years, Erikson wrote that the "subjective sense" of God as light "dwells on the very border of our conscious existence"; it is a "luminosity of awareness" and a sense of a divine center.[40] One's inner light can be sensed, he said. However, just as he had found for identity, when the light of one's spiritual center is looked at too long or examined too minutely, that light loses its radiance: "This numinosity . . . seems lost when it is too eagerly concentrated on for its own sake, as if one light were asked to illuminate another."[41] It is best found and experienced by focusing on others, that is, in acts that permit one's light to shine. One's light is the numinous, one that had first shone on the infant from mother who is "first joy."[42] In adolescence, the numinous resurfaces in the "ideological core" of identity.[43] If such a numinous core is at the heart of infancy and later adolescence, Erikson also came very close to placing that light into the essence of his thoughts on intimacy and generativity. He had held that one finds oneself by losing oneself in another and, by caring for others, becomes so involved that one's light of personal identity is seen by others and sensed by the self. In other words, love is the conduit to experiencing the light and to having an identity.[44]

The idea of God as a radiant core takes us to Freud. The skeptical Freud, too, Erikson said, had written about the numinous as "'illumination,'" as an attribute of consciousness, and as a God-given center that repels evil and darkness:

> Freud's . . . word translated as "illumination" is "die Leuchte," a word denoting, indeed, luminosity, and this in the two senses of the Galilean saying, that is, a "Leuchter"—a lamp—and a "Leuchte," i.e., a luminous quality, a shining light. This whole "skeptical" remark, then, in which our consciousness, whatever its worth, is compared with life itself, is in all its caution not too far from the psalmist's acknowledgment of a light given by the creator to the apple of the eye.[45]

Putting aside the question of Freud's association of light with God, Erikson found it likely that Freud had been a believer; yet Freud persisted in searching for the "darkness behind consciousness" and for the "structural divisions" in the psyche—of sickness, evil, and controlling passions.[46] In this observation is another of Erikson's revisions of Freudian thought. Erikson pursued evidence of light instead of darkness. Erikson's light is three dimensional. The first dimension is ego and spirit, the actual light of consciousness. The second dimension is that of a conscious awareness of being alive, whole, and well and of sensing one's spiritual self in changing ways throughout developmental time. The third dimension is the human's peripheral awareness of a God who created and creates, a brilliance that might be beyond the humans' physical world but that might just be here as well.

Erikson's premises about the representation of a God image also depart from Freud. As a young psychoanalyst, Erikson did not take issue with Freud that God is a projected father image. He then saw God the eternal Father as a wish-fulfilling substitute for the earthly, abandoning father. Later, Erikson saw it differently. By 1960, to him mother had become each infant's "primal other" and source of first light. Mother is the developmental basis of trust, hope, and faith, the beginning semblance of eternal light. "Mother *is* nature," he wrote; with mother, "love . . . in the form of care received, gives (the infant) . . . first hope."[47] As the "matrix" who provides all good things to the infant, she is the paradise from which the infant emerges, only to then seek that lost paradise forever.[48] Paradise eventually becomes a notion of the Kingdom of God, in whatever form that realm is envisioned and expressed. Without a hope-solidified first experience, mistrust is experienced as "hunger," as an insatiable, unmet need.[49] For trust is faith, a faith that counters hunger's "fear, anxiety, dread, and confusion."[50]

The polar opposite of paradise may or may not have been hell to Erikson, although he seems not to have dismissed this as a possibility. But anxiety certainly was Erikson's version of hell. In this, he captured the infant's 8-month stranger anxiety as the anxiety that can follow a person throughout life:

> The anxiety of being abandoned by what is familiar; the fear of being hexed by the evil eye; of being imposed on by strangers; or of being alone in a universe which does not care, a universe without a divine counter-player, without charity.[51]

Eternal paradise was also his idea of the "both/and" proposition of sensing and seeking the loving utopia of infancy and, later in life, of using the resource of early trust and hope to sense that one might just be worthy in the eyes of some actual God. To Erikson, infants who are not nurtured so as to develop trust and hope are candidates for failure at faith development in their adult years, when they need another kind of hope. Thus Erikson revised Freud's thought to claim that mother is the ontogenetic face of God. Without a palpably present, trusted mother in infancy, in the elder's waning years he or she may despair of attaining either hope in the continuity of the species, faith in the value of one life well lived, or trust in some eternal promise yet to be revealed. When one is very old or very ill, mother is the assurance, evoked in conscious remembrances and in an unconscious sense, that one was loved and cherished and retains that unblemished love. Mother continues to provide the basis for hope, faith, and trust even though she is likely long since departed.[52]

If mother is the developmental basis on which one can build a later trust in God, Erikson intermittently added father into the formula. Father is an ongoing need, the "guiding voice" and firm hand.[53] Erikson sometimes deviated to say that God was a parental, not just a maternal, image. By his middle years Erikson disputed as too limiting the idea that infantile regression and projection forward of a God image is the only Ultimate Other in the human or supernatural universe. In his writings, Erikson said that Sigmund Freud had reified the id, whereas Anna Freud had reified the ego.[54] "Why," one almost hears Erikson asking, "could not the Ultimate also have found a real, if not concrete, place in the Freuds' thinking?" Although "soul" had been thrown out with God and "theology," this did not make them "expendable either in life or in theory."[55]

Being spiritual is not entirely good news. The deeply spiritual dimension houses an existential sense of exquisite aloneness, estrangement, and dread.

Just as the psyche's compartments are permanently estranged one from another, Erikson wrote, and a "series of estrangements," beginning with fear
of abandonment, mark each developmental stage, the middle and later years
contain a sense of aloneness in the universe.[56] Adults can no longer repress
death, they harbor fears of "spiritual meaninglessness," and, among the old,
the experience of depleted time, space, and strength accentuate issues of
nonbeing.[57]Elders know "daily dread" in wondering when life will "suddenly stop."[58] There is a wish to "fuse" with another, with a God, with the
cosmos, or with one's "innermost self."[59] Among some, old-age dread leads
to a near total embrace of despair.[60] However, Erikson was quick to distinguish between existential dread and anxiety. Anxiety is the "psychotic
trend" in humans, he held.[61] "Anxiety may call for therapy, dread demands
faith."[62]

BUILDING HIS IMAGE

Erikson claimed that many more adults could attain the ethical, spiritual
level by developing insight into themselves, others, and the human condition, by caring responsibly, and by nurturing their childlike and spiritual tendencies. Such behaviors reinforce ethics; they also lead to a spirited, joyful
aliveness and engaged involvement with the world. However, Erikson saw
that ethical behavior was contingent on trust-ensuring, loving care in each
adult's infancy and youth, on the grooming of a positive conscience in childhood, and on the existence of a supportive social world. Not all were so fortunate to have had this wellspring filled so that they could grow and give in
kind. And so, the ethical and spiritual adult—with as little of the moral as
possible—is a rare, gifted, and honored image. It is the image Erikson himself spent his entire adult life creating. Between 1955 and his last publication
in 1985, he wrote more about this idea than about any other.

For these reasons, it is in this image that Erikson is least separable from
his work. It seems to be the case that all original thinkers, whether or not
they know or acknowledge it, use their work and their lives to search toward the design and intent of God. Erikson's image of the spiritual and ethical housed *his* search, a search made more difficult by the fact of his psychoanalytic lens, his mixed ethnic, national, and religious heritage, his early and
resurgent identity confusion, and the fact that he never knew his biological
father. Nonetheless, his writings about ethics, faith, and the spiritual show
both his quest for and his efforts to become the ethical-spiritual model that
he described for readers.

Erikson built his image by working on two levels. In the first of these, the
less subjective, he explored how it was that persons, in both mental normalcy and pathology, in both prior historical periods and contemporary
times, develop along the moral, ideological, ethical, and spiritual trajectory
and how they hold images of God. His second level was as a subject examin-

ing himself as subject. He pondered a changing Erik Erikson throughout his adult years, questioned what he himself made of his moral-ethical and spiritual development, and contemplated how he positioned himself against eternity and against the enigma he variously termed "Ultimate Other," "Great Spirit," "Final Other," "divine Thou," "absolute Being," "Grand Ultimate," "Numen," "Supreme Counterplayer," and "God."[63] After the passing years had led him deeply into middle age to experience his own ego's twilight, Erikson wrote increasingly about the association between an evolving, ethical identity and belief in the Ultimate. As noted, he found this tendency in every mature adult, even in the self-declared atheist Sigmund Freud.

By moving directly into the spiritual, existential, and ethical, and by placing the semi-impartial observer aside to build his image, Erikson strayed decidedly beyond Freud. Erikson said he understood Freud's desire to build a reasoned model of the human devoid of "common optimism and its illusions" about the existence of morality, God, and eternity, but he also maintained that Freud forgot to include himself, "the observer, the moral man" in his image.[64] Freud had taken "morality for granted" in excluding what he himself was doing when, in his advanced state in human evolution, he omitted his moral self from the model of human he unearthed.[65] To correct this error, Erikson placed himself, the moral observer and doer, back into the equation. In this way, and by uniting pre-Freudian concepts with second-generation psychoanalytic thought, Erikson believed he might be able to give psychoanalysis a pathway back from the mechanistic, fragmented, instinctual, captive, and controlled model it had created to one of organic wholeness, coherence, activity, unity, and self-reflection. This meant including the moral, thinking, conjecturing, and planning being and associating a strong ego with a responsible, affirming conscience. It meant seeing ego as soul and positioning a firm, evolving identity as the antagonist to estrangement from the whole self and from existential dread.[66] Erikson held that the thinking, caring, evolved adult is soul- and faith-connected. He countered Freud's pessimism, believing instead that one had to build on potential reserves and positive resources. "Faith," Erikson said, "is positive; doubt is negative."[67]

From Erikson's midlife on, many of the reasons for his need to isolate an image of the ethical-spiritual adult and to serve as that model through his writings are lodged in Kierkegaard's premises. In a number of places, Erikson said he knew he could not just conceptualize and write about only that which interested him aesthetically, Kierkegaard's first stage of adult development. His own development dictated movement to the final Kierkegaard stage, in which he could function as an ethical, spiritual adult.[68]

Further, Erikson maintained that he had to overturn Freud's position from one in which psychoanalysts, physicians, and related professionals were only scientific observers to one in which they were advocates. Indeed, his role was that of an observer of persons and their society. But he also believed deeply in "ethical intervention" and "advocacy."[69] For whether or not clinicians say so directly, their role requires that they align themselves with those who are inactivated by improper care, inordinate social pressures, or conflicting external values. As is true for his work in other areas, Erikson saw firsthand the social and family disorders that turn persons into distressed patients and deliver them to therapists for help. He gave credibility to the rage he felt on seeing patients who were unloved and mistreated by their families and society, individuals deprived of opportunities to develop and to be genuinely, uniquely themselves, respected by others just because they are human and have human needs. He had to transform Freud's stand.

To Erikson, the prevailing neuroses and psychoses of each historical era showed a collective, "inverted revolt against . . . the unmanageable or hypocritical values of the then existing establishment."[70] He disputed Freud's belief that "the psychoanalyst represents the ethics of scientific truth only and is committed to studying ethics (or morality) in a scientific way . . . leav[ing] *Weltanschauungen* (ethical world views) to others."[71] Instead, Erikson contended, "what the healing professions advocate . . . is always part of the value struggle of the times and, whether 'avowed' or not, will be—and therefore had better be—ethical intervention."[72] Humans could not long stand a "division of personal, professional, and political ethics," for this severs "the very fiber of our personal existence."[73]

With such thought in hand, Erikson detailed content for healthy behavior, an ethics of adult functioning, and the ethical basis for fostering developmental strengths in others. He lifted consciousness, insisting on speaking and writing about what he saw as the latest "underground," ethics.[74] To Freud and Freud's era, sexuality was the undiscussed underground. Erikson's own later time was one in which ethics was the undiscussed topic that had to be brought to the surface and talked about, particularly in light of its healthy, life-affirming dimensions.[75]

Building himself into his analysis and precepts and speaking out about ethics, about his ethical views, and about the connection between ethics and spiritual dimensions made Erikson less credible to many in a scientific, detached era.[76] However, to at least some reviewers, the way he joined belief and psyche, profession and person, made him more credible.[77] In fact, both his developmental thought and his spiritual, ethical persona are more believable because he *was* a psychoanalyst. He could have taken the less risky route of observing and mirroring the psyches of the times. Instead, he showed ways in which each era creates mental and moral problems for developing adults. He might also have left God as psyche's projection. Again he risked, choosing to give credibility to belief in the Ultimate. Erikson understood the extent to which the adult psyche will go to deny its eventual extinction. His psychoanalytic domain had led him to understand that belief in God is, in part, a projected image and a human need. Never one to forgo complexity or dissonance, he illustrated that until the later years of life, denial of death is a protective shield that permits work-committed functioning and living fully instead of cowering in fear of the end. Erikson's God occurs in action, even in that of denial; yet beyond image projection and denial, a real deity might exist.

Thus this image of Erikson's is one in which he joined the border at which psychology meets theology. It is Erikson's greatest move beyond psychology and farther afield of psychoanalytic restriction than any of his ideas about the latent potential of adults. His various notes lay bare his need to eventually show psychoanalysis as having cold feet, as too detached from its subjects and far too willing to illustrate emotional difficulties in the adult disconnected from what he saw as each person's need for faith.

In his revised model, belief had to have its place. Erikson saw belief as neither completely rational nor irrational. Rather, it is "a-rational," he said.[78] In this, he held that belief and faith have little to do with objective appraisal because limited human minds cannot reason their way to God. Yet he claimed that thinking adults can see evidence of the Ultimate's design within and beyond them. Within, there is the complexity of the human, with its multiple, coordinated systems and its integrated psyche-soma, a body and mind that reveal a prewired design and sequential unfolding. Beyond, a life-sustaining planet and multiple galaxies are in clear view.

The ethical-spiritual adult that Erikson portrayed is process and goal. It is an outward reaching, affirming state toward which one aims and which one never quite reaches. Erikson held to this as telos, an elusive aim and a developmental growth process. His notes leave little doubt that he depicted this goal and process as he in fact saw it. But describing ethics and spirituality in this way was also useful to his need to avoid an "either/or" mentality and its inherent reductionism. Retaining the duality of both movement and aim meant that Erikson could convey complexity by using ideas of tension and polarity, that he could show how persons develop individually and how the collective species might best evolve, and that he could illustrate the impossibility of developmental perfection in any human. To Erikson, healthy individual development throughout life always requires excursions outward toward others and the social world, from trust through care to hope, instead of reaching deeper into the dark recesses of the mistrusting, stagnating, and eventually despairing self. Thus, development is never complete. It always moves toward human others and toward the Ultimate Other. This applies to individuals and to their collection as a species.

When Erikson considered reasoning against belief, on analyzing others and himself he concluded that belief is both separate from reason and is superordinate to it. Thus higher level intellectual powers are not prerequisite to belief or to experiencing the Almighty. In fact, he held that when adults give primacy to reasoning, they occlude belief by tuning out the limbic part of the brain that lends greater access to a sense of a deity. Further, when they focus on the powers of the reasoning brain, adults tend to foster an aggrandized self-love for that which they had no role in creating. A psychoanalyst and a Kierkegaard scholar, Erikson placed the introspective subjective, the metasubjective, and the intersubjective above the objective. He valued these forms of knowing more highly than either objectivity or the human attributes that permit it.

The introspective subjective, in which one looks deeply into the self, is the point at which Erikson conceptualized insight and illustrated an insight-belief connection. He found that insight and belief frequently coincide, particularly in those adults who have the gifts of perceptive, reflective minds. In adults who are not particularly talented in this regard, insight might be learned. Belief and insight are thus nearly on par. They are mutual experiences of those who Erikson sometimes referred to as "sublime" persons.[79] Yet the modes of knowing of insight and belief are different, insight requiring subjective and intersubjective knowledge and belief requiring partial suspension of the modes of thinking through which the subjectively experienced world is known. Together, they walk parallel, sometimes joined, paths. One feeds the other. In adult life, particularly from midlife onward, assuming that a firm basis in trust had been established in infancy, it was his premise that insight combined with belief leads to the higher reaches of consciousness in which adults stand in awe before a designing and governing Almighty.

Late in his own life, there is evidence of a deeply spiritual Erikson. This is an Erikson who diffused his own thinking to foster inductive, shapeless connections among a sense of spirit, artistic symbols, and mystical ways of perceiving things differently. There are signs of this development in his earlier writing, but his spirituality comes forward markedly in the notes of his final decade of writing. At the time, Erikson was constructing his last conceptual work. He had rounded out his life-cycle elaboration with his 1977 book, *Toys and Reasons*. Afterward, then in his late 70s, he contemplated the Galilean Jesus' parables against the human sense of "I."[80]

Erikson's imagery is vibrant in those notes. Free, alliterative associations appear alongside biblical passages and geographic data. His handwritten thoughts appear in the various colored pens he was inclined to use, in pencilled sketches, and in his ideas about the religious symbolism of statues and paintings in various times. His imagery is spatial, symbolic, and allegorical. Notes and drawings of madonnas, crosses, weathervanes, animals, birds, and fiery angels compete with sensory notions and visionary images about worldviews. All are juxtaposed against the human in evolution, against adults in prior historical times, against contemporary humans, and against images of future time and space. In these, Erikson was developmental and existential. He wrote about the world as a place of beauty and darkness, as one in which God and evil are palpable. His was a view of the power of compelling principles, of the sanctity and violation of human life, and of the fundamental awe in which he held creation and the Great Spirit. To him, that Spirit captures and holds adults, especially after midlife.[81]

As noted earlier, Erikson was not religious if by this term we mean weekly attendance at worship services or adherence to an institutionalized code of beliefs. He was, he said, "determined to live on the shadowy borderline of the denominational ambiguities."[82] He thought from within Judeo-Christian monotheism and, on its basis, incorporated Hindu and ancient Chinese thought. However, he wrote that he had been drawn to the teachings of Jesus from an early age. In part, Erikson said, his sense of the "credal immediacy" of the Gospels, of the way of life of the first Christians, and of Christianity's "core values" originated in his youth.[83] His mother had led her son to believe that such values were not incongruent with his Jewish upbringing. She had also been a devoted reader of Kierkegaard, an interest she shared with her son. Both the acts and sayings of Jesus and the existential premises and adult stage progression of Kierkegaard are points of origin for many of Erikson's ideas.

In addition to biblical passages and Kierkegaard's diary and books, in his notes Erikson referenced the writings of St. Augustine, Nietzsche, Confucius, Freud, Angelus Silesius, and Shakespeare. He was attracted to the revisionist thought of Martin Luther, Mahatma Gandhi, and Albert Einstein. He particularly based his ideas on thought prior to the time when discrete fields of study took hold. This furthered his ability to think between twentieth-century disciplines and to maintain his creativity. Indeed, few besides an originator like Erikson, thinking outside faith systems and domains of inquiry, would have had the hubris to amend the Golden Rule.[84]

In his later writing period, after *Luther,* and particularly from 1961 on, Erikson's personal faith came to the fore. We see Joan Erikson's hand here. A daughter of an Episcopalian minister and a devout Christian, her influence on Erikson's thoughts, in this area as well as in other conceptual areas, has been underestimated. Based on Joan's suggestion, in a letter in 1976, Erikson said that he was a "Christian apprentice."[85] And, he said, he continued to study the "living implications of Christ's message" in light of original and ongoing meanings while not aligning himself with any particular version of its "institutional fate."[86] He held that a tight institutional fit would have precluded his "infinite search," just as it would have removed him from his combined Jewish and Gentile heritage, from his psychoanalytic orientation, and from his ongoing development as a thinker.[87] He was determined to remain unfettered.

Knowledge of Erikson's refusal to confine himself to any denomination or human belief system is essential to understanding his thinking about the religious element and ethics in adults. In an unpublished letter, he said that his convictions held "a Christian tentativeness" in belief that said "yes, maybe."[88] Erikson's "yes, maybe" is the "yes, maybe" of a number of adults who think deeply about faith, ethics, and the spiritual. Such persons hold the conviction that human artifacts of religious belonging constrain belief along institutional party lines instead of nurturing faith and unity among all who "search infinitely." He claimed that his nonbelonging housed his need to avoid abandoning personal responsibility to declare that something was wrong no matter which social, political, or religious convention it belonged to. Likely, his tentativeness also arose from his inability to fully believe in what he sometimes sensed but could not see. In his typically wry humor, he drew distinctions between intellectuals and those with precise religious affiliations, eschewing the limits of each. "Needless to say," he wrote, "neither intellectuals nor religious life can maintain itself on the high plane of such noble systems as Augustine's and Aquinas's. Intellectuals always cultivate simpler, starker antitheses in order to assure small victories in argument; while the religious-minded want to 'get there' faster."[89] There were also problems in the ways religion and science exclude each other. He agreed with Albert Einstein: "Science without religion is lame, religion without science is blind."[90]

Thus Erikson worked in conflict and in the zone in which psychoanalytic skepticism counters free-ranging belief. We can credit this conflict with his diffuse writing and with the inconsistencies in his published thought about spirituality and belief from one writing to another and, at times, in one and the same article, speech, or chapter. It is as though his knowledge of the unconscious, its projections and illusory wish fulfillment, sometimes did battle with faith to the point of diffidence, as though he was unsure whether and how to give belief its due while maintaining his position within the intellectual priesthood of psychoanalysis.

Erikson's fit within skepticism took several forms. Either he took the position of God as a projected human need or the position of God as transcendent reality. At times he vacillated between the two. When psychological premises dominated, Erikson implied that psychoanalytic thought might, for some, substitute for religious belief.[91] After all, its "free association" was a "Western form of meditation," and therapists were often expected to create fresh faith structures and rituals for their patients.[92] This is especially the case when religions fail to do so.[93] At other times he hedged or alternated between his early premise of God as "phantom" and his later view of God as a spiritual reality.[94] The best way to reconcile his competing positions is to place him in his profession and in his era, just as he did for those about whom he wrote. Erikson was embedded in his period of evolved Western thought. Despite his attempt to incorporate thought from as early as the sixth century B.C., by the time of Erikson's writing years, religion's hold on the post-Reformation Western mind had eroded. The trend line has been one in which scholars and the public have spent always decreasing time and effort gazing upward, as it were, to study premises about God and the Kingdom and ever more time gazing downward to study themselves and the many objects scattered around them. Particularly in what Erikson himself saw as a jaded U.S. society and era, self-conscious and self-focused adults had become disinclined to subordinate their pride in intellect and individualism and their faith in their own autonomous control to a controlling, higher power. Erikson was part of two remarkable countries and an equally remarkable twentieth century. Some of his writings thus reflect his native Germany and, later, his adoptive America's authorship of place and time, all from within an intellectual's, psychoanalytic zeitgeist.

Thus finding the most representative Erikson voice with respect to God and faith is difficult if not impossible. The difficulty is heightened by the fact that the entire body of his American publications span the years 1935 to 1985. It was a half century during which Erikson developed from a 33-year-old young adult into an 83-year-old elder, and, to him, the United States changed from one of Roosevelt-era hope in the promise of government to provide a better life to the era of post-Vietnam and Watergate suspicions about such government. There had to be changes, some of which occurred as values and society changed and as Erikson himself saw things differently because of those value shifts, because of his various studies, and because of personal changes due to experience and aging. For the latter, certain changes seem to have been the result of his own evolving adulthood and the changing context of his body and mind, which informed him differently, in effect from intimacy through care to old age and transcendence. Thus, three different periods and writing forms appear sequentially in his constructions. These are his theoretical period (1935–1960), his realistic, theoretical period (1961–1969), and his existential, experiential period (1970–1985).

Early on, in the first period, Erikson's was primarily the psychoanalyst's pen. Until his mid-50s, Erikson wrote as a theoretical clinician and as a positive, conflict theorist. At age 48, for example, writing in *Childhood and Society*, he projected forward the stage resolutions of older adulthood. At that time Erikson had had few, if any, clinical encounters with seniors. His "integrity" versus "despair" crisis and the best resolution of this in "wisdom" thus had to change when Erikson himself became old. Integrity then became "integrality," of working just to keep one's body, mind, psyche, and senses together. Then faith and hope replaced wisdom. For all of these reasons, he himself said that each of his writings was a separate "period piece."[95]

Further, when Martin Luther took hold of his ideas in 1955, Erikson changed substantially. He himself noted this in the preface to an unpublished manuscript, saying that when he reemerged from that "historical excursion to clinical work, I was not the same."[96] Life history no longer meant a person's pure and isolated personal history, nor could he pull patients or historical icons out of their life narratives, spiritual beliefs, and all of history to treat them as case histories. It was "illusory," he said, to think that psychoanalysis or its techniques can be advanced in such "anesthetic isolation."[97]

From the writing of *Luther* onward, Erikson merged insights from history and life narratives, clinical data, personal experience, self-analysis, biblical readings, and personal faith and combined these with his prior bent of infusing knowledge from earlier recorded time. By age 64, he was more reality and less theory based. He wrote that ultimate concerns are preeminent to seniors; however, in that realistic, still theoretical era of writing, he was content to leave such concerns to theologians and philosophers.

By age 72, Erikson was an existential-experiential writer who understood firsthand both bodily decline and the identity of one who is peripheral to working life. Newly marginalized, no longer integral to the institutions that foster identity, he changed his thinking to build in God, Jungian premises about gender archetypes and the soul, and old-age dread. By age 80, Erikson was a decidedly existential thinker; he had to give faith its due. *Faith* then became an alternate term for *integrity*. By then Erikson was no longer at such great psychoanalytic distance from belief. He gave faith high berth in his published thought.[98]

Harbingers of Erikson's existential thought that began with *Luther* occurred when a middle-aged Erikson looked back on his own troubled youth and young adulthood and looked deeply within as well. Erikson was in the sixth decade of life, a decade in which adults contemplate their lives against eternity. From that point on, Erikson remained attuned to the hazy terrain that is a meeting ground for the existential, the psychological, the ethical, and the spiritual. It seems natural for him to have moved his thought to the fringe of the temporal. Here psyche meets its version of theos and begins to soften its denial of death. As the ego perceives more clearly its future non-existence, many adults conceive of themselves as living on in some spiritual essence beyond one time- and space-bound location. Erikson understood such belief as the antidote to despair. Yet, according to his widow Joan Erikson, he and she hedged, understanding that "it is the only way humans *can* think."[99]

An Enraged Voice: Against Moralistic Religion, Toward a Wider, Postmoralistic Species

Erikson was at his writing best when his rage came through. One problem about which he vented considerable pique was the clustering of persons into bureaucracies. He held that all institutions thwart individuals' ethical development. As soon as they are established, institutions rigidify. This deadens vitality and its expression by living, breathing, affirming principles. In this conviction, he neither vacillated nor changed his mind over time. He was particularly incensed about the ways in which the very structures that are meant to be homes of faith and ethics keep adults at the undeveloped childish, dependent, moral level. These structures are institutional religions.

Erikson maintained that different religions and their inherent worldviews hold moralistic codes, ritualisms, and requirements that help to isolate, divide, and keep the peoples of the world apart. Their various "thou-shall-nots" and their guilt-sponsoring penitence captivate the faithful as prisoners of childhood morality. Religions are "dogmatic systems."[100] They encode and ritualize what humans already believe, that we have "always lived and will live hereafter."[101] But religions minus a "living ethics" are regressive;

they force one backward to the dependency state of the preautonomous child, using their own "law to . . . subdue the spirit."[102] Thus Erikson worked to take down religions' ritualistic artifacts and negatives while building toward belief in principles, community, unity, and a universal God image. In this, he attacked both the Judaic and Christian religions in the Western world orbit. Both "elaborated" human "infantile guilt into a universal sinfulness."[103]Religions and morality had to be "tamed."[104]

To Erikson, orthodox Judaism needed to cast aside its tendencies to inculcate scruples, compulsions, and superstitions.[105] "Phobic avoidances" and "compulsive purifications" are dangerous both to faith and to mental health.[106] Restrictive Judaic dietary proscriptions, for example, are leftover legalisms, for Jesus had converted the Mosaic law that had found foods and receptacles unclean.[107] Uncleanness comes from the weak or evil id within, not from anything that enters humans from outside. Further, the God of Judaism cannot serve either human or faith development as a "threatening and vengeful," eternity-denying God.[108] Erikson agreed with Einstein: Judaism houses moral covenants based on fear and negation. The Jewish God could not lead to a unified Kingdom or to a unified mankind if Judaic remnants continued on as nothing other than a "negation of superstition, an imaginary result of its elimination," a system of "moralism" and "pietism."[109] Thus, for Erikson as for Einstein, Judaism was not a "transcendent religion."[110]

To Erikson, Jesus was the model who showed "the way" to a transcendent form of humanity, belief, and behavior. Jesus was the "last true reformulator of existential 'I,'" Erikson wrote.[111] His "passion . . . made of all subsequent history a mere shadow."[112] As a result of Jesus' active, positive advance and his "healing mission," Judaism should shed its archaic morality.[113] Before Jesus, "the Way" had been that of Lao-Tse, the celebrated sixth-century B.C. founder of Taoism, whose teachings interested Erikson greatly. In Taoism moralizing and rites are renounced. Rites, in particular, are deadening. They come into the order of things when "the way" of being is lost, that is, when virtue, benevolence, and good faith decay.

As for Christianity, Erikson wanted it stripped of latter-day reconstructions, monetary influences, and superstitions. He espoused a return to the "virginal" sayings of Jesus, the pure Christianity that Jesus had taught and that Einstein said it should be, that is, "purged" of later "additions," especially those of "the priests."[114] To Erikson, there was a great disconnection between the way of living Jesus had shown and the "retail" religion that compromised his teachings far into the twentieth century.[115] An institutionalized avarice, replete with "Bible quoting bigotry," had replaced the love, care, and childlikeness of the parables.[116] Later editions turned those teachings into a self-righteousness that held an accountant's "imagery of accrued credit in heaven."[117] Particularly repugnant was Christianity's replacement of Judaic superstitions with Roman versions such as indulgences, "vegetable" relics, and confession. To Erikson these are primitive and magical. They associate soiling with sin. Purchasing power (indulgences and relics) and "penitentiary technique" (confession) are used to make one clean again.[118] Further, such magic requires believers' deference to the fathers of the church and to those patriarchs' changing whims of scriptural interpretation. This was too passive an adjustment by the faithful for Erikson's tastes. To Erikson, Christianity might be thought of as a unique "attempt to free mankind from the Oedipus."[119] But in trying to heal blindness, incest, and generational weakness, the new mythology had substituted bureaucratic blindness to the adaptive needs of humans.[120] Erikson posed that adults' developmental needs and their spiritual needs are one. Together they require moving beyond folklore and breast-beating confessional guilt.

Erikson had no use for the way that all religions, once they are institutionalized, self-serve their own political and bureaucratic survival needs. Throughout his life, he held that "religion exploits," for its own purposes, "the most infantile strivings in man."[121] Religion:

> has monopolized the traditional formulation and the ritual restoration of faith. It has shrewdly played into man's most child-like needs, not only by offering eternal guarantees for an omniscient power's benevolence (if properly appeased) but also by magic words and significant gestures, soothing sounds and soporific smells—an infant's world.[122]

"Ceremonial hallucination," chanting, and shared superstitions are mesmerizing strategies through which the reverent together master their anxieties about the great "unknown."[123] In this way, all religions channel and compromise belief. They substitute magical rites for the unrestrained freedom of individual pathways to God.[124] Religions' closed, authoritarian ways hold the faithful captive by feeding on fantasy, terror, alienation, and neuroses. As such, religions guard the heavenly gates with "convention and pretense."[125] To Erikson, this impairs faith, fosters flailing about in remorse, blame, and backward-looking guilt, and leads to self-judgment and to the judging and blaming of others.[126] Religions divorce belief from a "living ethics" in which adults might find a way to actively create the Kingdom through caring for family, community, and worthy sociopolitical goals.[127] In these ways, religions have a mighty hand in building the negative identity.

In his most caustic criticisms about religions and their moralisms, Erikson tried to show how religions, at their worst, mock what had been meant to be a living, doing creed. He did not castigate personal faith or the value of religious belonging as such. Beneath the surface of his harshest, sometimes overdramatized, criticism was his understanding that among all the ideologies of the world, religion alone holds restorative powers: It "recognizes the individual's most personal needs for existential nutriment."[128] In fact, although Erikson criticized religious structures and their constraints, he endorsed the community power of shared symbols. He also held that a symbiotic return to the magic of childlike song and prayer, wonder, and shared ritual might just be the state of mind that gives persons a sensory conduit to the Almighty. He wrote that such experiences can become a creative bridge between one's trust-filled infancy and a "hoped-for and eternal future."[129] Anticipating those who would criticize such experiences as merely regressive, he wrote that "we regress in our dreams too," but such regression is healthy and refreshing.[130] It prepares us to take up the next day rested, invigorated, and ready to work toward the future.

Throughout his writing life, Erikson emphasized New Testament thought, reading from the German Bible in Luther's translation. He had had a "lifelong fascination" with the Galilean sayings, he said.[131] New Covenant thought was in keeping with an active, affirming basis of life, health, faith, and caring works. Thereby, it was an essential departure from the older Judaic image of God as one to be obeyed in terrifying fear and immobility.[132] In Erikson's view, the teachings and sayings of Jesus represent a "leap" in human consciousness; they are a radically new way of seeing, of thinking, of acting, of believing, and of feeling. In them he found a "Jesovanic coherence" and a "new 'disposition of mind.'"[133] Here Erikson comes close to Jung. To both of these psychoanalysts, the development of Christianity was a necessary historical element in the development of human consciousness and reflective thought.

The Galilean's sayings likely played a decisive role in Erikson's premise that one should always determine what one can affirm, what one "can say yes to." Affirmative words and actions counter what, to him, are the negatives in early, and in later orthodox, Judaism. The sayings also align well with his wish to expand and widen human consciousness in order to advance healthy behavior and to deepen insight into the human condition. These were vehicles that might open an international system of social justice.

Knowing that the idea of the divine as a single creator is a late development in the history of the species, Erikson did not limit ideas of God.[134] Yet in his writing Erikson's God is always singular. Although this is consistent with Judaic-Christian convention, Erikson's use of the singular also seems to have been motivated by his effort to portray unity between the God of Abraham and the God of twentieth-century Christianity. Erikson's unification, one-God concept was based, in part, on his emphasis of organic and spiritual wholeness. Working at the metalevel of groups and societies, he thought in terms of a collection of all individuals, which he seems to have mentally accumulated and projected forward to full species' development as one enlightened, complete, joined body. He believed that this body could not come together in health and unity unless its various religious forms, those possessing inherently divided ways of seeing and believing, were somehow transcended. A unified collective that cared for humans was what he had in mind. This idea requires adults to move beyond institutional prejudices and their superstitious, sometimes faddish elements to establish a single-minded species that behaves along the uniform faith ways of caring for others. In other words, belief in one God had to be complemented by faith acts that define one species. To Erikson, humans need to experience, embody, and represent the creator in a new, and a newly unified, way.

REVISING THE LEXICON

As noted, Erikson did not adhere to English or to any other language. To him, words in daily use carry numerous definitions that obscure clarity.[135] He found English parlance particularly troublesome, for it contains so many formal and colloquial words that, depending on usage, synonyms might become antonyms. Hence he turned to etymological origins and to early and later meanings based on Greek and Latin roots. In the process, he sometimes made up new English terms for his ideas. In this way he enhanced his tendency to convey ancient concepts that express a unity of soul, ego, and psyche in the human. Turning to his native German, he countered English-language fragmentation. Erikson was a poststructure unifier. He worked to put the human back together again after the pressures of separatist religions, Freudian fragmentation, and modernity had divided persons both individually and collectively.

Working to illustrate the ethical-spiritual adult, seven words in particular undergird his moral imagery and are classic Erikson. These terms are *actuality*, *mutuality*, *adaptation*, *insight*, *soul*, *spirit*, and *virtue*. Erikson coined new meanings for two of these terms (*actuality* and *mutuality*); he adapted the others from existing definitions to serve his purposes. At times, he might combine such words or use them interchangeably. Actuality might become mutuality. Soul and spirit are Erikson synonyms; yet soul depicts location, whereas spirit shows activity or tension, as well as location. Such absence of specificity notwithstanding, the terms are unified by the fact that Erikson used each of them to illustrate how adults guide themselves, children, and key others along as they "steer" toward engaged and more consistently principled lives.[136]

Erikson did not align himself with the moral view of humanism, which has as its god the intellectual acceptance of evolution's determinism and some confidence in humanity's ability to shape part of it. To Erikson, such postulates are passive; they had to be converted to an activity that gives both God and adults their due roles. In Erikson's thought, humans necessarily fit into the niche in which evolution lodged them. However, being adult means piloting psychosocial evolution by adapting the world to make it a better place for all living creatures and by working actively to bring forth the best-case rendition of the Almighty's design. Thus, for adults, each of Erikson's seven important ethical and spiritual terms has an active, affirming, positive quality, whereas the antithesis of each carries a negative, deadening, and inactivating meaning. The dystonics of each of the eight stages chart the potential "estrangements" that arise sequentially and afflict persons throughout their lives.[137] Erikson wished to lead from *patiens* (enduring, suffering with, forbearing, being passive) to *agens* (acting, exerting power).[138] This was his way of fostering coherence, personal centrality, and initiative, as well as positive tension and movement. He illustrated the importance of the psyche's activation, a vitality in which *agens* is the lifeblood of an identity that resists personal fragmentation and disintegration. *Agens* sponsors personal engagement and work, not necessarily in the externals of overt behavior, but in the internal workings of an energized, active psyche.

For Erikson, sponsoring agency, initiative, and personal control are inherent in the Hippocratic principle. He repeatedly stated his opposition to having patients recline horizontally, inactively, on a couch. This fosters dependence, immobility, deactivation, and a position that is physically lower than, and spatially peripheral to, the psychoanalyst. This cannot provide equality in the relationship, nor can it foster clients' beliefs that they can gain control of their lives. Further, this position fails to activate any sensory encounters of seeing and experiencing the other. It fails as well to engage the client in shared participation. Movement away from the need for un-Hippocratic dependence was what Erikson had in mind; inactivation characterizes "patienthood" and leads to more of the same.[139] Whether in the therapeutic session, in understanding Luther and Gandhi, in the ethics of everyday life, or in working with and toward one's God, Erikson's ideology poses an upward posture and engaged participation. Just as Jesus put those seeking cures to work while he healed them, Erikson would have those who are inactivated by ill psyches or by ethical stagnation involve themselves and work for their own healing. In fact, Erikson's modeling of Jesus became more important to him over time. Beginning in earnest with *Luther* and culminating in his article on Jesus and the human sense of "I" in 1981, Erikson noted the similarity in methods between the Galilean healer, various emulators, and his own modeling of Jesus' behavior in twentieth-century psychological healing.

Actuality and Mutuality

In part, Erikson used the terms *actuality* and *mutuality* based on his close read of Freud in the original German. Taking these concepts in turn, *actuality* means participation, as well as an intersubjectivity between or among persons, and being "in the midst of". It is "the world verified in immediate immersion and interaction."[140] *Actuality* is close in meaning to the German term *Wirklichkeit,* a word that combines the ideas of action, efficacy, and reality. Erikson said he meant to illustrate the importance of shared participation with "a minimum of defensive maneuvering and a maximum of mutual activation."[141] This requires "unselfconscious immersion in reciprocal action."[142] Distinguishing between the terms *actuality* and *reality,* by *reality* he meant the verified world in a particular society, one that most participants would validate and agree on based on their shared, congruent observations and interpretations. *Reality* is the extant world; it can be seen but is passive. On the other hand, actuality means actively participating. *Actualize, actualizing,* and *actualization* mean the releasing of one's own and of another's ability to participate effectively. In the absence of actuality, Erikson said, "reality becomes a prison of stereotypes."[143]

Close in meaning to *actuality* is the term *mutuality*. *Mutuality* means "mutual activation" in which two persons, or a leader and his or her followers, are active and are activated by one another.[144] This requires leeway, Erikson's term for the freedom to be oneself and to grant such freedom to others. Leeway and participation are key qualities of mutuality, as are the transforming power of authenticity and good will. First experienced with the mother, mutuality was, to Erikson, the source of hope and of trust. This first source is essential to life, to mental health, and, when integrated on a higher developmental level in adulthood, to the ethical treatment of others. Erikson limited the number of "shoulds" and "musts" he placed before readers, but in this case he insisted that persons *should* be cared for in infancy in a way that ensures trust, hope in life, self-trust, and eventual trust in an Almighty. Throughout all of his writing, Erikson held that each person *must* be treated with a regard (mutuality) that says he or she is a unique, separate being who is free from the suffocating control of others.

In part, *mutuality* is the Kantian Erikson. It requires treating others as autonomous ends, never as the means to an end. It is as well a Gandhian Erikson: God and truth appear not as ideas or visions but in action. In action, no one is harmed or denigrated in any personal encounters. All players are activated. This transforms their roles, enabling them to participate as equals toward a goal. To Erikson, it was such coparticipation that leads to shared awareness and mutual interpretation of the context. This, in fact, heightens participation. Access to the context and mutual involvement in it foster joint understandings and energize all. Erikson used the example of the dignity Gandhi promoted among those who had been inactivated by British rule and oppressive conditions. Erikson's change of the Golden Rule to one in which individual growth is advanced for each counterplayer—no matter his or her differing, respective levels of development or prior involvement—met the Gandhian purpose of mutuality: Through the instrument of the self, both the doer and the one done with (instead of done *to*) can grow.

"Mutual activation" was the "crux" of mutuality to Erikson, an "ego actuality" in which persons are "inspired" to actively engage their selves, strengths, and abilities.[145] This is a concern for keeping egos active and alive instead of powerless and helpless. To him, mutuality was transference, a "mutual 'transfer' of energy (Freud called it libido, that is, love-energy)."[146] Erikson found parallels between Freud's concept of libido, Shakespeare's notion of virtues that shine on others and redound to the giver, and Jesus' feeling the loss of something vital when the woman who was hemorrhaging touched him. Mental health, ethical and spiritual health, and ego vitality are of the same cloth. Activity, mastery, mutual involvement, and initiative promote such health. In fact, mutual involvement helps the adult to function responsibly and to experience the self as a vital spirit. Neither ego health nor ethical and spiritual health are found in psychological paralysis or in reclusive retreat.

Adaptation

Erikson distinguished between adaptation and adjustment to convey the importance of active agency. His positive, active term is *adaptation*, whereas the passive term is *adjustment*. He was consistent, using these words deliberately and noninterchangeably. Adaptation means fitting the environment to one's needs and to the needs of others in society. On this basis he admired rebels in the persons of Luther, Gandhi, Martin Luther King, Jr., and Rosa Parks, who used their rage about inhuman conditions to improve the human lot. Rage is important. The principled use their rage honorably, intelligently, and effectively.

Adjustment is the antithesis of adaptation. Adjustment too readily means some passive acceptance of conditions which no one should have to accept. Erikson variously gave the examples of physical and verbal abuse, of prejudice, slavery, and the robbery of human worth by uprooting, banishing, and denigrating a group's or an individual's identity.[147] Interestingly, he also wrote that the more sensitive the adult, the more vulnerable he or she will be to control by the egocentric, the self-serving, and the unprincipled. In notes scattered among his Harvard papers, he further implied that sensitivity, a concomitant of insight into the needs of others and of the self, might well reflect attributes of character and of personal goodness in some persons.

Erikson's distinction between adaptation and adjustment is partly Darwinian. To him, some adjusters are chameleons who are readily overpowered by others or are compelled by family or external society to fit within imposed, sometimes harmful, conditions. Other adjusters have weak egos. They too are readily overcome by the more powerful. Strong egos are found in those who are able to adapt their environments to their own purposes, typically for the good of others as well. In this strength-versus-weakness connotation of adapters versus adjusters, Erikson broached, but did not fully conceptualize, beginning work on the meaning of intersubjectivity. In unpublished writings he noted that an individual's tendency toward personal coherence, ego strength, and principled behavior gains in power by spatial proximity to others whose ego strength and principles are equally palpable.[148] In his unpublished notes and in *Gandhi's Truth*, he wrote of the ways in which personal agency and control lead to environmental mastery and to hard-won change and of the power of some significant others who lend strength to a cause and its leader. This is the intersubjective, a charged mutual zone of support between persons. But Erikson was wary. He eschewed efforts to give anything other than formless renditions of the mysterious space between humans who, nonetheless, somehow use such space and proximity to others to catalyze another's, and their own, vigor.

When Erikson combined adaptation and mutuality, his purpose was to show how adults can engage the fellowship and dormant power of those who are held down so that the full species might develop ethically together. Using the vehicles of the youthful Luther and the middle-aged Gandhi, Erikson linked actuality, mutuality, adaptation, reasoned intellect, and passionate belief in a cause. He maintained that charismatic leaders such as these are the rare few who restore humanity's faith in itself, a goal they achieve by working through their own individual crises so as to activate the insight, power, energy, renewed vision, and spirit of the people in their place and time. Writing about children, he insisted that the greatest offense against ethics is that of extinguishing a person's "spirit"; the greatest advances are seen in restoring it, in helping others to become more alive, active, and whole.[149] For individuals or for any collection of them, whether liberated from the Mosaic law, unshackled from the institutional church, delivered from British rule, emancipated from South African apartheid, or released from white dominion in pre-civil-rights America, the spirit activated means that the people—all the people, oppressed and oppressors alike—are freed to think, to act, and to develop.

Insight

Erikson worked to advance modern understandings about insight. He disputed the dictionary's notion that insight is an "either/or" ability, that one might see "into a situation *or* into oneself"; rather, true insight requires both forms of seeing.[150] Insight means seeing into oneself and into external situations in unison. It is a third eye looking inward and, simultaneously, looking outward to examine the world. It emanates from and advances reflective thought and learning. In his mind, truth is a primary product of insight; it comes from silent contemplation and reflection. Finding Americans too garrulous to do much in the way of listening, reflecting, or silently contemplating ideas and convictions, Erikson gave his country a message. He wrote that he admired Gandhi's insistence on spending one full day each week in complete silence:

> Gandhi often spoke of his inner voice, which would speak unexpectedly in the preparedness of silence—but then with irreversible firmness and an irresistible demand for commitment. And, indeed, even Nietzsche, certainly the Mahatma's philosophical opposite, claimed that truth always approached "on the feet of doves." That is, the moment of truth is suddenly there—unannounced and pervasive in its stillness. But it comes only to him who has lived with facts and figures in such a way that he is always ready for a sudden synthesis and will not, from sheer surprise and fear, startle truth away.[151]

Insight is a process. It is also a way of life. Insight is a given, perceptual talent in some, predominantly women, he wrote. To others it arrives with midlife, and to still others it is a hard-won achievement. Insight leads to the mastery of various work, relationship, social, and civic contexts. At its peak, Erikson saw in it a powerful correlation with spirituality. It is a near-perfect, if elusive, way of seeing. It is an illumination. And it holds a sense of the

Almighty. Because such "knowledge obligates," Erikson wrote, at its best insight leads inexorably to wisdom and to ethical action.[152]

Erikson held that both meditative, "soul-searching prayer and self-analysis" can result in insight.[153] He saw confessional, introspective prayer as the forerunner of Freudian psychoanalysis, having found such self-analysis in the fourth-century autobiographical *Confessions of St. Augustine* and in the mid-nineteenth-century diary of Søren Kierkegaard. To Erikson, the aim of all analysis was insight and ethical functioning. Whether achieved through psychoanalysis, through piercing reflection, or through praying to one's God, the insight achieved expands one's consciousness about how other persons and the self might best develop and not be harmed. Insight creates the mental medium for an altered ethical stance. This stance is one in which adults necessarily know that they are responsible for nurturing and sustaining life on one small planet.

Throughout his own written reflections, we find that children were primary to Erikson's concerns about insight-ethics applications. A society and world is only as good as its ability to see in children a treasure in the present and for the future. Through caring responsibly for them, humans develop into true adults. It was children, their care and deprivations, who revealed to Erikson each adult's and every nation's developmental stature.

Reformulating the meaning of insight, Erikson disputed Freud, just as he had with respect to prejudice. Freud had insisted that, at least in intelligent patients, insight leads to reason and to rationally applied knowledge. Erikson found that, once patients had developed insight into the cause of their distress, Freud expected them to rationally cast aside the symptoms they then no longer needed. After all, he had "x-rayed them with uncorruptible insight."[154] As a concomitant of such insight development, Freud felt they should abandon inclinations to blame others or to retaliate for the personal injustices that had led to their difficulties.[155] Such moral improvement was, to Freud, a reasoned, natural consequence of insight development. A latter-day Erikson disagreed. To him, insight and behavioral change hold both rational and affective bases. As Freud had done in contemplating prejudice, Erikson once again found that Freud had omitted the emotional from the psyche and its machinations. Erikson understood that rational knowledge alone does not result in disgorging symptoms or in abandoning some gut-level wish for retribution. Rage, its manifestations and sequelae, are emotional, Erikson held. What a person knows emotionally is far different from what he or she knows intellectually. The form and depth of the feeling aroused—rage, fear, anxiety—are not so readily detached from the unconscious or from remembered experience. They cannot be easily altered, like a change of travel plans or socks. Emotions deeply compel behavior and, when insight into their origin and mechanisms is slowly gained, persons can, in part, understand their difficulties.[156] The knowledge that is insight does not mean that hurt is no longer felt or related behaviors abandoned. However, insight can and frequently does lead to personal growth. In abusive situations, insight leads to freedom from collusion with the abuser; it helps the person develop a theory about the unconscious, the emotions, and the workings of the psyche.[157] This yields strategies for approaching problems in the future. Reaching toward better ethical functioning, Erikson maintained that insight can grant to the individual a sound reason to believe in his or her own human worth and, with a firm basis in that belief, gain a foothold on the next higher rung of caring for the self and for others.

To Erikson, insight and an increasingly sturdy ego develop together in each person. Ethical change is closely tied to ego and insight development, but not in the rational way Freud had thought. As Erikson said about Luther, such change comes from concomitant insight development, ego development, and meaningful, affective development:

> for an affect to have a deep and lasting effect, or, as Luther would say, be *affectionalis* and *moralis*, it must not only be experienced as nearly overwhelming, but it must also in some way be affirmed by the ego as valid, almost as chosen: one means the affect, it signifies something meaningful, it is significant.[158]

The emotional basis of insight and of ethical functioning meant to Erikson that an adult cannot be other than that which has become integral to his or her knowledge, insight, and feelings and to what that adult "means" with his or her entire self. This is Erikson's reason for saying that

> a man who knows what is legal or illegal has not necessarily yet learned what is ethical. Highly moralistic people can do unethical things; whereas an ethical man's involvement in immoral doings becomes by inner necessity an occasion for tragedy.[159]

At the collective level, Erikson took his insight-affect-ethics equation to the universals of responsibility for successive generations. Adults need to create a medium in which they always ask themselves what they owe one another, their children, and their children's children. This level of insight development requires raising collective insight and consciousness and working to sustain the courage of life-affirming convictions in others. Collective insight means finding an ethics in which humans see themselves as more than a succession of adults who wind through the eras. Because Erikson believed that evolution had to be adapted to human needs, insight had to reach higher levels in the general population. Otherwise, because insight always lags behind knowledge and inventions, and because new traditions that sustain humans do not develop as rapidly as fresh knowledge and the changed technology that undermine it, highly technological societies were always adjusting after the fact to industrialization, to missiles, to computers, to vehicles, to pollution, and to other inventions and their consumer-driven by-products.[160] Developing tools that control us and manufacturing too many things that we either consume prodigiously or discard wastefully seemed to him to work at cross-purposes with nature and with real human needs. Erikson feared that humans would soon find themselves in such a deteriorated condition that it would soon be too late to build a liveable world. The historian in him held that when the masses perceive rapidly moving negative events to have overtaken their ability to override them, a collective anxiety results in paralysis. Erikson's expressed ethical role was to raise consciousness and to criticize in the various forums open to him. He aimed to raise a species' collective insight in order to avert the consequences he feared.

Spirit and Soul

The terms *spirit*, *soul*, and *psyche* were synonyms to Erikson. Soul is psyche, Erikson's meeting ground with Jung.[161] Spirit is also the locus, soul. As both location and movement, spirit is an animating, alive tension in the psyche. To Erikson, spirit is the activator that promotes vitality and repels deadness, fragmentation, and stagnation. "All systems," the human system included, "demand a Spirit."[162]

Erikson wrote more about the spiritual than he did about soul as a location. In his notes he wrote: "'Spiritual' as Christian neologism ──> actualisation"; that is, "spiritual" carries the meaning given in Genesis and reformulated by the first Christians.[163] It means the center and a way of being, an actuality, a vital energy. The ego is "the middle that holds the whole *(das Ganze)* of me together," he wrote; spirit and ego is "I myself."[164] Erikson contended that by middle adulthood, spiritual and ethical unity have become the core of the ego, the center that binds the self. Spirit ensures wholeness and health. Writing about spirit in this ancient way was Erikson's effort to glue together a fallen, broken Humpty Dumpty. Virtue, spirit, and strength had become interchangeable to him; they arise in unison developmentally. They are incorporated into each of the eight optimum outcomes of the stages of life he had depicted. They cement the life cycle and the generations together. Showing the linear dependence of one virtue on another, he wrote, "will cannot be trained until hope is secure, nor love become reciprocal until fidelity has proven reliable. But this means that the virtues are charted epigenetically."[165]

Such wholeness requires combining psychology with theology, a different sense of "I," he said, one that is a new borderline of valid study.[166] He was concerned that the portions of the Western world which had abandoned God, soul, theology, and vitalizing qualities of the spirit had evicted the essential marrow of a complete being. Spiritual qualities are not of the mind or affect alone. Mental and physical health require human wholeness, and the appraisal of such wholeness means including the spiritual and the spirited as one. Without this approach, Erikson believed that neither human proportion nor peril could be understood or health ensured.[167]

Erikson tried to safeguard holism in each person's current context and in his or her personal life cycle, aware that psychoanalysis and developmental thought had led to investigating the human in a broken, "sliced" way and that the comparatively recent separation of humans and their world into discrete fields of study had further dissected the subject.[168] Thus, to define and pull spirit back together, Erikson went to his native German language and found the word *Geistigkeit*.[169] This term was useful to his unifying purposes and helpful in showing how the English language and contemporary times had fragmented understandings:

> *Geistigkeit* . . . means an intrinsically German preoccupation with matters on the borderline between the spirit and the mind, the spiritual and the intellectual, at its best combining some of both, and at its worst serving neither. It means a lofty identification with great humanists, above all the olympian Goethe.[170]

Working to reunify the twentieth-century human to promote health and wholeness, Erikson kept spirit in the formula, resisting compartmentalizing according to the particulars of philosophy, theology, and psychology. However, he did show the adult as a split personality. There are two spatial "regna" (kingdoms; reigns), he wrote. These are the "realist" domain of "divine grace" and the "naturalist" domain of "animality"; both exist in each adult's "inner conflicts and . . . existential paradoxes."[171] The earthly, horizontal region and the divine, vertical region are "two personalities and two callings" that one maintains simultaneously, a dualism holding an inherent tension that cannot be broken.[172] In this split, Erikson found signs of the adult's spiritual core in the use of symbols to convey spiritual meanings, in the paradoxical existence of separate but potentially shared space between persons, in an upright stance, and in human tendencies to scan visually fore and aft. Erikson found posture, position, and spatial imagery useful for illustrating what he meant by spirit and by the spiritual in human connections with others and with God:

> As a Navajo medicine man recently put it when asked by a friend for a definition of what is human: indicating the figure of a cross, he said that a person was most human where the (vertical) connection between the ground of creation and the Great Spirit met the (horizontal) one between the individual and all other human beings.[173]

Expressing the meaning of soul, Erikson turned to ancient concepts about the unity of body and soul. Humility, charity, and the awareness of grace and sin characterize soul, he said.[174] Soul is the scene of great battles as he had shown in *Gandhi's Truth* and *Luther*. Passive resistance was Gandhi's truth and soul force.[175] Gandhi was Erikson's vehicle for illustrating the conflict between would-be heroic killing that might lead to temporary mortal glory versus the risk of loving the oppressed and one's enemy enough to die, thereby preserving the soul. The former might save a portion of the horizontal realm for a bit of current or posthumous merit, but it was the latter, the vertical connection with eternity, that most appealed to Erikson's sense of organic and spiritual wholeness. Wholeness means a here *and* a hereafter. Erikson thus posed identity conflict between the physical *now* and the spiritual *now and later*. In his newfound versus, he gave preeminence to the affirmative, the outward, the forward, and the upward, a cohering option of both "here" and "hereafter." This is countered by the negative, the solely horizontal place and plane of the earthly "here."

Erikson went even further to distinguish the soul as a perceiving place. He constructed soul as the site at which the feminine meets the masculine in an anima-animus twinning.[176] Here the Jungian Erikson comes through: Wholeness becomes developmentally more so when the adult's dominant sexual identification is joined and complemented by the dormant gender counterpart. As a result of this twinning and openness to a new self, soul is the repository of an enhanced interpersonal opening, of the ability to experience another as if he or she were the self.

This is the most radical change in Erikson's lexicon. He saw soul as the adult's "most bisexual part" and as most complete in that bisexuality.[177] In a lecture in 1957, he claimed that "bisexual confusion (is) inherent in all identity conflict."[178] He may have been somewhat self- descriptive when he wrote that "the man who creates must be something of a sensuous woman."[179] Thus, whether in the budding sexuality and identity of youth, in the bisexual dissonance of artistic creativity, or in the midlife adults' experience of the opposite gender within, it is in complementing the primary sexual self with the dormant sexual self that persons are most whole, aware, receptive, and soul tending. Adults pose that newly complete self against eternity. In this gender and existential conflict and complementarity, when the adult is most open to the untapped opposite, soul is the seat for experiencing God as the Divine Other and for mystically transcending a single gendered adult who had been held captive in one time, space, and single-sex body. To Erikson, that newly experienced soul is the existential locus where "I" meets we and God.[180]

In this vast claim, Erikson stretched the landscape considerably. In doing so, he may have unearthed something as significant as it is impenetrable and difficult to entertain. Whatever one makes of it, Erikson held that belief in God, as well as the moral conduit to ethical sight and behavior, is developmentally sown in the human. Erikson was not one to comport with the literal and the concrete, but he nonetheless claimed soul for ego and for God, an ephemeral locus and spirit. He found that this ego-soul composite develops early in some brilliant, troubled youngsters (Luther, St. Francis, himself) and in midlife in others (Gandhi). He seems to have been too uncomfortable about interpreting women's experiences to write about their lives. Yet he sometimes hinted that girls and young women were "soulful" early on in life whereas most males discovered their souls much later in the life span.

Virtue

Virtue is ego and personal strength. Virtue is the successful outcome of each Eriksonian life stage. It is something a person accomplishes, something he or she has learned to do well.[181] Cumulatively, the eight virtues build. They bind with one another to build a stronger and more complete person. Although he was unclear about the exact source of his term *virtu,* Erikson equated ego strength with *Grundtugend,* meaning "cardinal virtue," and with Shakespeare's use of the term as a vital, potent quality that resists dissipation over time.[182] It radiates to others, showing them the way and fortifying the self on deflection. The term is redolent of Taoist and Confucian mysticism, of "the Way" attributed to Lao-Tse. In this use, virtue is that which reflects the inner quality and eventually the integration of one's complete character.[183] Writing about his use of the term, Erikson also referenced Mark's Gospel's (5:29–34) rendition of the woman who had been hemorrhaging and touched Jesus' garments so that his "virtue" would heal her.[184] He also reversed the reference points of Buddhism. Here he looked to Schopenhauer's interpretation: that Buddhism begins with cardinal vices as the "antitheses or negations" that the "cardinal virtues" must dispute.[185] Thus virtue means ego strength, character, and ethical vitality. It reflects ancient Eastern thought, the parables, an analytic Shakespeare, and what Erikson himself saw as making and keeping persons strong, vital, healthy, and whole. Notably, other than for will, the outcome of Erikson's second stage, there is a parallel construction in which each healthy outcome of the stages he defined is found in the radiated strengths of Jesus' meanings.[186] In a letter in 1972, Erikson described the stepwise strengths of each stage and their growing cumulation in words reflective of St. Paul: "Thus on each step what had been 'in part,' will now be recognized and interacted within its wholeness."[187]

In true Erikson style, writing somewhat like Kierkegaard, Erikson named the various virtues to which his ego strengths referred but, other than in his full-scale analyses of Luther and of Gandhi, he gave few specific examples. In part, this was his way of subtly planting his messages so that readers and listeners could apply it to the particulars of their own lives rather than dismissing them out of hand. It was also Erikson's way of avoiding moralizing and blaming, qualities he found onerous. Further, remaining abstract and generic was useful to Erikson's wish to see his thought applied across cultures and societies. He knew that persons in different cultures would be more likely to see the virtues as part of their lives and contexts if they did not hear them in the concrete examples of one society.

Erikson insisted that the basic values he had unearthed laid claim to the foundational strengths and virtues which various cultures, religions, and worldviews share. "The well-established identity," he wrote, "has arranged itself around basic values which cultures have in common."[188] Nonetheless, as much as he saw those virtues as the essence of transcendent values and strengths, he believed they were but a beginning point of departure. It was one of Erikson's primary desires to show the necessity of building one unified world. To do this, he thought, scholars and others would have to determine the permutations of those virtues as they could be envisioned and acted on in the lifeblood of each different culture. That would be the basis, he said, for making them cohere politically and internationally.[189] Values will only endure, he said, when they are useful economically, politically, and socially.[190] Because values change over time, he held that this work would require intensive, lengthy, and unending study.

Developmentally, Erikson's stage hierarchy illustrates the specific attributes of the human that he believed are at risk in each specific developmental period of life.[191] In his concept of dovetailing, he meant to demonstrate that the eight strengths—hope, will, purpose, competence, fidelity, love, generativity, and their completion in integrality and wisdom (hope)—are those that must be developed individually, as well as transferred to and strengthened in subsequent generations.[192] At the metalevel of assessing generations and societies, he wrote that his study of virtues revealed cohering principles that hold the generations and institutions together, as well as "defects in the 'fiber' of generations and institutions."[193] To those who would find such virtues and him utopian, Erikson had a ready retort: Persons denigrate such virtues as too "lofty" and idealistic when those very virtues are most socially "weakened."[194] Thus to Erikson the antithesis of virtue is not "vice." Rather it is a "weakness" that is manifest in "disorder, dysfunction, disintegration, anomie."[195] At the individual level, such weakness mixes with rage when persons feel blocked from pursuing their talents, strengths, active agency, and personal coherence. At the societal level, he maintained that the mental disturbances that typify an era are amplifications of the value struggles of that period which, at some level, all persons experience. Whether true of the possessed of ancient eras, the hysterics of Freud's time, or certain of the debilitating anxiety, depression, and character disorders that Erikson saw beginning to build, such disorders reflect both social value struggles and interpersonal disturbances.[196] To him, understanding those disturbances is basic to healing them. It is also basic to knowing what it is that adults "owe" each other. This, he said, is the foundation on which psychoanalysts and all adults build their ethical roles in each institution and in every family, not just for the mentally ill few but for all persons in contemporary times and for future generations. The human collective body can develop only when it does so as a strong, virtue- and value-grounded, ego-solid whole.

Erikson presented a demanding agenda. He also knew that he sounded sanguine at times, seeming to give the adult virtues in particular an optimistic and easily come by cast. He said he did not underestimate the effort that is required to bring about such strengths in the self and in others. He wrote that the virtues are not "gay and easy accomplishments" any more than they are "idealistic pretences [sic]"[197]

Virtue weakness is sin. Considering his use of the terms *virtue* to mean ego strength and *weakness* to convey an incompleteness or a relative absence of both ego strength and solidity, we might wonder what Erikson made of sin. In fact, he looked at sin and evil from various angles, sometimes using the

words themselves but more often painting a picture that described their pervasive presence. Depending on his subject and slant, sin could be weakness,
need, failure, or evil. He wrote that he believed in the existence of "original
sin" and, as a psychologist, also saw such sin as an element of the adult's
"curse" that he or she "cannot believe otherwise."[198] Being "guilty of guilt"
is a developmental sin, and everyone has two kinds of this sin.[199]The first of
these is moral guilt, that of "repression and inhibition," the effort to retain
qualities of goodness by "*not doing* and not even thinking" beyond a region
that is under careful superego surveillance.[200] This form of guilt is a haven
for a vindictive moralism that is often unleashed on children. In fact, Erikson wondered if it was ever possible to "yield power without evil."[201] The
second kind of guilt is the "repression of guilt itself," a "bland guiltlessness"
shown in a refusal to question one's own or a community's motives and, as
well, to prevent others from asking piercing questions.[202] Yet, to Erikson, all
such guilt represents lower order faults than thinking evil and intentionally
acting on it. At least guilt is a developmental given, and when recognized for
what it is, its presence and effects can be partially controlled.

Writing developmentally, particularly after his Gandhi period in the mid-
1960s, Erikson equated hope with faith and associated both self-gratifica-
tion and will with sin. He wrote that because will is developmentally inescapable in healthy child development, it is likely the ontogenetic source of
sin, that both will and willfulness, autonomy and sin, are paradoxically inherent in infancy and in childhood development.[203] Further, the id contains
evil that comes from within.[204] Id is "the strangeness of the 'animal' inside."[205] Id inactivates the "I."[206] Autonomy (will) and willful self-interest
(sin) raise their heads in unison; they are products of the second stage of life,
of autonomy versus shame and doubt. Yet, Erikson said, a healthy id is normal and essential in the infant and young child, whereas an impulsive id is
abnormal and a sign of selfishness, weakness, or worse in the adult.

If such is the fabric both of strength in the developing individual infant
and child and of weakness and unhealthy behavior in the individual adult,
at the family level it was weakness, sin, and maladaptation that Erikson
wanted adults to monitor. That is, he believed that strengths, as well as
weaknesses, are transported along the ancestral tree from generation to generation. This intergenerational transfer of weakness was what Erikson had
in mind by writing about primal sin. Such sin was Erikson's Augustinian-
based premise that evil is ontogenetically sown by the personal weakness
of parents and earlier progenitors. Erikson used the example of Gandhi,
whose father had forced him to marry when Gandhi was too young and
developmentally ill prepared to be either a nurturing husband or a good father. In addition to this, Gandhi's father had inculcated in his young
son, during his early years, a controlling, relentless conscience. This, said
Erikson, led to Gandhi's various lifelong guilt feelings. One most painful,
unending guilt feeling was Gandhi's sense of "sin" in choosing to recline

with his pregnant wife just when his father was dying.[207] In the next generation, Gandhi's son Harry, himself deprived of a tangible father in his youth, and verbally castigated by that father in young adulthood, became despondent and suicidal.

A related example is found in Erikson's retrospective account of Dr. Isak Borg. Borg is the 76-year-old protagonist in Ingmar Bergman's film *Wild Strawberries* and the main character in Erikson's 1976 article, "Reflections on Dr. Borg's Life Cycle." A physician, Borg learned too late in life of the lifelong intimacy he had sacrificed. His mother's coldness and the absence of intimacy between his parents had led him to "overdefine" his intellectual life and professional role. In young adulthood, Borg relinquished Sara, the love of his life, because of his emotional distance from her. Borg then failed the generative intimacy of fatherhood and, by late adulthood, was sadly withdrawn from all intimacy and society with others. Borg transferred his own absence of intimacy and caring along to his son and, although the story ends there, readers sense that the generational weakness may well continue on down the line, unless some healthy, more complete adult can fortuitously rescue the current and later generations.

The figure on page 108 shows what Erikson had in mind in writing about the intergenerational transfer of strength (virtue) or weakness. In the figure, a young adult is moving into the intimacy stage of life. If virtues, identifications, and ego strengths had been well grounded in the first four strengths of hope, will, purpose, and competence, if identity is in hand in at least some beginning, firm way, and if the young person's key caregivers had themselves developed a favorable ratio of seven strengths, culminating in their care of that youth, then adulthood begins on a secure basis. Care, the ethical basis of the adult's prime years, is the essential link between each person's life cycle and both the prior and future generations. For "childhood stages are characterized by the dominance of growing parts over the whole. Therefore, the child's ego is as yet weak, and can survive only if verified, on every step, by the adults' love, care, and wholeness."[208] Culture must be supportive as well, for it sponsors or thwarts identity. When society is in disorder, when it fails to nurture its young, or when it prejudicially closes down to youth, a firm, positive identity is impossible in the years that are critical for its development. Writing about Gandhi's father and Borg's parents, Erikson illustrated weaknesses that had been "perseverated" down through the generations.[209]

Thus the ethics of care must be sown. Ethics is as inherent as rage.[210] It is as prewired in developing humans as are a variety of human instincts; however, the ethical is only a propensity.[211] It must be developed by caregivers, by personal insight, by a supportive and principled society, and by the bedrock of a nurturing childhood and adolescence. Otherwise, ethical tendencies cannot ripen, nor can either ego strength or the ability to love and care for oneself. These, then, permit one to extend such love to others.

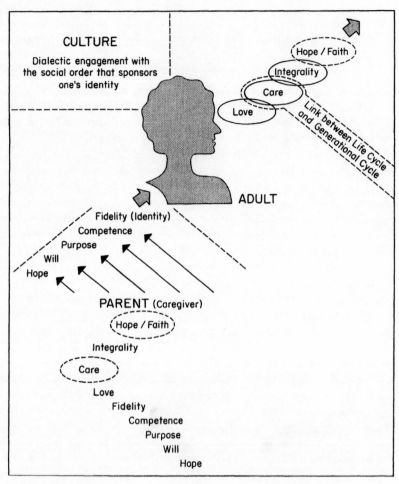

CULTURE

Dialectic engagement with
the social order that sponsors
one's identity

Hope / Faith

Integrality

Care

Love

ADULT

Link between Life Cycle
and Generational Cycle

Fidelity (Identity)

Competence

Purpose

Will

Hope

PARENT (Caregiver)

Hope / Faith

Integrality

Care

Love

Fidelity

Competence

Purpose

Will

Hope

Stage Progression and Vital Stage "Strengths" in Erikson's Theory of Human Development

REVISION AND RISK

Erikson's is revisionist thought. He successfully transformed Freud by placing himself, the moral-ethical observer, into the developmental model of the human. In this, he showed how morals can sabotage the best intentioned adult. He provided convincing reasons to believe that the *moral* is never fully outgrown. Objective data, from which Erikson distanced himself, support his findings that abuse and poor parenting lead to more of the same in later generations as grown children, by then fully imprinted on their parents or caregivers, do for and to others as they had been shown and done to. At the collective level, highly moralistic and exclusionary societies thwart the ethics of inclusion and, thus, of care to ensure that all persons develop together. Erikson transcended Freud's thought, showing it as limited, era-specific, and first-stage psychoanalytic insight.

Erikson's idea that ethics is primary to the "we" zones of adulthood has the ring of truth. There can be little in the way of care if there is no one for whom to be responsible. It is in the context of adults' putting their needs off-stage consistently that they actually become that which they have learned to do repeatedly. In effect, such care is a self-channeling or grooving of behavior. Erikson's risk in placing himself inside the adult as a moral-ethical observer, and then outside as an advocate of ethical care, led to both excoriation and admiration. He extended beyond developmental theorizing once he moved into the role of intervening, criticizing, and advocating; yet his voice compelled many to rethink what it is that the terms "development" and "adult" mean.

Many of Erikson's concepts about nurturing others and about the harm of exclusion are now fundamental to developmental thought; however, Erikson is rarely referenced other than in the display of his 8-stage grid and in citing his identity construct. His understandings about the moral residuals that exist in ethical adults and about the affective basis of both development and of ethics have yet to be written into texts on human development or ethics. Thus this portion of Erikson's cross-disciplinary thought has, so far, eluded any number of readers.

Erikson moved decidedly beyond theory in his revisionist belief system. He captured the inverted thought of Jesus, Einstein, and Luther, writing that contemporary adults can now see from within an altered "space-time" in which God's judgment is not one of deferred punishment or elevation but that of living by faith, by care, and by a sight that comes with and from use of the limbic brain. In effect, in his later life, Erikson fully reversed the idea that "seeing is believing." He noted that there are "higher truths" and held that "believing is seeing."[212] To believe became a new way to see, a feeling and seeing that had been helped along by his own insight, by his study of Luther and Luther's retranslation of the Bible and reconstitution of faith, by the ecumenical spirit of Erikson's own time, and by Einstein's advances in concepts of physical matter, space, and time. "To the ego," Erikson wrote, "eternity is always now."[213] It is thus in the "now" that one finds identity, spirit, and the divine, the now of making the Kingdom come to be in the present:

> if the Kingdom is so vague in its temporal boundaries, *where* is it? This question Jesus answers in another context: "Behold the kingdom of God is in the midst of you" (Luke 17:21). The Greek original, *entos hymon*, presumably can mean "between you" as well as "within you," for Luther's translation, "inwendig in Euch," claims just that.[214]

In this changed location for the Kingdom, Erikson borrowed Tolstoy's concept that "the kingdom of God is within you."[215] Erikson's studies of Luther had taken him to that concept.

Luther, a changed time-space concept, and Erikson's own ideas on weakness and sin came together in his thoughts about moving beyond weakness, guilt, and sin to place them in the past of developmental time. Erikson saw this spatially. Persons turn around to look at the past of the self, and then turn around to look to the future of a new self who elects ethical actions, the affirmation of self and others, and positive anticipation:

> Thus, repentance as an active choice (and the Greek word for it is *metanoia*, translated by Luther as "umkehr"—"turnabout") makes one central to one's life-space. With all the pain of penitence inherent in the word, one need not be inactivated by bad conscience, nor banned by divine judgment; and this seems to be a step toward the alertness of the sense of *I*, which is also implied in that repeated encouragement: "Be aware! Be wakeful! Watch!"[216]

Other than his ability to show how the moral self of childhood remains in the adult self, to illustrate the importance of ethical functioning in order to ensure the development of children, other adults, and the self, Erikson's greatest contribution to theory may prove to have been in the realm of social cognition or perceptual, emotional intellect. The roots of affective intellect, that is, of the ability to reside within the context and space-time of another, have yet to be deciphered. Another of Erikson's legacies is his refusal to permit other than active control by each person in his or her own system of space, time, and meaning making. Further, he ably illustrated how the imposed artifacts of religions and institutional requirements can deaden the "I" and its ethical development.

There are three aspects that call for some gentle criticism. First, Erikson himself transgressed into the terrain of the *shoulds*, of moralistic thought. As broad a brush as he used in his writing on ethics, he wrote from within the moral position as soon as he moved from theory to advocacy, critical commentary, and requirements. He knew this. In an unpublished tract from an early draft of *Luther*, he wrote: "If each new vital focus of psychoanalytic research inadvertently leads to a seemingly implied value-system, we should really call this psychoanalyism."[217]

It seems rather small to criticize Erikson for ethical advocacy, for telling readers what he had seen to go wrong in development, and for pointing to what can go right, for saying what adults must do to avoid the inactivation and harm of others. Care is indeed positive. Neglect of others is negative. But the unresolved question is the extent to which Erikson's thought was itself a string of moralisms. This does not appear to be generally the case, but it is important to know that he too was occasionally trapped by the moral in his moral-ethical adult characteristics and to be alert to this in his work.

A second point of criticism is Erikson's use of relativism and absolutism. At times he wrote from within the perspective of relativism, of the ways in which relativism holds sway in moral thought and must be appreciated for its use in debunking moral absolutes. At other times, he wrote from the vantage point of a teleological and absolutist view. These offsetting viewpoints carry a "both/and" premise that does not quite hold. Time and cross-cultural evidence will tell whether or not there are true competing relativities in the human moral-ethical universe or whether there is some mutual developmental endpoint about which all systems, ideologies, and mature adults can agree and hold sacred.

Third, it is evident that Erikson wrote for his readers, for those who could afford to have and to consider morality, ethics, and its ramifications—the middle class. They alone possess the resources that are needed to entertain such ideas and, perhaps, the inclination to consider heightened ethical and spiritual selves and a more just world. To those who are homeless, hungry, desperately poor, or mentally ill, there is slim opportunity to be moral, much less to strive to better an ego ideal through heightened ethical functioning.

6

Playing, Childlike Adult

The opposite of play is death.

— Erikson, "Godkin
Lectures"

Holding aside the specifics of stages once more, Erikson's writings provide a wealth of insight into play and potential childlikeness in the grown adult and about how one might reclaim some of childhood's lost power. It was clear to him that too many persons lose vitality, joy, and a sense of wonder en route to full adulthood. To Erikson, the adult version of play exists in ideas and plans, in drama and scenarios, in visions, models, and worldviews. But childlikeness is an entirely different matter, a giant step beyond play. Adult childlikeness requires combining play with wonder and trust, a blend found only in the rarest of persons. Further, in the broad span of life called "maturity," Erikson found that only the most extraordinary adult could see in children generally, and in his or her own internalized child specifically, anything other than weaknesses that had to be variously restrained, controlled, or brought up to stature. By full adulthood, wonder, the ability to see things delightfully anew, had been forfeited, and distrust and cynicism had replaced much of childhood's trust. This is one reason for Erikson's change in the negative poles for adult resolutions. He saw that identity, in its evolving adult forms, cannot coexist with cynicism, isolation, and rejection. Solid development, positive adaptation, and good mental health require acceptance of oneself, of other persons, and of viable social roles, instead of role refusal, withdrawal, stagnation, and bitterness mixed with self-disgust.[1]

Erikson saw the suppression of children, and the dual repression and suppression of the child within the adult, as very much related. Adults resist and "stereotype" children.[2] They burden childhood with ideas of littleness, immaturity, helplessness, and nonseriousness. They see children as irresponsible, irrational, weak, and unconcerned about important matters. After all, children do not work and cannot contribute to central concerns of life in productive, caring roles. Further, children, and one's own small child inside, are not physically "big." This is a deficit model for the child, framed in terms of what the adult hopes he or she is against what the child is not. Size, responsibility, and burdens reign supreme in adults' minds, leading them to believe they must be more perfect, restricted, serious, and austere than their own younger selves. Such beliefs provide a sense of safety and of control; they shore up adults' false notions that they alone occupy the only protected place in the mortal universe. Seeing competence in children and in one's prior, now-subverted, child would unseat security. Dismantling such defenses provokes anxiety; retaining them promotes the illusion of safety.[3]

In keeping such defensive needs and mechanisms intact, Erikson saw adults to project their own fears and negative identities. In this way, adults dominate youth and "colonialize" both their own vitality and children around them in an ongoing way.[4] Originality, creativity, genuine play, wonder, abandon, and leeway are variously restrained. Erikson enjoyed the *Peanuts* comics. Likely he would have approved of cartoonist Charles Schulz's insight that adults might unearth remarkable potentials in themselves if they could keep alive the glee and imagination of children, entertaining life "the way a child skips rope and a mouse waltzes."[5]

Surveying Erikson's lifetime of writings, children's play and each child's needs were of primary importance to Erikson.[6] Child's play appears in the articles of his Vienna, years and he returned to this topic in his very last book. Perhaps this emphasis is not surprising as he had been trained as a Montessori teacher, had taught children in the Burlingham-Rosenfeld School in Vienna, and, in Freud's circle, had worked to develop the specialty of child psychoanalysis under Anna Freud's watchful eye. Erikson departed markedly from Freudian thought, but he had found in Anna Freud's *Kinderseminar* a wellspring of inspiration. Thus, whether in Vienna in the late 1920s and early 1930s, as Boston's first child psychoanalyst in the mid-1930s, or in the Child Guidance Studies project at the University of California at Berkeley in the 1940s, childhood and play framed Erikson's early psychoanalytic thinking. He incorporated his early studies of play into his influential book, *Childhood and Society*.[7]

In the mid-1950s, Erikson left childhood and play behind to develop his thinking about ego evolution in adolescence. He then conceptualized adult intimacy and generativity, after which he returned full circle to the topic of play, this time in its adult forms.[8] In the 1970s, he connected his notions about children's play with adult vision for the 1970 Loyola Symposium and, later, for the 1972 Godkin Lectures at Harvard (published as *Toys and Reasons*).[9] He then associated rare forms of adult play with childlike wonder and linked healthy adult ego evolution and childlikeness to faith.[10] Thus the play of children was important to Erikson's thought from his psychoanalytic origins and, although adult childlikeness appears in a number of his earlier writings, he conceptualized both adult play and childlikeness after he retired from full-time institutionally sponsored work in 1970.[11]

Erikson prized his own play with artistic, visual-spatial dimensions and his ability to see things anew, to "behold" them with a freshness of appreciation. Further, as a keen observer, he was deeply interested in the many ways in which the social and physical worlds represent themselves in individual psyches and group ideas and in how such imprintings then play themselves out in the social scene. To Erikson, ours is a precategorized and ververbalized world in which it is far too easy to overrate the importance of words and their meanings.[12] To him, the careful study of humans meant that one could not afford to overlook that which actions say and words omit.

In his later years Erikson said that play had always been his primary resource, just as dreams had been Freud's. "Thank God . . . for the little children," he wrote; they " . . . play it all out before our eyes."[13] Play and the visual forms it produced were a close fit with Erikson's native talents, but he also felt that his "preoccupation" with the "revelations" of children's play was an intense "reaction ('with a vengeance')" to his training analysis when he, "born to be a painter," had to convert his mental pictures into words and then, during his long clinical years, had to re-convert patients' dream images into verbal interpretations.[14]

When we know Erikson's background, talents, and beliefs and recognize that he had arrived in the United States understanding just several hundred words of English, his affinity for play is apparent. The toy world is one in which children act out their thinking through representational constructions. In that world they play out their ideas, joys, conflicts, and traumas, and they do so with an innocence and honesty that Erikson admired. Erikson needed few English words in his early years in America to understand what children were trying to say. They showed him.

By the time Erikson focused specifically on adult development, he was articulate in the English language; yet behavior and its messages continued to hold his attention. He found that adults too play out their concerns, at times honestly and freely, sometimes blinded by illusion, and often wearing masks of deception and self-deceit. Rarely are they childlike. In adults he saw the very deficit model that such "grown-ups" project onto children. To him it was children who obeyed developmental laws with consuming grace and boundless joy. And so one more polarity appears in his unpublished writing, a "Joy versus Superego" opposition in which he showed how weighty guilt and conscience development exact their price in the years after infancy.[15] Joy is subdued because of the sequential experience of shame and then of guilt—shame in the toddler years, on learning the "civilized" and safe limits of autonomy, and guilt in the next higher level of the play age, at which one internalizes mores, norms, rituals, rights, and wrongs. "Shame is an inside and outside matter: fear that someone will laugh at us." "Guilt is entirely inner."[16] Thus shame and the eventual incorporation of cultural mores and conscience into an increasingly interior mental life replace much of life's early abandon, glee, surprise, and wonder—the realm of joy.[17]

PLAY: OVERARCHING ATTRIBUTES

When considering Erikson's ideas about adult play and childlikeness, it is useful to keep four elements in mind. These are, first, Erikson's close fit of play to psychoanalytic tenets and methods and, within these, his use of spatial form, artistic ideas, and cognitive premises; second, his tendency to connect adult play to and yet to separate it from adult childlikeness; third, in his mainstream writings, Erikson's placement of play at the center of the child's and the adult's primary working concerns; and fourth, two important conceptual changes he made in his mid- and later life in which he, respectively, linked psychosocial development with cognitive development and inferred that adult intimacy and work deftly take away true play. I will consider these in turn.

With the first of these, in writing about play, whether describing the scanning and playful infant, the block- and toy-consumed child, or the visioning, idea-inspired adult, Erikson remained closer to psychoanalysis than he did with any other topic. Considering his tendency to work in the borders of thought and to bridge his thought with anthropology, sociology, and history in particular, his border thinking and other disciplines are remarkably absent. An inveterate psychoanalyst in the play realm, even when he eventually considered Einstein's childlike wonder and play with ideas, Erikson looked only to those elements that would "arouse a psychoanalyst's reflectiveness."[18]

In play Erikson found the analogue of dreams, if with several key differences. In dreams, turmoil from the external fabric of life plays itself out in the "inner world." Dreams are typically seen on a night screen. They are projections in the dark, made when one is "more deeply regressed and . . . immobilized" than during the day when one is active and functional.[19] Day work shows up in the play of children who demonstrate their inner concerns actively in externalized bodily motions and toy designs and in the play of adult ideas brought forward through the myriad forms of blueprints, plans, experiments, theories, models, and drama. To Erikson, who was much more interested in what he could see in persons when they were active, absorbed, healthy, and ego-involved, the engaged activities of children and adults in the light of day met his needs to emphasize mental health over disturbance and to show activity and forward movement over regression.

Within Erikson's tight fit of play to psychoanalysis, paintings and sculpture, spatial notions, and symbolic ideas were his essentials. His youthful talents and experiences had a role in this. As an adolescent, he had believed in his visual and artistic talents, had held hopes of sharing his biological father's artistic ability, and had given reign to such hopes and aspirations when wandering about as an artist. Psychoanalysis became his substitute for art. The content of his writing shows access to visual ideas and to a preferred, inductive, surveying mode of thinking and writing. He pictured content. To Erikson, great artists were natural psychoanalysts playing skillfully at their crafts. They showed concretely, in silent form, that which twentieth-century psychoanalysis uses words to express. In various notes, he jotted down similarities between the amorphous shapes and ideas expressed in art, the adult psyche that is revealed in plans, concepts, and visions, and the child psyche at work in play. Interestingly, Erikson saw children as "natural but, alas, mostly shortlived artists."[20] Growing up means using more and more words and, eventually, semantic concepts that lead one inexorably away from the visual and the concrete.[21]

Further, as others before and after him, Erikson saw similarities between mental illness and art. An undated note shows him portraying psychiatric disturbances and modern art as metaphors for each other, in which he found mentally disturbed persons to occupy, and painters to portray, a surreal position somewhere "between chaos and form."[22] Like water captured well on canvas, he wrote, "a feeling of twilight, something of the borderline (results)."[23] Erikson himself seems to have functioned in a near-borderline way when gleaning impressions of others. In a note found among his papers he cryptically described his ability to tap his unconscious by "diffus(ing) the point of contact" between himself and another person and to then "project the diffusion on that person."[24] Somewhat like a "refractory . . . prism," he said, this permits the unconscious to "receive the 'rays'" which the "conscious mind blocks."[25] The "rays reconverge deep inside" (the unconscious, only then to) "enter consciousness."[26] The result is an "immediate impression of person or group."[27] Without an exact context for interpretation, those few words of Erikson's might seem to carry little weight; yet in various writings, notes, and audiorecordings Erikson retrospectively self-diagnosed himself as having been a borderline personality when in his 20s. He may well have retained the ability to function in an altered ego state, in effect placing conscious reality and its stimuli aside in order to garner a gestalt of unconscious impressions.

In the second overarching attribute of his work, Erikson sometimes considered adult play alone, whereas, at other times he connected adult play with childlikeness. As a developmental thinker, Erikson knew that adults can try to, but can never fully, reclaim the realm of childhood, for life and personal development have taken them beyond it. Yet it was important to Erikson that he mine the possibility, to consider how adults might tap some of the lost potential of childhood. And it was important to him that adults themselves work to recover their childhood resources. Only in this way could one regain the vitality of the moment-absorbed child, muster the childlike ability to somehow put aside cares and to work within them, and experience the composite of trust, joy, and seeing afresh. In such tension, Erikson created a difficult opposition indeed, that of living and engaging as authentically and freely as a child, all the while knowing that one cannot again occupy that space. For childlikeness within the role responsibilities of adult life means exploring undeveloped potentials, repelling cynicism, playing with ideas, questioning staid thought, behaving honestly, and engaging freely. Together these seem mightily antagonistic to development's fourfold burden of shame, guilt, repression of childhood, and schooled reasoning, all within daily work environments in which psychological safety and mistrust are frequently modern-day synonyms. Said somewhat differently, joy is the province of childhood, whereas the adult is an "artful perverter of joy."[28]

Erikson believed that psychoanalysis had colluded in the universal loss of childhood by emphasizing negatives and deviancy. Seeing persons as universally "driven," asking "only what has to be defended against," his discipline had undermined belief in adult talents, resources, and untapped possibilities.[29] Erikson wished to correct this errant focus.

The third key attribute of Erikson's ideas is his insistence that, for children and for adults, play occurs at the center of each person's developmental competence and at the focal point of life's concerns at that moment in time. Here, he disappointed those waiting to hear him say something startling about the role of play in releasing humans from work's toil. It was not to be. To Erikson, each healthy person, at every developmental level, needed engaged work that alone shows one's play. Among children and adults, he believed that genuine play renews the psyche; like refreshing sleep, it prepares one to take up new challenges and demands. Among adults, good work provides release from emotional demands; it permits play with content and ideas. Thus, to the Erikson who remained very much the psychoanalyst in his approach to the topic, play is not that which occurs when one departs from concerns. Writing early or late, whether considering children, adolescents, or adults, his points address the human need for the psychological space and the social permission to be authentic and to play in work genuinely—within one's developmental level and context, through the display of one's competence and important concerns, and through engagement in the society of one's historical era. To him, good, free, uninterrupted play was the essence of work, a vital, engaged immersion for all. Play is "the ego at work," a vehicle for regaining self-esteem, for expressing mastery and ideas, and for working through the requirements of a stage of life.[30] A future directional arrow, play is a realm for trying out new roles and skills toward heightened, more integrated competence and a more expansive reality. He wrote, "What more extended body of not yet organized elements of experience does the ego attempt to synthesize at a given time? Look for it in Play."[31]

Play intrigued Erikson. In fact, his unpublished papers show a nearly tireless interest in the many ways in which genuine play showed itself. As a natural concomitant, Erikson studied play disruption and inhibition, for in these he found manifestations of personal, family, and societal problems. He saw the psychological harm that comes to children when they are reared by adults who ignore them, who are psychologically distant, or who treat them like budding criminals according to some restricted stereotype of what children should turn out to be as adults.[32] In the first case, a "habitually unresponsive adult" is perceived by the child as a hostile, "inimical other": "The unresponsive eye becomes an evil one."[33] In the second, children are made "manageable by making them feel sinful."[34] Such youths are sometimes so constrained that they cannot play freely as children, nor can they later engage genuinely with others as adults. "Lost ease" with self and others is mental *"disease."*[35] Further, children who cannot play have found some reason to mistrust, a distrust manifest in such a loss of personal self and ego agency that they are unable to "say 'I.'"[36] Approaching his eighth decade, Erikson returned to one of his early premises, that defective interplay with the principal caregiver is antecedent to, if not directly causative of, at least some psychoses.[37] Such defects produce fractured egos. The inhibition of play prejudices healthy development; it speaks of impaired ego vitality. Play is aliveness itself. "The opposite of play is death."[38]

For children and in all the later years of adulthood, impeded play induces frustration, intense anger, rage, and hate or such a numbing sense of paralysis that persons feel dead.[39] Restricted, on the outside of play, children passively observe from the sidelines. Then and later they mistrust blending play with freedom, and play with interplay, excluding all of these from work. When development is stunted, something always grows in its place. In this case the qualities that grow are either "an impulsive need to coerce by violent means, and a dark impulse to negate others" or the overwrought, obsessive need to exclude all vitality and play from work, from that which is central to the adult self.[40] The ease of play and interplay ensure the safety of free energies, freely used, and "mutuality" with others, whereas in the extreme, interfering with play dampens affect and denies autonomy; this deadly combination leads to depression, aggression, and a wish to kill.[41] Hostility is the negative pole of interplay; it necessarily results when a psyche is confined.[42] Those who imperil the free work, space, self-determination, and mastery that together define play "must be annihilated."[43] Curtailing play is thus risky business for perpetrators, as well as for the victims, for whether one is a child or an adult, in a family, institution, or society, any person or structure that requires "excessive compliance" only ends up "endangering itself."[44]

Not all of adult play's absence can be laid at the feet of childhood experiences. Many adults restrict themselves, abandoning aliveness and genuine interplay with others. Through his analysis of Dr. Isak Borg, the protagonist in Ingmar Bergman's screenplay *Wild Strawberries*, Erikson showed how an otherwise mature person had himself abandoned freedom and play.[45] A physician then nearing the end of his life, Borg's reveries, dreams, and interpersonal exchanges show us a man who had immersed himself too deeply in his profession. He had surrendered himself to his role to such a degree that "restricted his spontaneity and playfulness and made him, in fact, the compulsive character that he became."[46]

Implicit in all of the foregoing is the fourth overarching point about his thoughts, that throughout his theoretical years Erikson was largely consistent in interpreting play. Writing the Godkin Lectures in 1972, at the end of his most prolific years of writing, Erikson said that he had not changed his mind about the meaning of play or its approach and had found no reason to alter his concepts on play as written in his first book.[47] He was substantially correct, for he always wrote psychoanalytically about play space and spheres of play, about the limits and freedom of play in childhood, about adolescents' play with the idea of an ideological self that is projected into a future time and space, and about the projected psychological visual field and space that ideational adults create. Yet he did make two changes. The first of these is his shift in thinking, in which he moved his own ideas about play closer to cognitive developmental premises. The second change is more problematic than the first, for in his retirement years Erikson overturned one of his most important points, that for adults play occurs through work alone.

Taking these changes in turn, with respect to his nod in the direction of cognitive development, Erikson's meetings with Piaget figure importantly. After his discussions with Piaget and others in Geneva in early 1955 and his observations of Inhelder's methods and findings on the same occasion, Erikson saw beyond the developmental psyche alone.[48] He then positioned himself closer to a view in which he combined the psychological apparatus with cognitive structures for infants, children, and adolescents.[49] He associated infants', children's, and adults' explorations of ever greater physical space with both cognitive understanding and with libido in its broadest meaning, agreeing with Piaget that at every developmental level humans assimilate visual and symbolic representations that go beyond psychological adaptive needs.[50] Piagetian concepts first appeared in his writings in 1958 and, by the time of his 1970 Loyola Symposium and 1972 Godkin Lectures, they were integral to his thinking.[51]

Erikson variously referenced cognitive concepts such as "operations," search strategies, "hypothetical propositions," and the necessity of "construct(ing)" and "re-invent(ing)" something so as to understand it.[52] However, as closely as he associated cognition with psyche in visioning, entertaining ideas, and interplaying with others in life's widening radius, Erikson kept psyche apart, more fluid, affective, and subjective, and on a higher plane than thinking. In Erikson's notion of psyche at work in play, he portrayed possibility and forward movement. Play resolves the past and hosts the future. In part, a child or adult plays to explore a "new identity element" that is lodged in a fresh idea of community and, in doing so, sees where such "experience . . . might lead."[53] In other words, the ritual of play connects a life in its narrative and in one niche of history; one conjures and resolves the past and apprehends the roles, abilities, events, and possibilities that are yet ahead.[54]

The second, unrelated, change is our theorist's late-life overturning of one of his own claims, apparently unwittingly. Until his retirement, Erikson had insisted that adult play and work occur together, that one does not play if and when work is pushed to life's periphery; rather, work itself *is* the adult person's play. He found the best of adult play in the fresh ideas that arrive in a time-out-of-mind zone of mentally leaping, intuiting, and creating and scorned the "vitalists," those who wear themselves out in endless recreation.[55] Using themselves up through exhausting play, such adults harbored some "counter-Calvinist" need to see play as its own end, as though only those activities constituting childhood play could be considered play in adulthood.[56] This is obsessive, a "post Puritan purism," a denial of what adulthood is about.[57] No wonder," he wrote, that the "'identity crisis' both fit and took (in the U.S.) for there can be little doubt, that America in its homes, schools, and colleges overdeveloped in both sexes the kind of identity that was based on childhood stages when initiative and industry are the strengths to be developed."[58] Antagonistic to their Calvinistic tendencies, Americans did not see that they had transferred those overdeveloped work strengths to their off-work pursuits. However, in his eighth decade of life, well after he had left full-time employment, Erikson's observations lead us to conclude that the identity, intimacy, and generativity years themselves create a second latency period, this time for childlike play instead of oedipal sexuality. Erikson then noticed that the postwork period of life brings the opportunity to play again, if in a different way. One can then escape the "overdefined" work definitions and gender roles that had held one captive during adulthood's prime years. Thinking along with him in the writings and interviews of his last lucid decade, we infer that the older adult may well become a more complete psychosensual person as well. Less bifurcated as half of a single-gendered organism and more of a human who has become both-gendered, the elder becomes a person who feels and thinks more as a whole being, both from within the gender that had been dominant and within the previously dormant gender that now opens up.

Considering this later shift in view, a change that he himself may not have fully known he was making, we might look to the extent to which the context of Erikson's own life shaped his thought. He worked hard during his years of theorizing; thus, in part, he gave a theoretical view of play as he then saw it, in terms of work's meaning to his own ego and needs and to the egos and needs of others. In his retirement, play came to mean something far different. It meant freedom to jettison earlier adulthood restrictions, those that intimacy and work requirements themselves create. And it meant experiencing the sensual, bigendered self and the natural world more deeply.

SPHERES AND LEAPS

Moving now to Erikson's play concepts generally and then to adult play specifically, I discuss three notions that were important to him during his theoretical period. These are the sphere or arena of play itself, the idea of play as the ability to leap freely, and the importance of vision. In Erikson's major stream of thought, play is work. Play occurs on location, is a created and projected psychological-visual field, and is a territory for representing ideas and conflicts.

By *sphere*, the first of his key notions, Erikson meant the zone or area for play. For infants, Erikson labeled the play space the "autosphere," the body of self and of mother.[59] This is the initial human "geography," he wrote, one in which the baby first explores the mother with taste, touch, and sight and later plays within the zone of his or her own infant body.[60] The mother's facial topography is particularly important, for, to the infant, it is an extension of that baby's being. In seeing and touching the mysterious protrusions, openings, and flat surfaces of that loved face babies learn all there is to know about their universe at that point in time. Mother is universe. Touch, taste, smells, and sounds unite with vision as an organizer of what is seen and experienced to create a fully sensory cosmos. And in that first sphere, babies try out behaviors, in effect finding ways to attract and habituate others to their needs.[61]

For children, Erikson wrote about play configurations that are constructed in a *microsphere*. By "configurations," he meant the arrangements that children make with toys and blocks in three-dimensional space and the forms that such constructions take.[62] Erikson used the term *microsphere* (sometimes *microcosm*) to delineate the actual physical space in which children create their toy constructions. It meant the flat surfaces of a table or floor on which toys are displayed, as well as the boundaries of that area. The child's use of space and toy forms and the way toys are symbolically used paint a picture of that child's ideas, imaginings, fantasies, and conflicts. This microarena is a suspended reality, a world for imagining, for developing and showing competence, for mastering reality, for expressing an "ego ideal," and for refreshing the ego when the big world of people and things overwhelms the young psyche.[63] After Johan Huizinga, Erikson saw microspheres to represent "temporary worlds within the ordinary world, dedicated to the performance of an act apart."[64] In this "temporary world," the child tries out "new identity elements," learns and dramatizes what is within and out of bounds, expresses "territoriality," models others, and learns how to use toy objects (miniature cars and trucks, toy animals, blocks, tiny wooden dolls) to represent persons, conflicts, and fantasies.[65]

Each microreality is the young child's work zone and escape realm, a safe harbor to which he or she can flee adults' rituals and weighty surveillance in order to create new rituals.[66] In this realm, the healthy child loses the self in creativity, and in that one small territorial world, play offsets the "burden of morality."[67] The child is momentarily free to act out desires and goals unfettered by adults or by his or her own young conscience. Erikson saw psychological and cognitive development as one. Interpreting from the vantage point of the projective medium of child's play, he variously wrote that play serves ego development, aids the child's unmitigated curiosity for learning and for experiencing surprise, serves as a vehicle for deploying the developing cognitive apparatus, permits symbolic improvisations, and allows the child to try on the unique "role pretensions" that each society's rendition of reality presents.[68] Play is an outlet for imagination and for the release of tensions. Play is serious, a work of the ego.[69] Similar to the time-diffused commitment moratorium of adolescence, the fantasy of play suspends time, permitting a halted arena from which the child can step forward developmentally.[70] In this singular realm, the child sees what is both "'fun to do' and *pleasurable* in its repetition."[71] In the earliest stage a sense of the numinous had been built by the infant's growth in trust colored by mistrust, and in the second stage a sense of the judicious and lawful emanated from rule-learning in the period of autonomy, which incorporates shame and doubt. Now a sense of the dramatic develops as a result of time-out-of-mind play initiative, a drama that holds its portion of conscience and guilt.[72]

Expanding upward developmentally and outward spatially, Erikson's term *macrosphere* means the school environment and other large contexts. For the older child, it is the space in which he or she expands the cognitive-psychological equipment by gaining competence in working with things, learning to share, and understanding new freedoms and limits in the larger physical structure and space to which ideas are attached. In the school age proper, the child learns the skills of "methodical performance."[73] Play is thereby transformed into concrete work and formal skills. Imagination is lost to duty.

For adolescents and adults, Erikson's *microsphere* describes ways in which adolescents in their high ideology and adults in their work project a field of vision, as well as the ideas, plans, and models that fit within that field. Adolescent microspheres are values and utopian ideas projected against the prevailing macrosphere of the social and political arena that encases the problems of the day. But another uniquely adolescent macro environment also exists for such youth. This is the sports field, an engaged zone for competitive action which youths carry along with them into adult life. In those later, larger, adult arenas, youths turn the comparatively benign sportsmanship of the teen years into political prowess, gaming, and, for some, tactical war maneuvers. All games reflect psychological, social, physical, and cognitive abilities; games also reflect "models of power" and of aggression, both in process and in outcome.[74]

To the adult, *microsphere* is theory and theater, the eye and visual field projected. Play becomes the "polis" of the macro political sphere, as well as the representational drama of theater, of play acting in the work roles of life, and of entertaining a microcosm of ideas. Erikson's take on ideas was that they are each rational adult's mental playing field, the abstract world that cognitively developed adults themselves construct. Thus Erikson substituted the mental leaps of adults for the physical leaps of young children. Yet, to Erikson, the ideation of adolescents and of adults was but a poor substitute for the play of children. He wrote that the play he saw in childhood had no comparable form in adult life other than in rare "creative moments."[75] And, agreeing with Anna Freud, he held that the pubertal "fire of sexuality" displaces childlike play forever; the adolescent ego weakens under its pressure and genuine playfulness then ends.[76]

It is hard to disagree with Erikson about the adult loss of play. In adulthood, work compartmentalizes and streamlines life, tact and politeness replace directness, and fear of encroachment by dangerous others prohibits originality, freedom, spontaneity, genuineness, and creativity. Role responsibilities require dutiful, not imaginative, attention. And the sexuality of adult life, with its staid, bifurcated gender roles, creates its own neediness; the casualty is play and the result rigidity.

The second major notion that is important in Erikson's concepts on play appears in two ideas that he linked. These ideas are found in Plato's claim that "the leap" is the best model for the play of the young and in the German word *Spielraum*, in which Erikson found a unique idea of freedom. For the leap, Plato wrote in his Laws that all young animals "leap and bound, they dance and frolic, as it were with glee."[77] Applied to play, the idea of using the earth as a "springboard," of testing the "leeway" of prevailing limits, of moving easily, and of returning to ground safely and "resiliently" appealed to Erikson. When thinking abstractly, adults leave behind their concrete lodgings in the physical here and now to leap into some time-out-of-mind zone. Ideas, plans, drama and scenarios, visions, models, and worldviews result. *Spielraum* became Erikson's metaphor for the leeway attained when one leaves the concrete ground, thus temporarily offsetting the gravity of place and time, of gaining freedom from cognitive, psychological, and physical restrictions that hold humans captive. This means that one can spring freely, committed to that choice and engaged in the act, yet within a safe harbor, as on the "lee side" of the wind.[78] Thus free physical space and at least temporary psychological distance from encroaching others are necessary. No one can play without the space and freedom to do so.

Translated literally, *Spielraum* means "elbow room" or "clearance." Thus play is "easy and free movement within a set of firm limits," as well as freedom from those who might curtail initiative or crowd one's psyche.[79] The primary role of play is to create *Spielraum*, a leeway of engaged, unfettered motion within boundaries.[80] For children's play, Erikson used this dual idea both literally and metaphorically. For adults, leaping and *Spielraum* was a combined metaphor for abstractly engaging when at work, when creating scenarios, and when attending dramatic theater. But as usual, *Spielraum* carried a responsibility, for it is vintage Erikson that any gift has its price. In this case, a free adult is one who extends freedom to others, one who "increases spielraum for self *and* for interplaying others."[81] Similarly, all superior theories open avenues to fresh leeway for humans, whether for thought, for action, or for the space to exist freely.[82]

By *Spielraum*, Erikson meant providing the interpersonal space that frees others to act and interacting freely with others. He meant both interpersonal and intergenerational mutuality, equality, and reciprocal space and interchange. He did not specify how to do this, leaving it for readers and audiences to determine this in their own lives. However, with respect to how one uses the self to energize others, an obscure note finds him saying that the adult intentionally "polarises" the self.[83] Typically, Erikson had used the term *polarity* to mean two poles that oppose each other, one attracting and the other negating, repelling, and self-repelling. But he now meant the ability to keep two seemingly opposite qualities operational. He moved to the idea of optic polarization, in which a light can produce unique effects in different planes. This was his way of thinking about how, just as one can make light waves vibrate, a person uses the energy of self actively to provide energizing actuality for the self (on one plane) and for others (on other planes). Wary of reifying the physical space between persons, "polarise" meant energy of self when interacting with others across that space. As light rays brighten and vibrate, the validating energy of self invigorates and animates another.

The third important notion in Erikson's approach to play is vision. The sphere is essential; it is "the eye projected."[84] Erikson meant two things by this brief statement. First, he meant that the infant's vision and, with it, the ability to "drink in impressions" is the earliest organizing element in life, that humans retain early visual pictures from their prelinguistic years, and that such images are transported into later ideas, such as worldviews and notions of God.[85] Second, Erikson saw adult visual ideas as the individual's construction of reality, a partial but future-projecting reality. Individual reality is only partial because humans must reduce the more complex, complete external reality so that their limited human minds can assimilate and handle it. In this, he borrowed Walter Lippmann's interpretation that the mind takes in material from the larger environment and "reconstructs" it on a smaller, simpler scale in order to work with it.[86] There is a three-way relationship among "the scene of action, the human picture of that scene, and the human response to that picture working itself out upon the scene of action."[87] The adult's tendency to absorb a limited, reduced rendition of reality and to reorder and remake that reality, as it is visually, mentally reconstructed and portrayed fits hand in glove with one's ideological views and values and with the projection of these into visions and a hoped-for future. For "we never can exist without mental visions which go beyond what sensory vision can grasp or our grasp of things can confirm."[88]

ADULT PLAY: EGO VITALITY, AN IDEATIONAL UNIVERSE, AND WONDER

Erikson portrayed adult play in a rather restricted way: He showed play within psychoanalytic thought alone, refraining from crossing into other disciplines, used only his own theory about the optimum in life span development as the convoy for thinking about such play, and illustrated how play can be used either to free one's and others' energies or to lie, in effect creating visual ideas that are meant to deceive. In those adults whom he found competent in the positives of play, two key overlapping qualities function. First, playing adults are those who can find and engage the playing child within themselves in an ongoing way and, when their own play has been disrupted in service to consuming, detail-driven work, they know how to unshackle themselves, freeing their intellects, reclaiming personal choice and initiative, and liberating their spirits. Such adults willingly extend the freedom of such rights to others. Their relationships with others are equal, mutual, and genuine. Second, playing adults use a mature cognitive, psychological apparatus to envision and create ideas, in effect leaping into a space and sphere that capture and permit projection of the mind's eye and thought. This occurs on site in work, as well as in tendencies to plan and to entertain visions, political ideas, and drama.

In both attributes, Erikson's explicit dictum holds: Playfulness is manifest aliveness, vitality itself. Playing adults are engaged, adaptive, and resilient. They retain and foster freedom, leeway, and range in the various roles, modes, and activities in which they function. Thus play is the freedom of actual persons and of their roles and role latitude; play is not an attribute of activities that somehow resemble the block-constructing, ball-playing, gaming enterprises of children. Implicitly, his view leads away from the considerable restraints that curtail behavior in the daily roles and purposes of contemporary life, thus countering role ossification and adult rigidity.

All adults live simultaneously in two contemporary, present-tense worlds, whether or not they are conscious, or always conscious, of this. These are the current adult world of mature life and the prior childhood world, that which is now inside the psyche in a vivid or vague, truthful or vastly reconstructed, form of once-young life. In this fact lies the first of Erikson's major findings. In some adults, particularly those whose vitality had been nurtured when they were young, who had been permitted to develop their talents according to personal choices and interests, and whose imagination and initiative were permitted to range, those very childhood resources remain accessible and renewable within the requirements of adulthood.[89] These adults live in a mature skin that has detached itself from childhood, yet they are uniquely aware of developmental continuity between their maturity and their earlier youth. Gender, work, civic, and social roles require allegiance and time commitments; they are sponsored by a body-mind-psyche that cannot again function as a child. Yet these vital adults feel unconstrained by such tolls to live freely and autonomously. Keeping trust and honesty intact, they exhibit spontaneity and authenticity of being and relate genuinely with others.

Throughout his years of theory building, Erikson noticed such adults, but he did not publish his observations. In his last set of interviews, those with middle-aged and older adults for the *Vital Involvement* book, he interviewed adults who had been participants in the Berkeley Child Guidance Study.[90] Not only was he struck by a surprising similarity of content and form in the play constructions of participants when they had been 12 years old and in the themes and content of their lives 40 years later, but he found that those who had been able to play freely as youths were the same persons who showed vitality in their maturity. They had renewed themselves throughout the many years and travails of adult life and showed amazing resilience.

In these and other vital adults he noted the absence of pretensions that, if worn, would mask the real self. Refusing to forfeit authenticity, spontaneity, and autonomy, these adults seemed to eschew living as disguised persons in feigned personalities, an attribute of narrowness and rigidity.[91] He noted that affectations show up in those who have relinquished the desire to learn, to take a chance, and to free the self for new opportunities. This becomes a death of sorts, both for the self who cannot risk and for relationships, as those who feel they must disguise themselves close down. They cannot freely, genuinely engage with fresh thought, with new content, or with others. Erikson's resilient adults counter such tendencies. They live and relate only as they are, genuinely.

Genuineness captures the naturalness and openness of children. In adults, this appears as receptivity to insight, to fresh styles of living, and to potentially different ways of being in the world. Erikson saw some of this in those who were open to seeing things anew through Eastern mysticism, to thinking and worshiping differently in the ecumenical movement of his day, and to immersing themselves in fresh forms of music.[92] These are adults who feel rejuvenated in the presence of young children, a fact that is not surprising, as they had been happy and felt safe in childhood play when young. As adults, their vitality continues. They have greater access than most to joy and laughter, to aliveness and abandon. They shed blinderlike restrictions that would mask both observation and living in the moment. Mentally healthy, they have "free . . . flexible energies . . . [that can be] used in different ways."[93]

To the contrary, in those who had known harsh, restrictive upbringing, playful vitality frequently dies, both for childhood and for later years. And among those who had grown up in overly serious homes, imagination often withers and, with it, access to a free play with ideas and a sense of the ridiculous. Further, so many of the persons we call *adult* are characterized as such just because they are serious and have lost their spirit of play. Erikson saw dramatic examples of this in those who had accumulated such a superabundance of wealth, and thus extensive leeway, that they and their children were "paralyzed . . . (and) stifled," and, at the far extreme of this, in those of such poverty that they were completely deprived of leeway and their potential for play.[94] Between these two extreme versions the overly grim others reside, those who have abandoned the glee, trust, and wonder of the child within. That internalized child is now experienced as a defect, as a deep splinter. When felt it must be removed.

Although his primary publications on the topic reveal an Erikson who portrayed adult play as a form of vitality that seems heavy, markedly devoid of humor, and what we might call *fun*, his notes and earlier writings show that this was not completely the case. To him, intimacy with one's loved partner carries the joy of abandon, of free play with the sexual powers, process, and sensations of self joined with another in interplay, pleasure, and playfulness.[95] A frolicsome gaiety comes through in his descriptions of Gandhi and St. Francis.[96] And humor is one of his essentials, not as a "humorless wit" that is "aggressive" but as humor that "reconciles the situation and the persons in the encounter."[97] He could not abide wry jesting that harms another, that is used to "exploit . . . (or to) diminish."[98] Here the Kantian, ethical Erikson surfaces, the theorist who required treating others as loved, or at least valued, ends but never as the means to an end. Whether engaged in relationships with loved others or when relating to others in the commerce of daily life, no one could be cheaply used as a mere object.

A free identity and freedom of play are opposites of cynicism, the distrust of people's goodness and sincerity. Yet our theorist, who renounced cynicism and the aggressive wit that contains it, is the same one who applauded sarcasm, a quality that is cynicism's cousin. He agreed with Ivan Illych that sarcasm helps to keep one free; it laughs at the artificiality of social forms and structures, but not at persons themselves.[99] Used as the tool of probing satire, sarcasm is that which insightful people use to unmask the illusions that permeate all institutions and societies. One way or another, adults are taken in by the importance of the social and institutional roles they play. And to our final hour, playing in one role or another somehow captivates us.[100] Yet investing oneself too completely in occupational, title-impressed roles is none other than delusional because such roles are overlaid with conceit and deception. Taking on the mantle of roles as though they represent the real self leads to a counterfeit life in which adults give up both "inner and outer spielraum" through illusions that prevent insight and its companion, freedom.[101] Enter sarcasm, the mature playing adult's ability to satirize the illusory pretensions that work roles and their sponsoring institutions promote.

Adult play is found in those who can reclaim the glee of childhood and the "sportiveness" of adolescence.[102] There is an utter necessity of keeping play and leeway alive in the core of adult concerns and work and of learning how to emulate those who know how to energize both the leeway and breadth of their own and of others' central functions and activities. Without such freedom, range, and interplay, adult egos die, and hence all human institutions as well.

This then is the essence: Self-renewing adults somehow keep their internal youthfulness alive, contributing their energies to work; yet in the play and leeway of genuine work, they resist becoming work's, an institution's, or a superior's marionette.[103] Giving up personal freedom as work's slave suffocates the ego and, through a wrongful claim to necessity, creates automatons who are dulled by formalized, work-habituated rigidities.[104] Likely, they are dulled by society's norms for success as well. Like Marx, Erikson was concerned that one could too readily become a "craft idiot," caught up in work's drudgery and in the tools and structures which then govern the adult.[105] The centrality of play in work, and of work with playfulness, is Erikson's main theme and requirement. It is use of the mind's eye and the mental visual field to leap into, to create, and to work within a macrosphere, to project adult ideas and vision, theories and plans, projects and blueprints, using the freedom of a nonsubservient ego. How else to gleefully elude forces that would crush an ego's vitality?

The second major finding relates closely to the first, that adult play requires toying with ideas on the stages of life that are primary to adulthood. This occurs on site—in work, in political concepts and ideological visions, in generative care of others, and in all else central to adulthood's unique position of maintaining the business of the world. Because no sane person requires children to do their work of play in some place foreign to them, neither can the play of adults happen in a location that is "extraterritorial" to their principal contexts and concerns.[106] Work is a gift. It provides access to, contributions in, and inclusion by mainstream society. Work structures time, engaging the mind and psyche; thus work is essential to adult mental health.

The play that is contextually central to the business of being adult lurks in adult reason.[107] Play enters theories and imagination. In those who can freely use their imaginations where it feels safe to do so, psychological safety comes from knowing that their imaginations and creativity operate in environments in which they are free to take risks.[108] When children's environments or adults' work or home contexts thwart the ability to take chances freely, an absence of safety compromises human functioning. In such conditions, persons "store up aggression in search for (more or less) sanctioned outlets."[109] Adults and children who are denied mental space and personal security become defensive. They show frustration, anger, and rage. Depression sometimes results as anger is diverted inward. On the other hand, leeway, *Spielraum*, is the "soul of adult play," the genuine gift of "free to be, you and me," a safe harbor for work, imagination, and creativity.

If such leeway seems a mighty utopian departure from the contemporary reality of codified behavior, formalized structures, and the politics of power in institutions, Erikson had something powerful in mind. This was Isaac Newton's sense of what his own adult work had been like:

> I do not know what I may appear to the world; but to myself I seem to have been only like a boy playing on the sea-shore, and diverting myself in now and then finding a smoother pebble or a prettier shell than ordinary, while the great ocean of truth lay all undiscovered before me.[110]

Newton's impressions of his life's work conjure up notions of searching play at the front line and forward rim of thought, play as "active learning," a play-work that advances knowledge and understanding.[111] It is a play with thought similar to the theory-building Erikson himself did and wished all could have, a play with ideas so free from corruption by industrial or utilitarian profit motives that its work is fascinating, engaging, and incapable of subordination to such extraneous purposes and pressures.

Einstein's Childlike Play

Albert Einstein was Erikson's favorite person for showing how an adult can keep childhood curiosity and wonder alive in work. In fact, Erikson saw similarities between Einstein and himself, not by way of their equal stature as discoverers but because of certain shared talents and styles of thinking. Einstein and Erikson were both highly visual thinkers who placed less stock in words than in spatial concepts.[112] Both men played ideationally with polarities. They associated, juxtaposed, and combined elements, freely rummaging through possibilities. Both were inductive, surveying thinkers who made bold intuitive leaps. They worked on the meta level, projecting thought into their own version of the macrosphere. Both were free thinking as youth, resisting standardized formulas and rigid ways of seeing. To Einstein this meant resisting childhood schooling in the mechanistic, Germanic curricula; to Erikson it meant resisting a similarly rote Germanic curriculum and spending a childhood living and breathing Goethe, Kierkegaard, and Eastern mysticism. Both venerated the world and creation, holding these in awe and with great personal humility. Einstein, the self-proclaimed citizen of the world, foreswore national boundaries; both men avoided captivity by doctrinaire religion. Throughout his handwritten notes and jottings, one finds an Erikson who modeled the great scientist in pressing for originality, in using inductive, noncompartmentalized thinking, and in working to take thought to the next level instead of burrowing along established lines.[113]

Einstein used symbols and images that he mentally juggled, replicated, and connected, a way of thinking that both men spoke of as "combinatory" or "associative" visual play. Erikson epitomized this play as *begriffen*, a free play with concepts in which Einstein engaged his mind in a ranging survey, in *"uebersicht,"* an "overview (or) free scanning of a wide area."[114] Searching an expansive ideational terrain, Einstein worked in a style Erikson called *"Anschauung,* a way of looking at things that is both focused and encompassing."[115] Having emulated Einstein, Erikson titled his last book of largely unpublished writings *A Way of Looking at Things*, meaning *Anschauung*.[116]

Active, "intuitive 'beholding,'" *"begreiflichkeit,"* characterized Einstein's thought, from which his perceptions and "leap(s) of intuition" then forecast the order of phenomena.[117] When intuiting, Einstein placed his mind within the realm he studied, suspending self and control, "all that our central, active, selective, aware, effective, and inclusive ego fears most."[118] Thereby he could see and position himself amid the "swirling" forms that seemed to swim before him.[119] In such a state, he eventually pondered how light waves would seem to someone who was in stride with them, and in that step, made his most important discovery.[120]

Einstein's childhood had fostered his imagination, trust, and intellect. Dearly loved as a child, his parents had trusted his normalcy and abilities despite his delayed speech. According to Erikson, Einstein himself later transferred the trust placed in him to the entire cosmos. In his adulthood he continued to ask questions only children would ask, engaging and relying on a range of senses, much as a child will do. Creativity was Einstein's most "basic urge"; this and his innate wonder kept his affinity for play and learning alive.[121] As well, he held to the earliest impressions of his childhood years, continuing to see the sphere as a primary, unifying element in the universe. He thought aesthetically, with symbols instead of with words whose logic can trick the mind, burdening it with arbitrary categories and deceptive notions. He suspended interpretations and conclusions for long periods, something Erikson called "a delayed 'I see' phenomenon."[122] And he laughed infectiously, delighting in humor. He enjoyed immersion in the natural world which fed his thought. He worked silently and alone, engendering an isolated creativity. Trusting in physical simplicity, unity, and order, but not in a simplified, reduced universe, he held to his faith that the most remarkable fact about the world is its inherent "comprehensibility."[123]

Throughout life, sustained playfulness extended into Einstein's deepest thoughts.[124] He was uniquely able to play with ideas that seemed to reside in the stratosphere, while working on site and in the present, blending symbolic thought with philosophical and physical ideas and maintaining an extraordinary personal reverence for the overall order in which he believed. His inventiveness held a creativity and grasp of the "extra personal world," a supreme effort to see a sector of the physical universe and creation as does God.[125] Erikson synthesized Einstein's work-play as that of trusting the world but not necessarily how others or prior theories and laws view the world; Einstein resisted deductive enterprises, observed with wonder, and scanned widely, senses attuned. Erikson called his unique outcome a "rendezvous in the here and now, between man's scientific insight and the universal Logos."[126]

Described is an Einstein who developed a gestalt, a picture, as the outcome of his mental imagery. And in writing about such imaginings, Erikson's rhetorical questions appear: Might it be that adults who are best able to play, to create through their work, are those who maintain, as Einstein did, a questioning curiosity and wonder? Are they good inductive, scanning thinkers, not quick or glib, and do they resist, stubbornly perhaps, ways of seeing that are incomplete, arbitrary, or too well accepted? Do they necessarily and as a result avoid premature closure? Do they keep their senses alive, trusting them and the observations that come from them? Do they prefer to ponder ideas and reflect on them, and do they work best when silent and alone? These *are* Erikson's implications about the best of creative play in work. An additional implication must be added, one that Erikson did not say but that exists as a soft undercurrent in his papers, the inference that immersion in nature, away from the stricture of artificial work structures, environments, and requirements fosters reflective thought.

Playing, Playful, *and* Childlike Adult

For the essence of his final theory-building book, *Toys and Reasons*, Erikson appropriated William Blake's insight, "The child's toys and the old man's reasons are the fruits of the two seasons."[127] Erikson meant that ideational toys and reasons emanate from the last phase of reasoning adulthood, just as toys are the deployed and discarded fruit of childhood play. By *reasons*, Erikson referred to the rational and philosophical adult, for as he wrote, "the child "plays," the adolescent is "wild," and the adult is a "philosopher."[128] Complex as always, just as he illustrated human effects in what he saw as corollary periods of childhood play and play in adulthood reasoning, he wanted to again show how, in its near completion, the closing of life incorporates and returns, full circle, to early life. Old reasons and reasoning can be "blessed (again) by playful childlikeness."[129] Knowing his subtlety, it cannot escape notice that Erikson may also have meant the "old man" in Blake as a self-referent. Here was a 70-year-old Erikson who had had his reasons for theory constructing throughout his life and would now show connections between a reasoning, toying psyche and visions, between projected visual-mental microspheres and his version of developmental utopia, and between illusory reasons and what was then afoot in the killing minds of those who orchestrated the American side of the Vietnam War.

But we need to look beyond adult play to see what he meant by the childlikeness that is a major step beyond the play of psyche in thought and reasons. In fact, when one looks beyond Erikson's concepts of play in adult work alone, his notions about childlikeness stand out more clearly. These thoughts appear in the *Galilean Sayings*, in his *Psychoanalytic Reflections on Einstein's Centenary*, and in thoughts scattered throughout his earlier writings and notes.[130]

In portraying the childlike adult, Erikson wrote descriptively, explaining childlike qualities but avoiding deep conceptualizations. He seems to have been unsure about how, exactly, one goes about recapturing childlike trust, wonder, and joy, of how one abandons the developmental burdens while bolstering the gains of adulthood. This is a "both/and" polarity so extreme as to create difficulties even for Erikson. But his thoughts on the subject are essential reading. To his last writing years Erikson remained convinced that the pathway to heightened development came about through the "metanoia" he had described for the spiritual adult: One must turn back to again see and find renewal in the child forms and ways of being in the world in order to live completely and freely, eyes open for fresh opportunities, for new learning, and for a different kind of innocent trust.

From his first paper in 1930 onward, Erikson quoted Freud on the subject.[131] Freud mourned bitterly the toll that development exacts, the loss of "the radiant intelligence of the child."[132] Noting this observation as the extent of Freud's insight, as Freud had not treated children clinically, Erikson expanded: As each child grows into an adult, cognitive development and accumulated knowledge dull young senses with facts and reason. The objective world readily displaces the subjective. The delight of simply being, learning, and basking in the given world of self, nature, and a deeply affective existence are lost. As adults, one will never again love as completely as when one was very young. The tinge of choice, reason, purpose, need, and duty cloud first loves. And the purity of feeling deeply, with a mingled body, psyche, and soul, evaporate. Conscience and its associated shame and guilt replace abandon. Awe, surprise, and spontaneity too readily give way to stilted rules, roles, and ingrained ways of seeing. No longer free or capable of experiencing newness, vision narrows and learning wilts. Defensive egos result. Radiant intelligence dies.

Growing knowledge about the self and increasing information about the world add anxieties to the multiple losses—loss of subjectivity, of affective unity, of sensory awareness, of loving completely, and of living in an astonishing present that extends interminably. Erikson described six major sources of this anxiety in adults. First, there is the sure and increasingly palpable knowledge that one will die. Anxiety from this source is buttressed by the second, the adult's existential dread of aloneness in the universe, disenfranchised or forgotten by a Supreme Other, that Power which the objective, deducing adult brain fears may not exist anyway. These dual anxieties are reinforced by the four major scientific discoveries of the last five centuries which seem to confirm that one is negligible in the universe, a momentary bundle of water and protoplasm, an organism whose anxieties about death and God's likely absence seem clearly well founded. With Freud, Erikson credited three major sources of this anxiety in the discoveries of Copernicus, Darwin, and Freud himself, and then added Einstein as the fourth. Together these originators' discoveries stole away the validity of human belief in its centrality and supremacy of place, of species, of consciousness, and of time. Copernicus relieved us of the security of the earth's, and therefore the human's, centrality in the universe; Darwin divested human stature of its elect, created, separate position among creatures; Einstein stripped away the absolutes of space and time; and Freud disrobed the psyche, showing it both entangled and devoid of consciousness alone as lord of its house.[133]

When the multiple losses of childhood accumulate and mingle with an objective, abstract brain, and these join up with anxieties about death, anxieties about the potential absence of God and any waiting eternity, and anxieties born of loss of illusions regarding human preeminence due to the handiwork of scientific discoveries, these together crush what is left of a childlike psyche. How then to unseat these "gains" to reclaim childhood's trust, abandon, joy, awe, and confidence in safety and protection?

Although his notes tell us that one cannot fully discard adulthood's development to reclaim childhood once again, Erikson believed that adults can regain some of the power of the child by reversing the deficit model, by seeing adulthood as deficient against childhood. And he surely gave us his version of adult childlikeness. It is advancement to the highest plane, that of affective subjectivity combined with, but not obstructed by, reason. It is a "naive zest" for life, a vitality, happiness, amazement in nature and in the moment, and an intentional resurfacing of the joy of learning.[134] But childlikeness in adults means an "old child" as well, the love and longing for a childhood that cannot again exist, either as it was or as we have idealistically reconstructed it.[135]

Among the main implications of this topic, we find four sets of complex ideas. The first of these includes the characteristics of a child that adults can partially regain; the second follows from this, that of what it is adults must do to reclaim a childlike nature; the third is Erikson's polarity of young and old in the self-same childlike adult; and the fourth is found in his loose associations about existing in nature, sensual experiences, and reflective learning and creativity.

First, there are the characteristics of children that some adults can, with effort, again find within their being. Erikson believed that someone who is truly adult can recapitulate the strengths of childhood within all subsequent stages.[136] Infancy, childhood, and adolescence are inside, challenging each adult to find his or her own "continuity . . . (in the) discontinuity" that developing, growing new powers and processes, and seeing the world differently, through the lens of objectivity and reasoning, brings.[137] This means avoiding one's suppression and working through the repression of childhood, of incorporating childhood into and bringing it up to the present.

To our theorist, the childlike qualities that one can mine are the following: Children are happy and joyful. They have a peace about them that comes not from external objects but from inner peace and the "inner space."[138] They are graceful; they show uninhibited, engaged movement with a mission. Children are animated and alive, unconstrained by convention. One sees in them the "joy of self expression," an enthusiastic "inviolacy of spirit."[139] They are resourceful and inventive, are readily lost in the abandon of creative, highly unique endeavors.[140] They exist in and with wonder, imagination, and surprise. They live in and with nature, and their bodies and minds freely interplay together instead of functioning separately. They are not constrained by ingrained overdiscipline, self-restriction, or avoidance of risk. They show an eloquence of simplicity, spontaneity, and sincerity.[141] Until we show them how to be otherwise, they are gentle, honest, direct, courageous, benevolent, and positive. They are meek but stubborn of purpose; they don't readily make deals, nor do they know the meaning of pretense.

Children speak with unabashed pleasure, telling their stories eagerly.[142]

They hold in awe some special occasions, remembrances, sights, ceremonies, and persons. They love deeply and unconditionally, cherishing those who love them most. They live in a highly affective state. Highly visual and aesthetic, they are mesmerized by beauty. They love music and the dance. They trust their senses and the knowledge that comes from those sources. Theirs is an "uncorrupted core," the "'innocent eye' and ear" which knows faith but not ambition, trust without question, and the glee of curiosity and learning when quiet or raucous.[143] They discover. Correctly and sometimes incorrectly, they know many inspired "aha experience(s)," in what is "not an entirely logical step but a sensory and sense step."[144]

Second, therefore, what must one do to live at least partially as a child while coexisting as an adult? Most important, each adult will understand and avoid the price of alienating him- or herself from the child inside. The price is loss of the qualities just described, including loss of freedom, of deep loves, of creativity, of learning, and of trust. This requires that one not "suffocate," in oneself, in other adults, or in children, the "creatively good," the "genius" that is "the child in every human being."[145] If adults were not so fearful of becoming dependent or "helpless" once again, they might well be more creative, more "magnanimous," and less ambivalent about their own childlike qualities and about children.[146] Erikson found that even the many writings on children's play reflect distance from children and an "intense ambivalence" about them.[147] He suggested that adults might well emulate children. They might spend time with children and adopt their ways of being in life. Like the unconscious, children are playful and good natured, filled with humor. In their presence we learn about ourselves, we relearn spontaneity, joy, and genuineness, and we learn about the inner machinations of the unaware psyche, theirs and ours.

Included is the requirement that material goods and roles cannot possess the adult, ruling and owning his or her life. Like neuroses, we can have them but we cannot let them have us. Some few possessions that one cares for and about and some monies that one spends "relevantly" are concomitants of adult autonomy, but inordinate attention to the goods of this world alters one's existence; they enslave one to that which is at most a means, not the end.[148] As for roles, many adults "submit" to too-standardized roles and find themselves in bondage to them. Adult childlike potentials die off; they are unused, or deemed unnecessary, or are so blatantly "inimical" to role requirements that they are discarded.[149] In overadjusting to roles, adults become standardized. They lose uniqueness, freedom, and flexibility. Consolidating risk and change, adults become risk-aversive and anti-child. They "submit" to reality, having moved from the play of childhood through adolescence and quickly into the "dominant means of production" or, in these days, of service or of information or economy manipulation.[150] Role playing debases play. Instead of freeing the ego, roles imprison and restrain it. Adults then display ego needs which, at their boisterous worst, loudly shout, "Look at me, look at me." This diminishes interchange with others, for the ego-needy adult builds the self up and keeps others down, apart, or unequal. There can be "no interplay between perceived unequals."[151]

Surrendering to the requirements of others' and organizations' realities means that by the time middle age arrives, adults are typecast, staid, and rigid. There is scant room for playful variation. They "pretend to be free and natural"; in fact, they "play free and equal" but exist at the behest of roles, a mass market, bureaucratization, consumerism, and convention.[152] These are traps, or in Erikson's words, "infantilisms."[153] Play is gone from work, freedom is subjugated to structures, things, and tight role performance; childlikeness has left the persona. What Erikson defined, of course, is stagnation due to a loss of leeway and potential for variation. Conformity rules.[154] Sheer repetitive habit leads to rigidity and loss of joy, whether or not the adult wants this.[155] His point applies as well today as in the 1960s or 1970s, for, as any photograph of a group of middle-agers in their workday environment shows, forced smiles notwithstanding, their faces do not typify a free or happy lot.

As our theorist said, adolescents see this. Adults appear like "robots" to youth, especially those adults who are the "most technocratically dominant."[156] Owing to years of "self-repression and restriction," the "mature" are sewn up by their infantilisms.[157] Therefore, adults desperately need those they call great, those they can look up to and admire, for only such persons can "provide images" of adult possibility to those who are "trapped" by stagnation.[158]

To reclaim the child, Erikson wrote that the adult must dispel too harsh a superego, for it is a "self-violence"; it weighs down the 'I.' The "weight of excessive guilt . . . leads to repression in thought and to inhibition in initiative."[159] We might say that the inhibited, conscience-riven adult attempts somehow to become a *perfected child*, an oxymoron as a term but an expression that captures what he meant. To become perfected is to become rigidified, meaning that one is very much not a child at all. Where there is obsessive perfection, childhood has fled. Childlikeness is abandoned in routinization, in duty, in the fear of making mistakes or of being wrong, and in one's sense of obligation, whether or not that obligation is actual. It is difficult to feel and to be weighted down, the moral and moralistic adult in perpetuity, while maintaining childlikeness. Humans cannot jump in and out of different skins. Creativity, the very "peculiarity of . . . uniqueness," is sacrificed.[160]

Erikson also claimed that adults need to abandon at least some of their adulation of things that work. He implied that in our various illusions about the importance of technology, materials, and tools, of being self-impressed with our human ability to control things, adults too readily transfer this notion to controlling other persons. Instead of ends, others become manipulable cogs in our psyches, the means to some other, likely ambitious, end. Even if technological prowess is one's talent and work life, he believed that developmentally advanced adults could free themselves from becoming robotic technocrats who could neither think well nor feel deeply.

He had many other suggestions, several of which he repeated time and again and thus bear including here. See children as a gift, he wrote, both one's own and those of others. Avoid seeing each child as that which the adult is better than (weak, mischievous, immature, careless); instead see the child as one who has what so many adults have managed to lose—energy, a willing laugh, the bounce of glee, and motives devoid of greed and self-promotion. Avoid the childish petulance of older life, the moralizing, judging, and disinclusion of others. Love deeply and deeply trust some few others. Deflect authoritarianism and cynicism. Don't fix on the past, but live in the present while anticipating the future optimistically. Eschew that "pervasive boredom" that comes with mere "affluence and power."[161] Instead, let the adult self be tickled by the absurd, including the absurdity of rules, roles, structures, and things. And avoid the trap of overwork. Work that is too psychologically strenuous, too taxing, or too prescriptive is grueling; it stunts freedom, blunts abilities, and blocks creative potentials.

The third set of thoughts holds Erikson's view of seasoned elders who are both old and wise, young and childlike. Erikson did not tightly conceptualize his points; in fact, they are largely scattered throughout his notes and writings. But he gave this synopsis:

> The polarity of being an eternal child and yet also a wise old man at the same time is in fact a traditional configuration, if of a rare and August type; there are gods, saints (St. Francis), and true savants like that. There are Jesus' astounding references to the eternal promise of becoming like children. Laotse's very name seems to refer to the fact that he was born with a little white beard. And in Einstein's home culture, Goethe once declared himself a Weltkind (a world child) sitting among the prophets.[162]

In that one telling passage, Erikson wrote of the five men who, in one way or another, best personified wise, older, childlike adults to him. Throughout his own adulthood, four of those men had claimed his interest. Joan Erikson added St. Francis to his repertoire.[163]

Erikson's reference to Jesus points to the New Testament descriptions of children, to how one must turn and become like children, a metanoia. Jesus had "insisted" that grown-up faith "demands the continuation into maturity of a true childlikeness and youthfulness."[164] These alone insure adult faith. "Childhood and the kingdom . . . (are) coincident and dependent on one another . . . (for both) anticipate the future," Erikson wrote.[165] Further," wisdom demands table fellowship, not asceticism"; there is a "joyousness of we-ness fusing a basic source of I-ness: to imbibe while looking in each others' eyes, recognizing each other's faith."[166]

Lao-Tse (also known as Lao Tzu) likely lived in the fourth century B.C., but the sayings attributed to him were written down during the second half of the third century B.C. Throughout his *Wanderschaft* moratorium, Erikson had carried some writings of Lao-Tse with him as he hiked. That small book of writings now appears among the Erikson Harvard collection. Translated, Lao-Tzu means "old master," "old boy," or "ancient child."[167] Erikson occasionally spoke about Lao-Tse in German as a "greiskind," an "old man, child."[168] Writing about historically acclaimed leaders who, in resolving their personal identity crises, resolved the needs of their era, he wrote about Martin Luther as one of several young-old men who became old-young men, thus illustrating the ancient child: "The chosen young man . . . extends the problem of his identity to the borders of existence in the known universe. . . . No wonder that he is something of an old man (a *philosophus*, and a sad one) when his age-mates are young, or that he remains something of a child when they age with finality. The name Lao-Tse, I understand, means just that."[169]

Erikson connected the actions of the disciples of Jesus with the translated wisdom in the words and the translated meaning of "Lao-Tse." Chinese texts were sometimes named after their author, as in "*the* Lao-Tzu." This text carries the corresponding title "Tao Te Ching." *Ching* is translated as "classic" and *tao* as "the way," and "*te*" means virtue.[170] Erikson wrote that Christ's disciples spoke of their following of Jesus as "the way," and, in the Harvard papers we find this cryptic note:"Wisdom = Way"; The Way = Laotse."[171] Because thoughts about the meaning of virtue appear in "Lao-Tzu," the text may well have been one origin of Erikson's term "virtu" or strength that, when each is balanced by its negative force, will emanate as the best case resolution of each life stage. He did not hide this fact from those who might pay close attention to his writings. In Erikson's primary autobiographical
accounts, he wrote that he and his friends had toted knapsacks containing some "distilled passages" of Lao-Tse, Nietzsche, Angelus Silesius, and Schopenhauer as they roamed the Black Forest together.[172]

In his notes about the old child in Einstein, Erikson was taken with the scientist's ability to maintain a childlike wonder into his later years. Einstein's tendency to express awe, his wide open eyes looking directly into the camera, struck Erikson as a signal of old-age childlikeness. Einstein had kept his curiosity, his sense of things in context, and his sensory acuity intact. It is "the senses (that) help to keep one in context."[173] For the lyrical Goethe, the poet who lived into his 80s, who uncovered the unconscious before Freud, and who showed Erikson the sequential unfolding of intimacy, generativity, and integrity in adulthood, it was cynicism that adults must avoid. That "world child" could create only by leaving home, by observing but detaching himself from his era, and by keeping his own identity in barely bridled evolution.

Henri Matisse is one other old-child who appears in Erikson's notes. Showing how an elder can harness and exhibit some good share of childlikeness, Erikson pointed to the Matisse Chapel of the Rosary in Vence, France, writing:

a dramatic example of a determined breakthrough of . . . childlikeness, paired with the wisdom of a matured craft, can be seen in Matisse's chapel in Vence. His sketches show how he decided to abandon a life time's tricks of prettification and to sketch the waystations with childlike dissonance.[174]

These fragments of thought suggest that one need not age into a brittle, terminal state; wrinkled skin need not mean stagnant, antique mentation that has lost its childlike sense and forms. If adulthood is a bridge to senior life, then with some retained energy, wit, desire, and good fortune, the approaches, stances, and qualities of childlikeness are there for the finding. In his retirement, Erikson wrote that he found "healthy aging almost shocking."[175] He was surprised to see that content and psychological resources waited yet ahead, something that an "ego can work with."[176] Perhaps in his earlier adulthood, during his prime years of theorizing, there were too few elders about who, as a critical mass, showed him the vitality of childlike ways.

Fourth, Erikson implied a substantial connection between a child's existence in the senses, in nature, and in a deeply affective life as a unity and some adults' abilities to think reflectively and creatively; such adults had persisted in immersing themselves in their senses and in the natural world. He saw a relationship between many adults' alienation from the senses and from their "inner nature(s)" and their separateness from nature itself.[177] In childhood, the ego is a "body-ego" that holds psyche and body as one, he wrote.[178] Children are unified parcels, and they unite with nature in an affective, total experience. Young children love music, love having their mothers sing to them, and they closely engage the other, eye to eye. For Freud, Gandhi, Einstein, Jung, St. Francis, himself, and numerous less original others, he implied that play with ideas and notions, the work of imagination and mental constructions, was best experienced when vacating routine responsibilities to immerse in nature and luxuriate in uninterrupted thought.[179] Einstein, for one, loved the outdoors and found in it a resource that nurtured his thinking. Whether enjoying unadorned nature or reading the psalms, there was to him an "'intoxicated joy and amazement at the beauty and grandeur of this world . . . joy (from which science) draws its spiritual sustenance.'"[180] Thus Erikson equated living in the inner and sensory world and in the world of nature, freed from human artifacts, with joy, beauty, grandeur, awe, imagination, a freed psyche, learning, and creativity.

Immersion in the outdoors is calming; it is a great medium for childlikeness and reflection, a respite from an otherwise chatty world. In numerous asides, Erikson showed his disfavor with a too-talkative species that, emulating Gandhi, would profit from a weekly day of silence. Take your mental life outdoors and into the senses, Erikson seems to say. Talk less. Listen to yourself more. See apart from strictures, enclosures, and others' narrow views. Children and childlike adults exist in the affective world of sensing, loving, and creating. Highly ideational adults may or may not glory in nature, but in such adults reflection and creativity come from silence, from peace, and from an inner space.

Contemporary institutions provide scant escape to permit contemplative, deroutinized mental excursions, particularly outdoors. And, as Erikson himself noted, there is a modern-day bind, for the institutions of adult life sponsor two forms of denial, denial of play and denial of death. Because work institutions are essential to the ways that contemporary adults live out their prime years, this means that most adults are bound to a work life in which they are captive of a "double defensiveness."[181] Adults are denied and deny themselves the free range of the leeway of play and of childlikeness in work. We deny as well the sure, everyday fact that the opportunity to play, whether as a child or as a child-atrophied adult, will not go on forever.

ERIKSON'S GIFT AND SEVERAL BLINDERS

More than for any other topic, Erikson's writing on play and childlikeness capture one's imagery and sense of adulthood as possibility. His was the psychoanalyst's lens, his the connection between cognition and psyche, his an ability to show spatial effects and visual-mental work in the concrete play of children and in the abstract projections of adults. Simply and aesthetically, but not simplistically, he illustrated that ideas are visual-cognitive-psychological constructions and miniature reconstructions, that the public sphere replays itself on a collapsed personal, visual-mental screen. He told of the positives adults leave behind when they retreat from childhood, creating difficulties for themselves. And he showed that many views of childhood are deficit-based but that one can invert the model to reclaim attributes of childlikeness. Reading his thoughts on play and childlikeness is a gift, just as children are a gift. He shows, as none other before or after him, how trust, autonomy, and play within a happy childhood are early and lifelong resources. If less harsh, his message is the same as Blake's. In ourselves and for our children:

> He who mocks the Infants Faith
> Shall be mock'd in Age & Death
> He who shall teach the Child to Doubt
> the rotting Grave shall neer get out
> He who respects the Infant's faith
> Triumphs over Hell & Death[182]

We see in Erikson's concepts a compelling rendition of the ideational playground of adults. But Erikson, then late in his career, sometimes comes across as heavy, prescriptive, and arbitrary. *Toys and Reasons* in particular lacks adequate inclusion of content about the joy of children and of mature childlikeness in at least some working adults some of the time. His text was written for an academic audience, which explains some of its ponderous tone. Yet by viewing adult play only through Erikson's lens, play's vitality seems to flee. For his scholarly *Godkin* audience and in a period that had come down on his thinking rather critically, he had to remain within psychoanalytic thinking, for that is the principal credibility of his view. But how distorting or incomplete this view might be, and how much it may press beyond a justifiable stretch at times, is worth questioning. Erikson himself said he was one with a "psychoanalyst's overtrained eye."[183] We understand this. And he was in the process, in his 70s, of conceptualizing fresh ideas. He said that his *Godkin Lectures,* thus *Toys and Reasons,* the *Loyola Symposium,* and related notes as well, were a "program . . . only a playful vision" that was "one thin lane of approach."[184] Yet when he asks what the adult "must do and be" when he or she plays, his thoughts carry a confining element that play and interplay, in the visioning and work realm he described, is best when it escapes.[185] He conveyed a moralistic set of "shoulds" and "should nots," an Erikson *playism* of sorts.

Related to this is the difficulty that a search for play is completely absent from the actual *Vital Involvement* study, conducted, for the most part, after his writings on adult play and childlikeness were complete.[186] Searching through the Harvard files, notes, interview schedule, and interpretations makes it clear that the Eriksons did not consider play or childlikeness among that group of adults. There is no mention of wonder, creativity, or joy. At most, one finds Erikson's notation of "sensory aesthetic" in the margin of an occasional record.[187] This is both fascinating and problematic in light of our theorist's point that the content and struggles of every stage move on to the next and subsequent stages of the life sequence, in which they are recapitulated in light of then-present issues.

Writing on play, Erikson showed how he linked, combined, and surveyed. He presents evidence of a mode of thinking similar to Einstein's. There is suspension of ego, scanning, inducing, and overview. He sometimes tacked a string of associations and assumptions together. He himself wrote that certain of his work was "speculative."[188] He showed how he played with ideas, sometimes free associating and sometimes searching for word roots to locate meanings. He found ideational relationships among *thea, thauma, theory* and *theatre.*[189] If this places his empirics in question, it also shows a creating mind. It shows as well that it is the human's eventual corruption by categories, numbers, and language restrictions that, in part, leaves us less able to exist in fresh awe, surprise, and wonder at the physical and ideational universe. Imaginative, original discoveries are nearly always made by those who are comparatively new to their disciplines, who are farthest from narrow categories, microscopic lines of inquiry, and rigidity-inducing concepts. Linear aging alone does not bring this about. Erikson himself kept freshness alive longer than might have otherwise been the case because, for a time, he kept his thought in the interstitial web between disciplines instead of entrenching himself within any one.

Yet in his notes Erikson implied that his own years of overdiscipline, of hard and focused work, had taken its toll on his playfulness. He might have added that play and childlikeness must and will exit when one's work narrows thinking to the width of one's shoulders. Adults can see and entertain only so much of play, interplay, and ideas, much less childlike joy, abandon, and awe, when they are encased in any one ideational playground, however free and engaging that sphere may be. The restrictive way in which he viewed play may well have been a result of his driven nature and of working very hard to conceptualize children's and adult's development.

It is also important to recognize that, in writing about the space to play in work, Erikson's notions about Newton, Einstein, Freud, and other discoverers apply best to upper-echelon thinkers, those whose cognitive development, skills, and credentials permit a latitude of choice in occupations, whose personal capacities and work climates engender thinking abstractly, who have the luxury of rather expansive time to reflect as they perform their jobs, and who are comparatively free from economic pressures. The Erikson who insisted that adults must have the space and freedom to play within the work zone is the same theorist who noticed that in various discoverers play with ideas and notions, the work of imagination and mental constructions, is best experienced on vacating routine responsibilities, immersing in nature, and luxuriating in uninterrupted thought.[190] We take no issue here. Vacating, either literally or ideationally, in order to work freely is of the essence. But such is not the daily experience of adults who grind away on assembly lines or heavy machines, who toil in hourly service, or who are pressed by daily production deadlines. It is not the case for those whose jobs, and perhaps cognitive development as well, sire only concrete thought. Economic necessity always obliterates play and *Spielraum;* concrete thinking begets more of the same.

Important as well is his reminder that play in the adult psyche means the ability to stand back, wake up, and learn to be conscious of what we are doing in an ongoing way. Developmentally advanced adults can observe themselves. They see themselves as real persons who interact genuinely with others. They understand the difference between flawless technique and its products and the use of such to exploit the world, others, and themselves. They understand as well that humans live in a societal context. It is not unusual that when Erikson moved from his microlevel of individual humans to their collection in the U.S. aggregate, he saw democracy too as a form of interplay within limits. To our theorist, it is a dynamic in which the "executive, the judicial, and the legislative . . . fight with each other constantly."[191] In this societal dynamic he captured structures, interplay, and tensions not very different from those of the warring id, ego, and superego.

One great blinder appears throughout his writing. Erikson's concepts on child play and childlikeness come from the male view of mid- to late-twentieth-century psychoanalysis and through his study of himself and other men alone. It is a lopsided view. Erikson himself wrote that, as a rule, women are more privy to the inner workings of the psyche and an inner life. They are more "soulful" and introspective than many men. Women, unless they are busy emulating men, have free and flexible egos. Women rigidify less readily than men and do so later in life. Why then did he miss the possibility that many more women might remain playful and childlike than is the case for men? Young mothers play with their children (as do many young fathers these days), and we see their joy, wonder, and smiles when they do so. Do not these mothers, perhaps particularly those who are close enough in age to their own childhoods to remember them clearly, rediscover their own childlike qualities in the abandon, glee, and total trust of being with their infants and toddlers, in effect absorbing those attributes to find and reinforce such qualities in their hidden selves? As a male who was immersed in a male-normed view, who was focused and work immersed and frequently absent from his own children, his tilt to the male side of experience is understandable but unacceptable.

This recognition leaves unsaid, if only for the moment, the fact that until the end of Erikson's writing years, he considered anatomy as one's destiny. He interpreted early play constructions and later themes as gender representations. Women have an enclosure, an inner, (uterine) space, whereas men have an outer, projecting reproductive tool. To him the inner space and the outer projection are seen in the forms and configurations of gender-typed childhood play and, variously, in later life as well. Thus anatomy was inescapable, a dated agreement with Freud's thought.

Despite Erikson's several blinders, the final words here must reiterate the gift of Erikson's message. We abandon play and the child inside at considerable risk. Benign neglect brings rigidity. Malignant neglect fosters cynicism and a willful disregard for the radiance of play in our work, for the child in ourselves and in others, and for children around us. The consolidated adult work we do and the way we live out our lives is a great crossover system that in overcompliance endangers its own resilience. Absence of leeway, in work, in community endeavors, or at home, and limitations in the interplay one is permitted and within which one is considered human—trusted and autonomous—seriously harm the psyche and inhibit functioning. We can hope, as he did, that among the elements written into the human code is an affective bond with playing and interplaying children, a quality whose existence makes adults see to the survival of children within and among us.

7

Historically and Culturally Relative Adult

Relativism is *not* the same thing as relativity. For the
person who masters relativity there is a definite order
and obligation to everything he does.

> — Erikson, "Erik Erikson on Play,
> Vision, and Deception"

To have an identity combined with a sense of its own
relativity, now that would be a *new* identity.

> — Erikson, "Jefferson Lectures"

In describing the adult who knows the self as historically and culturally relative, Erikson portrayed a highly sophisticated person, one who thinks at the
metacognitive level of abstraction, is knowledgeable about history and cultural differences, and cares to be insightful about and open to other persons
and ways of being in the world. Such an adult perceives that he or she lives in
the total stream of history, in one unique life history, and in one sociopolitical
system that is skewed culturally and era specifically. This is an adult who functions amid a disorienting awareness of distortion, who knows that his or her
own way of living and of seeing things is particular to one cultural-societal
niche, to one childhood and adulthood in one life, to one upbringing, to one
social position, and to the one historical period in which he or she was somehow deposited. It is also the adult who is not narrow of mind or so self-
centered that he or she cannot place his or her unique self in someone else's
perspective of role, culture, or way of viewing life. Necessarily, this adult understands his or her biases and groomed need for them, all the while renounc-
ing ethnic, racial, class, religious, and historical superiority.

Erikson believed that few would entertain and live with relativity as a preferred way of thinking and of viewing phenomena. But from his early studies of Sioux and Yurok native life and of German and American national characteristics in the 1930s and 1940s, this *was* the view he tenaciously pressed. Running counter to some interpretations of relativity, he held that the adult who appreciates the true meaning of relativity, of living as one person within a great universe that holds a "'manyness' of outlooks," must be principled, for living with such disequilibrium requires knowledge, as well as solid ethical footing and functioning.[1] To the person "who can think in relativity and act in it . . . who masters relativity, there is a definite order and obligation to everything he does."[2]

Among cognitively undeveloped or less knowledgeable adults, among those who are parochial or intolerant of differences, and among the unethical, a misunderstanding or intentional misuse of relativity and its tenets can readily deteriorate into relativism. Erikson isolated three primary forms of relativism, those of judgmental moralism, of an "anything goes" narcissism, and of anxious "nihilism," the last of which harbors the uneasy conviction that existence holds no meaning.[3] By 1970, Erikson identified narcissism as a growing disorder and trend, one that he saw in the character neuroses of individuals and, structurally, in the consumerist, possession-driven mentality of American society. In particular, he warned about the influence of narcissistic "enthusiasts," those who learn superficially about, but do not comprehend, the psychosocial relativity that was inspired by Einstein's physical relativity and by expanding knowledge about cultural differences.[4] At their worst, given to "rationalization" and "opportunism," such persons misunderstand that, in all of its complexity and stringency, relativity does not mean lapsing into or condoning situational pragmatism, a human chameleon with the mantra, "What works is good and what feels good is better."[5]

An originating psychoanalyst, Erikson functioned at two large-scale, intersecting, and previously undeveloped crossroads of developmental thought. The first of these is the point at which evolution and the social history of the species meet the present. This historical crossroads holds remnants of the genetic, developmental past, and, in each person, carries a sense of some collective past as well as a remembered, a *memorial*, conscious and unconscious individual past. The second, simultaneous crossroads is that at which one form of cultural, racial, ethnic, or societal human meets another. It was Erikson's view that the entire species, in its great historical length and cultural breadth, had to understand and accept itself if it was to ever come together. The all-human species had to somehow see itself both in location and connected, earliest-to-latest human and here-to-the-far-reaches-of-the-globe human, if it was to stop murdering itself. Thus he identified two wide-reaching polarities that live and breathe in each adult, those of "wider, *universal* identity vs. ethnicism" and of historical relativity vs. era-centrism.[6] Envisioning the positive side of each pole, he held that in true maturity, adults would be more inclined to avoid criticizing or trying to reshape other persons' and groups' perceptions and behavior, just as they would eschew reconstructing history to judge adults from prior times as somehow deficient against later-day knowledge, understandings, beliefs, and conduct.

In this chapter, we consider the culturally and historically relative adult separately, understanding at the outset that one includes the other. Erikson modified some of his views over time as he saw from within his own changing lens in one lifetime against altered social values, expanded technology and communications, greater media penetration, modified transportation and mobility patterns, increasingly dispersed living conditions, and heightened class and cross-generational separation. Nonetheless, although his writings span a half century of changes, they largely show a consistency in viewpoint and approach. It is this continuity in thought we consider, avoiding those arbitrary or dated points which, if incorporated, would detract from, if not sabotage, his otherwise unified view.

CULTURALLY RELATIVE ADULT

Erikson illustrated that each person is embedded in the fabric of family, culture, society, and nation, that for some persons in some areas and times, this fabric is homogeneous and integrated, whereas, for others and in different eras, the fabric is loose and heterogeneous. Culture is both inside and outside the human. It is inside the individual's ideational and linguistic psychological apparatus and is integral to the way persons construct and perceive their reality. Culture is external to the self as well, for it exists in the shared notions of a group's ideas, symbols, values, modes of thought, and behavioral norms. Further, the physical environment of landscape, spatial attributes, and topography is internal to the self as well, for these enter and feed each psychological structure and idea system with terms and metaphors and with ideas of free-ranging opportunity and access, restriction, exclusion, and danger. Erikson held that in a number of primitive groups, the geophysical topography feeds collective and individual ideas and leads to magical beliefs, superstitions, supernatural constructs, and "parallel" ideas in which persons build associations between the external land, outcroppings, space, rivers, and oceans and internal human anatomical structures, their strength, and functioning.[7]

When he visited the Yurok and the Sioux, Erikson found that geographical and spatial ideas infiltrated and distorted natives' ideas about the external world. Such ideas became a guidance system for behavior. For example, early in the last century the Yurok of the Pacific Coast did not know the discrete directions of north, south, east, and west. There was only an "upstream," "downstream," "toward the river," and "away from the river." The Yurok experience of life, depicted in its language and habits, was one of a "centripetal" world in which salmon were central to a small circle of geography. Space was bounded by the rim of sky, which sent forth game, and by the coast, which provided a bounty of shell money. These terms conveyed notions of a geographically restricted, spatially unique zone. Within that zone the natives' actions reflected their perceptions of the topography and its provisions. The Yurok lived in "horror of unrestricted radius"; thus the realm beyond the zone was one in which danger lurked and one dared not venture.[8] Diametrically opposite to the carefully bounded, "centripetal" world of the Yurok, the Sioux of the South Dakota plains lived with concepts that were shaped by the immense prairie they roamed and the language and behavior that expressed it. Ideas of far-ranging "centrifugal" expanse informed their ideas, language, and behavior as they roamed in groups, following buffalo and smaller game.

In technologically sophisticated societies, geography and space are important as well. In the United States, for example, ideas about an expanding "frontier" (to the west and into space), "waves" of immigrants, and its location between two oceans (from "sea to shining sea") are key to a sense of freedom and to isolationist ideas and policies, when this becomes politically expedient.[9] To Erikson, early in its history the massive United States, self-contained on a continent with imposing natural borders, could afford its insular freedom. Its metaphors and individual behaviors, then and now, reflect this. Exploration and expansion, "ranger" ideation, and the equation of a new, spatially separate, independent nation with the "self-made" man who can make many things (including remaking the self again and again) exist in its imagery and in a people's psychologically grounded sense of self. Sensational "newness" becomes an "invigorating" and "obsessive" replacement for absent national ideas about community and tradition.[10] Its democracy, its unique form of "extroversion," and its genial, optimistic attitudes reflect a spacious, open country in which "the sky's the limit."[11] The American imagination could thus become as broad as its continent and as vast as its spirit, success, and messianic zeal.

In contrast, in the Germany of the 1940s the "Maginot Line" and the "Limes Wall" were among the "subverbal" ideas which, as mental remnants of physical barriers, captured individual and national thought to "dominate and narrow imagination."[12] A Germany that was and felt spatially encircled and trapped by its borders led to fears and internal divisions which altered the course of a people. Erikson's point is that national opportunity and threat, historically built, seep into ideas that inform and persuade the psychological apparatus. These reverberate in each person, in family life, and in the nation to yield mutual impressions, shared "slogans," understandings, and a people's sense of past and future.[13]

Erikson's placement of society and the external world as realities that exist within the psyche was a bold leap beyond the Freuds. Although the Freuds credited the importance of the social world, to Sigmund Freud the group was completely external to the self and was only of random influence, however imposing that group might be in swaying thought through mob, crowd, or group appeal. Anna Freud was slightly closer to Erikson's thought, yet to her the group held only some chance, spurious ability to influence but not to infuse and infiltrate human ideas and imagery or the ego's centrality and competence.[14] Erikson saw things differently. He asked how the society of one's life, the culture, and the external environment become internal to the person, how an ethos of cultural understanding is conveyed to the infant, and how this ethos builds as the child grows into an adult, incorporating social perceptions, interpretations, conventions, and a group ethos along the way. To him developmental and psychoanalytic understandings and applications were "deficient" to the extent that they did not take stock of "the cultural relativity of symptoms and adaptive patterns, and variations in external reality."[15]

Thus each person's internalization of reality, particularly as it represents a group ethos, is powerful and persuasive. One's fit within the ethos of the group and that group's fit within the broader national society are critical. To Erikson, *ethos* meant the "interdependence of persons" and the way persons are organized so as to relate to one another.[16] Its "inner logic" of shared ideas, values, mores, linguistic symbols, and customs gives a unified way of seeing and interpreting phenomena.[17] However strange it might seem to those outside the group, each ethos is a nested set of wombs—of family, cultural group, and society—that transports principles of living to infants and children in order to direct, channel, and sublimate behavior. Its modes and values of living wrap together desires, needs, norms, and traditions to infuse each individual's conscious and unconscious. Its consistency makes one's very self and the society of one's life seem permanent, even though both are temporary.[18] Thus ethos is a living code that cements the social structure. It builds uniform views, customs, attitudes, and habits, and, therefore, the "character" of a people.[19] Due to an elongated period of human child rearing, youth cannot help but be inducted into a system that regulates actions, emphasizing some over other forms of behaving, identifying, relating, defending, exhibiting and sublimating rage, and casting off devils. In primitive cultures or in technological, more reason-driven societies, absorbed ideas, early and enduring myths and fables, and learned behaviors that are both explicitly taught and imitated lead irrevocably to an image of the self, family, group, and world and of the self within those larger constellations. These, consciously and unconsciously, inform and power the ego.

When Erikson wrote, he sometimes used the term "culture" interchangeably with "society," whereas on other occasions *culture* meant the tight, partly inherited characteristics and behavioral patterns of a specific, racially separate group of people. In general, *culture* in his work carries three dominant meanings. For an indigenous people living together within a common racial or ethnic heritage, culture meant prevailing mores, beliefs, and traditions that unite. Together these create a collective ideology, a sense of some uniform ancestral past, shared notions about the present and future, and ideas about the Almighty. Most commonly, and early in his work, he wrote about the Sioux and Yurok natives as illustrating this form. It is a *homogeneous* group of people.

For a less homogeneous but geographically contained and linguistically uniform society, culture meant the *volksgeist* of a people, that is, their historical spirit and understandings and the language, symbols, and meanings that had developed, historically, within a nation. One finds this form in his early writings, particularly those about Germany and its adolescents, about Hitler's imagery and Gorky's childhood, and, later, in his writings about Gandhi and India. A sense of *volksgeist* also permeates his thought about the spirit of a *heterogeneous* people, one that springs from and develops along with its nationhood. In this respect, both early and later in his work, Erikson wrote about the United States and its origins as a continent with an ethos of national independence, personal freedoms, individualism, and democratic spirit that, however privileged for some and closed to others, infiltrates bureaucratic, legal, religious, and personal ideals and images.

"Culture" in his work might also reference the *zeitgeist* of the times or of a *homogeneous* age group, that is, an ethos of understanding that cross-permeates a number of countries simultaneously in an era (the Alexandrian Age, the Renaissance, the Enlightenment, the Post-Absolutist Era) or some uniform ideas that hold meaning for a decade of age groups (adolescents, for example, or elders), widely dispersed as they might be in different regions or nations. And he used the idea of culture as *zeitgeist* to denote regional differences as well, for example, in describing regional German people, Californians, or U.S. Easterners, among whom he lived and found particular views, styles of living, and ways of experiencing and seeing life that differed markedly from other areas of each country.

Erikson knew that his findings about cultural groups would soon be dated, for even the most homogeneous, change-resisting group is altered by external forces and new ways of seeing themselves, their society, and the world. The Native American, Germanic, Eastern European, native American, U.S. white American, and U.S. African American characteristics he described in the 1930s, 1940s, 1950s, 1960s, and 1970s were vastly different from those cultures' and their members' sense of things today, as are prevailing views in different locales, regions, and nations. In 1974, he wrote of his concern that some of his terms that were based on earlier times had become "obsolete" in just two decades.[20] Referencing his prior thoughts about the Native Americans he wrote, "Words like 'rehabilitation,' 'relocation' and even 'education' have had their historical time. . . . What all this reinforces in me is the conviction of how important it is to understand the unavoidable time-boundedness of our conceptions and cultural observations."[21] Further, the widespread infiltration of technology and media takes its toll. Erikson was not a fan of either of these forces, finding technology threatening and the media manipulative of thought.[22] He variously wrote that no one living in 1944 sensed the peril of nuclear destruction at each and every moment the way all nations and generations did after the first use of the atomic bomb in

1945. And, as important as the media could be in removing blinders, few living in the United States after the Vietnam War and seeing photojournalistic evidence of its carnage, and few reading about or watching the Watergate hearings and feeling justifiably betrayed, would trust those in power as so many had before. No one could hide or insulate the self again. These were penetrating, inescapable powers that changed life, views, and the psychological self dramatically.

Given that contemporary adults have somehow adjusted to the irreversible fact of living in a nuclear and information age and understanding that many of the Erikson's observations about culture and society are now dated, we ask what he saw that has applicability today for the adult who understands and lives with cultural and societal relativity. What concepts, truths, and principles operate even as societies, races, ethnicities, and the spirit of the times yield to new forces? These overarching understandings fall naturally into two main areas. The first area holds his originating concepts about the conscious and unconscious ways in which culturally and nationally unique ideas portray themselves in individual development. The culturally relative does not change developmental absolutes; yet it plays these absolutes out differently. The second area is that of his metasystems view of the group and the way each group as an aggregate reflects individual ideas, attributes, and a sense of opportunity and restriction. Viewing individual attributes from their collection in any society, Erikson posed that each cultural and national amalgam of persons has a "group ego" that incorporates and reflects individual characteristics, society, and the times. Some such characteristics are adaptive and health promoting, but others are symptomatic of an "asocial" picture and of social and class disjunctions.

Individual Physical Absolutes against Cultural Relativities

Erikson wrote about intraindividual, intracultural, and intrasocietal patterns. He also described differences between primitive, native groups and technologically sophisticated, rationalized groups. In his published writings, he largely avoided straying into true ethnological comparisons of customs, traditions, and folkways that contrast different groups of people. In fact, other than for his comparisons of the Yurok and Sioux natives, he wrote as from within the person and his or her cultural or national group, deviating from this only to provide his rendition of social criticism about national or cross-national threats to developmental health. Thus he functioned more as a developmental Darwinist and an anthropologically attuned psychoanalyst than as someone we might today think of as a cross-cultural developmentalist. Further, Erikson conceptualized the person in and against society to consider the myriad ways in which societal ideas, ideals, and views are sown into the individual psyche in, for example, the symbols a person uses, his or her sense of freedom and individual coherence, and ideas of self.

With respect to individual development, he showed continuities and discontinuities between developmental needs and the ways different societies abet or thwart development. However, he did not pose any specific developmental progression in the way a culture, nation, or spirit of the times might differentially infuse the psyche. And, although some such content is subtly woven into his concepts about the moral child, the highly ideological adolescent, and the ethical adult, concepts about qualitative developmental changes in the appreciation of cultural relativity do not appear in his published thoughts or in his notes. In fact, as was noted for the moral and prejudiced adult, Erikson found conscience and identity development to take one down, not up, a developmental ladder toward maturity of viewpoint and openness to others. Instead of becoming more permeable to and accepting of personal differences born of unique cultural and national settings, too many adults deteriorate into moral, and therefore moralistic, habituation to their own ways of being in the world, becoming critical and judgmental of other ways and persons.

When one searches for the specifics of Erikson's thought that remain current and that illustrate what he meant by cultural relativity, the primary content that emerges is that of developmental absolutes against cultural variance. Erikson wrote that there is cultural and national variance in the intensity, length, and duration of stages of individual development, depending on the traits a given society will emphasize and suppress. However, because the order and progression of development are determined by physical readiness and the way such readiness is permitted expression, the absolutes of universal development in each person meet up with social norms for the expression, sublimation, and restriction of traits and characteristics. There are, for example, universals in the discrete age bands at which an infant will crawl, stand, and walk, develop speech, and, later, communicate with a growing number of people. A universal developmental period exists during which each normal child will be ready to learn the reading, writing, and psychomotor skills of society; in later youth, an established age band defines puberty and excursions into abstract thought. In early adulthood, a wider but no less absolute age period exists for peak sexual interest, fertility, and production of the most normal ova and sperm for procreating. And, in middle age, another universal time-determined age band occurs for the extinction of fertility in women and the waning of sperm quantity and normalcy in men.

Such developmental absolutes meet up with the relativities inherent in cultural expression and emphasis. Child training methods, informal skill training, formalized schooling, puberty rites, norms for procreating and raising children, and social modes for separating from one's young and for aging are the ways that different cultures variously channel and modify impulses, guide and force sublimation of various energies, and synthesize traits. Such channeling, sublimating, and synthesizing lead to cooperation, forms of preferred or thwarted independence, modes of achievement, styles of living, and mechanisms of acceptable or unacceptable displacement. Models of acceptance, collaboration, propriety, and efficiency result. Adults are those who bring the next generation into existence, who design, sponsor, and continue various rituals for child nurturing and training, both inside the family and outside its enclosure. These rituals and methods, a culture's or society's unique ways of patterning behavior and living, of working, playing, loving, and seeing, provide comfort to those inside a culture's protective shell. They offer a solidarity of viewpoint, reduce anxiety among children and adults, and provide the offer and promise of fitting in.

Because infantile, childhood, and adolescent understandings are the "psychological raw material" that each human presents to his or her adulthood and society, and because each culture will choose, stress, and intensify certain infantile characteristics and ways of behaving over others, cultures will look, and will actually be, different from one another in their living forms.[23] This occurs despite the fact that all societies and cultures work with the selfsame physical being whose development proceeds according to a preordained design. Erikson found that there is far less congruence between cultures in the clusters of traits that are highlighted and thwarted than outsiders will choose to believe and to accept. It seems that adults the world over will project their own and their society's preferred views.

Among Erikson's specifics, he found cultural differences in *trait emphasis*, in *stage length*, and in the tendency to adapt children's *developmental readiness* and inclusion needs to group norms. Taking these in turn, in terms of *trait emphasis*, some cultural or societal groups emphasize oral tendencies, other such groups focus their efforts on developing autonomous aggressive characteristics, and some groups emphasize wealth accumulation, either for the benefit of the collective group, the family, or the individual, the latter who "sit in isolation on their possessions."[24] Certain societies more than others depend "heavily on guilt," others on shaming and shunning.[25] These points of emphasis are built into child-training methods and later show up in adults of the society. The various obsessions and anxieties of adults that arise from these are developed and mirrored in the obsessions and anxieties of its children.

Speaking to the cultural variability of *stage length*, in more primitive societies (for example, the Yurok), children who experience extended years of breast feeding show a lengthened trust/mistrust phase. Such conditioning tends toward heightened oral manifestations in adulthood. In mainstream United States, an elongated period of schooling and skill development prolongs the period of identity formation. And, in societies in which arranged marriages are the norm for young adolescents (for example, in Gandhi's India), or in those with numerous teen pregnancies, childhood is shortened and identity short-circuited. In such cases, adolescents care for their young while they themselves are young, their identities loose and undefined.

In addition to variability in *trait emphasis* and *stage length*, Erikson observed that some cultures seem more attuned to children's *developmental readiness* than others. As he found among the Native Americans he studied, such groups tended to match such readiness with skill development and with adult tribal needs. Amazed at the "defeatism" of white Americans, such natives trusted their children to develop in step with the culture's expectations for their competency and participation.[26] Tribal adults were confident that their youth would naturally seek cooperation with the norms and activities of their society; thus there was no need to apply studied methods of subduing and domesticating children or of routinizing them in clocklike precision. To Erikson, tribal natives were adept at matching the child's development of language, of locomotion, of exploration, of autonomy, and of readiness for skill development with tribal provisions for such growth and for inclusion.

Compared with what he saw in the harshness of compatriot Euro-Americans, in "our worries and our warfare with children in homes and nurseries" and our tendencies to pronounce "cruel . . . verdicts of 'constitutional inferiority' on children," the natives were astute in their knowledge and use of developmental readiness, confident in themselves, and generous in their love for the young.[27] The primary preoccupation of the Yurok mother, he said, was "to secure for the child an easy birth and a basic inclination to wake up and live."[28] Among the Crow he found a stable, tightly knit community, one in which children were incorporated early on into an ancestral tradition that provided acceptance and coherence, thus inducing little childhood trauma and anxiety.[29] And among the Sioux, he noted the absence of "hostility" and "verbal abuse" of children in the tender period when the young are learning about their bodies and their relationships to adults.[30] Only later were young Sioux molded to tribal customs. The conscience of each youth then meshed with community traditions and beliefs and was made "strong and durable even under conditions of imposed change."[31] Contrary to the "every-family-for-itself culture" of white America with its various "prisons" of single families, its "isolated places for childhood," and its great divisions between childhood and adulthood, such care and incorporation into communal life made for a sense of oneness with the tribe and among natives of various ages.[32] There one could see continuity and a sense of shared participation, all of which lent an "unequivocal firmness on which mental health is based."[33]

Erikson gave two generic thoughts about the meaning of cultural inclusion. First, cultural homogeneity and inclusion are surrogates for what is lost from the mother. Her earlier "availability, reliability, and firmness" are impermanent, but they are always needed and sought.[34] When there is a self-same coherence with one's society and inclusion in it, the loss of earlier maternal securities can be partially substituted. This is particularly the case when mothers securely "mediate" between youth and society and between society and the child's sense of his or her own later grown self, complete with ideals and purposes.[35] Second, the closer the match between cultural (or societal) traditions, rituals, customs, and beliefs and that culture's development of children's abilities when these are most ready to be developed, the less anxiety will occur among its children and the fewer rifts between children and adults. The history of a people, its economy, and its living patterns are strengthened to the extent that each individual child and adult is strengthened. Coherence in each individual's small universe reflects the coherence of the larger society to which the individual belongs.

Unique cultural methods and styles, however internally consistent, frequently seem mightily "strange" to outsiders.[36] In fact, the stronger a culture, race, or society, and the greater its coherence, the more difficult it is for outsiders to understand it.[37] As though one knows "only the nouns of a foreign language," but not its verbs, adjectives, or clauses, outsiders might glean some sense of a culture's important values and meanings but will not understand what the traits, habits, routines, and ceremonies are actually saying, preferring, emphasizing, and omitting, or why this is the case.[38] Implicit in its traditions are a culture's concepts of space and time. Such concepts unify ideas and beliefs to create some of the greatest differences between one group and another. Each society, Erikson found, adeptly organizes its unique beliefs and just as "cleverly conceals its irrationalities."[39] Beliefs and irrationalities are the nucleus of rituals, traits, child-rearing methods, and ceremonies, of that which is found beautiful and endearing and that which is repugnant. And although a variety of beliefs are "magical," this does not make them any less potent.[40] In fact, outsiders must understand that denying the validity of such beliefs will not diminish their reality or power. All humans have their special version of magic and superstitions. These serve as a "collective mastery of the unknown," permitting us to say almost aloud: "I see you! I recognize you!"[41] Such magic and mastery reside in the group's image of itself, complete with vision and conscience, the latter tailored with a "peculiar logic" that keeps it whole and secure.[42] Vision, self-image, magic, conscience, and mastery—together these preside with "hypnotic power" over group ideation.[43] Sometimes consciously, but primarily unconsciously, we accept our own forms of logic and illogic. Yet humans are remarkable in their ability to counter and resist the existence and importance of such logic in other social forms:

> what to one country appears to be the life and death struggle of a vital vision supporting a hard-won national identity—a vision for which groups of persons will stand together or kneel together, march together, or fall together—in another country may be perceived as not more than a curious revelation of idiosyncracies and pretensions.[44]

In the adult who would work to appreciate cultural relativity, more than tolerance is required. One must "respect the truth" in another as he or she experiences that truth.[45] Not to accept others in their worldviews, cultural-ethnic perspectives, developmental progressions, belief systems, and states of knowledge and experience, replete with magic and biases, shows arrested cognitive development, lack of knowledge, and irrational "ambivalence" at best.[46] At worst, denying others the right to their own unique cultural views shows a "petty and righteous cruelty."[47] Grant others, Erikson wrote, the "charity of identification," for truth is relative, as are our "experiments" with it.[48] And, we might add, we can hope for reciprocal respect in return, whether or not it is forthcoming.

The foregoing synthesizes Erikson's most applicable thought about developmental absolutes against the relative emphases and characteristics of discrete cultures and the call to those who are able and who wish to more fully appreciate cultural relativity. Specifics about the acceptance of individuals in their families and societies appear in his clinical case studies of individual patients, in which he tailored his insight to each person in one unique life and its setting. For such persons, he directed attention to the way a child's or youth's family fostered development and buffered social effects. In this, the family was always central, a cocoon from which the child emerged either whole or battered—sometimes incapacitated. The family itself was his second point of detailed emphasis. A family might be in step or at odds with society. One family might exist in the mainstream of the larger world, accepted, included, and rewarded, whereas, for various reasons, another was peripheral, excluded, and dependent. For the family and its various generations and society, Erikson used two metaphors, the notions of *dovetailing* and *cogwheeling*. *Dovetailing* was Erikson's term for showing how each child's increasing abilities and "strengths" interlock with the strengths of a growing number of persons who are "arranged around" the child, first in the family and then in the expanding radius of school, neighborhood, and social order.[49] By *cogwheeling*, Erikson meant to show how the various life stages of persons interconnect with the stages of other-generational persons and how that series of generational wheels supports and moves each other along through time.[50] At their best, these operate with strength and support, functioning as a set of tightly connected, smoothly fitting cogs that bolster abilities and ease transitions instead of roughly abrading or disconnecting.

The Group Ego: A Giant Reflecting Pool

Moving outward from the person and family and spatially upward to the larger group and society, Erikson, who wrote abstractly about cultural relativity, became even more obscure at the meta-systems level. When he considered the cultural group in this respect, it was in terms of its potential cohesiveness versus loose heterogeneity, a tight identity compared with a broad diffuseness for the individual and its aggregate. Here the idea of a "group ego" enters his thought and, with it, his implication that such an ego is a giant collecting pool that holds, registers, and reflects all individuals egos that live within its ethos. He used the term "group ego" not as a metaphor but as a distinct, if amorphous, corporate reality. "Group ego" is the "organized and organizing core of a culture situated as it is in its constituent individual egos."[51] Three points are essential here: *coherence, autonomy* needs in groups and individuals, and the salience to a culture and its members of *inactivation* and forced dependence.

For the first of these, Erikson wrote that in any culture the "group ego . . . tends to take stock of and synthesize what has been selected, accepted, and preserved."[52] Each person develops and maintains a "conceptual synthesis of the inner and outer environment" and, to a greater or lesser extent, each single conscience is "part of a communal one."[53] The person lives in a social context that either is *coherent* to and with the person, is hostile, non-cohering, inimical and repelling, or is somewhere between these two extremes. Coherence or its absence can exist throughout an individual's lifetime or can vary by periods of a life. For example, youngsters can face the wall of rejection early in life to the extent that they are excluded from opportunities for talent development and inclusion throughout all of life. Or some youths might be fortunate indeed when young, their abilities developed and adapted to societal needs, their skills used, and their talents rewarded, only later, as older, no-longer-useful adults, to be cast aside. Coherence and symmetry with that society is then lost forever. For the person and for any group, incorporation into the larger national ethos is key to synthesis and coherence with the self, the group, and the society of the group and its times.

For the second of his points that relate to group ego, Erikson implied a match between individuals and groups in their needs for ego *autonomy*. If the individual is to become an adult of responsibility, immersed in an identity and in the roles of that identity, one whose ego is free, actively engaged, and whole, personal autonomy is crucial. The same principle holds at the level of the cultural group. For any culture to be "viable," its autonomy and a concurrent "sense of free will" must exist.[54] Thus there is a parity between the cultural group's needs for autonomy and those of each person; one reflects the other. This concept is important to Erikson's belief that democracy and a wider, all-species identity would have to eventually replace ethnic identities and their respective, narrow homogeneity if humans were to move beyond prejudice and each groups' insular sense of self with its own brand of autonomy.

The third of Erikson's points is how a group of people, and therefore its pooled ego, can be *inactivated*, in effect forced into a dependency existence of sacrificed autonomy, passivity, and loss of the essential spirit that once gave it energy. His best example of this in terms of culture, symbols, and the livelihood of a people is that of the Sioux. There were, Erikson wrote, "three inseparable horsemen of their history's apocalypse . . . the migration of foreign people, the death of the buffalo, and soil erosion":[55]

It is said that when the buffalo died, the Sioux died, ethnically and spiritually. The buffalo's body had provided not only food and material for clothing, covering and shelter, but such utilities as bags and boats, strings for bows and for sewing, cups and spoons. Medicines and ornaments were made of buffalo parts; his droppings, sun-dried, served as fuel in winter. Societies and seasons, ceremonies and dances, mythology and children's play extolled his name and image.[56]

Sioux customs, ideas, beliefs, roaming behaviors, child upbringing, and a cherished standard of living had been based on the "age-old abundance of game," which vanished at their own hand and on the intrusion of the white man, who made an otherwise "'natural' change traumatic."[57] The American natives of the plains would comprehend very gradually that the foreign, bleached-skin invader was a permanent occupant of *their* land, that he would not turn back to cross the great sea over which he had come. In some respects, they were like Americans of the 1970s who waited in vain for the giant steel mills to return. Reversal of circumstance was the only way to reclaim a life-sustaining tradition.

Not only did the white man stay, but he corralled Sioux freedom, curtailed their nomadic life, imposed his schooling and standards of achievement, and made them dependent on him. Their "group ego" was thereby deprived of spirit, land ownership, ways of being in the world, and an ability to support themselves. Forced to their knees and dependent, bankruptcy of autonomy led to passivity, depression, and forced accommodation to the "economic problems of the lower strata" of some other society.[58] Further, white society had foreign, rigid notions about the meaning of achievement, which it imposed on Native children. Boarding school requirements and children's forced removal from parents and tribal ways aside, foreign standards led to passivity and minimal success. Americans required a "perfectionism" of them that "we would hardly ask of ourselves, and . . . the acquisition of our neuroses."[59]

There are two salient messages for today: First, the defeat of autonomy and of what a group holds high as the standard for its communal ego defaces the group and each person in it. As was true of the Sioux, this leads to depression and may result in rage turned inward as "self-torture."[60] Group ego annihilation leads to self-abuse, which punctuates the loss of self and an end to "overt revolt" against the usurpers of freedom.[61] For the person and for its group, constricted opportunities and forced dependence necessarily lead to psychological "defeat."[62] Second, when those in power insist on "perfectionism" in a striving accomplishment system that is foreign to a group's concepts of development, appropriate behavior, and progress, mere "surface achievement" is the likely result.[63] There can be no ego vitality when duty requires subservience to others' ways and models.

HISTORICALLY RELATIVE ADULT

From the beginning to the end of Erikson's writing life, history proper, each person's life history, and the meeting ground of history and psychology were enormously important to him. In the first chapter of his first book (*Childhood and Society*, 1950), he told how and why adults must understand historical relativity and claimed that in the psychoanalysis of persons and in psychologically understanding society, historical appraisals are essential. In the text of that chapter, he showed how a crisis in 5-year-old Sam was "identical" with his mother's deepest conflict, and how dormant, long-standing conflicts born of a family's perceptions of its race's history and of the contemporary fit of that race in the larger society met up with crises in the family and between its generations.[64] In young Sam, and later in the chapter, describing a war-stressed marine whose ego fracture echoed childhood traumas, he showed how a person's body will comply with deep-seated psychological experiences, needs, and fears to sabotage the ego and to produce physical illness. Although a person's concern may be primary to one of the three giant biopsychosocial systems and processes, it is codetermined by "its meaning in the other two."[65]

By 1957, Erikson was making his first full-scale psychological excursion into history proper, or "psycho-history" as he purposely hyphenated the bridge terrain in which one discipline meets the other. His hyphen meant a "compost heap," the interdisciplinary endeavor through which fresh methods and a new field of sustained inquiry can bloom.[66] To Erikson history was a remnant of, as well as a negotiator between, each current era and the personal mind and life. Thus psycho-history was not the application of one to the other field but a meeting ground in which the processes of history and of development join up to interact and influence each other. Pulling a person out of his or her own history and out of history proper, as clinical and social studies tend to do, augers against complete understanding.[67]

Erikson was attracted to Luther as he would later be to Gandhi. When he returned to clinical work in the late 1950s after studying Luther, the reformer's conflicts, and era, he said he was "not the same."[68] He knew personally and felt deeply that history is palpably connected to each and every person. For each cohort of adults who finds itself planted in one historical period together, there are shared views, understandings, and perceptions that differ from those of other age groups living in coexisting generations and that differ once again from persons in distant centuries. That is, highly variable understandings are born not just of linear time but of historical variance and of era-specific and life-stage ways of seeing. Just as no one can know another without understanding his or her memories, no one can know earlier adults without understanding their views and beliefs within the prevailing ethos of the times. History does not lodge persons in a period and leave them there unattended but works from inside as well. It winds its way into and through psychological interpretations, remembrances, a sense of one unique life, and the deep meanings that arise from where and who one is and was. One's life and its values interact with and reflect the times.

With a developmental psychoanalyst's depth, Erikson pressed an elaboration of Collingwood's view that "'history is the life of the mind itself which is not mind except so far as it both lives in the historical process and knows itself as so living.'"[69] To our theorist, a mind that lives in and assesses history exists in "systematic subjectivity" to its subject.[70] However it might aim for objectivity, the subjective reigns over and clouds the objective.[71]

Therefore, he wanted cognitively able adults to lift to the level of conscious awareness their approach to history and its information, to develop greater appreciations of historical relativity, and to understand the needs of their own unconscious selves as they look at the past. What, he asked, are the concealed "value implications" in our efforts to understand history?[72] How might we better understand how some who speak for their eras manage to frame immutable messages even in the face of change and seemingly insurmountable resistance? How might we understand the relativity of our own work, views, and the motivations that exist within our unique positions in the life span and in our eras as we also learn to become aware of the work, views, motivations, and life-stage relativities of the various key actors in history? And how should we frame all of this against those who wrote down the events and of the historians who reviewed and interpreted it all?[73] How can we make explicit the understanding that some events were recorded whereas others were omitted, a fact which is inseparable from the points of view of the recorders themselves? Such knowledge requires a conscious awareness of the systematic subjectivities that preside over each person's view of the historically relative. To this Erikson added a Hippocratic obligation. We are responsible to the past, he wrote, to not damn an era or violate another person's being. As much as the present, history deserves that we do it no harm, that we leave its principals in at least as good a condition as we found them.

Clearly, Erikson was not a reconstructionist. His great gift to psychological historical interpretation was to define the adult who appreciates historical relativity as one who understands that we cannot hold up a mirror to look backward over our collective shoulder, in effect seeing and reshaping the past according to later-day views and knowledge. Doing so signals one or another deficit—inadequate cognitive development, insufficient understanding, thoughtlessness, moralism, or arrogance. It shows an era-centrist supremacy of time, place, and knowledge. This applies to facts and theories, as well as to various ways of life and perceptions: We do not have the "right," he said, "later to judge a theory 'wrong' which, rooted in the spirit of its time, has established a firm first step essential to all later theories, attuned as they may be to *their* time and its dominant or contending world images."[74] Nor should we, as we nonetheless do, indict earlier thinkers for purposely spoiling our later endeavors that belong to a far different era and way of seeing.[75] An adult's thoughts are always related to the "main currents" of the era, to the "mood" of one life and period, to the existing "moral climate," and to the "lineage" of thought and discoveries that had occurred up to that point in time.[76] Each era has its own inner "logic."[77] As is true for other aspects of human existence, no one is impenetrable to the surrounding world and era. Thus the past is a stage seen backward in time, a visualized retrospective that leaves past values and perceptions intact. Agreeing with Daniel Boorstin, Erikson held that history is not a mere collection of dates, events, and words but a series of scenes through which adults can understand the ways our predecessors confronted timeless and "ancient problems" of the species, minus later values and vanities.[78]

Yet every era "recreates history" in terms of "what it needs the past to have been" for its present and future people.[79] This historical rethinking serves the future as a guidance system. Other than by connecting each of us to important others in our personal lives and collective past, sometimes in service to narcissism, the past is useless unless it projects forward to a desirable, hoped for, "predictable" future.[80] In that past-to-future connection, mentally recapitulating the past permits a society and world to retain worthy elements and to discard the harmful. History against the future foretells actions worth repeating and errors that must not be duplicated.

As is true of the culturally relative, adults who think within understandings about historical relativity face the challenge of Einstein's centipede, of walking on many legs—here and now, there and then—nearly suffering paralysis due to the difficulty of simultaneously self-observing and looking back at their prior selves and other prior selves as they try to labor forward. Such adults see the self in personal history and in all of history, a subjective view of subject and of past subjects and objects. This view is distorted by the past's intrusion on the present, by its interaction with current needs and motivations. We remake our memories, Erikson wrote, seeing the past again as we believe it was and reinterpreting it in light of present needs. Importantly, significant persons from the personal past come to live with us again in the persons of those who are currently important and are here with us today, a largely unconscious transference phenomenon. Thus even the adult who is highly attuned to history, that is to history proper, to its relativity, and to living in one historical niche in all of living history still yields to the unknown unconscious and to various unknown motivations.

The person who appreciates historical relativity endures living with a great complexity of thought and understanding. Yet the difficulties are somewhat less arduous than for appreciating cultural relativity, for history removes emotion from the equation. Those from prior times are not among us; they cannot grate on us with their peculiar traits and habits, with different ways of seeing and of being in the world. They cannot argue with us or usurp our terrain. And we can excuse the dead, almost deceiving ourselves that they did not know things nearly as well or care as deeply as we do today.

Erikson's view was primarily that of each person in society and times and of one period against another. Although he was not explicit, his notes lead us in the direction of two interpretations that apply developmentally: First, that a deep interest in the past comes into its own in the middle years of life; second, that some highly abstract, metacognitive adults heighten their cognitive development in life's middle years, partly based on their own prior cognitive development and partly because some such adults are unique in their abilities to perceive the self in the flow of all history.

First, adults unconsciously merge all of history and the history of their childhoods into a unified "time environment," a consolidation that is one and the same.[81] We "fuse" our personal past and the great generic history into a combined "pre-history" which, for each person, becomes the "child-hood of mankind."[82] In that blended past environment, one structures an arena of past "helplessness" and humiliations against current masteries.[83] The unification of historical zones, of the personal and the generic, is one that lengthens with expanding life. As the adult grows in years, always ex-tending the time left behind, history itself lengthens, and so do the connec-tions and similarities one sees among various human behaviors and events. The adult mind operates to distort, in part repressing and suppressing the emotions of childhood, wishing to never again feel as small, powerless, and incompetent. Having grown a rational mind, adults deprive themselves of the awareness of their own complete histories and of the sensual knowledge of the world before it was overly rationalized and thus swept too clean of af-fect. Nonetheless, as adults' time in life expands, as their histories lengthen and their insights into human behavior in history deepen, they develop greater interest in history proper. By the middle years of life, what we might term *historical sentience,* a peak awareness of history itself, comes into full bloom. The relativity of one life in one cadre of interlocking generational lives is now posed against the lives of all who have gone before, and adults become philosophical, positioning themselves in a linear, metaphysical se-quence that goes beyond the current context. Not only does one then gain a "comradeship" with persons of prior times, with their quests, desires, bat-tles, and demons, but such continuity also reduces anxiety: Joined in history, we are not alone in the universe as we had feared.[84]

Because the "I" is "the experiencing center," there must be some abun-dance in "I time" behind one in order to best appreciate and understand his-tory.[85] For this reason, a deep affinity for history and an interest in learning more about it come to the fore in the middle years of life. As the denial of death slowly evaporates, replaced as it is by the understanding that life will end in the not-too-distant future, middle-aged adults engage in history telling, sometimes accurately and sometimes with improved renditions. Telling history makes values durable, somehow immutable in the face of cur-rent and expected change.[86]

The second inference that surfaces applies to cognitive development. Al-though he did not say so, Erikson's thought leads to the conclusion that among cognitively advanced middle-agers, the expansive scope of past time that arrives with that period of life interacts with a highly abstract thinking apparatus. Together these integrated attributes lift such adults' mental ex-cursions to a higher rung of the cognitively abstract ladder and deeper into meta-understandings about historical continuity and relativity. Implied is a thinking elite, one that will be reduced in size by the proportion of per-sons who are self- or era-centric, who lack insight or interest in historical processes, or who are concrete thinkers.

The great mass of adults may not be able to develop their cognitive apparatuses in order to appreciate ideas with the full complexity that is required. For his own part, Erikson believed that most adults lack either the ability, the interest, or both. They learn only enough about advances and engage only in such thought as will be sufficient to make them anxious, as he believed remaining at the superficial level will do. In fact, most of us reduce thought, cherishing one or another side of a complexity so much that the other must be excluded. In U.S. society one of the great continuing anxieties is that, in accepting a theory of human evolution, with or without its ancestral lineage of hairy primates, such acceptance necessarily excludes a deity and that deity's creating hand. If one were to attempt to influence such either-or thinkers to place their mind's eye within the relativities of each era, against its available knowledge, and within its "cultural, scientific, and technological conditions," the further demands of such knowledge and thought complexity, with the added requirement of a nonmoralizing openness to alternate ways of being, would be resisted and, along the way, greater anxiety evoked.[87] As we know, anxiety frequently deters one's quest for further knowledge. A downward spiral is initiated. Partial knowledge leads to anxiety and anxiety to the reinforcing of one or another of life's preferred reductions.

When we ask what it is besides the awareness of historical relativity and our obligations to it and to earlier adults that Erikson would have us bring to the level of consciousness, his key points fall into three main areas. First, there is the fact of historical change and adults' resistance to it; second is Erikson's claim that each era brings forth its unique psychological pathologies; and third are the adult's needs and abuses of those persons whom history has elected as its great. We consider these in turn.

Resisting Change

As for other social scientists of the mid-to late twentieth century, Erikson was acutely aware of the increasing rapidity of sociotechnological change and the personal disorientation this brings. In fact, change interested him greatly. He was primarily interested in how individuals and whole groups of people keep their preferred views intact and resist information that might challenge their biases and lead them to accept diverse others. He illustrated this in his concepts about the pseudospecies mentality, the prejudiced adult. Particularly in times of great and threatening change a people will cling to the ideas, preferences, and fears that shore up the uniqueness of their own special group and its attributes. Backing away from others, retreating deeply to their kindred kind, fear and hate of other kinds of peoples become pathological. And, Erikson wrote, fears, as the "conditioning" element in group ideation, are conveyed from one generation to the next; they are transmitted more readily than memories.[88]

Related to his points about the prejudiced and the highly moralistic adult, he wrote that all adults show an age-related decline in the ability to adapt to change. Adults become habituated to their preferred ways of thinking, biases, and habits. Comforting and protective, these are difficult to disgorge. Further, an enormous difference exists between high-speed technological and, thus, social change and the snail's pace of human evolution. In many respects, humans are physiologically closer to their hunter-gatherer ancestors than to the requirements of a fast-paced, jet-speed, computer-accelerated era.

Erikson concurred with Freud that the superego, the moral and moralistic part of us that is based on earlier traditions and on the parental conscience, is that which maintains continuity with that past, holding onto and transmitting ancestral convention. In this way, the superego is that which "resists historical change."[89] Adults fight changes in tradition and in what they see as correct. They greatly fear "deconsolidation" of their achieved adult roles, ways, and privileges, shoring up their preferred patterns and building great bulwarks against any revolution which they did not help to inspire or advance.[90] And, because their own risk-taking, revolutionary spirit left them along with the exit of their youthfulness, superego is now sturdily in charge. All comparatively small changes, as well as larger revolutions, are fought with near equal vigor.

In this way, adults are always in the position of staid change resistance, whereas youths are at the vanguard of innovation. In fact, adolescents are the very vehicles of social change. As each life meets history proper, youths together share experiences that their elders have not known. Unified in ways that an increasingly heterogenous and divided group of elders cannot be, youth forces the older generation to follow along. Change is youth's standard, its slogan being "with it."[91]

Thus older adults are soon "outdated" by the vitality of the young and their "possession of the future."[92] Time is on the "side" of youth and so, it seems, is history itself.[93] Among the young, a self-possessed sense of control and mastery, an autonomy stage in fresh garb, declares itself newly and forever free of its prior adult captors. Adults who have nurtured the young, if not their change-invoking ways, unimpressed with youth's brashness and opposition to mature standards and to them as adult standard bearers, find themselves in the position of resisting both the changes and those at the helm, youth itself.

Depending on the times, the young might either herald ideas and ideals, issues and values, with confrontations, demonstrations, marches, protest, and dissent in loud and blatant demands, or they might incorporate themselves into changes already in process and, feeling identical with such changes, help them along. The United States saw the first of these forms in the civil rights and Vietnam War protests of the 1960s and the second in the current computer revolution with which youths feel at home, having grown up integral to its technology. Look to the songs and music of each new generation of the young, Erikson suggested. These tell what is important, inspiring, and abhorrent to the young and frequently indicate where their passions congeal and their spirit will lead.

Because every relationship contains a measure of ambivalence and opposition, so too in the aggregate must youths establish themselves in opposition to parents, teachers, and older values. To develop ego agency, a sense of being central, in charge, and nonperipheral, they must keep elders at bay—in effect, ruling the rulers. They do this by stepping outside traditional standards and meaning systems to create their own meanings and traditions which will later fall at the hands of their own children. Thus the adolescent relates the self to the "ideology" and the technology of the day, whereas the adult is tied to the superego, to that which is linked to the "morality of yesteryear."[94] Youths' high ideology recaptures the "fantasy" they had put aside with their toys and childlike ways. And in their newly created ideological matrix, they integrate ideology with peer identifications to substitute for the mother with whom they had once felt integral.[95] As they break with the past to structure themselves and to restructure society, new utopias enter life. Youthful passion and fresh forays into reason combine with an attraction to change and to risk.

In addition to youth, another group is important to change. This is the elite of society, those who do not enact change but, in their prerogatives and privileges, their advantages and license, signal ways of behaving and freedoms worth usurping. Here Erikson followed the lead of the German sociologist Max Weber, who showed that, in their identification with the rights of the elite, the masses gradually insist on such privileges for themselves. Thus, Erikson wrote, "there came to be something of the French chevalier in every Frenchman, of the Anglo-Saxon gentleman in every Englishman, and of the rebellious aristocrat in every American."[96] Near the end of his writing years, Erikson watched as the world became a smaller place due to high-speed travel, media penetration, and migration. He believed that the overarching idea of democracy was the one value that was replacing separate cultural values, intragroup homogeneity, race, and class. The ideal of democracy was the new elite, a set of cherished freedoms that all peoples of the world wished to own. Democracy had replaced status as the preeminent privilege.

History as an Asylum

"History," Erikson said, "is a gigantic psychiatric hospital."[97] In that particular statement he referenced the way singular leaders in history have been able to ride their own and their era's conflicts to speak for the period. Such voices were raised for the people. But Erikson also meant that history is not a bland composite of passing times, events, and places but a choir of muted distress in which those with mental disturbances sing forth the problems held in common by all persons in their society and epoch. In effect, such illnesses give a "critique of the period."[98] Pathology and its various symptoms are related to values and goals, to how each era permits certain personalities to thrive whereas others crumble under its various pressures.

As is true of other areas of his work, Erikson wrote in generalities. When speaking of era-specific difficulties, he did not provide hard data. But he did say that the possessed of ancient times showed the problems of the biblical era, the hysterics the sexual repressions of Freud's day, the "schizoid characters" the distress of a "mechanized" era, and the more recent "plastic" character disorders the difficulties of the postindustrial world.[99] In all of these, society's values and its core pathologies are "two sides of the same ethos."[100] Whether or not we wish to look at them and consider what they tell us about the larger society, the disturbed are a lens into the value struggles of the era. Such struggles and pathologies exist at some level in every person in society.

Further, in his Harvard papers Erikson claimed that the pathologies that are typical for a society and a time may well represent the larger community's pattern of stage-related emphases. A society in which mistrust and cynicism reign may favor "delusional addictive" disorders, those given to emphasizing shame over autonomy, the "compulsive-impulsive" pathologies, and those which stress guilt more than initiative, the hysterical pattern.[101] He knew that it would be impossible to assess the extent to which the earlier, more primitive psychological apparatus showed its pathologies through hysteria, conversion reactions, or possession by devils. In fact, many such disturbances evaporated with industrialization and a better educated populace. But, although Erikson gave us a near-impossible relationship to study, it would be hard to explain away his points. When egos are invalidated, inactivated, fragmented, or isolated, the absence or destruction of social support and interchange are certain to have preceded pathology.[102]

Erikson held that U.S. society, with its legal structures and rules, is embedded in Stage 2 development, autonomy versus shame and doubt, replete with do's and don'ts, quid pro quos, diagnostic labels, and categorical exclusions.[103] Those who fall apart under such pressures are set aside; the disturbed and the failures among us are sometimes lumped together in a depersonalized way. Gaining insight into such effects lifts the conscience of a society, he wrote, perhaps leading to at least one form of a more "inclusive identity."[104]

The claim is not that those who suffer as the mentally distressed examples of a society's and era's problems are less able or potentially less vital. Rather, they are the more sensitive among us, the weather vanes and barometers of the special strains each period will wield. Society's pressures, as they are evidenced by those who are mentally incapacitated, must be looked at and carefully attenuated so that all persons, the distressed and the normal, are supported and validated. If the key neuroses of each era show an "*inverted revolt* against the values of the existing order," if patients are those who are most "inactivated" by the "inner conflicts" that operate in every person, the "traffic" between society and the inner world should be assessed.[105] We know the importance of understanding the way persons are accepted and supported in their interpersonal networks. Information regarding such acceptance at the societal level seems similarly important. The human is permeable to society and interacts with his or her community and its values. If Erikson presented a difficult problem for study, such knowledge is nonetheless an important part of every intelligent adult's repertoire, important information that begs inclusion in conscious awareness.

Needing the Great

As his psychobiographies show, Erikson was deeply interested in revolutionaries, creators, and leaders in history who were exemplars of insight, ethics, and justice. The gifted men about whom he wrote helped move humanity to a more inclusive identity. With decisive spiritual and political leadership, they changed largely negative identities into positive, affirming identities. Their indignities about repression of the masses advanced a principal cause of their times. Thus he chose to write about Martin Luther, his book largely a construction that considered the traumas and contributions of one of the great borderline personalities of history, and about Mahatma Gandhi, the latter-day originator of nonviolent resistance.[106] Shorter works and notes show his interest in the intellectual vitality of Einstein and the political leadership of Jefferson, in the originating Freud and the philosophical Kierkegaard. Summing up his own life's work, he cryptically noted that "eros" was Freud's theme, whereas the wider identity was his own.[107] Erikson was primarily interested in those who showed the way to a more inclusive rendition of humankind.

The question that concerns us here is why adults so need those they can call great. What power and image do such persons have that we find absent in ourselves? Why do we hallow them and curse them, raise them up and then cast them aside? For those few who put themselves at great risk in order to change history itself, what do they awaken in us and how do they, with all their human needs, rise above the masses to express and to show what others feel but cannot say? What is it in all of this that adults who appreciate historical relativity might bring to the level of consciousness in order to understand themselves better?

Two points about Erikson's interpretations bear stating at the outset. First, he said little about how the great come to see themselves as historical revisionists and revolutionaries. Along with the great gift of artistic expression, Erikson, like Freud, believed that greatness defies analysis. Second, in appraising contemporary leaders or those who are immortalized in the history books, he felt that adults should look at their own transference onto the great. Once we look directly at the contemporary needs in every age to bestow the word *great* on some few visionaries, leaders, and originators, we can no longer so easily conceal the similarity between our own small-scale traumas and those who lifted their conflicts to central, large-scale proportions. Clearly, such central figures become our ego ideals. But why do we call them great, why "surrender" to them, erect statues of them, and later revise them in our books, sometimes finding them so flawed that we wonder about our initial impressions? And when does the ego ideal enter our developmental world?

It is in the play age, the third stage of psychosexual development, that Erikson found the ego ideal to enter each person's world for the first time. Trust/mistrust have been met, and autonomy/shame and doubt internalized. Now, with the entry of the two counterplayers initiative and guilt, each child begins to establish that which is worth looking up to and emulating, ideals worth striving for, and purposes worth serving. The ego ideal builds through the stages of childhood and is revitalized with each new form of competence. In adulthood, the ego ideal of the self is counterposed against the ideal counterparts in the adult's era and against those who have been relegated to history. Looking to history, great creators, discoverers, and originators serve us differently in different periods. In the first phase they appear heroic and nearly flawless. As historians rewrite history, such historic egos are forced to comply with then-current needs as their biographers successively amplify one aspect of a personality or contribution and subdue others. Some historians will reconstruct the past and the great altogether, arbitrarily forcing both to comply with later values, ideas, and discoveries which the prior time and its key persons could not have experienced or understood.

Erikson's view of the role played by the great was the same as Freud's, that the superego of an era is:

> based on the impression left behind by the personalities of great leaders—
> men of overwhelming force of mind or men in whom one of the human
> impulses has found its strongest and purest, and therefore often its most
> one- sided, impression.[108]

The great lift their own conflicts and neuroses to a grand scale and ride them for all to see. They give content to what adults might become if they were not locked into various infantile needs. They permit us to see ourselves as the heroes we wish we could be instead of the weak and crippled cowards we fear we are. Perhaps due to a lengthy childhood, we humans always seek older persons to endorse the "license" we take.[109] As for the great, they "flatter" us, allowing us to share in their likeness, an image which we helped to shape.[110] The great are also a grand mirror of sorts, showing the timeless problems of humanity in their era's unique way. Yet such leaders seem able to control the conflicts that hamper others and, in so doing, release the common adult's vitality. Particularly in those in whom one finds some similarity of personality and views, their struggles and high values seen in light of our own will reaffirm our convictions and actions in a harsh world. Thus the great validate and liberate adults, freeing the better side of each self to do battle with the demons and doubts shared by all.

It is not that great leaders do not have their problems. In fact, they have what Erikson called "oversized identity problems."[111] Earlier conflicts with their own fathers were often deep and troubling, in many ways making them the parent to their fathers and a spiritual parent to all. Showing great energy beset by restlessness, they seem a conduit to immortality itself. Appearing to face death unflinchingly, they temporarily permit all others to deny its existence. Their self-love becomes "charisma," their very "illusions" "shared utopias," and their belief in "omnipotence" an energetic aliveness for those who follow along behind.[112] They work on such a grand scale that contemporaries fall by the way, for few can face similar problems in such self-solidarity or with such zest.

Thus the great create images for all. They and their ideology bolster individual egos among the masses.[113] Believing in them, one can trust the self, including the personal ego ideal which now can better keep the paltry id and the negative identity at bay. And the great grow greater still to the extent that they show great empathy with humans in their plight, are contemptuous of personal ambition and self-gain, and show the way to a joint future that proceeds from the fragments of the past. Thus will adults love and cherish their portraits and sayings, words and deeds, holding them and their gifts in superior esteem and crowning them variously—until we find, as we do, that they too were flawed and imperfect.

As for the great, they need followers to give their work significance. Here Erikson noted that the human is not an "isolated 'closed system.'"[114] Followers project on the great some "unlived" and "unrealized" aspect of themselves.[115] Renewed in mastery, feeling momentarily lifted from the mediocre, those who are vitalized will lift their leader up just as he or she lifted them. Followers create a grander-than-grand image of the leader and, with near-adolescent idealism and awe, portray an icon, a guru, a saint, and a savior. But this station is most temporary. It exists until we no longer need them or until we need them in some revised version.

COMMENTARY

Erikson's gift was to show the necessity and the discipline of consciously understanding each culture unto itself and each era in history as unique to its times, discoveries, and ways of seeing. He reminded his readers of the human tendency to project personal experiences and views in era-centric and ethnocentric ways, proclivities that auger against understanding historical relativity and the wide identity we share as a species, if in different patterns of emphasis. He extended his early work on the cultural uniqueness of the Yurok and the Sioux into his psychohistorical studies. There the artist, the "radical man" who "had wandered into psychoanalysis," wandered into history, having become "bored" with his life-stage scheme and its "egotistic" qualities.[116] He then took up his friend Margaret Mead's admonition that his life-stage view was too "closed" a system, that he had to open its edges to permit historical variation.[117] We have profited because he did so. He straddled the thin dividing line between radical relativism and cultural or era stereotyping, sometimes showing the strain of attempting to say anything about a people or period without typecasting either one. If anything, he was closer to the dangers of cultural than of relativistic excess.

Three critical comments are in order. First, writing on the topic of relativity, itself difficult to pin down under the best of circumstances, Erikson's tendency to write amorphously without crisp detail magnifies problems. The reader continually struggles to find his meaning. Erikson himself knew this but had ongoing difficulties with precision.

Second, with respect to historical relativity, Erikson wrote in terms of one's position in recorded history. This is a Western-world lens that does not include the view of those who see the self in many cycles of progenitors, immortals, and eternity itself. Erikson did nod in the direction of an Eastern worldview in *Gandhi's Truth*, but that nodding was partial at best. His view reflects Western European and American society alone.

Third, Erikson was self-critical about his own work in one important dimension. Of necessity he had assessed those leaders in history who, by virtue of autobiographies and voluble center-stage activities, had provided a wealth of material for analysis. He knew that this approach, as essential as it was to his work, "disqualified" from appraisal those who worked in silence and within the restrictions of national security.[118] Thus his choice of leaders, particularly of Luther and of Gandhi, yielded information based on high profiles and self-reflective writings.

Except for these difficulties, Erikson's was an observer's analytical eye and an innovator's mind. Before it seemed conceivable to think in such a way, Erikson was writing about the cultural, social, and topographical landscape that exist inside the psychological human. And, for psychohistory, although he said that history writing has always carried some implicit psychological approach, Erikson made explicit an approach and a consciously psychosocial way of thinking about history, its changes, and its era specifics. His subtly planted message that a developed adult is one who will press the self to think in terms of both a culturally and a historically relative view takes us to new understandings and a higher level of developmental thought.

8

Insightful Adult

Insight begins in oneself.
— Erikson, "The Leverage
of Truth"

Considering that Erikson held adult insight in high esteem as the preeminent quality which makes one more human and humane, he had less to say directly about this attribute than about other characteristics and renditions of adulthood. He held that insight development is necessary if one is to understand the self as one who is prejudiced, is less than optimally childlike, and tends toward the moralistic and the historically, culturally biased. However, although he described insight at those outcome levels, he said little about the process, that is, about how one goes about developing insight. Erikson himself said that his theoretical work was lacking when it came to defining and elaborating insight; yet, because he emphasized this attribute as a capacity and tool of the highly developed adult, insight requires our separate consideration.[1]

Insight is "discernment."[2] It is "heightened reality."[3] As a perceptual talent, insight is the ability to see behind the immediately apparent and below surface manifestations. It requires appraisal, the ability to be introspective and analytical, and an observing, reflective intellect that cares to see to the heart of a matter and to the inner nature of things. Insight requires "an active attitude of contemplative inquiry."[4] It demands "systematic self-analysis" and "systematic self- awareness" as ongoing tools and depends on senses, on the emotions and empathy, and on listening with the heart.[5] Insight is the dual "power or act of seeing into a situation *and* into (the) . . . self *at the same time*," an act that searches inward and outward in unison.[6] To Erikson, insight is separate from rational knowledge and exists on a higher plane. Thus it must be valued as a separate entity and nurtured as such. Using Kierkegaard's thought, Erikson implicated insight as the principal developmental tool that moves adults to the ethical level of behavior. Developmentally, movement from engaging in the youthful interests and passions that absorb the self to the higher plane of functioning within ethical commitments requires a decisive, conscious turn in behavior. The higher plane is generativity, and the turn of being toward functioning as a generative adult is based on insight, that is, on the perceptual awareness of one's responsibilities. Thus insight and its correlate in ethical behavior define and describe adults who develop a higher consciousness and a commitment to conscientious action. From that plane of development, retreat is unlikely.

Erikson frequently associated insight with intuition, with the tacit, unspoken, and unprovable sense of things. In this, intuition was frequently an immediate perceptual sense, as well as a form of disciplined "personal judgment."[7] In its immediate form, intuition is a sudden awareness, a response to subtle messages and to perceived relationships. A "sudden synthesis," it is "the 'aha' experience . . . not an entirely logical step but a sensory and sense step" in which there can be a "revelation, that is, a sudden inner flooding with light."[8] But insight can also come about as the result of a more prolonged probing and searching, a disciplined listening to one's inner voice.

The world of enhanced insight is found by looking deeply within oneself as one looks outward and listens carefully to the way the external world reverberates inside one's perceptions. That external world might be jarring or harmonious; it may be disquieting or comfortably concordant with one's interior psyche and one's sense of how things should be. When relating to others, insight requires that one develop consciousness about where it is that the other exists in his or her position in life and context as that life stage and social condition resemble or differ from one's own. This requires adults to very nearly reside within the other to experience that person's uniqueness in the perceptual world and social context. It is impossible to fully abandon one's own life space, but in a "self-analytical" and "analytical" alternation of experiencing the self and then the other, the other's motives and needs reveal themselves, as do the perceiver's own desires, motives, and prejudices.[9] Erikson held that this was the one way to see the good in another and the positives and negatives in the self. Experiencing the other requires subduing censorship of the other and of oneself. It requires the ability to intentionally hold onto gleaned impressions while delaying their interpretation and judgment. Insight thus requires that one not alienate others or the self. One attends to the senses with an inner eye and mind, listens with active receptivity, and gives credibility to perceptions. This permits an intuitive picture to emerge in which one trusts what feels right or wrong, truthful or distorting.

Insight, Erikson held, balances knowledge. He accepted the Socratic premise that insight depends on, but occurs after, knowledge in the learning sequence. Although knowledge alone can enslave humans, insight takes us beyond knowledge, for insight is an "inquisitive approach by which we learn something essential about ourselves even as we master the facts around us."[10] This, to him, was true mastery, for insight requires learning how to "master nature" without destroying the species and nature, all the while facing the fact that there is a lower, irrational, and self-serving essence in all humans, oneself included.[11] Thus insight requires one to accept the existence of a variety of unknown traits and motives which characterize the self. Adults have to accept that there is a functioning unconscious in each of us, a substratum that moves us and of whose role we are largely unaware. But Erikson also meant working to glimpse and understand the unconscious as a condition of self-mastery. This means that aware adults will then understand how it is that each person's "secret guilt and repressed rage" prevent true insight.[12]

Of necessity, insightful adults understand that the fear of losing control terrifies each of us at some deep level. A sense of being in control is something that one works to develop early on in life, and maintenance of such control is a perpetual need throughout all of life. But it is the fear of losing such centrality, authority, and power that hampers the adult's "ability to be magnanimous," accepting of others, and unprejudiced.[13] At its extreme, forcing the control of "infantile dependence" on others only achieves the opposite effect; it makes adults less free than those held captive.[14]

Erikson held that many women are superior to men in possessing and demonstrating the gifts of tacit, perceptual insight. More empathic and compassionate, gentler and more peace-loving, they showed him a "finer discrimination for things seen, touched, and heard."[15] Equating the inner life and "inward mind" with the "domain of women," he credited women with the ability to find the "Ultimate" in the "immediate," for they more readily discern the needs of others and respond to those needs.[16] But Erikson also equated female anatomy with destiny as had Freud, and he interpreted the interior domestic household spaces that he saw in female play constructions as reflecting the "inner space" of a uterine compartment. Both interpretations are sadly dated, old bromides bottled in Freud's pharmacopeia as structural, anatomical determinism. The product of a paternalistic era, until late in his life Erikson did not see his own error in this respect. Then, in a shaky handwritten note in the margin of a previously published article found among his Harvard papers, he wrote "embarrassing" about a statement that had placed women in a dependent, infantile, and unequal position.[17] However, despite having concluded that he had made this error, he never changed his mind about what he saw as the direct correlation between inner and outer space, a remnant of the Freudian school and, perhaps, of his early interpretations of Yurok topographical imagery as well.

As for the male gender, men are too partial to "'what works' and . . . what man can make, whether it helps to build or to destroy," he said.[18] Keen on their machines and on penetrating into outer space, Erikson held that empathy comes to them with difficulty, as does insight into their own prejudices and "defensive maleness."[19] "The culmination of male dreams," he wrote, "is to intrude into God's space; into the Cosmos!"[20] Insight development is hampered by male aggression, by a masculine love of objectivity and "machine tooling," and by men's addiction to "mercantile" competition.[21] Men are too easily controlled by the very technology and business trades they had created and are blind to the ways in which these manipulate them.

If insight comes only as a lopsided gift, as a talent with which one is born and which, without good genes and preferably the female gender, is impossible to attain, then one half of the species is left in a rather hopeless, nondevelopmental condition. This was not Erikson's contention. It was his premise that enhanced awareness and heightened consciousness can lead to insight, assuming that one is adequately motivated. He implied that some adults can themselves nurture insight development whereas, in others, guidance or therapeutic help are needed. Erikson described himself as a visual person who garnered a gestalt of impressions.[22] His own perceptual acuity came through the use of himself as an "instrument" with a "band of receptivity," he said.[23] To him it was a condition of insight development that each person had to learn the best use of his or her unique receptive abilities while also learning the obligations of intruding into another's world. Never abandon sensory awareness, he said. The sensory complement "sharpens our awareness."[24] Without the senses there is a "vacuum of impressions," and one is easy prey to "indoctrination" and "thought reform."[25] Erikson did not trust thought that had not been digested and appraised by the senses, for distortion, lies, and vanities are only revealed when one engages all of the self.[26] The total self includes the sensory apparatus that many adults discard en route to maturity, qualities they scuttle along with their imagination, creativity, trust, and other childlike attributes. As a result, adults are only "selectively aware—(they are) overwhelmed or deprived of sensations."[27]

Critical of his own field, he reminded readers to appraise discoveries in terms of the context of the times in which those discoveries were made, in light of key originators, and in terms of the contemporary state of knowledge at the time of discovery. Because Freud's originating thought was dependent on energy dynamics, Erikson held that Freud had made far less of the human's various affects and sensory modalities than of instinctual, sexual attributes and their presumed quantities. Wanting intellectual parity with the sciences, Freud had placed little emphasis on sensory knowledge, on empathy, and on grasping a comprehensive overview in the form of an "active and intuitive 'beholding.'"[28] Further restricting the adult, Freud had required his patients to recline on a couch, with himself well beyond their view. This was primarily because he abhorred patients' tendencies to stare at him. This motive aside, his method deprived those seeking help from using their eyes as they garnered impressions. The Freud school deprived adults in other ways as well. Erikson agreed with Margaret Mead who, early in their professional relationship, expressed her concern that, to Freudians, the person has no limbs, only orifices.[29] Freud's total view excluded the arms and legs that permit one to actively move about, and, I might add, to touch, feel, and experience the world. Thus it is a further deprivation which, when coupled with that of the visual, depletes one's full awareness.

We must recognize that although Erikson's concepts extend considerably beyond Freud's, his too are lodged in that early psychoanalytic school. This may explain Erikson's incomplete efforts to codify insight as a developmental process and to fully elaborate the talents, sensory knowledge, and perceptual awareness that are included in the full composite of abilities which are now referenced by the single term *insight*. To him, insight was process and product. Insight alerts us to "what is worth studying, and it is also what emerges from our studies. If we put together everything we know, we still need insight for orientation and action."[30]

INSIGHT AND ETHICS

Erikson's one book that has the word *insight* in its title (*Insight and Responsibility*, 1964) says little about the development or demonstration of this quality.[31] But in its frontispiece, the author quoted Shakespeare in *Measure for Measure* to tell the reader what insight ultimately requires:

> Heaven does with us as we with torches do
> Not light them for themselves. For if our virtues
> Did not go forth of us, 'twere all alike
> As if we had them not.[32]

Although his message was indirect, an elaboration of his dedication of the edition to Anna Freud, who, he thereby implied, had shed light onto his professional pathway, Erikson meant that insight necessarily requires ethical performance in which one shows others the way. Ethics is shown by the profound commitments of life, thus by the qualities of middle age. Ethics comes after the passions and interests of young adulthood, themselves an important step in the developmental sequence. However, to him, young adults' passionate beliefs and convictions are more likely to be held within the mind's eye of the ideological self and, as such, are largely devoid of sustained, action-engaged commitments. Ethics, on the other hand, requires both ideology and active commitment. Responsible, conscious, long-term, committed actions emanate from ideological principles and passionate beliefs and are forged by the insight that life holds adults accountable at the behavioral level.

Yet the passionate interests and deeply held convictions of young adulthood are important, for insight emanates from the fervor of profound beliefs, from the principled convictions that begin in the high ideology of youth.[33] In fact, holding onto one's passionate feelings and convictions was a lifelong requirement, something Erikson found absent in those who attended only to the intellectual compartment of life. Erikson cited two examples of intellectual lopsidedness in Bertrand Russell and Charles Darwin. In later life Russell deeply regretted his lost ability to feel deeply about concerns, whereas Darwin felt that he had lost his esthetic sense of things, having become a lopsided "theorizing machine."[34]

Unfortunately, Erikson was highly abstract in describing what he meant by ethics. He seems to have wanted readers to reach their own conclusions about the meaning of such commitments in their own lives. Like the highly abstruse Kierkegaard, Erikson also may have feared that expressing his thoughts specifically would bring the "most dreadful contrasts into action."[35] But pinning down his few specifics, he precisely said that "the ethical consolidation of adulthood is based on insight" and that, by ethics, he meant a guidance system that moves adults beyond mere "blind obedience" to the precepts and requirements of others and to what one must not do.[36] One had to enlist the self in an "insightful assent to human values" held in common and to work thoughtfully, with reasoning well intact.[37] To him, a preeminent value was that of recognizing the wider all-human identity which binds the species and to which committed work is required. Always, ethics and working to invoke cherished human values were affirmations that led individuals and the species forward. The passives and negatives of what adults did not and must not do had to turn into the active positives of engaged effort.

Ethics is the "final ego-ideal of adulthood," an active ego-ideal that embodies social justice and truth in action, one of Erikson's reasons for exploring the adult life and political activism of Gandhi.[38] Ethics, he said, "is transmitted with informed persuasion" of others and with social modeling but cannot be "enforced with absolute interdicts."[39] But ethics also means that one can and should feel free to use "indignation" as a "tool of adult care," a tool that is "sharpened by knowledge and insight."[40] Thus there are times when objective distance has to be abandoned, when the care of and for others insists on our intervention, in theory, in research, and in practice, in order to improve conditions for those who are harmed by individual, personal circumstances or by unjust social conditions at the collective level.

Although he did not elaborate on the idea publicly, Erikson believed most strongly that ethics is built into the evolutionary process at the individual and at the species levels. Ethics is as inherited as is "our instinctive and instinctual equipment."[41] It was in the order of things ahead that adults would learn to foster and to care for the inborn ethical capacity which, when insight joined up with "political organization," would necessarily result in a universal idea of species-wide humanity.[42]

Kierkegaard in Erikson. In his ideas about adults' developmental movement from the passionate aesthetic to the committed ethical based on the use of insight as a developmental tool, it was the existentialist Søren Kierkegaard who supplied Erikson's theoretical model. Writing in the first half of the nineteenth century, Kierkegaard described beliefs, sensitivities, and early convictions as a form of passions, feeling tones, and interests, an aesthetics of youth and of the first stage of adulthood. One can either immerse in one's passions and follow appealing interests that are satisfying and ego gratifying or one can place such interests behind one developmentally and move forward to work within, and through, one's ethical commitments. This is Erikson's generative adult in full form, the cynicism-aversive adult who engages the self in the work of the world. The generative is the developmental stage that occurs before the final stage of psychosocial life; it is a stage of the continuing, but slowly fading, denial of death, as one clings to the daily functioning that requires such denial. This bridge period of the middle years is one in which the adult develops the profound insight that personal products, progeny, ideas, and the gifts of self to others are all that can be left behind in this world.

Kierkegaard "inspired" him to make a "serious and methodical turn to social and political conditions."[43] As a result, Erikson said he knew that he could not live a mere aesthetically interesting existence, although this would have been pleasing and might naturally follow from a "stepson's" tendency to avoid belonging, to continue working between disciplines. He felt that he had to transform certain concepts within their social dimensions to show, for example, the origins and meaning of prejudice and to contribute to understandings about nonviolent strategies. Thus he made a "conceptual turn" away from theoretical and clinically applied psychoanalysis, his "aesthetics," toward the ethical work of studying and revealing the "social and historical implications" of the revolutionary thought and actions of Luther and Gandhi.[44]

Kierkegaard's stages of adulthood move from the aesthetic to the scientific, and from there to the ethical and then to the religious. These are closely related to Erikson's sense of the passionate intimacy of young adulthood, the ethical generativity of middle life, and the spiritual integrality of the elder years. The self is not static, both thinkers held, but evolves in qualitative leaps as the person develops from the aesthetic through the ethical into a religious (Kierkegaard) or spiritual (Erikson) being. To both thinkers, the subjective and intersubjective were superior to the rational.

With respect to insight's role in leading one to the ethical level, Erikson was an avid student of Kierkegaard's thought, witnessed by the nearly 100 pages of notes, clippings, and thoughts about Kierkegaard as a thinker and as a case study in his unpublished Harvard papers. Erikson showed interest in Kierkegaard's mental aberrations, in the philosopher's concept of polarities, of stages, and of the successive unfolding of stages, and in his ideas about sympathic and antipathic tensions which, in Erikson's thought, became the positive, or syntonic, and the negative, dystonic, tensions of each life stage. In Kierkegaard, Erikson found the idea of adult evolution and qualitative becoming. This is an active process, a self that "relates to itself," one that is partially preconstituted by the Creator but which alters itself through its own agency and through commitment to some compelling idea.[45] In the "Journals," Kierkegaard said, "the thing is to find a truth which is true *for me*, to find *the idea for which I can live and die*."[46] This is Erikson's "individual . . . choices and decisions which will, with increasing immediacy, lead to a more final self-definition, to irreversible role pattern, and thus to commitments 'for life.'"[47] In important respects, both thinkers described an identity that, in the middle years, becomes a generative identity.

Kierkegaard's three stages of adulthood—the aesthetic, the ethical, and the religious self—are adult orientations in which forward movement from one to the next occurs because one recognizes and assents to obligations and because one becomes more aware of the eternal and of the "Ultimate" Other. Kierkegaard's aesthetic is a close match to the content of Erikson's "Intimacy-Isolation" stage of young adulthood. The young adult engages the pleasure, pathos, and passions of life. Here are lodged the beginnings of insight and of ethics that will drive one toward generativity. Insight, Erikson said, is an outgrowth of "passionate experience" as much as it is based on perceptions of content and obligations.[48] "Care," the strength of the generative adult of the middle years, unfolds from "love (that) . . . pervades the intimacy of individuals, and it is thus the basis of ethical concern."[49]

Kierkegaard's ethical stage conforms to Erikson's middle adult, who lives with the tensions of generativity and stagnation. To Erikson, ethical consolidation is the developmental telos to the morality of childhood and the ideology of adolescence. Now in the center of caring for progeny, ideas, commitments, and other products of adult life, the ethical adult can do no other than nurture these. Kierkegaard did not specify exact commitments or what the ethical self must become, but, as for Erikson, that philosopher had meant ethics as action. In the "Journals," Kierkegaard wrote that "the highest of all is not to understand the highest but to act upon it," a commitment that both the philosopher and the psychologist found in the caritas of Christianity.[50] Kierkegaard maintained:

> To the Christian love is the works of love. To say that love is a feeling or anything of the kind is an unchristian conception of life. That is the aesthetic definition and therefore fits the erotic and everything of that nature. But to the Christian love is the works of love. Christ's love was not an inner feeling, a full heart and what not, it was the work of love which was his life.[51]

That interpretation is very close to Erikson's illustration of the ethical person through the life of Gandhi: "Now what Gandhi meant by truth would be impossible to discuss in brief—if at all. 'God,' he once said, 'occurs to you not in person, but in action.'"[52]

To Kierkegaard, ethics required decision, intention, and behavior. Ethical positions and actions are consistent in Erikson as well, based, as in Kierkegaard, on insight. If one is perceptually aware of something, this is but an essential precursor to the responsibility that must follow. To both thinkers, choices must be made, a turn to the ethical as a path. *Actuality* was Erikson's term for describing interaction, shared participation, and mutual activation, a mirror of Kierkegaard's *ethical action* and *actuality*.[53] Both stake out a moral high ground that leads the adult to use the self as an instrument which validates and activates self and others.

In a number of other ways, Kierkegaard was Erikson's resource. In both thinkers we find successive stages for the adult. Kierkegaard calls these "Stages on Life's Way," in content and processes that anticipate Erikson's stages of adulthood and their commitments.[54] In both writers, each sequential stage does not replace the former. It builds on earlier stages. Life is that which is "successively unfolding."[55] This sequencing is one that Erikson called "successive differentiation" early in his work and "decisive unfolding" in later editions, a combination of the philosopher's words.[56]

Kierkegaard was not a practicing therapist, but Erikson credited him, not Freud, as the first psychoanalyst. Erikson, on the other hand, frequently addressed clinicians directly, requiring more than adherence to the Hippocratic injunction of *do no harm*, itself a rather passive absence of action. Instead, therapeutic action had to go beyond inactivity, leading to insight and to transformed perspectives for both the clinician and for the patient.[57] Generalizing beyond clinicians, Erikson portrayed ethical action expansively for all whom he could legitimately call *adult*.[58] He was most concerned about adults' responsibilities to develop a new relationship to children:

> That shift in self-awareness . . . cannot remain confined to professional partnerships such as the observer's with the observed, or the doctor's with his patient. It implies a fundamentally new *ethical orientation of adult man's relationship to childhood*: to his own childhood, now behind and within him; to his own child before him; and to every man's children around him.[59]

It may well be that his own childhood experiences of rejection led to his sensitivity to children in general and to how societies can deprive them of acceptance, inclusion, and, ultimately, vital identities.

THE NET EFFECTS OF INSIGHT

The principal effects of insight development are found in awareness and mastery of the self, in perceptual acuity about other persons, external surroundings, and events, and in the ongoing tendency to study human behavior and motivations. In this, one uses equally all the powers of knowing, not abandoning the senses but giving them equal berth along with the reasoning brain. This is "wholeness," complete use of faculties and peak self-knowledge. It is not surprising that Erikson also equated such wholeness with mental health. Insight is that which keeps the adult "indivisible," aware of self and of others, an active, central player in the unfolding drama of life.[60]

Insight development means self-knowledge about one's own motives and "inclinations," that is, an adult who will stand back, wake up, and become more conscious and honest about the needs of the self and about the self's sometimes unconscious intentions and actions.[61] Here Erikson seems to require that adults become armchair psychoanalysts of sorts. In particular, this demand comes to the fore in his many writings on prejudice. He wanted the adult to understand how much each of us projects the negative identity, seeing all too clearly in other persons that which "one is unable to recognize in oneself."[62] Adults need their resistances, projections, and various other mechanisms of self-defense; these are "symptoms . . . signs of an inner ambivalence of long standing."[63] "If part of us were not on the side of the temptation," he wrote, "we would not need symptoms to defend ourselves with."[64] By "temptation" he meant the wish, however unconscious, to cast off the positive values that long years of childhood grooming had built and which habit had solidified. Positive values are the attributes which one associates with established ideas about virtues. Examples are initiative, competence, industriousness, cleanliness, and socially or culturally specific versions of goodness, manners, ways of communicating, trustworthiness, notions about the divine, and other group- or family-specific merits. Adults castigate others for not having the virtues which seem so clearly manifest in themselves, fearing, of course, that they are not so clearly manifest. In their castigation of others, adults often employ their well-developed "puritan conscience," which, in its moralizing tone, may achieve little more than that of exhausting both themselves and the accused.[65] Meanwhile, the accuser secretly wishes to let down the guard, however occasionally, to become the villain, one who is so mercifully free of constraining virtues.

Further, insight helps us to recognize ourselves as the territorial animals we are. Each person "fights for the territory he has staked out for himself, his place on earth, and his progeny."[66] There are regions and boundaries inside the psyche as well which we variously project on those who dare to usurp the rights we feel we do not have: "In order to be good (we) . . . repress parts of ourselves, that is, create within ourselves areas out of bounds for ourselves."[67] We then project those areas externally for those we believe to have dramatically strayed into territory which we ourselves dare not traverse. In such a way, "we believe it to be a matter of justice as well as logic that transgressors must be incarcerated."[68]

If humans are prone to taking that which is inside, projecting it onto others and the external world, Erikson would have us understand that a two-way street exists. Highly permeable to the social world and its institutions, the external environment enters and lives in the psyche as well. Insight development thus leads to an awareness about the various ways that social opportunity and deprivation infuse the human sense of self and personal notions about future possibility and of the ways in which institutional roles shape adult role definitions and their rigidities. And it seems that insight also serves as a sword that can slash its vulnerable owner, for insight is associated with personal sensitivity. The worldly institutions of commerce and trade tend to "favor" the unsavory and "ruthless," whereas the "more sensitive and insightful" become "enslaved," mere marionettes precisely because they see to the heart of the mercenary game and will not play.[69] The insightful know that all human institutions, however worthy their aims, are self-serving and, as such, exploitative. But such insight, and the concomitant refusal to participate in exploitation of self or of others, also keeps them at the periphery of competitive life.

Erikson expected insight to serve ethics, a turn to the responsible and committed life. But he also held that the peak illumination that comes with insight leads to knowing the self as a spiritual being, a conduit to one's sense of the Almighty and to the extraterritorial realm of the divine. Wanting to understand "religious genius," he had studied Luther and Gandhi, finding in them, as well as in Freud, a higher consciousness of the Ultimate Other, that, propelled by insight, the monk and the political activist credited but that Freud denied.[70] Insight was one of the many tools which "God has given us."[71] Thus it is important to study that tool and to use it fully as a pathway to the Maker.

Erikson required a great deal of enlightened adults, for he wished them to become students of human development, as well as of psychoanalysis. In particular, he held that such adults would see in themselves the content, as well as the positives and negatives, of development. They would recognize that highly defined roles and consolidated versions of adulthood had honed their abilities and skills just as they had also built up various rigidities and a deep resistance to change. They would have the ability to look carefully at what had been abandoned en route to those consolidations, in particular to the lost wonder and zest of childhood and to the trust which various work institutions force adults to relinquish. They would have insight into the ways in which the moral can lead to the ethical through the ideology of adolescence and would perceive the adult tendency to balance an ethical sense with moral imperatives, sometimes regressing fully to the moralistic. Insight into the moral-ethical might well result, he held, in purposeful use of the self as an agent of affirmation. Identity is positive, he wrote. Its absence is found in the negatives of cynicism and prejudice. Belief and faith are positive; doubt is negative. Ethics lets us know what to say "yes" to; morals and moralism tell us what to say "no" to. Insight and ethics together strengthen the ego; they keep the caustic, judgmental superego at bay. And ethics does for others that which will aid their growth, a quantum, positive leap beyond moral reciprocity. Insight thus leads adults to know how to be positive and affirming, to listen for the negatives in their own speech, and to watch for acts that repel. Such awareness prepares them to actively change their words, tones, and acts into those which are positive. Thus, as is the case for other areas of his thought, Erikson conceptualized a stance of nonviolence toward all. This, to him, embodied a truly liberated consciousness.

In many ways insight also defines the wise adult, at least in the changed rendition of Erikson's later years. In wisdom, the insightful adult is and does that which is given in the natural developmental order of things. The passionate intimacy of young adulthood yields to the middle years of functioning as caring, ethical progenitors of children and of other worthy products. Later, an age-advancing elder keeps the integrated self together, an affirming resource to the young. Here then is Erikson's developmental utopia, those wise enough to grow in step with the unfolding possibilities which mature life offers.

ERIKSON'S VIEW IN PERSPECTIVE

Compared with other areas of his thought, Erikson's concepts about adult insight are far less developed. He wrote abstractly and in a product-oriented way, describing neither the process nor the developmental pathway of insight. Nonetheless, he forces a view into qualities of perceiving that few other theorists have elaborated.

Among the positives of his view, Erikson leads one to look to the ways any number of adults have not developed or have abandoned the use of their full sensory complement. His thinking thus gives balance to the reasoning brain. He held perceptual intuition in high esteem as a quality that is much more than what has been denigrated as a gut-level, feminine gestalt. And he makes one consider how nonmasterful adults are unless they bore through to apprehend their own unconscious motives and needs, all the while understanding the extent to which they need a sense of conscious control. There is strength in Erikson's pointing to the thing-world as that which commands attention, blinding adults to insight into universal human tendencies and needs. And, as always, his is a directional pathway that leads adults to recognize a universal, species-wide humanity, a point to which all need attend.

There is merit in his statement that "systematic self-awareness" is an ongoing growth process, just as there is value in forcing attention to enhanced awareness about the self that functions as a receptive tool with Hippocratic obligations. He forces a compelling look to the ways in which the Freudian method of an inactivated, nonseeing person on the couch deprived both psychoanalysis and early developmental thought of qualities of seeing, touching, feeling, and experiencing. And, as a route to affirmation and ethical action, Erikson makes one aware that there are obligations to the years and powers of adulthood, but that it is for each adult to determine what those are. Active energies are required in the work of the world, positive and decisive steps that are much more than what adults understand as negatively embroidered prohibitions.

Erikson's excursion into the ethical takes him well beyond psychology.

He justified that move on the basis of Kierkegaard's existential philosophy. It is a not-so-subtle move away from describing adults to the prescriptive, ethical, and spiritual. In this, Erikson was himself projecting the needs and actions of his middle-age and early senior years, a fact borne out by the dates, as well as by the content, of his writings on insight. However, his insight-ethics connection carries more weight than his insight-spirituality connection. Indeed, becoming attuned to the motives and needs of self and of others may well result in movement to higher ethical functioning; awareness frequently leads to positive behavioral change. But there is little evidence in support of Erikson's contention that insight is a pathway to the Ultimate. It is the case that studies into this human transcendent equation have not been conducted. It is also true that insight expands in the middle years at about the time at which adults show greater forays into Bible study and reading spiritual material. Clearly, this finding of correlation is not necessarily one of causation. Nonetheless, a suspended interpretation may be the best temporary alternative to criticizing his premises.

It is evident that Erikson was incomplete in describing the process of insight as an adult condition. It seems equally clear that insight is one tool of the highly developed adult, that its powers can be credited with heightened mastery. Perhaps sharing some similarity to the vitality of mental health, insight is also best seen in its absence, in those adults who, for a variety of reasons, are ill attuned to their own needs and perceptions and to those of others around them.

9

Wise Adult

Wisdom is justified by her deeds.
— Erikson, "The Galilean Sayings
and the Sense of 'I'"

In his later years, Erikson overturned his lifelong belief that integrity and wisdom are products of the last stage of life. He then acknowledged that as a middle-aged theorist he had erroneously projected forward his assumptions about the fruits waiting at the end of a long, productive, engaged life. As a comparatively youthful theorist, he had held that wisdom, the "oldest virtue," would accrue only to those who had managed an adequate length of life, maturity, and the ability to see events in their historical continuity.[1] Later, as an elder theorist, he realized that wisdom and integrity were "somewhat grandiose designations of old-age strengths," particularly for those facing life's end.[2] He wrote: "The demand to develop integrity and wisdom in old age seems to be somewhat unfair, especially when made by middle-aged theorists—as, indeed, we then were."[3] Thus he abandoned his prior view of wisdom as a "final overview—with some wit to spare."[4] He changed integrity to "integrality," the ability to maintain a sense of wholeness in the face of bodily and sometimes mental and psychological deterioration, and replaced wisdom with faith as the final form of achievable, existential hope.[5]

But throughout his lifetime of writing, the idea of the wise adult figured prominently in his work in two principal forms that he never abandoned. First, wisdom characterizes those who follow the blueprint that nature has given the adult, intimate when young, caring and productive in the middle years, and ratifying of life and some fundamental, learned principles when old. Here is housed Erikson's generative adult and, to a lesser extent, his version of intimate and integrated adults. The paramount achievement of such practical, grounded wisdom is the ability to care for others. Second, wisdom describes those who provide evidence of maturity, sound judgment, and able reasoning. Here the thoughtful, principled adult appears, the person of convictions and of careful, deliberate action. In both meanings, wise adults are those whom others emulate, who show others "the way" to be and to act. Clearly, the best case rendition is the combination of both qualities in the same person. In fact, in many wise adults the two appear as one inseparable entity. However, because Erikson delineated two distinct sets of attributes, these linked notions require separate consideration.

WISE, CARING ADULT: THE ABILITY TO DECENTRATE

Erikson noted how Einstein had described his own change in direction from a concern for self and others to the *it* world of physical principles.[6] In so doing, Erikson implicated his own focus on the adult who could decentrate in a different way, to become concerned about the "we" instead of the "self" and the "it" worlds. This is the adult who nurtures those with and for whom he or she is intimately engaged and ultimately responsible. Such nurturing entails the ability to function in a "post-narcissistic" way, to care so deeply about others that one's own needs are placed off stage.[7] This is accomplished only by those in the central portions of adulthood, in the adult periods when "we are what we love" and "we are what we originate and can take care of."[8] Before and after those periods, the self is focused on the development of the "I" as a unique, comparatively isolated entity. In earlier life, the "I" forges its way toward a circumscribed, individual identity whereas, in postgenerative late life, there is a return to the "I" and its newly self-centered needs. The elder contemplates who the "I" is because of what he or she has been, has done, and has cared for, and each elder contemplates the existential sense of a solitary "I" in relationship to an Ultimate Other.

To the extent to which the adult decenters the "I" in the principal bands of adult life, the "we"-focused adult exists in full form, the person who nurtures others as part of the in-charge generation's dictum of doing that which is given in the natural order of possibilities. That is, wisdom means behaving in accord with personal competencies, opportunities, and requirements at each adult stage. For the young adult, expressing the self in a mutually intimate relationship with one primary other person and joining in intimate friendships within a small circle of like-minded associates represent the ego's wisdom at that point in life. For later young adulthood and in the middle years, wisdom is defined by generating, loving, and caring for children, by creating products and ideas, and by adhering to honored principles and convictions. This, then, is ego integrity, a wisdom of functioning to which Erikson subscribed throughout his lifetime of work. As he said, integrity only "grows" in the person "who in some way has taken care of things and people and has adapted himself to the triumphs and disappointments adherent to being, by necessity, the originator of others and the generator of things and ideas."[9] In this sense, then, wisdom is seen by the acts and deeds of adult life, by the actions and products which are desired, mentored, sponsored, and cared for. By no means is this a fully conscious function at every step of the way. The unconscious informs adult desires and behaviors to such an extent that "What man, at a given stage, had wanted unconsciously, became that stage, and the sum of such stages, man."[10]

Erikson's reference to the "sum" of stages points to his earlier reasons for placing integrity and wisdom last among life's accomplishments. Despite his antagonism to views of his theory as an achievement script, he largely described older adulthood as a result of the younger adult's contributions to his or her own "self-perfectability."[11] In fact, he held to this view throughout his life. He firmly believed that all adults make choices that will either improve their current and later developmental lots or will cause these to deteriorate. Adults can choose to love more and to engage more with others instead of living in isolated self-interest; they can care generously and responsibly for others instead of sequestering themselves inside their own self-serving needs; they can elect to accept one life and its satisfactions over rejection, self-rejection, and disgust. As per Freud's insight, Erikson held that each adult had to face his or her own negative tendencies in order to free the self to deal with the difficulties inherent in one temporary life. Here, then, is the clue to Erikson's choice of terms for the neurotic negatives that oppose intimacy and generativity: "I think, he [Freud] made the point that only when man has faced his neurotic isolation and stagnation, is he free to let his imagination and his sense of truth come up against the existential dilemmas which transcend passing realities."[12] Freud thus supplied Erikson's notion that intimacy counters isolation in young adulthood, whereas generativity opposes stagnation in middle adulthood.[13] Developmental growth and resistance to neurosis always require reaching out to others in the social world and within one's circle of family and intimates. Syntonic, positive qualities (trust, autonomy, initiative, industry, identity, intimacy, generativity, and integrality) are "integrators," whereas the dystonic, negative attributes (mistrust, doubt, guilt, inferiority, cynicism, isolation, rejectivity, and despair) are disintegrators.[14] Throughout each cumulative life, the former will build toward psychosocial unity and wholeness, the latter toward fragmentation and absence of coherence.

It is with respect to parenting and adults' general responsibilities to the next generation that Erikson's points about the wise, mature adult compel the greatest attention. Although he softened his position somewhat over time, eventually implying that adults need not themselves have children in order to show their care and wisdom, he always held adults responsible for the coming generation. Each generation of adults was called to ensure the resource of trust among those in the next generation. Trust is a "safe treasure," a legacy that makes development possible.[15] The child without "trustworthy caretakers" may "'find his thumb, and damn the world.'"[16] Further, it is incumbent on those who elect parenthood to be "tangibly" accessible to the young and to avoid "burdening" youth with the negatives which they themselves had inherited from the prior generation.[17] We "'do violence' to children and arouse inner rage in them wherever we withhold from them a guidance without which they cannot develop fully—or force on them decisions for which they are not ready."[18] Nor should adults require that their children live out their own unachieved dreams, for, in fact, "generativity ends where we transmit the curse of unlived potentials to coming generations."[19] "Wherever we let our children down," he wrote, "we become their demons."[20]

If such other-centered care strikes one as a dramatic form of altruism, this is not entirely the case. Not only do care, love, and concern foster the development of the young, but they are also gifts to the adult self. Adults require the challenge and the gratification of needing to be needed. This lends coherence to the adult's sense of functioning on the central stage of life and provides a sense of participating in ensuring species continuity. The reward of self-verification occurs through such labors. Nothing other than nurturing and caring for children will ensure a measure of immortality; nothing other than cherishing and sponsoring the young will ward off the "deep depressions of middle life" and the despair and self-rejectivity of older life.[21]

Intimacy's Wisdom

Intimacy is the first "we" stage. It depends on a well-grounded ego identity, an "I" that is formed to such an extent that its firmness of self and ideological convictions are comparatively solid. Thereby, intimate joining with another will not threaten the ego's indivisibility. Further, recalling Erikson's theoretical change, it is not identity against identity confusion or diffusion that he ultimately saw as the dialectic that must be resolved prior to intimacy with another but identity against cynicism. Cynics have great difficulty accepting the sincerity and worthy motives of others. As such, they repudiate intimacy, for it is antithetical to engage genuinely and deeply with a loved other all the while questioning that other's goodness and *real* intentions.

Meeting the needs of two partners, intimacy also meets the species' needs for continuity. Thus Erikson found wisdom in the young adult's ability to develop and sustain a commitment to another. Intimacy can be developed in a number of friendships and affiliations as well, but it is clear that love with one cherished other is the ultimate intimacy to which Erikson referred. Beyond mere sexuality, the person expresses a "selectivity of love in a shared identity."[22] In this there is a "mutual verification," an "experience of finding oneself, as one loses oneself, in another."[23] Such unity and solidarity prepare the way for the development of a new generation. In effect, identity now evolves into an interdependent identity. One loses oneself and newly finds the self through a shared commitment, a cooperative style of living, and shared convictions. In effect, the ideological self is reconfigured through its relationship with a primary, intimate other.

A key basis for intimacy is mutuality, defined as the dependence of each partner on the other so as to develop each person's "respective strengths."[24] Mutuality requires an interdependence of will and of resources and the capacity to commit oneself permanently. In this, the ethical self comes into being for the first possible time. There is "ethical strength" in each person's behaving in a way that will honor commitments despite the "significant sacrifices and compromises" these entail.[25] Likewise, polarization of the genders now makes its debut. Earlier developmental strengths are either intersexual or asexual, whereas intimacy achievement depends on the distinct operation of two different sexes who function jointly. Polarity means the differences in the functions of procreation, distinctions which, at best, will integrate and unify the partners.[26]

Along with Freud, Erikson held that only "mature genitality" will result in "intellectual clarity, sexual mutuality, and considerate love."[27] But going beyond Freud, he implied that in intimacy is found the origin of wisdom and of ethical behavior for each human adult. The careful choice of an intimate partner, along with intimacy's products of children, give evidence of who the adult is in that stage of life and at the end. Such commitments and products eventually provide a "last but firm whisper of confirmation."[28] Choices made, commitments adhered to, and children entrusted to the world become a reflective mirror of a judicious, foresighted, balanced self. These are clear indicators of wisdom.

The Wisdom of Generativity

In defining the wisdom of functioning as a caring, generative adult, Erikson departed considerably from psychology. He took the position of an ethicist, perhaps even that of a theologian of sorts, as Gutmann claimed.[29] In effect, Erikson joined the horizontal plane of concrete work and of the ethical behavior inherent in reaching out to care for others with the vertical plane of transmitting principles of worthy living to such an extent that one justifies the self in the eyes of the Almighty. Yet it is his very departure from psychology that permitted him to say what it is that the mature adult needs to have been as the primary resource in that self-same person's postgenerative stage of older adulthood. For without having brought up and cared for children successfully or in the absence of legitimizing one's middle years by productive, worthy, careful work, an old adult will find little joy in remembrances. The fact of too few worthy accomplishments means scant pleasure in what it is that elders can claim for themselves as contributions to the world they will depart. As Erikson found, adults' highest platform seems to be that of the anal station; adults are always concerned about what it is they can leave behind.[30] Thus we can say that, just as the ego holds the self together, keeping it whole, coherent, and unfragmented, the generative years of middle adulthood hold the aging self together, both then and for the later years. As Erikson showed in the case of the elder Isak Borg, the protagonist of Ingmar Bergman's film *Wild Strawberries* and the principal character as well in his own article about Borg's adult life, failures at intimacy and generativity trail along with adults into their later years.[31] Such failures ably seed the path toward despair, disgust, depression, and, eventually, rejection and self-rejection. An elder needs to remember the past as a "visual lullaby" that soothes psyche and soul instead of abrading that elder with details of lost opportunity and failed possibility.[32]

Generativity is a sublimation of genital sexuality. Its pathological absence is "narcissism," a self-love so needy that such adults cannot, or elect not to, transcend their own gratifications.[33] Thus care for others is an ego sublimation that, paradoxically, bolsters the ego. If, as Erikson wrote, "so far in man's total development, adulthood and maturity have rarely been synonymous," here is his version of the mature adult: a generosity of being, a vital interplay with cherished others, and a "we-ness" instead of "asceticism."[34] It is acceptance of a narrowing of choices because of commitments made and a real basis for the mental health of the adult self in the middle and later years, as well as of those who depend on that adult's love and care.

Of note is Erikson's ambivalence about the role of child rearing as a primary requirement for attaining generativity. Originally, he had posed an either-or stipulation: Adults could either elect to engage in "establishing and guiding the next generation" or, in the absence of such "enrichment," would find themselves in a condition of "stagnation and interpersonal impoverishment."[35] By 1963 and the second edition of *Childhood and Society*, he abandoned his parenting requirement. "There are the leaders, of course, and the thinkers, who round out long productive lives in positions in which wisdom is of the essence and is of service."[36] And "there are individuals who, through misfortune or because of special and genuine gifts in other directions, do not apply this drive to their own offspring."[37] Misfortune aside (he likely meant absence of a marriage partner or infertility), his softened stance may have been in response to criticisms of his earlier position or may have been the result of an effort to broaden generativity's definition so that those who could not parent would nonetheless feel responsible for the next generation.[38] Whatever his reasons, his papers show that adults were never off his hook. Generativity primarily means such faith in the species and in the future that adults, all adults, will sublimate their own needs to somehow care for the young and, in so doing, ensure the species into the future. His was an adult developmental requirement that harmonized with a species requirement.

In late life, Erikson returned to his earlier conviction that parenthood is the "procreative core" of generative adulthood.[39] Such care for the young requires solicitude and attention to biological, psychosocial, and learning needs, concerns which have an "invigorating impact on both sexes."[40] Logic and truth are kept alive by performing the teaching and modeling functions.

Because human offspring have such long childhoods, such teaching inculcates children into an ethos of living and a style of relating to others.

Among the dominant contributions such thought makes to understandings about the wisdom of ego investments in the broadest span of adulthood called middle life, two ideas stand out. First, Erikson depicts active psychological energy through investments in and care for others as the person moves toward greater complexity, synthesis, and eventual completeness as an integrated human. Second, the adult is defined as one who is integral to the cycle of generations. Here there is an interlocking reciprocity. The generative adult is now the linchpin, the essential human medium who ensures physical certainty for continuity of the species and for the beginnings of mental health in the young generation. In this view, adults' lives and those of their children are tightly interdependent, for "the generational cycle links life cycles together by confronting the older generation's generativity with the younger one's readiness to grow."[41] "The adult," Erikson wrote, "is so constituted as to need to be needed."[42] The accumulated strengths are essential to the cultivation of strength in the next generation, a task from which the adult gains yet another strength. Thus generativity is a fresh arena for growth. It is an amplified form of Freud's adulthood, which he is said to have defined as a time "to love and to work."

Here reflective, temperate judgments and actions replace erotic encounters and other immediate ego gratifications and interests. Wisdom exists in "maintaining the world."[43] Clearly, this is an ego ideal, that of the ethical adult in full form. The alternative is not particularly attractive, for in it one sees some "retardation" in the ability to develop caring qualities.[44] "The reasons are often to be found in early childhood impressions; in faulty identification with parents; in excessive self-love based on a too strenuously self-made personality; and in the lack of some faith, some 'belief in the species,' which would make a child appear to be a welcome trust."[45] Nongenerative adults frequently become self-indulgent, acting "as if they were their one and only child."[46] In such narcissism, regression may occur to the point of "an obsessive need for pseudointimacy" with the effects of "stagnation, boredom, and interpersonal impoverishment."[47] Psychological or physical "invalidism" may then occur as the manifestations of singular self-care and of pervasive egocentric concern.[48]

Thus Erikson eventually changed the antipathic counterpart of generativity from stagnation to rejectivity. Failing to develop the capacity to determine who to care for, nongenerative adults turn on others as a form of outward rejection and turn against themselves in inner self-rejection.[49] Or, in those who have children, rejection may manifest itself in cruelty toward their own children and in prejudices directed toward portions of the family or community.[50] Such adults tend to repudiate others who are deemed so different from the self that they are considered dangerous, a manifestation of prejudice. On the other side of the coin, there are always some adults who are so unwise as to create or to accumulate more than they can possibly care for. Here Erikson was scathing. To him, it was the propensity of contemporary adults, particularly those of affluence, to create, to build, to garner to the self, and to then uncaringly abandon or discard. It was in old age that he saw the fruits of able care, that of some few things well cared for and of a grand generativity in which adults show an active if detached concern for life itself, for grandchildren, and for the wider species.[51] Old-age generativity holds elders together against the indisputable awareness that their own lives will soon be forfeited.

Wise, Integrated Adult

Despite Erikson's late-life departure from his early claim that "wisdom" is the explicit domain of older adulthood, there are some continuities in his thought that give credibility to a wisdom that continues on from earlier life and, at least in one respect, achieves a higher level. But the main point is that wisdom does not begin in old age if it was not present long before; neither does wisdom end just because one is old.

In the older years of life, adult wisdom is found in maintaining bodily and psychological coherence, in integrating a lifetime of memories, in developing an affinity with humans in different places and prior times, in developing some final sense of faith in the species, and in juxtaposing a newly solitary "I" against the Ultimate Other. "What is demanded here could be simply called 'integrality,' a tendency to keep things together."[52] There is a "timeless love for those few 'others' who have become the main counterplayer's in life's most significant contexts" and, at best, an ability to transcend one life while affirming all of life.[53] There is strength in acknowledging the meaning and power of one human existence, and there is practical wisdom in maintaining psychological order and meaning even as the physical, mental self deteriorates. Here is the greatest ego challenge in all of life, the life period that "leads man to the portals of nothingness, or at any rate to the station of having been."[54] Wisdom is found in an enduring hope in the species and in finding ongoing meaning in life even as it begins to elude one. As existence becomes constricted, identity is limited to what one once was and to one's past contributions, to the vital involvements permitted one, and to the wisdom of some existential hope.[55] Hope exists "in the form of (then, adult) faith as a part of wisdom."[56]

Here is the highest level of development, "one of emotional self-reliance, completion in rounding itself out and in connecting one life to the cycle of generations."[57] It is a return to the "I" and to trust, the essential strength of the first stage of life. Against a very real "tedium vitae," a wearisomeness with life, integration is shown by the ability to find meaning in life while "counteracting" the personal knowledge of "multiple disintegration" from which there is no escape.[58]

The elder pulls inward to the self as a necessary concomitant of diminished physical energies and because of increased introspection and self-assessment. A once-widening social radius is now increasingly constricted as friends die, commitments decrease, and energy is parceled out more sparingly. Through seeing backward to an intimate and a generative self, adults turn inward to nurture one ego, to bring it to some final fruition by integrating the past of the self with a feeling of embeddedness in the species and its ongoing evolution. Here, then, a higher level is reached in one respect. Adults can gain overall understanding and perspective only through experiencing the cumulative periods and requirements of all of life. Through understanding a wide purview of engagements, wisdom comes into its own. In effect, adults cannot know this, cannot identify with the problems and joys of each earlier and current period of life, until they have known all of these firsthand, experientially. This includes sensing the proximity of death, for it is only in the elder years that one can no longer engage in a denial of death. In the intimacy and generativity years, denial of death is important to functional ability and to the ability to defer one's own needs so as to engage in the needs of others and the practical problems of living. In the years of old-age integrality, on the other hand, death's reality is integrated into human functioning, as each elder juxtaposes the self against eternity and the dissolution of the "I."

Such feats require active work. At best, identity is now a self-assessed compendium of accumulated strengths and some failures. A transcendent identity supplants each adult's earlier vocationally based identity. Nonetheless, the fruits of one's work in the generativity stage are particularly important to the elder, for only those who have taken care of persons and things can find meaning in those very elements that one must transcend. One must be able to look at what he or she has generated and find those contributions good, thus affording an inner worth in which the adult can say, "All in all, I would do this over again."[59] But, as well, there is a renewed identity crisis. A sense of "I am what I contributed and what I once was" eventually becomes "I am what survives of me."[60] Adding to the burden, there is scant retreat from requirements to sponsor the development of those who will survive the self. Adults are always those who offer "continuous solutions" to the generations which will follow along behind.[61] Such sponsorship includes conveying "some forms of faith to coming generations."[62]

In their ego integration, elders become contemplative and philosophical. Such adults leave behind deep passions and prior resentments to attain perspective, acceptance, and a serenity born of knowing where one stands in ethical space. Freed from the full tilt of productive work, older adults can enjoy a "liberated wonder," a time for expanding the senses, and "time 'to play with.'"[63] There is a slower, deeper experience of time and a period for new interests and fresh discoveries. Fresh vitality occurs through a "sensory aesthetic" of knowing and appreciating various experiences fully and of treasuring beauty anew.[64] Nature can be experienced afresh, its smells, sights, sounds, and tactile sensations known more fully. Declining sexuality is replaced by a "generalized sensuality," and one experiences the opposite gender as part of the self.[65] Each man finds "his own female self" and each woman her male counterpart.[66]

Some older adults can maintain a sense of wonder and of childlike wisdom. Erikson saw wonder in the wide-eyed persona of Albert Einstein, someone who always seemed intent on asking questions the way children do, with a curiosity and mesmerized sense of being which was astounded at the magnificence of the world. As well, he found evidence of a "childlikeness paired with the wisdom of a matured craft" in the late-life art of Henri Matisse, particularly in Matisse's chapel in Vence, France, in which he had transformed "prettification" into "childlike dissonance."[67] The potential continuance of the child in the old adult was particularly expressed to Erikson by the name and teachings of Lao-Tse, the ancient Chinese sage whose name means "old child."[68] Lao-Tse's was "the way" to live as an elder.

In those adults who seem unable to find meaning in life, to maintain wholeness, and to integrate one complete life narrative, a prevailing sense of despair results. Such older adults traverse their final years with a foreboding sense that their lifetime of contributions was inadequate and that their lives are thereby bereft of meaning in important respects. They feel an overriding sense of waste.[69] Among some adults, ongoing stagnation and rejection may be on a continuum with the failures of the prior stage of life.[70] In the later years a final opportunity exists for offering waning energies to the world, but "self-isolation" and mourning are overwhelming.[71] There is a "dread of emptiness"; there are "resentments over being 'retired'" and unwanted.[72] Unable to transcend a failing body, there is a despair in feeling that "nothing works."[73]

Depression reigns, as do pervasive feelings of disgust, rejection of others, and self-loathing. "Pettiness" and "pretenses" may become mainstays of existence and "dogmatism" the primary defense.[74] Erikson found that "adult consolidation suffers from a persistent dread of de- consolidation" to the extent that it needs "to classify and ward off deviancy with political, religious, legal, and medical means."[75] When despairing elders possess some form of family or monetary power as well, dogmatism can turn into a pretentious wisdom ("sapientism") and a "coercive orthodoxy."[76] Thus do some manage, from their wills and graves, to rule and to control the living. These attributes show "autocracy," "possessiveness," "ossification," and "misery."[77] Such misery is, of course, readily transmitted down through the generations.

WISDOM: PRINCIPLES, REASON, AND EXPERIENCE

In the second form of wisdom that Erikson described, knowledge and convictions result in "principles, reason, and experience."[78] In this meaning, wisdom emanates from insight and from ethical beliefs. Here there is sustained reflection, sensitivity to the needs of others, sound judgment, prudence, and responsible action. Such attributes are found particularly in his psychobiographies of Martin Luther and Mahatma Gandhi and in his Harvard notes about St. Francis, Kierkegaard, Einstein, Jefferson, and Lincoln.

Erikson's association of wisdom with insight and ethics was partly the result of his dictionary dependence,[79] in this case based on his awareness that *wis*, and the earlier *wys*, derive from *vise*, the pluperfect stem of *videre*, which means "to see."[80] *Wis* also comes from "moral" and "certain." Thus we find a reference to those who show others the way by guiding, directing, leading, or by exemplifying prudent conduct. *Dom* is a designation of honor.[81] In German, *Weise* means a wise person or sage; *Weisheit* means wisdom or prudence.[82] Thus "wisdom" is an honorific title, one attributed to those who can see and who, in their conduct, show others a depth of discernment and a high ground of behavior worth emulating. As Erikson found, such wisdom becomes a preferred and consistent way of life. Wisdom embodies insight and principled action.

In his mid-60s, Erikson implied that he had erred in placing wisdom last among life's accomplishments. The date was August 6, 1968, Erikson's occasion to deliver the T.B. Davie Memorial Lecture at the University of Cape Town, South Africa. The ceremony marked the 23rd anniversary of the bombing of Hiroshima. John and Robert Kennedy and Martin Luther King, Jr., had recently been assassinated in the United States; protests about the Vietnam War were escalating, and civil rights protests had barely ebbed. It was not long after the Cuban Missile Crisis. Revising his prior thought, Erikson held that wisdom can and, in fact, must be situated earlier than the last stage of life if humanity is to survive its destructive tendencies. Speaking of Gandhi and Freud, he said that men of great insight are "usually best known to us from portraits taken late in their lives when they seem so forbiddingly wise," but that "one need not be old and detached in order to have insight."[83] Perceptions, insight, empathy, and integrity are then easily obscured or invalidated. His association of insight and wisdom is striking. Erikson had originally placed wisdom last among life's strengths based on biblical sources and on Socrates' conclusion that insight is based on, but comes after, knowledge. However, in his Cape Town lecture, Erikson implicated wisdom and its compatriot of insight as qualities that belong squarely in the center of both human affairs and of the generative concerns of each person's life. In part, he moved from Socrates to Kierkegaard and to the high ideology of his own identity construct. As is true of his concepts about insight, he argued that wisdom develops after, but is based on, the ideological convictions of youth and the passionate beliefs and interests of young adulthood. Drawing examples from Freud and Gandhi, he held that the prodigious discoveries and leadership that come to fruition in the middle years necessarily emanate from the knowledge, insight, and fervor such persons showed as young adults. Only later did they mature into their full forms.

Making his case for repositioning sound judgment and active leadership, Erikson held that "in office" one needs to function as a Confucian and "in retirement" as a Taoist.[84] The Confucian is a "pole-star," a guidance tool for others.[85] The Taoist is transcendent. In retirement it is far too late to influence much of the world. Therefore, he repositioned insight and wisdom, for these qualities are essential on the primary stage of adulthood when others can see and emulate the acts through which these are revealed. Later, referencing the elderly and wisdom, he held that such "ancient words [are] much too high sounding . . . for the experience of the unpretentious, not to speak of the powerless among us."[86]

When one asks what it is that Erikson saw as defining those of wisdom, a number of attributes appear. Wise adults engage in careful planning.[87] They are temperate and deliberate, refraining from quick responses, impulsive conclusions, or immediate actions. Yet he noticed that wisdom had become synonymous with "posture" and that some people, wanting immediate expertise, were mightily impatient with those who took their time to offer it.[88] They conveyed an attitude of "'Don't think too hard; just give me your wisdom.'"[89] But wisdom was not a "short circuit between knowledge and conviction"; wisdom means "seasoned" experience born of careful study, observation, and processes of exploration.[90] Those of wisdom take the required time to draw conclusions responsibly. As such, they demonstrate conscientiousness and, when applicable, able workmanship.[91]

Behaving ethically, those of wisdom eschew judging or stereotyping others. They hold to principles and human values in a material world. They behave authentically, shirking affectations born of pretense or of the defensive need to appear other than as genuine, unique persons. They relate well with others and are sensitive to their needs, contributing their efforts in a manner that does not require quid pro quo reciprocity. They treat others as ends, not as the means to some self-centered end.

As a result, such adults tend to become ethical, and sometimes spiritual, leaders. Although they may not choose leadership roles, they are emulated as role models, for their consistently principled, wise behavior shows sound judgment, high ideals, courage, purpose, responsible action, and unswerving convictions that are worth following. They are Confucian pole-stars to others. In part, Erikson validated the founder's thoughts: "As Freud concluded, 'men are strong as long as they represent a strong idea. They become impotent when they turn against it.'"[92] Potency and strength of principle are hallmarks of wisdom, a vitality that age alone can neither instill nor dislodge.

There is obvious crossover between certain characteristics of the wise adult and those of the ethical and the insightful adult. Attributes of the childlike adult also appear. Yet wisdom stands on its own in important respects. Among these, good and careful reasoning, substantial experience, sound judgment, deliberate, purposeful behavior, and skilled craftsmanship are prominent. Further, in a number of wise adults Erikson found an "economy" and directedness of effort that focused their work.[93]

In its many definitions wisdom is similar to intelligence in that it exists in the eye of the beholder or concept constructor and suffers from as many views as there are societies, definers, and abilities waiting to be elaborated. Erikson's version is unique in that its full constellation includes the functional attributes of behaving in accord with nature's blueprint of biological competencies, at least for the intimate period of adulthood, of showing one's mettle as a person of conviction and care, and of manifesting good reasoning and able judgment. Among the adults he studied, not one measured up to those qualities entirely. Gandhi begat and discarded, Luther was obscene, verbally violent, and a "colossal crybaby"; Freud was rigidly dogmatic and God-negating; and Kierkegaard was too troubled to be taken completely seriously.[94] Only St. Francis, Charles Darwin, Thomas Jefferson, and Abraham Lincoln emerged comparatively unscathed by Erikson's scrutiny, but he had studied not one of those men's adult lives in depth. Surely he would have found in them some "inner arrest" that is "peculiar to adulthood," just as he had found in the others.[95]

We know this much: that wisdom is a process and result of adult life. It is a way of living in which there is eventually a verification by one's deeds. This implies that adults cannot claim wisdom unto themselves. Wisdom is in fact an honorific, a title of merit that can only be attributed by others who are watching along the way. In the final appraisal, as St. Paul said and Erikson often repeated, they are known even as they have been known.[96]

ERIKSON'S ALTERED VIEW

Erikson astutely portrayed wisdom as a developmental adult attribute, even if he was neither the first nor the last to do so. But he was the first to illustrate how the adult "I" can decenter, how the "we" of love, work, and care occupy and depict the wisdom of the adult years. In this connotation, wisdom is an achievement. Conceptualizing this, he showed the courage of intentionally committing the naturalistic fallacy. This led critics to accuse him of being an ethicist, of theorizing prescriptively, and of fostering idealistic, utopian thought. Erikson knew this. He countered such criticism, saying that knowing what can go awry in development had led him to depict the behaviors that are required so that mental health and positive development will result.[97]

Erikson's late-life shift, that of placing wisdom earlier in adult life, is a different concern. The change shows that in his middle years he had conjectured about older adulthood. He had projected forward his assumptions about elders' strengths and vulnerabilities. This begs the question of what else he may have conjectured. And it shows that not even an able theorist can know the possibilities and difficulties of any one period of life unless and until he or she knows them as an experienced subject or has accumulated sufficient data from a critical mass of persons thus situated.

Yet the deed basis of Erikson's connotations of wisdom and his holding to wisdom as a preferential way of living through adult time carry weight.

From earliest times, dating to the Egypt of 2500 B.C., and from the first books of the Bible to the current day, philosophers and others have concerned themselves with wisdom's meaning and manifestations. Some traditions interpret wisdom as a talent, aligning it with intelligence. Others see wisdom as a product of careful study, as an achievement. Erikson's concepts owe a great deal to the thought of Socrates, Plato, Aristotle, Confucius, Lao Tse, and various biblical sources. Taken in their entirety, such sources originally led him to place wisdom within the province of old age. The courage he showed in repositioning his thinking in order to show wisdom as a unique form of extending outward to others and of caring to engage in constructive, thoughtful, principled behavior go far to assuage his earlier misstep.

10

Acclaim and Criticism for Erikson's Theory and His Concepts of the Adult

I just wanted you to say it's nice.
—Erikson to Kurt von Fritz

In the previous chapters we considered Erikson's largely unknown concepts about the adult, keeping his depictions of various adult stages, crises, and turning points mostly aside. Erikson was concerned about what it means to be an adult and what the adult might yet become. "What is the adult *sui generis*," he asked. Why do we take adulthood "for granted?"[1] What potentials and powers might reveal themselves were we not so entangled with childhood-based notions that elasticize into adulthood? Why do we use as benchmarks the behavior of other adults scattered around us, and why are notions about the adult sometimes restricted by the very moralisms which, in the best of development, adults avoid?

Searching his papers and notes, one finds that Erikson had answered many of his own questions about what it means to be adult. In addition to the intimate and caring variants of the adult that he had described for the sixth and seventh stages of life, Erikson showed adults as prejudiced, as moral-ethical and spiritual, as playing and potentially childlike, as historically and culturally embedded, and as variously insightful and wise. There are reasons for the best of the developmental excursions that he described and for their limitations. Psychological and cognitive advances permit some adults to understand themselves as necessarily prejudiced due to a single-family upbringing in a particular sociocultural niche and in one historical era against all of history, whereas those with restrictive psyches and limited cognitive development cannot come to such knowledge. Lifting our consciousness about the limitations to human comprehension, he showed how to think about the self as a perceiving adult who must diminish and reconstruct the more complete and multidimensional external reality on a limited, skewed, and far-reduced scale in order to assimilate and manipulate it inside a tiny brain. He described the transition to the moral-ethical in adulthood from its basis in childhood morality and adolescent ideology and illustrated how the trust of infancy can lead to mature spirituality. He showed how adulthood is, in so many ways, deficient against childhood and led thinking along a line in which children can function as participants with parents and other elders. His understanding of insight as a process and product relegates mere knowledge to an inferior status and, in his later years, his perspectives on wisdom placed that rare quality earlier in the adult years than he had previously held. He showed the malignancy of ethnic, racial, and similar forms of prejudice as a negative human warping that must be understood and intentionally abandoned if adults are to apprehend that all are partners in one species which can only survive if it is united. And, in myriad ways, he helped adults to watch for and find the machinations of the omnipresent unconscious.

There are some problems with his thought. For the identity that winds its way into adult life, certain renditions of the adult are more characteristic of mid- to late-twentieth-century Western world adults than of adults across all societies, cultures, and times. Autonomous Western-centric identity development is not universal, and the world of Judeo-Christian thought in which his concepts are embedded cannot characterize the full realm of spiritual, religious understandings or the sense some adults have of participating in a more complete ancestral world. Yet insofar as Erikson tilted toward the cognitive by, for example, showing the adult ideation that is play's developmental advance and illustrating the unique adult ability to see the self in the flow of historical time, certain of his adult concepts may well show cross-cultural developmental invariance. Indeed, across the world, we can wonder how many adults would question Erikson's point that some attributes of what we call adulthood, in whichever nation or culture one finds them, are vastly deficient compared with those of children. In adults cynicism creeps in, various prejudices accumulate, authenticity is forfeited, and rigidities build.

As a psychoanalyst, Erikson's thought is contiguous, if not continuous, with Freud's. Erikson converted Freud's psychosexual motif to one that is principally psychosocial. He placed the social and historical inside the psyche instead of only beyond its enclosure, and he searched for what it is that brings humans forward in development instead of harkening backward, as had Freud, to infantile origins. Erikson looked for the constituents of normalcy instead of deviance, constructed from a positive, healthy view of life instead of on the basis of its negatives, and asked what it is that the adult can yet become instead of what it is that adults must defend themselves against. In many ways, he pursued the vitality and light that energize the ego in its forward journey instead of focusing on passivity, darkness, and retreat. Throughout his work he gave the gift of lifting our consciousness about what adulthood brings and takes away. He showed how we are led along by characteristics of which we are largely unaware, depicted group and cultural preferences, and illustrated adult tendencies toward era-centricity. He countered the rubber-band fallacy, showing that concepts about adulthood need not be restricted by the childhood notions on which basis its development originated; yet, in his complex way, he led us to understand that one is always part and parcel of a lifelong narrative that began and continues on from infancy.

A key to understanding Erikson's focus on adults and their potentials, as well as his distance from Freud, lies in his last book, *Toys and Reasons*. He titled the second section "Ritualization in Everyday Life," thus showing his departure from Freud, who had titled one of his books *Psychopathology of Everyday Life*.[2] In his altered wording, Erikson meant to illustrate his efforts to understand and portray the normal, healthy psyche and his view that one must know each psyche on the basis of its contemporary location in the self and society as the point of departure for all else, mental disturbance included. This is a significant revision of Freud, who used the broken "archeological mound"[3] of the ill mind, traced back to its origins in infancy, as his frame for understanding normalcy. Erikson would not accept the premise that mental health should be understood on the basis of deviance from it, nor did he believe that the origins of psychological life in infancy hold all of the answers. Persons continue to adapt to life as it progresses, and early support or difficulties cannot chart the entire course. Origins are not rigidly deterministic.

However, as much as he had transcended Freud, Erikson said that he was a Freudian and wished to be known that way.[4] In several autobiographical accounts, he wrote that alliance with Freudian thought meant acceptance of six "principal constituents," those of the *unconscious* and of *resistance*, *repression*, and *transference*, that of the *"etiological significance of sexual life,"* and that of the *"importance of infantile experiences."*[5] Accepting those elements and the founder's methodology made him a Freudian, even if he did not accept one tenet embedded in Freud's notions of early experiences, the view that everything can be traced back to infantile origins.

Mining Freud, Erikson turned repeatedly to Freud's writings, citing him throughout his own works. And, as perusal of Erikson's personal library readily shows, he read Freud in the German original, translating Freud's writings himself.[6] He picked up and used as a springboard the thread of culture he had found in the writings of Freud's last period and used Freud's sketch of Leonardo da Vinci as his prototype for *Luther*. Freud was his "teacher," and he the imprinting "duckling."[7] Thus no one has the right to take the Freudian lineage away from him.

In the final analysis, it does not greatly matter where we place Erikson theoretically. He crossed the borders of thought, stepping outside psychoanalysis to show the adult's need for spirituality and faith, asking adults to better themselves as ethical beings. He linked his later thought to cognitive concepts of development and wrote for the intelligent reading public instead of for his colleague psychoanalysts. Thus not even psychoanalysis captures him completely. He was more the creator than a thought conformist, more an innovator than a follower.

REVIEWERS' THOUGHTS

In the remainder of this chapter, I place Erikson in the stream of the acclaim and criticism that followed on his work. Like all originating thinkers, he enjoyed great accolades and suffered excoriating rebuke. At times the criticism of his work is apt, and at other times it appears to have arisen because he had been so bold as to revise Freud's thought, because the reviewers had misread him, or because Erikson arbitrarily committed the naturalistic fallacy of changing an *is* to an *ought*. That is, by eschewing merely mirroring what he saw in adults, he risked his own standing in saying what adults *ought* to do to ensure their own best development and that of others.

Nearly all of the critiques of Erikson's work have addressed his theoretical views in general, his psychohistories, or his many thoughts about child and adolescent development. In the following sections I look only to the criticisms of his overarching theoretical perspectives in general and to the less complete criticism of his work on adulthood. However, at the outset I must highlight the fact that the qualities of adults that appear in the six prior chapters of this book are generally known only to the limited extent that some of those attributes are dispersed throughout parts of his books and articles. Thus, because reviewers have not analyzed Erikson's unpublished papers and because his diffuse published content about the adult has not been synthesized, we cannot hold critics responsible for material that does not exist as a published, organized body of thought.

First, I review Erikson's work with respect to his stature as an originator. Following this, I consider his revisionist theory and the inferential nature of his work. I then take up the points that he was an idealistic, utopian thinker and that he fostered a conservative, conformist, and male-normed view of development.

Erikson's Stature

In 1966, having asked 31 psychoanalysts to list the most prominent living psychoanalysts, Arnold Rogow found that Anna Freud headed the list, followed closely by Heinz Hartmann and Erik Erikson.[8] Similarly, a 1980 study of the opinions of members of the Boston, New York, and San Francisco psychoanalytic institutes placed Erikson third in prominence, immediately after Heinz Hartmann and Ernst Kris.[9] Along with Reik, Bernfeld, and Fromm, Erikson held high status as one of the four most prominent refugee lay psychoanalysts.[10] In fact, one reviewer placed Erikson alongside Freud,

Rank, Jung, and Roheim as one of the handful of thinkers to originate important psychoanalytic concepts.[11]

Erikson has been variously acclaimed as the "most creative psychoanalytic mind since Freud,"[12] as the "most eminent" of the ego psychologists,[13] and as the most prominent psychoanalyst in the world.[14] For moving psychoanalysis in the direction of the social world, he has been described as the "most significant" of all post-Freudian thinkers.[15] His life-span framework has been recognized for its singular effort to portray the essence and completeness of development,[16] and he has been credited with bringing Einstein's relativity into contemporary understandings of humans in their development. For these and other reasons, he has been acclaimed for authenticating understandings once considered "deviant" by analysts.[17]

With his books published in more than a dozen languages,[18] Erikson's thought has led to two intellectual biographies[19] and 13 additional books on his thought. Numerous chapters and dissertations supplement such work, and it is a rare text in human development, psychology, or personality that does not include some rendition of his life-span model and his identity construct. Since 1950, more than 300 critiques of his work have appeared in journal articles and newspaper book reviews. In these he has been described as a "pioneer," a "transformer," a "guru," an "innovator," and as either a major Freudian "revisionist," "extender," or "refiner," as the one person who single-handedly reshaped psychoanalytic views, and a "genius" with great "imaginative reach" and humanity.[20] Whether credited with infusing psychoanalytic thought with new viewpoints or with creating a "yawning gap" between psychoanalytic dogma and his own theory, reviewers have commended him for infusing mainstream intellectual thought with contemporary psychological understandings.[21] The views that best describe Erikson's distance from Freud are those that mark him as moving beyond doctrinaire orthodoxy, as the theorist who discarded mechanistic views while retaining and synthesizing viable organic, psychological content, and as the thinker who integrated across fields of knowledge to show the dialectic interchanges one has with others and with society.[22] In these, he moved from dogma to a multifaceted position, countered tendencies to reify structures, advanced from concerns about the Freudian id to consider ego needs, and showed the difference between anxiety and the normal angst of life.[23]

Erikson's "independent vision" of psychoanalytic theory has been held as "dominating" the discipline to the extent that the "limitations" of his thought are seen by some as the "field's limitations."[24] With his excursions into the psychological plights of Hitler and Gorky, and later of Luther and Gandhi, he has been deemed the originator of psychohistory.[25] Due to such studies, as well as to his life-span perspective, his work became a springboard to life narrative studies. His sensitivity to diversity and human needs has been applauded, particularly in its potential applications to the medical and related professions.[26]More than any other psychoanalytic theorist, his thought has been acclaimed and vilified for its ethical stand and values, for showing what it is that professionals in the helping fields can and must say *yes* to and what they must decry.[27] And there is always the fact of the "sparsity," if not the complete absence, of theoretical views on the totality of lifespan development, on the meaning of functioning as an adult, on psychohistory, and on issues of nonviolence to which one can compare his thought.[28] In these he stands alone.

In addition to the positive reviews and acclaim that followed Erikson's published thought, another way to look at his prominence is in terms of the theorists whose subsequent work he inspired. Erikson's model of adult development is at the core of Levinson's thought about the seasons and created legacies of adult life and is fundamental as well to the adulthood concepts of Gould and Vaillant.[29] Based on Erikson's thought, Clayton developed stages of wisdom, Peck developed transcendent stages for old age, Goethals and Klos established substages of intimacy, Loevinger identified stages of ego development, and Marcia distinguished unique forms of identity development and incompleteness, largely for the period of late adolescence.[30] Fowler has incorporated Erikson's thought into his stages of faith, and for both Browning and Kotre, Erikson's thoughts on generative care inspired their own versions of generativity as the apex for the developed adult.[31] Even Gilligan, who has criticized Erikson's theory as male normed, countering with two gender-specific forms of adult moral perspectives, has implicated generative care as that which best illustrates mature ethical behavior.[32]

Erikson conceptualized in terms of the principal psychological energies that capture the motives and investments of the human at various points in the life span. Thus he was not in favor of tendencies to distill, reduce, operationalize, or scale his thought. Nonetheless, as Bourne found for the period of 1962 through 1977 alone, 50 separate investigations had sought to denote identity in operational terms that would be suitable for testing.[33] Since then, efforts have proliferated; the tendency to operationalize all of Erikson's constructs, despite even his changed mind about certain adult content and meanings, has expanded.

There are restrictions to Erikson's appeal and to the inroads made by his thought. It has been claimed that Erikson has suffered William James's fate in that both thinkers' concepts are respected, studied, and cited beyond the walls of psychoanalysis more so than within.[34] Indeed, there has been far greater interest in Erikson's thought among various university audiences and among the interested reading public than within the psychoanalytic community.[35] A number of factors have been important in this development. As Friedman claimed, the decades of the 1950s and 1960s in the United States were high points for interdisciplinary studies,[36] and, to Crunden, the 1960s, the years of Erikson's peak reputation, was the very decade of the country's cresting interest in psychological issues.[37] These tendencies, plus Erikson's inclination to avoid writing for the psychoanalytic community alone, enhanced his standing among academics and an intellectual readership although his theory was not particularly followed by analysts, nor was much of it incorporated into the tenets of psychoanalysis and its institutes.

Erikson's disinterest in establishing a psychoanalytic school, replete with followers to expand his thought, may also have limited his ability to make incursions into psychoanalytic premises.[38] Some have held that Erikson was not concerned with systematizing and testing his thought in any rigorous way and that his growing disenchantment with orthodox psychoanalytic theory in general increased his marginalization among colleagues.[39] Cavell combined a number of these points, claiming that Erikson's wide appeal beyond, and nonintegration within, psychoanalysis was a result of his "disdain for jargon, the breadth of his interest, and the fact that he cared more . . . for the life lived than for theory."[40]

Erikson did write for a wide audience. He did not tightly scaffold his premises for psychoanalysis alone, possibly because this would have sacrificed his broad appeal. Yet it is an error to amalgamate his thought, writing, or professional interests as though these did not change over more than four decades of work. Early on, Erikson presented papers at formal psychoanalytic gatherings and wrote more clinically than was the case later in his career. There is, for example, a vast difference between his seminal article on "The Problem of Ego Identity," presented in 1953 at meetings of the American Psychoanalytic Asssociation and published in 1956 in the *Journal of the American Psychoanalytic Association*, and his "Reflections on the Dissent of Contemporary Youth," published in 1970 in *Daedalus*.[41] Between 1953 and 1970, he moved afield of the analytic hour and patients' concerns to spend far more time inside the University academy, increasingly concerned with social problems and with ethics. Even in his books that were addressed to graduate students and to the public, his growing distance from psychoanalysis is evident. *Young Man Luther* is replete with analytic thought, whereas, in *Gandhi's Truth* such content is lean.[42] While writing *Luther* in the mid-1950s, he was on a brief sabbatical from clinical practice at Austen Riggs, and his writings of *Gandhi* took place in the mid- to late 1960s, when he was at Harvard and had exited daily psychoanalytic work.

The psychoanalytic and psychiatric literature does include some of Erikson's life-span and social contextual premises but not much in the way of referencing him as their originator. Erikson anticipated any number of theorists, including Bowlby and Ainsworth in attachment theory and Jaques with respect to the midlife crisis, but he is rarely cited as a proponent of infant relational and attachment needs or of the middle ager's growing inability to deny the reality of death.[43] Scrutinizing the object relations thinkers who contributed to self psychology, Bacal and Newman completely excluded Erikson's role, and Kohut, in his three books, referenced Erikson only sparsely.[44] Although Lichtenstein[45] held that Erikson alone had successively revealed the enigma, dimensions, and societal consciousness of identity, Wallerstein[46] observed that Modell had remarkably little to say about Erikson's work in four separate publications.[47] With Erikson's thought largely dismissed as some leftover of the personality theory movement of yesteryear, Wallerstein has held that his limited recognition in psychoanalysis is due to the fact that constructs such as identity did not readily mesh with the prevailing ego-psychoanalytic views of the day, that the id-ego-superego constellation and the "impulse-defense" ideation so prominent in the institutes could not be readily reconciled with Erikson's identity, cross-generational, epigenetic, and contextual views.[48] Wallerstein also claimed that Erikson was unable to change the institutes' prevailing focus from psychopathology to mental health. There is little surprise in this last point. As we know, psychoanalysts are expected to conceive of and treat mental illness, not to promote mental health among the healthy.

Nonetheless, identity difficulties are now included among psychiatric nomenclature and, in at least some current psychoanalytic literature, the social world is depicted inside, as well as surrounding, the psyche. Erikson's own concepts about adults' developmental progression have been incorporated into various psychiatric notions of stage-based adult differentials in motives, needs, content, and resolutions. Erikson led a number of psychoanalysts to see that Freud's thoughts and methods were only beginning points of inquiry.[49] Mentally healthy adults are no longer described on the basis of comparisons with those who are highly neurotic or mentally ill,[50] and hierarchical levels of mental mechanisms such as Vaillant's equate adult development with more mature defenses, such as sublimation, humor, anticipation, and suppression.[51] Despite such infusions, the tendency of the psychoanalytic establishment has been to view the totality of Erikson's psychosocial thought with suspicion or to cast it aside into some popularized "limbo."[52] Clearly, in later years, his tendency to stretch beyond the confines of psychoanalysis to consider transcendent identity contributed to his marginal status, as did the evaluation that his thought was "common sense."[53] The eloquence of his writing, his "painterly prose" as some have called it, furthered his marginality.[54] Indeed, Erikson was one to paint a picture, not to write along the tight lines of formal logic or argument.

Assessing Erikson's Theory

There have been two sequential periods in the appraisal of Erikson's theory. In the first period, largely in the 1950s and early 1960s, Erikson's thought was applauded exuberantly. It was held to represent a fresh psychoanalytic perspective that led us to think holistically about the human. For the first time, we thought about life in terms of unified, developmental progression from its beginning to its end and considered the human parcel as a trinity of psychosocial and biological complements. We entertained the ways in which the human is both open to and bounded by society and history. We pondered the importance of identity as a stage-specific challenge that bridges into adulthood.

Few reviews appeared in the late 1960s, but in the second period of criticism, from 1970 on, his work received arch criticism, as well as positive acclaim. His work was given the greatest scrutiny between 1974 and 1977, a period that saw more than 100 published reviews of his thought. Particularly after his excursions into psychohistorical publications, first with *Luther* and then with *Gandhi*, his work raised eyebrows. Yet, irrespective of whether one applauds, partially accepts, or discards his analytic depictions of those who are no longer alive to be psychoanalyzed or to complain, Erikson had earlier contributed enormously to developmental thought, a fact that many latter-day skeptics of his work seem to have forgotten. It is the case that once new thought is absorbed, it no longer seems novel or as important. "Oh," we seem to say, "we always knew that." Seeming to abandon all of Erikson's thought, some critics showed this tendency; their reviews were negatively weighted and were frequently capricious. Other reviews were balanced and made important points. It is the latter to which we look, first considering Erikson's theory and then his concepts about the adult.

Beginning with the many positive points about his theory, Erikson's lifespan perspective has been credited for its comprehensiveness and for the way it depicts life as serial, eventually cumulative, development that moves from birth through the final years.[55] The person is "indivisible," one who cannot be removed from the context of one entire life or the world of that life.[56] After Freud's fragmented zones, modes, and urges, Erikson represents a new wholeness, a sense of human coherence and unity. Many have credited Erikson's thought as a robust open-systems view that effectively counters Freud's closed perspective.[57] The person is permeable to new developmental content at each step of advancing life and is open as well to other persons and to the social, historically niched world.[58] The theory is grounded in evolving, developmental, biological (epigenetic) factors, many of which exist but are not fully apparent in earlier life;[59] yet earlier life does not fully or "mechanically" hold all of life's later evolution.[60] Some reviewers have found great worth in the fact that Erikson depicted essential psychosocial content that exists throughout all of life despite its stage-specific prominence. For example, the rudiments of generativity are seen in early life, when children's primary concerns are those of trust, autonomy, and initiative, whereas older adults who are concerned with generativity and integration as the dominant issues will continue to grapple with the need for transcendent trust and for autonomy and mastery.[61]

By asking new, broad questions, many of which prior psychoanalytic thinkers had skirted, Erikson widened the focus;[62] and he supplied new meanings for terms such as *mutuality*, *actuality*, and *adaptation* by which students of development and behavior could understand both the intricacy of humans and their needs to exist in parity with their world and in partnership with others. Further, he explained human vulnerability to others, to the social environment, and to oneself.[63] Examples of these are seen in the various ways that children's anxiety mirrors that of adults in their group and in the way some forms of identity failure and their expression as depression and rage reflect deprivation of opportunity. He also illustrated that adults are vulnerable to the unconscious deals they make with themselves and the societal deals with which they collude.[64] Thus Erikson's efforts to link psyche, soma, and society are held as true integrators, not just as the juxtaposition of one set of factors, contents, or disciplines against the others.[65] He showed how developmental needs mesh with the family and broader institutions of society, even illustrating how the prevailing content of various periods of life is expressed in social forms, functions, and establishments. For example, trust is elaborated in religion, autonomy in the law, play and initiative in dramatic theater and politics, and competence in the business and technological establishment.

More recently, Erikson has been taken to task and even taken apart. Both Lipset and Coles have pointed out that we may have come to expect far too much of him just because he has contributed so much to our thought.[66] As Erikson suggested to Coles, we may have become "disenchanted lovers."[67] We now see holes in his conceptual base, even though it is the case, and Snarey's point, that no sweeping, "grand theory" such as Erikson's is internally congruent at every point.[68] Nonetheless, some criticisms have been appropriate.

With respect to his overarching view, Erikson's thinking implies an artificial parity and equal weighting of the three complements of soma, psyche, and society. This does not show how lopsided the equation actually is, for the psychological apparatus relies far more on its body than it does on society.[69] Eager to unite the human and to conceptualize across various disciplines, Erikson also seems culpable of having divested certain content of its complexity as he bridged from one field to another.[70] His knowledge in the sciences, especially in the highly relevant areas of human anatomy and physiology, was limited, as he himself noted.[71] This is also the case with his partial knowledge of sociology and anthropology and, to a lesser extent, of history as a field and methodology of study. It is true that functioning in the amorphous terrain between disciplines permitted him to make important discoveries about humans who do not reduce to one or another field, but doing this also meant that he had to think broadly and diffusely, thereby abandoning depth, as well as some particulars and precision, in the process. His tendency to think from a position halfway between the person and society has led to the gentle rebuke that he had "compromised" the previous psychoanalytic focus on the person's deep sense of him- or herself in that experience of self, as well as in the external world,[72] and that his focus on the unconscious has led to diminished attention to the centrality of consciousness.[73] Some critics have claimed that he generalized to an extent that stretched believability. In particular, by attaching identity to adolescence and then to all of adult development, including spirituality, ethics, prejudice, and group and national belonging, identity's credibility sagged.[74] And yet Erikson's "monopoly" of identity as an ideological-vocational, future-oriented sense of self in society has held despite his tendency to fan it out more broadly using a Western-world connotation.[75] Appropriately, Erikson's projection of middle-class, Euro-American identity as the gold standard for all has caused him the most difficulties.[76] Further, some have wondered if he overgeneralized the experience of his own cohort [77] and the extent to which he represented various group phenomena as though he believed they actually were, in fact, an amalgamated form of attributes accumulated from individuals' characteristics.[78]

Erikson's tendency to generalize and to speculate eventually found him in some difficulties. Although it is not the purpose of this book to examine his psychohistorical studies, his books on Martin Luther and Mahatma Gandhi, as well as related writings about identity protagonists, show that his were, at least partially, constructions. As identity icons, the subjects of such writings were Erikson's vehicles for the display of identity crises, for his developmental thoughts and poetic expressions, and, at times, his unique way to get "a lot off my chest."[79] He stretched beyond data and speculated considerably. For example, writing *Luther*, he used the problems of a seminarian of mid-twentieth-century America as the prototype for the Luther of sixteenth-century Germany. An early draft of the book finds him saying that he lacked data and had relied on several limited sources.[80] He stretched beyond available knowledge by claiming that Luther's conversion was a spiritual manifestation whereas St. Paul's was "intra-psychic."[81] He could not have known that the "clerical proletariat" of Luther's day were "totally subservient and unprincipled,"[82] and readers must question whether it is true that any "future orator must, first of all, learn silence."[83] Most comments such as "come to think of it" and "in scattered remarks throughout this book" were edited out,[84] and statements such as "we can only sketch" and "we can only outline what we are reasonably competent to perceive" should have been.[85]

In *Gandhi*, he could not have known that the Mahatma's mother was an "utterly undogmatic religious person," that as a boy Gandhi was "straight and yet not stiff; shy and yet not withdrawn . . . willful and yet not stubborn" or that "in his presence *one could not tell a lie.*" [86] It was a stretch to conclude that Gandhi was "delighted to be arrested" or that, unless he himself suffered, "he never felt happy in making life harder for others."[87] He could only have surmised that Gandhi appeared "to have been almost anxiously eager to know" what those who had studied Freud might say about him; and Erikson speculated that "a teased government . . . becomes brutal until it learns to respond parsimoniously to a new weapon."[88] These examples do not even take into account Erikson's psychoanalytic conjectures, some of which were based on the leaflets that Gandhi and his followers distributed.

Thus, as beautifully written as they are, his psychohistories are appropriately criticized for going beyond the available information to embroider, exaggerate, or conjecture.[89] In fact, Erikson's two psychobiographies seem to have been a key reason for scholars' looking more closely at his thinking and calling into question his theoretical views, however well grounded many of them are. Distortions tend to diminish a thinker's reputation.

In addition, there is the curious fact that the Erikson who wrote two important case analyses in his psychoanalytic dissections of Luther and Gandhi told very little about the people he worked with as a therapist. At Riggs, Erikson did treat a seminarian who became his model for the angst of Luther, but beyond that one person, the actual people who lived out the real problems of their lives are largely absent from his writings. A perusal of Erikson's restricted clinical files in the Harvard papers shows the extent to which this is the case. Yet, giving him the benefit of the doubt, it is likely that Erikson considered such persons and problems in an anonymous aggregate but was so concerned about issues of confidentiality that he did not isolate out case examples in his writing.

Other criticism seems to fit with Lipset's and Coles's points that we have wanted more of Erikson than he could possibly have given in one lifetime. Some have misread him, apparently believing that he had held that his thought was inviolate, as though humans would not change through advancing historical time. According to Coles, Erikson understood from the very beginning of his professional life that truth and facts are not immutable, whereas "a viewpoint or a manner of inquiry" were much more inclined to stand the test of time.[90] Speaking of his stage content, Erikson cautioned that it was not a "definitive 'inventory'"; " I speak only," he said, "of a developing capacity to perceive and to abide by values established by a particular living system."[91] Nonetheless, some have reviewed his theory as that which was meant as a timeless system or as the achievement scale he warned against. He said that there was no one who could have successfully completed all the life crises he had illustrated and, if so, "I never hope to meet such a person."[92]

When we look specifically to views about his adulthood concepts, in general Erikson has been held in high esteem for the very fact that he was the first to focus on the meaning of adulthood.[93] He was among the first to consider the adult years as terrain for ongoing development.[94] He shifted the focus, first from childhood to adolescence, and later from adolescence to adulthood. His anti-originology stand did not permit the subordination of later developmental issues to the earliest, nor did he permit Freud's final position of genital maturity to stand as the endpoint for development. It may not seem so now, but these alone were groundbreaking accomplishments in a century of the child.

Rather suddenly, psychologists and others began to pay attention to qualitative changes in the content of adulthood and to the meaning adults give to their lives.[95] Taken with his illustrations about the complexity of ongoing life, seeing the adult years as a unified terrain of developmental purpose, content, and direction,[96] and focusing on the meaning of the "we" years of intimacy and care,[97] reviewers initially acclaimed his thought. Then, any number found it lacking. Some held that identity, as a stage-specific crisis and fulcrum and as an ongoing medium for development in the adult years, was credible. To them, once established with some firmness, identity is necessarily portable. It is the ongoing ground and vehicle for psychosocial development, not a stage-specific construct and adolescent endpoint alone.[98] To others, identity lost its meaning and Erikson his credibility once he claimed it as the engine and fuel of all content beyond, as well as particular to, adolescence.[99] They asked how identity could mean everything, from the identity of early ideological and vocational commitment through identity achieved through adult love and caring, all the way through to a transcendent identity. On the one hand, Erikson's loss of status as a theory developer for identity as a specific, age-linked crisis seems fitting. On the other hand, we would have lost so much had he stopped there. He might then have failed to show identity's essence in an adult's sense of him- or herself and its very plasticity for the meaning making that shows varied mature forms.

Some have discarded the entirety of Erikson's work due to his ongoing use of identity to depict adult meaning and development. Further, they claim that he has not explained the process of development, of just *how*, for example, one moves from the "I" years of youth to the "we" years of central adulthood and that applications are absent in all of his work.[100] Others have viewed his thought as an evolution throughout his own adult years, thought that, as is true for all who work with psychological content, has its own portion of "minor blemishes"[101] and cannot have done all that we may now wish. He has shown the importance of understanding adults as those who are interdependent with each other, with children, and with their unique society and historical era. He has been credited for showing how each sequential generational cohort invigorates the social institutions that also determine its values and development.[102] His ability to show the content and activity of the functioning unconscious,[103] to show that the child continues to reside in each adult, to illustrate how the developing adult needs play in his or her work,[104] and to show that ongoing fuel for development exists even in the elder years of life have been valued as considerable accomplishments.

If any other aspect of Erikson's thought has endangered his credibility as much as his multiple extensions of identity and uses of historical data for psychoanalytic speculation, it is his focus on ethical behavior and spirituality in adult development and in his profession. Erikson comes across as a Christian statesman. In fact, he himself said that he was a "Christian apprentice"[105] and an advocate of heightened ethics. It is telling that his writings have had greater appeal to religious studies and divinity schools than to psychoanalysis and its institutes. His *was* the naturalistic fallacy, if it is fallacious to state what must be done to keep development on track, having recognized the mental dysfunction that occurs when persons are ill treated. To some, Erikson's inclusion of the ethical placed his thought in question. To others, his bold step generated applause. It showed conviction, courage, and leadership. Most reviewers and followers of his thought fall into the latter camp. He became an edifying voice to those who had long since tired of mere objectivity without a viewpoint.

Yet, in that he included human spiritual needs and the Ultimate Other in certain of his writings, some critics claimed that psychoanalysis was his tool for spiritual thought and for his nearly theological agenda,[106] that he had moved from describing human attributes to spiritual values. He had left observational objectivity behind, they said, sponsoring instead a subjective, ethical stand and extending from psychological structures and methods to a blend of thought that included psychology, Kierkegaard's philosophy, St. Augustine's confessional musings, and Scripture. In fact, this is partly the case. Quoting the fourth-century thought of St. Augustine, Erikson wrote that "God gave (man) . . . a mind and a memory, and thus the rudiments of an identity."[107] He reflected as well Kierkegaard's view that faith and identity are compatriots. And, although there are multiple sources for his ideas of polarities, Zock has pointed out that Erikson found in Proverbs a basis for a unified "world order" and for the interaction of the poles "good and evil, negative and positive."[108]

An evolution to greater spirituality is not unusual among adults. For Erikson, it seems to have been expectable. Married to a Christian, having heard Kierkegaard read at his mother's knee, and, as a youth, experiencing the Lord's Prayer in awe, prepared the way.[109] In his later years, he deepened his lifelong emphasis on *Geistigkeit*, the "intrinsically German preoccupation with matters on the borderline between the spirit and the mind," a *Geistigkeit* he had found in the humanistic thought of the "Olympian Goethe"[110] and myriad others in the traditions of his Germanic homeland. We can only wish that Erikson had remained more generic in his nod toward the spiritual. Instead he largely bowed to one religious tradition and excluded other traditions and their adherents. It is not Eriksonian to exclude.

Further, contemporary, objectified views in the Western world no longer permit the equation of soul, ego, and spirit as a combined entity and energy that can be studied in unity. Erikson's ventures in that direction led critics to accuse him of "prescribing" values and becoming an "ethicist," of "moralizing" and "preaching," and even of "haranguing."[111] In a way, he had combined church and state by integrating spirit, the Ultimate, and ethics with psychoanalytic tenets. Erikson concurred that he was guilty of the title "hidden preacher,"[112] but held that labeling him as such "unhappily . . . gives my colleagues such an easy way out of considering what I have to say."[113] His important messages were thus easily discarded.

Further, we must know the difference between theorizing from the position that values, ethics, and spirit are integral to human functioning and judging from a position of "easy moral superiority."[114] He eschewed the latter. If Jefferson was racist, then that was us; Nixon's election as president was a mirror of the American people and their condition at the time.

Erikson held that a moral code is written into the script of each human's development and that a spiritual essence is at the core of each person. With his belief that psychoanalysis is not objective but holds a disciplined subjectivity and intersubjectivity in its approach, it was but a short distance to his largely latter-day thought about the existential and value driven in adults and in human affairs. This later position permitted him to insist that humans have to be known in their entirety, not as some reduced versions of themselves, and that such an entirety includes each person's sense of a moral, or moral-ethical, and existential self. "One pole of any identity," he said, "relates man to what is forever contemporary, namely, eternity."[115] For the practice of healing, he insisted that ethics could not be divorced from clinical methods because psychoanalytic work includes nonneutral advocacy for its patients and that values always exist in such practice whether or not analysts are willing to recognize and explicitly state those values. We need not quibble with his points. Searching toward the periphery of their lives, most, if not all, adults contemplate the meaning of their lives against eternity. And all practitioners of the healing and teaching arts incorporate values into their practice.   Irrespective of the extent to which one accepts or resists this awareness, values are at the bottom of the content selected and the manner in which these are offered to clients and students.

However, Erikson was not a religious thinker, nor was he an advocate of institutionalized faith. He subverted Freud's atheistic devaluation of religion, noting that many adults need their homes of faith. But he also took religions and their bureaucratic structures, ramparts, and ritualisms apart. Such artifacts, made by humans, too readily prejudice its participants, induce rigidities, and ultimately lead away from an active, faith-filled way of living.

In addition to his heavy leanings toward Christian beliefs, one compelling criticism of Erikson's ethical position is that he had wrapped both his psychoanalytic observations and ethical advocacy in a liberal ideology. Had he limited his ventures to advocacy, even to the ethical and spiritual needs of humans, he would have remained on more firm ground. But he also veered into politically charged terrain and, in so doing, went beyond the acceptable. Among others, Crews questioned which came first, psychological thought or liberal politics.[116] To proceed from psychological observations to what it is that humans need for mental health in a society that liberally supports it is one thing; to move from an a priori liberal ideology to psychological principles in support of that ideology is quite another. Indeed, Erikson tacked back and forth between the two, and it is unclear which came first.

There is also the question of what we are to make of Erikson's own changes in his thought. As Gutmann has claimed, Erikson became a "revisionist Eriksonian."[117] His identity and his sense of himself and of his fit in psychoanalysis remained diffuse and insecure. One could say that Erikson's was a built-in personal redundancy. He resolved his own identity crisis again and again. In many respects, Erikson is inseparable from his work. As to his ongoing additions and revisions to identity as a concept, Gutmann noted the tendency of originators, particularly in their older years, "to turn against their own innovations."[118] He noted as well Erikson's "fear" of being "categorically defined once and for all," as a person and an innovator and in terms of the ideas he had generated.[119] Thus he rejected both himself and his prior concepts in the vein of an autoimmune reaction.[120]

Erikson also engaged in projection as he conceptualized. In his middle years, he had projected forward his hopeful view that older adults were wiser adults, that they, and eventually he, would come to some grand ego integrity and wisdom as the fruits of lives well lived. When he reached that part of his life, he saw that he had erred. At best, one can accomplish some semblance of integration in the face of bodily and psychosocial disintegration. And, when an elder of 76 years of age then experiencing the negatives of aging, he changed his mind again. It was not identity against identity confusion or diffusion that represented the crisis of late adolescence but that of identity against cynicism, of role refusal. Exclusivity then came to represent the negative pole of intimacy and rejectivity to portray the negative pole of generativity. He had projected optimism forward when he was younger, and he seems to have projected the negative view of cynicism, exclusion, and rejection backward through time when older.

Erikson's Writing and Thinking: Questions of Vagueness, Reduction, and Inference

Particularly given Erikson's vocational origins as an artist and his graceful, poetic writing, insofar as he generalized and wrote vaguely at times, and because he conceptualized on the grounds of psychoanalytic, inferential, and discreet patient information, the validity of his thought has been questioned. Indeed, the credibility of psychoanalysis itself has been challenged. Its methods and data are held suspect, and it has been found lacking in meeting standards of empirics. Critics complain that it is devoid of objectivity's requirements of close reasoning, "hard" data, validity, and replicability. Particularly in a medication era, in which psychotropics have had decided treatment successes and in which there are few health care dollars for long-term psychotherapy, criticism of Erikson and of his field sometimes blur as though they were one.

Looking to the criticisms of Erikson's writings, reviewers have not agreed with each other. The great bulk of reviews in this area, positive and negative, has largely focused on his writing style, the question of reductionism, and his data. Some have claimed that Erikson's writing, and thus his thought, is imprecise and ambiguous. Others have held that his thought is so deeply contextualized that he requires more than a quick reading or a lopsided perusal that isolates one or another point without grasping his total thought. One body of critics has held that he is a reductionist, whereas others have maintained that he is very much the nonreductionist. Some have held that his thought was not psychoanalytic or developmental, but was philosophical or phenomenological; others have held him in high esteem as the preeminent psychoanalyst, one who wrote broadly and sometimes philosophically so as to avoid narrowing the human. Any number of critics have maintained that he lacked objective, empirical data, whereas others have rebutted that he did indeed have data but that such data did not comport with objectified, and therefore dehumanized and simplified, measures and criteria.

Taking these points in turn, it was Erikson's tendency to paint impressionistically as he wrote. At times he wrote imprecisely. On listening to his audiotapes, one finds that his lectures and presentations were more direct than when they were later placed into text. The first drafts of his manuscripts were more exact and clearer by far than later, published versions. By the time Erikson's words appeared in print, he had softened or hedged his points. As he said, he would sometimes "re-write with characterization rather than facts."[121] Thus his writing is often as vague as it is profound, as amorphous and elusive as it is elegant of phrase and subtle in the use of nuance. Coles has claimed that Erikson wrote abstractly to prevent an ossification of his points in which readers might lose the full meaning he meant to convey.[122] And, in fact, attributes such as identity are so heavily weighted with the unconscious that it is nigh impossible to pin them down precisely in writing. On doing so the unconscious tends to vanish. This applies to other concepts as well. How does one explain in exact, testable terms that prejudice leads to rage among those who are its victims and that prejudicial exclusion leads to a failure of more complete development, both for the excluded and for the excluder? How can one express, with specific, provable words and hypothetico-deductive lines of proof, that adults invoke the cultural attributes they have transported along with them since they had integrated those mores, norms, and viewpoints as children? Even if expressions were adequate to the concept, we now know that there is no nonconditioned group of control adults with whom others can be compared.

His were profound concepts. Yet they were often written with such eloquence and literary symmetry that meanings became obscured. Sometimes, only when he elaborated on similar material in various sources, does one or another of Erikson's ideas become clear. Speaking to such difficulties, Kovel said, "try to remember what he has said and a cloud tends to form."[123]

Related to his opaque writing tendency is the issue of his word associations. Sometimes Erikson associated words to convey a sense of the ridiculous among his readers. At other times, reasons for their intrusions are unclear. Whatever his intentions may have been, this tendency in his work leads one to question what kind of theoretical validity he may have attached to such associations. Is there some need to juxtapose "monkhood, its monkishness, and its monkery?"[124] What has *adult* to do with *adultery* except by idea opposition? What has repression to do with both suppression and oppression, as Gutmann questioned?[125] Such associations do not support his case, however historically embedded in the origin of ideas those word concepts may be.

As to the claim of reductionism, those who have accused him of this are half the number of those who have said he was very much the nonreductionist. In fact, Erikson made every effort to avoid this human tendency and was highly successful in most of his work. His representation of the person as a biopsychosocial composite avoided distilling the human according to the biopsychological alone. Thus he counters Freudian biological determinism and mechanistic rigidity. Critics who see distillation in his work fail to recognize the extent to which he balanced nature with the nurture of ongoing life, of caring persons, and of resource-rich contexts.[126] Erikson's illustration of the way development presses forward into and through adulthood further counters claims of reduction. He did not reduce culture to some trifling or insignificant status. And he avoided simplified diagnostic labels for persons and nations, a tendency of those who reduce phenomena. Further, just as Blos noted, Erikson's depiction of life in terms of competing polarities counters reductionism.[127] However, it is the case that psychoanalysis is itself a reductionist system and manner of thought.[128] To the extent that Erikson employed it unilaterally, that portion of his work evinces such distillation. Certain indications of this tendency appear in *Luther*, as has been claimed.[129] Further, when representing individual psychological attributes as a collection in society, he performed a kind of reduction through recapitulation in the aggregate.[130]

It is also the case, and White Riley's point, that stage theories are reductions and, in fact, that they represent age reifications as well.[131] However, it is also the case that just as Erikson avoided deterministic ideation, refusing to attach ages to his various stages and writing in broad brush strokes about the psychosocial content of them, his efforts have been undone by those who have themselves reduced his thought. It is unseemly to hold him responsible for the simplifications of others, even if greater precision, clarity, and evidence have sometimes resulted. Any such gains are more than offset by a loss in the complexity of his thought.

Accusations that Erikson was more the philosopher and phenomenologist than the psychoanalyst oppose claims of reduction. Erikson wrote psychoanalytically and philosophically. He had a viewpoint. However, one must know that the rubric under which we place his thought depends on the particular publication in question, as well as the purpose of its writing, the period of his life in which he was then writing, and the sociopolitical context of the time and, therefore, of his thought. Erikson himself does not reduce to a snapshot view or to a particular line of thought. We recall the statement with which he closed the first chapter of *Luther*, saying that he would use the term "existential" as *he* meant it, "mindful that no school of thought has any monopoly on it."[132]

To the extent that Erikson wrote philosophically,[133] one finds Blake and Hegel in his work. The dialectics of thesis and antithesis, of conflicting polarities in the self-same stage of development, and life as a series of tensions and contradictions are systematic Hegelian notions. All three of these thinkers—Blake, Hegel, and Erikson—held that life is an evolution of oppositional contraries. As to claims that Erikson was a phenomenologist,[134] if by such a label is meant that he observed and described attributes without bothering to explain them, the criticism is unfounded. His thought does resemble that of the German phenomenologists Heidegger and Husserl, just as Yankelovich and Barrett maintained.[135] Yet his closeness to them, as is true of his similarity to Goethe and Hegel, is due more to a spiritual brotherhood of thought and style than to content. Erikson conveyed the unique German spirit of his day. It evokes a range of oppositional, unquelled emotions, of youthful pining and melancholy, of wanderlust and tradition, of joy and despondency. It holds, as well, more than a nugget of Eastern mysticism and of Hindu tradition.

Finally, Erikson's reasoning and the viability of his data have been questioned. Those who claimed that he sometimes represented himself as having reasoned by analogy are correct. In particular, he applied analogical thinking to epigenesis and to pseudo-speciation (prejudice). His tendency to think in terms of metaphors likely made such correspondences appealing. Concerning epigenesis, he had limited knowledge in the sciences and seems not to have known that this concept is apt only for thinking about ongoing development, not for scientifically explaining it. Weiland too recognized this error in his thought.[136] Throughout the evolution we call "development," context, genetics, and motivations interact to create less than uniform results from one person to the next. Except for puberty and menopause, which are standard age-linked events, humans do not unfold uniformly. When Erikson entertained notions of prejudice, he wrote analogically about the presumed correspondence between pacifism in humans and animals, sometimes slipping into anthropomorphism. He even implied that institutions show functional forms of individual human development and evolution. However noble his intentions or metaphorical his meanings, such meager reasoning was his Achilles heel.[137]

Questions of whether or not his data meet standards of objective, replicable science plagued Erikson. They placed him and his thought in doubt. Yet such questions apply to psychoanalysis as an entirety, not specifically to one or another of its practitioners. Edelson, for one, has said that science is objective and "conservative,"[138] whereas, as we know, psychoanalysis is subjective and intersubjective. Psychoanalysis arose from a liberal, revolutionary movement whose aim, to this day, is to free persons from restrictive influences, whether these are harsh superegos, brutal families, or limiting societies. Thus psychoanalysis remains at variance with demands for confirmation, proof, and efficacy and, as such, is pretheoretic, as critics such as Edelson have held. Yet truth, fact, confirmation, and proof can and do exist in the individual situation. That such personal truth frequently remains at variance with truth in other human lives and conditions and, as such, cannot comply with the rigors of generalizable scientific objectivity does not erase its existence in fact. Each individual world is a whole world, a world of one subject. And, as contemporary thinkers recognize, no mind can be arbitrarily extracted from itself or its social context.[139] Hence, individual uniqueness and single-subject, nonobjectivity define the terrain. Motivation and highly personal meanings define subjectivity, whereas, just as Kakar has held, the sciences fail to attend to subjects' reasons for actions.[140]

Thus Edelson's and others' question about "whether there is a methodology that is *logically* capable of assessing the scientific credibility of psychoanalytic hypotheses" is not the issue, for psychoanalysis cannot be tested empirically or proven objectively.[141] It prides itself on not reducing the human in such a way, on validating personal, idiosyncratic attributes, knowledge, and experience. On the other hand, as Schnell put it, science has progressed by "rejecting such personal knowledge . . . by stripping away the unique and idiosyncratic," seeking instead the uniform and the deterministic.[142] Because psychoanalysis can be neither purely objective nor neutral does not mean that it is less than pure science; rather, it is different from objective science.

Erikson: A Conformist, Utopian Ideology in a Male-Normed View?

There is a subtle relationship between claims that Erikson espoused a conformist, conservative bias and that his was an idealistic view. These two charges align with claims that he theorized from a male-normed developmental model. I consider these in turn.

Many who have charged Erikson with conformism to a conservative and, in fact, a "success ideology" claimed that although his was a "romanticization" of rebels, his concepts buttressed the view of an ego that needs to adapt to prevailing social roles and expectations.[143] Portions of this appraisal ring true. In Erikson's life, and in that which he depicted as the most harmonious mode for others, he was concerned with the person's integration into prevailing mores, with the synthesis between the individual and his or her culture. But was his a "parochial" conformism, as has been claimed?[144] Did he espouse a form of ego restriction that is markedly conservative? Did he thereby unduly affirm the "status quo?"[145] And was his a social achievement ideology born of middle-class values?

Once again, critics have expected a great deal of one good thinker. Yes, he was most concerned with the fit between the person and society. If he overemphasized this point, perhaps partially projecting his own ego needs and the way the society of his youth failed to integrate him, must we also now expect him to have illustrated how average persons might do well to avoid fitting in? He did show this when writing about the revolutionaries Luther and Gandhi, although those men were anything but average, everyday persons. He admired those who were left of center and, in fact, he himself was liberal in his politics. But his primary concern was to show how incorporation into society counters alienation and anomie. He seems also to have known that society needs only so many rebels. The claims that he was representative of a normative existence are correct. He was concerned about "expectable" lives.[146]Just as he emphasized the healthy and the "homeostatic" as opposed to mental disturbances, Erikson held that society is the petri dish that feeds such homeostasis.[147] But he did not advance notions of mere adjustment to society. Instead, he espoused adapting the social milieu, its institutions, roles, and mores to the self to the extent possible. Hence his consistent use of the term "adaptation."

In his normative view of adults, the life he admired was the generative life of "marriage, heterosexuality, and the raising of children," just as Roazen has held.[148] And his was the middle-class bias. In fact, in his early years of psychoanalysis, those who traveled to Vienna for analysis were from the affluent upper echelon of society. It was largely their children whom Erikson taught, observed, and sometimes treated. Among them were children of Dorothy Tiffany Burlingham and Eva Rosenfeld.[149] In the United States he became part of the prosperous medical establishment. As Hale pointed out, even psychoanalytic clinic patients were from the middle class in those days.[150] Few were blue- or pink-collar workers. In the post–World War II years, he wrote from within a "surplus economy" and celebrated the person's autonomy.[151] Surplus and privilege do make for choice, even if one chooses to fit in. Autonomy also reflects the freedoms of his adopted country and its constitution.

Attention should be paid to potential reasons for the harsh tone in the reviews of those who have rebutted his thought about the fit of the person in society. Many reviewers have sounded angry, reactionary, and defensive in refuting this part of Erikson's work. As individuals who need to feel in control, in charge, always our own agents and resources, perhaps, as Piers and Berry contended, Erikson "injured" our "narcissism":[152] We now see that we are as much shaped by society as we are capable of shaping it and our futures. His view bothers and offends any number who contend that we can ride our individually determined destinies.

As to claims of his idealism, affirmative stance, and utopianism, there is little to dispute. Erikson himself said that he was idealistic and knew that he sounded utopianist.[153] Most reviewers have been harsh in criticizing him for these tendencies, whereas some have found his hopeful, positive perspective refreshing, an antidote to the negativism of Freud. One finds that many reviewers who have found optimism so pervasive in Erikson's thought and have censured him for it seem to have not learned the lesson of context, either that of society as a context or that of the context of an individual in his or her changing life through its time. They have taken Erikson out of his position in the United States, avoiding seeing the role of this hopeful country in Erikson's theorizing. Arriving into the United States in a New Deal era, coming form a poor and war-defiled Europe, he was taken with possibility. Just as Crews said, even his identity concept was "launched on a prevailing updraft of nationalistic idealism."[154] His thought was imbued with Germanic longing as well. To Manuel and Manuel, who placed Erikson in the late twilight of such thought, utopias are nostalgias.[155] Such nostalgia suffuses his early work, pointing a directional arrow to a better future.

If Erikson sound meliorist in his more youthful writing, captured by the idealistic view that society tends to improve over time, such hope was embedded in a "can do" mentality and in the ongoing glow of practical, democratic reform tactics. Yet as is true for other changes in his thought, Erikson would not be so optimistic in his later years. By the era of Vietnam, civil rights protests and violence, and missiles launched into space, it is difficult to avoid seeing the negatives in his writing. In that period, he originated his concept of pseudo-speciation and wrote less about the ego ideal, harmony, and faith in progress than he did about the negative identity of prejudice and the dissent of youth. He could yet hope that the species would find its universalist affinity, but life had become far less benevolent, society less benign, and this was due to the context of the society and times, as well as to an aging man's view from within the older years of adulthood.

In a publication that studies only his writings about wisdom and integration, I noted a changing tone in Erikson's work through time.[156] Comparing his writings at the ages of 48- to 64-years, when he was in his middle and early-old-age years, and those at the ages of 72 to 81, when he was in middle and late old age, it is clear that his writings became more negative as he aged. Excluding concepts classified as general, as social commentary, or as those which reference pathology, in the first of those periods 19 statements portrayed a positive resolution, tone, or content, and 4 conveyed negative content or affect. In the second period, the trend is reversed. There are 13 negative and 6 positive statements during his oldest years.

Clearly, utopias are preferred states, not realistic places or states of being. In Erikson's work, early or late, he wrote in terms of possibility and of the desirable middle and late estates of life. His writing is indeed "edifying," a "testament to moral courage."[157] Some of those who have criticized his ideas and ideals seem to have had few of their own. But, in fact, in order to see in a way that permitted him to write about what adults might yet become, he had to blindfold himself to the facts around him, that adults are frequently more narrow and non-end-state oriented than he might have cared to have seen.

As to his portraiture of women, Erikson's view is neither accurate nor appealing. Despite the fact that he softened his own position over time, having questioned himself as a result of attacks from those in the women's movement, he seems never to have understood women well enough to accurately represent them theoretically. Compared with boys and young men, he treated fewer girls and young women as patients. He did not write about any women in his psychobiographical or related accounts, and even his book *Identity: Youth and Crisis* is devoid of representations of young women.[158] Among the 268 items in the composition section of his papers donated to Harvard, only three pertain specifically to women, and those few show his bias that anatomical spaces and projections preordain development.[159] His writings evince the Germanic and chauvinistic male norm minus Freud's misogynism. He equated female morphology, the "inner space," with nurturance, and male morphology with intrusion into "outer space."[160] Here too he reasoned by analogy. His was the single developmental pathway born of the ideals of male autonomy from which women somehow deviated. Erikson thus became the whipping post for all of women's anger that had been building up ever greater steam since Freud claimed anatomy as destiny, a rejoinder to Napoleon's "history is destiny."

Erikson's skewed views about women are largely absent from the chapters in this book. Thus, although little should now be said about his male-normed concepts, it seems inappropriate to completely skirt those biases as though they did not exist or are unimportant.

The greatest faults with Erikson's view are twofold. First, he of all people did not see the extent to which women's behavior reflects the social context that either excludes, allows, or encourages their full participation in vocational and related roles. Behavior reflects role modeling and social permission. Thus the children's and youths' play constructions, on which basis he concluded that gender distinctions arise because of differences in anatomical morphology, likely reflected what those young subjects saw in the roles of the adult men and women in society. As late as the 1950s in this country, most married women did not work except within the enclosed spaces of their homes. In those years, granting a woman admission to medical school carried a deficit connotation, that of taking away such an opportunity from a man. In the 1960s, women's earnings were completely excluded from calculations used to obtain home loans. Conceptualizing primarily in the mid-twentieth century, Erikson did not foresee how quickly women would change, given the opportunity. Second, although he nodded in the direction of gender distinctions, he did not portray equality in those differences, nor did he see that there might just be two very different, but equal, developmental pathways. It seems that Erikson, a complex thinker who was antagonistic to reductionism, did not just speak in the male voice of chauvinism. He seriously oversimplified the lives, perspectives, and developmental differences of women and placed women in a position of dependence on men and accommodation to a male developmental pathway that is not their own.

Further, Erikson lauded male-normed autonomy in identity to the exclusion of the relational in identity. As Gilligan and others have pointed out, women consider issues in terms of relationship, connection, and attachment and from the moral voice of care, whereas men's view is that of separation, independence, and individuation and the moral voice of justice.[161] Erikson had not seen the extent to which, in his adherence to prior male-normed theory, as well as in his work and in his writing, he was largely in the company of men. His biases went unchallenged by that company.

Although in his later years Erikson held that "Freud's general judgment of women was probably the weakest part of his theory," Erikson continued that theoretical weakness.[162] But it is also the case that Erikson admired women. Wright and Piers and Berry were correct in saying that he criticized our "male-dominated heritage," that he was not "anti-feminist" but an "advocate" of a "more 'feminized' world."[163] To him, the conflicts in the world were "crudely male."[164] He held that man's identity is "based on a fondness for 'what works' and for what man can make, whether it helps to build or to destroy."[165] He eventually regretted his own use of the term "virtue" because it sounded so masculine.[166] He applauded Emma Jung's "woman's voice against patriarchal exploitation" and the highly generative tone of her letter to Freud.[167]

He did not comport with women's exclusion and, in fact, held great expectations of their potential roles. He wanted women to provide fresh hope for the future in that they alone could somehow deconstruct the path toward nuclear annihilation with a new "ethics which may yet—because it must—surpass man's proud inventions."[168] In other words, men had torn the fabric, the safety net, of the prebomb era, and women would have to mend it. How much women might resent this fresh requirement is difficult to say.

Erikson wanted women's voices and leadership to be heard and seen, but he knew that he could not speak for them. In his remarks on student unrest at a White House forum in 1969, he asked why there was not even one woman included among those invited.[169] He also knew that he did not understand women. Writing to Margaret Mead, he complimented her on her book about Ruth Benedict. "Wonderful," he said, "most of all, how you say and document something new about Woman. I hope to understand what it is, before long."[170]

Yet in his final years, Erikson knew that he had miscued in characterizing women as inferior.[171] He had cast women in a dependent position and, at least for that portion of his thought, had come to regret his antiquated view.

CLOSING WORDS

Erikson's concepts about the adult are a testimony to his thought, to his unswerving belief in humanity, and to a humanist's hope that adults could transcend themselves. He held that adults can reclaim the trust of childhood and that they can become more ethical, wise, and caring persons and more open to others. Contrary to Freud, Erikson loved humanity. He wrote elegantly and profoundly and led a quiet revolution against prior negative renditions of adults and their purported limits. A testimony to him as an adult, reviewers have noted his humor, tact, and honesty and the way he fostered transference among his readers. We cannot know if it was sometimes difficult for him to state and restate his requirements for adults in the face of those who scorned such thought. We do know that he repeated, in various texts, articles, lectures, and presentations, and in any number of ways, that functioning as an adult means having insight into the immaturities that had been handed on from prior generations and having the wisdom to avoid transmitting them to future generations.

Although he wrote from interstitial terrain instead of narrowly within any one discipline, Erikson was anything but a psychoanalytic pretender. He observed himself as he wrote. His psychological thought shows great breadth, encompassing childhood, adolescence, and a range of forms in which adults see their world, consciously and unconsciously, and live in it. If we are prejudiced—and everyone is—it is in recognizing it that we can self-correct. All adults are at least moral persons. Some of those who are moral, and therefore moralistic, can move forward into the higher form of ethical functioning. Adults are spiritual, and irrespective of their diverse religious convictions or comparative absence of exact beliefs, they can accept and share in the fact that spirituality is part of our common humanity. If some adults are gratingly rigid or negative, there may still be time and the occasion for them to find the childlike joy that resides deep within and to more fully use their unique adult form of play to create positive ideas, concepts, visions, and plans and to open themselves to others.

Adults are, but some may not know that they are, culturally and historically relative. Knowing the self in such a way may lead to aborting ideas of national, ethnic, or racial superiority and era-centricity and might enhance one's personal humility. There are many ways of being in this one large world, and knowledge about the way we reduce and skew reality, for reasons of sanity as well as for sheer maintenance of the ability to function, might lead adults to become more accepting of others who have the self-same tendencies. Some adults are insightful; some are also wise. Their love and care are manifestations of wisdom, as are the products of their generative lives and their occasions of able thought and leadership. Reflecting on the qualities and products of insight and on Erikson's renditions of wisdom might just inculcate a greater tendency in those directions.

Erikson's work is not perfect. His thought and writings have their share of limitations. That he stretched his points and overgeneralized at times, tilted toward ethicism and preaching, wrote from within the male view, and seemed sometimes to believe that analogical reasoning was sufficient reasoning are not good motives for discarding the majority of his thought, which is otherwise solid and profound.

Here was a thinker whose contributions were substantial. Erikson appears to have cared deeply about his readers as well and about the way his work was received. He showed great empathy, even when he could not refrain from saying what some did not wish to hear. That his empathy was sometimes not matched by those who reviewed his work is the price of originality.

Erikson's total work on adulthood will likely be studied again and again. It is a body of thought that has more to say for itself than anything that can be said against it. We can only wish he had known this. Likely, he did not. On one occasion, perhaps worn down by criticism, noting that reviewers seemed bent on "destroying . . . all aesthetic context" in his work, Erikson told about a small boy to whom he compared himself.[172] On having one of his sketches reviewed, analyzed, and dissected, the child said, "I just wanted you to say it's nice." And so, the final words must be these: "It *is* nice, Professor Erikson. It is *very* nice."[173]

Notes

Preface

1. Barney G. Glaser and Anselm L. Strauss, *The Discovery of Grounded Theory* (Chicago: Aldine, 1967).
2. Robert Coles, "The Engaged Campus: Organizing to Serve Society's Needs," (keynote address presented to the National Conference of the American Association on Higher Education, Washington, D.C., March, 1995).

Chapter 1: Introduction

1. See, for example, Gerald Holton, "Introduction," in *The Twentieth-Century Sciences: Studies in the Biography of Ideas*, ed. G. Holton (New York: Norton, 1972), vii–xiv.
2. "The most influential living psychoanalyst," is from a review of *Life History and the Historical Moment* by Erik H. Erikson (unknown author); found in "Clippings and reviews of *Life History and the Historical Moment*," Item 1552, The Papers of Erik and Joan Erikson, bMS Am 2031, The Houghton Library of Harvard University (hereafter cited as Erikson Hrvd. Pprs.); from *Time*, 17 March 1975. "The last of the psychoanalytic gurus" is from Alan Chaikin, "Summing Up," *The Virginia Pilot*, 6 April 1975. "A healer and an interpreter of ourselves and our times" is from Janna T. Steed, "The Man Who Gave Us Our 'Identity Crisis,'" *The Berkshire Eagle*, 26 April 1975.
3. Fawn M. Brodie, "How History is Analyzed as Psychodrama," *Los Angeles Times Book Reviews*, 20 April 1975, review of *Life History and the Historical Moment* by Erik H. Erikson; found in "Clippings and Reviews of *Life History and the Historical Moment*," Item 1552, Erikson Hrvd. Pprs.
4. "Developmental Considerations," 4 November 1984, Item 1633, Erikson Hrvd. Pprs.
5. Robert Coles, *Erik H. Erikson: The Growth of His Work* (Boston: Little, Brown, 1970), xvi.
6. Steven Weiland, "Erik H. Erikson on America: *Childhood and Society* and National Identity," in *Intellectual Craftsmen: Ways and Works in American Scholarship, 1935–1990*, ed. S. Weiland (New Brunswick, N.J.: Transaction, 1991), 54; Paul Roazen, *The Power and Limits of a Vision* (New York: Free

Press, 1976), 43, 48; Robert M. Crunden, "Freud, Erikson, and the Historian: A Bibliographical Survey," *The Canadian Review of American Studies* 4, no. 1 (Spring 1973): 48–64; 60.

7. Erik H. Erikson, *Young Man Luther* (New York: Norton, 1958).

8. Erik H. Erikson,"Reflections on the Dissent of Contemporary Youth," *Daedalus* 97, no. 1 (Winter 1970): 154–176; 175.

Chapter 2: Erikson's Thought in Context

1. Erik H. Erikson, "Autobiographic Notes on the Identity Crisis," in *The Twentieth Century Sciences: Studies in the Biography of Ideas*, ed. G. Holton, (New York: Norton, 1972), 15.

2. "Quietly convinced," is from "Autobiographical Remarks," 22 June 1977, Item 1580, Erikson Hrvd. Pprs; "very kind people" is from Gauss Seminars in Criticism, 2 April 1970, Audiotape 1, Erik Erikson Lecture Series, Seeley G. Mudd Manuscript Library, Princeton University Archives (hereafter cited as Erikson Gauss Lectures).

3. "Further Autobiographic Remarks," August 1977, Item 1581, Erikson Hrvd. Pprs.

4. Erikson, "Autobiographic Notes on the Identity Crisis," Holton, ed., *The Twentieth Century Sciences*, 16.

5. Erikson Gauss Lectures, Audiotape 1.

6. Erikson, "Autobiographic Notes on the Identity Crisis," 16.

7. Erikson to Hope G. Curfman, 30 December 1976, Item 811, Erikson Hrvd. Pprs.

8. Erik H. Erikson, "Autobiographic Notes on the Identity Crisis," *Daedalus* 99, no. 4 (Fall, 1970): 745.

9. Erikson to Curfman, 30 December 1976, Item 811, Erikson Hrvd. Pprs.

10. Erikson, "Autobiographic Notes," *Daedalus,* 744.

11. Erik H. Erikson, "A Memorandum on Identity and Negro Youth," in *A Way of Looking at Things*, ed. S. Schlein, (New York: Norton, 1987), 656. First published in *The Journal of Social Issues* 20, no. 4 (1964): 29–42.

12. Erik H. Erikson, *Life History and the Historical Moment* (New York: Norton, 1975), 26.

13. Ibid., 131.

14. Erikson Gauss Lectures, Audiotape 1.

15. Ibid.

16. Erikson, *Life History*, 28.

17. Erikson Gauss Lectures, Audiotape 1.

18. Ibid.

19. Erikson, "Autobiographic Notes," *Daedalus,* 740–741.

20. Joan M. Erikson, interview by author, Harwich, Mass., 11 October 1995. See also Erikson, "Memorandum for the Freud Archives," October 1977, Item 1583, Erikson Hrvd. Pprs.

21. Answer to Per Bloland," 1977, Item 1584, Erikson Hrvd. Pprs. (Per Bloland is a grandson of Erikson.)

22. Erikson Gauss Lectures, Audiotape 1.

23. Among those articles, one considered adults' motives for enrolling in evening classes, and three focused on adults' learning abilities.

24. Richard I. Evans, *Dialogue with Erik Erikson* (New York: Harper and Row, 1967), 61.

25. Erik H. Erikson,"Observations on Sioux Education," *Journal of Psychology* 7 (1939): 101–156.

26. Erik H. Erikson, "Observations on the Yurok: Childhood and World Image," *University of California Publications in American Archeology and Ethnology* 35, No. 10 (1943): 257–301.

27. Erikson implied that he would one day write his autobiography. See "Notes on my parentage," circa 1977, Item 1590, Erikson Hrvd. Pprs.

28. On interview, Stephen Schlein spoke about Erikson's lifelong insecurity. Stephen Schlein, interview by author, Lexington, Mass., 18 October 1995. With respect to Erikson's name change, see Sue Erikson Bloland, "Fame: The Power and Cost of a Fantasy," *Atlantic Monthly* 284, No. 5 (November 1999): 51–62. Further, Angelus Silesius, whom Erikson was careful to reference in his autobiographic comments about the identity crisis, may have been an identity model for him with respect to adopting a different last name. Angelus Silesius was the self-adopted name of Johann Scheffler, the seventeenth-century German mystic. On finding that he was an orphan, at age 15 Scheffler changed his religion, his domain of inquiry, and his name. See, for example, Angelus Silesius, *Angelus Silesius: The Cherubinic Wanderer*, trans. Maria Shrady (New York: Paulist Press, 1986), and Sister Mary Hilda Godecker, "Angelus Silesius' Personality Through His Ecclesiologia" (Ph.D. diss., The Catholic University of America, 1938).

29. In 1939 the maternal mortality rate for white women was 353 in 100,000 live births and for African American women, 762 in 100,000 live births.

30. Developmental Considerations," 4 November 1984, Item 1633, Erikson Hrvd. Pprs.

31. Erik H. Erikson, *Childhood and Society* (New York: Norton, 1950), 229.

32. Ibid.

33. Robert Knight, M.D., was then the medical director of the Austen Riggs Center, Stockbridge, Mass. Erikson had considered an appointment at the Menninger Clinic, but internal politics there persuaded him otherwise.

34. "Autobiographic statement," undated, Item 1644, Erikson Hrvd. Pprs.

35. Erikson, *Young Man Luther*. See p. 9.

36. As Wohl said, Erikson tended to lecture and to present papers only when students, not administrators, invited him to do so. Hellmut Wohl, interview by author, Stockbridge, Mass., 12 February 1996. An example of this is Erikson's "Insight and Freedom" address, given on invitation by students as the T. B. Davie Memorial Lecture at the University of Cape Town, South Africa, 6 August 1968, Item 1499, Erikson Hrvd. Pprs.

37. Erikson to Mead, 2 March 1966, Container B-4, Mead Papers, The Library of Congress (hereafter cited as Mead Papers). The commission on the Year 2000 was a commission which, in the spirit of the period, addressed future concerns.

38. "Memorandum," to the commission on the Year 2000, Container B-4, Mead Papers.

39. Ibid.

40. "Loyola University symposium, notes," April 1970, Item 1510, Erikson Hrvd. Pprs.

41. Of those 13 articles, 5 considered education, learning, and perceptual acuity; 4 addressed mental health, body-mind functions, adjustment problems, and psychology. One each considered middle-age lifestyles, religion, relationships with children, and adult tuberous sclerosis.

42. See the following: Erik H. Erikson, "Sex Differences in the Play Configurations of Preadolescents," *American Journal of Orthopsychiatry* 21 (1951):

667–692; Erik H. Erikson, "Cross-Cultural Patterns in the Adjustment and Maladjustment of Children: I. Deviations from Normal Child Development with Reference to Cross-Cultural patterns"; "II. Etiology of Maladjustment in the Environment of the Child," in *Scandinavian Seminar on Child Psychiatry and Child Guidance* (Geneva: World Health Organization, 1952), 19–23, 26–28; and Erik H. Erikson, "Remarks Made at an Interagency Conference" at Princeton, New Jersey, 21–25 September, 1951, in *Healthy Personality Development in Children: As Related to Programs of the Federal Government* (New York: Josiah Macy, Jr., Foundation, 1952), 91–146.

43. Erik H. Erikson, "On the Sense of Inner Identity," in *Health and Human Relations* (New York: Balkiston, 1953), 124–143.

44. Erik H. Erikson, "Identity and Totality: Psychoanalytic Observations on the Problems of Youth," *Human Development Bulletin*, 5th Annual Symposium (1954), 50–82. Chicago: The Human Development Student Organization.

45. Erik H. Erikson, "The Syndrome of Identity Diffusion in Adolescents and Young Adults," in *Discussions on Child Development*, ed. J. M. Tanner and Barbel Inhelder Proceedings of the Third Meeting of the Child Study Group, World Health Organization, vol. 3. (New York: International Universities Press, 1958), 133–167. For Erikson's reference to a "unified theory," see p. 143.

46. Erik H. Erikson, *Toys and Reasons: Stages in the Ritualization of Experience* (New York: Norton, 1977). *Toys and Reasons* was Erikson's completion of his life-span theory. He presented an early draft of this book as the Godkin Lectures, Harvard University, 1972 (hereafter cited as Godkin Lectures), after his retirement from Harvard as professor of human development and lecturer in psychiatry, 1960–1970.

47. Erikson to Dorothy Burlingham, 14 October 1974, Item 765, Erikson Hrvd. Pprs.
See also Erikson letter to Lois Barclay Murphy, 15 December 1980, Item 1151, Erikson Hrvd. Pprs, in which Erikson said he had wished to "round out his theory of the life cycle by paying special attention to adulthood and old age."

48. "The Freud-Jung correspondence; selected issues," circa 15 November 1978, Item 1597, Erikson Hrvd. Pprs.

49. Erik H. Erikson, "The Human Life Cycle," in *A Way of Looking at Things*, ed. S. Schlein (New York: Norton, 1987), 598; first published in the *International Encyclopedia of the Social Sciences* (New York: Crowell-Collier, 1968), 286–292.

50. Ibid., 595.

51. Erik H. Erikson and Joan M. Erikson, "Introduction: Reflections on Aging," in *Aging and the Elderly: Humanistic Perspectives in Gerontology*, ed. S. Spicker, K. Woodward, and D. Van Tassel (Atlantic Highlands, N. J.: Humanities Press, 1978), 2.

52. The two papers on Freud are: Erik H. Erikson, "The Dream Specimen of Psychoanalysis," *Journal of the American Psychoanalytic Association* 2 (1954): 5–56; and Erik H. Erikson, "Freud's 'The Origins of Psychoanalysis,'" *International Journal of Psycho-analysis* 36 (1955): 1–15. The article on ego identity is Erik H. Erikson, "The Problem of Ego Identity," *Journal of the American Psychoanalytic Association* 4 (1956): 56–121.

53. In his 1955 panel presentation for the World Health Organization, Erikson said that his 1956 paper was then in press. It was published as "The Syndrome of Identity Diffusion in Adolescents and Young Adults," 1958. See p. 140 of that article.

54. See, for example, Erik H. Erikson, "Hitler's Imagery and German Youth," *Psychiatry* 5 (1942): 475–493.

55. Erikson, "The Syndrome of Identity Diffusion," 140.

56. Erik H. Erikson, *Childhood and Society*, 360.

57. Erikson, "The Dream Specimen"; Erikson, "Freud's 'The Origins'"; Erikson, "The First Psychoanalyst,"*Yale Review* 46 (1956): 40–62; Erikson, *Young Man Luther*.

58. "Planning Conference on the Adult," 18–19 September 1971, Item 1516, Erikson Hrvd. Pprs.

59. Erikson, "Hitler's Imagery," 475, footnote 2.

60. "Gauss Seminars in Criticism. Princeton University: miscellaneous papers," 1969, Item 1506, Erikson Hrvd. Pprs.

61. See Erik H. Erikson, "Psychoanalysis and Ongoing History: Problems of Identity, Hatred and Nonviolence"; *American Journal of Psychiatry* 122 (1965): 241–250; Erikson, "A Memorandum on Identity and Negro Youth;" Erik H. Erikson, "The Concept of Identity in Race Relations: Notes and Queries," *Daedalus* 95, no. 1 (1966): 145–170; Erik H. Erikson, *Insight and Freedom*, University of Cape Town, 6 August 1968, Item 1499, Erikson Hrvd. Pprs; Erik H. Erikson,"On Student Unrest," 10–11 May 1969, Item 1501, Erikson Hrvd. Pprs; and Erik H. Erikson, *Gandhi's Truth* (New York: Norton, 1969).

62. See Erikson, *Toys and Reasons*; Erik H. Erikson, *Insight and Responsibility* (New York: Norton, 1964); and Erik H. Erikson, "The Golden Rule and the Cycle of Life" (the George W. Gay Lecture on Medical Ethics, presented at Harvard Medical School on 4 May 1962), 412–428, in *The Study of Lives: Essays on Personality in Honor of Henry A. Murray*, ed. R. White (New York: Prentice-Hall, 1964); and Erikson, *Insight and Responsibility*. See also Erik H. Erikson, "Remarks on the 'Wider Identity'" (presented to the Catholic Worker, Tivoli, New York) and remarks made at a senatorial dinner (Washington, D.C., 1966), in Schlein, *A Way of Looking at Things*, 497–502.

63. "Miscellaneous Papers and Notes," various dates, Item 95M-2, Erikson Hrvd. Pprs.

64. Erikson, "Memorandum on Adulthood," September 1971, Item 1515, Erikson Hrvd. Pprs.

65. Erikson, *Gandhi's Truth*.

66. Erikson, *Toys and Reasons*, 11.

67. Ibid., 19.

68. Ibid., 22.

69. "University College Lectures," 28 February 1977, Item 1571, Erikson Hrvd. Pprs.

70. "Godkin Lectures," (manuscript drafts and revisions), April 1972, Item 1524, Erikson Hrvd. Pprs.

71. Ibid.

72. Erik H. Erikson, "The Galilean Sayings and the Sense of 'I'," *The Yale Review* 70 (April 1981): 321–362.

73. Erik H. Erikson, "Reflections on the Last Stage—and the First," *Psychoanalytic Study of the Child* 39 (1984): 155–165; 163.

74. "Planning Conference on the Adult," 18–19 September 1971, Item 1516, Erikson Hrvd. Pprs.

75. "Report to Vikram: Further Reflections on the Life Cycle," February 1977, Item 1573, Erikson Hrvd. Pprs.

Chapter 3: Erikson and Rethinking the Meaning of "Adult"

1. Erikson to Peter Blos, 4 November 1974, Item 739, Erikson Hrvd. Pprs.

2. "Memorandum on Adulthood," for the "Planning Conference on the Adult," September 1971, Item 1515, Erikson Hrvd. Pprs.

3. Ibid.

4. Ibid.

5. Ibid.

6. *Erikson on Erikson* (Chicago: Parents Magazine Films, Inc., 1977), film.

7. "Memorandum on Adulthood," for the "Planning Conference on the Adult," September 1971, Item 1515, Erikson Hrvd. Pprs.

8. *Oxford Latin Dictionary,* 1968, s.v. *adultus.* According to this source, the term was first used to describe humans, animals, seasons, the sun, and various other forms by T. Maccius Plautus, who died in 184 B.C.

9. Erikson to H. Lynd, November 1957, container 1, reel 1, Lynd Papers, the Library of Congress.

10. In Evans, *Dialogue with Erik Erikson.*

11. Eliot Jaques, "Death and the Mid-life Crisis," *International Journal of Psycho- Analysis* 46, no. 2 (1965): 502–514; Daniel J. Levinson, *The Seasons of a Man's Life* (New York: Ballantine Books, 1978).

12. Erikson, Gauss Seminars in Criticism, Audiotape 1, Erikson Gauss Lectures.

13. Ibid.

14. Ibid.

15. See, for example, *Webster's New Twentieth Century Dictionary of the English Language,* 2d ed., unabridged (Cleveland: World Collins 1975). See pages 1811–1818 and 1827–1830.

16. "Memorandum on Adulthood," for the "Planning Conference on the Adult," September 1971, Item 1515, Erikson Hrvd. Pprs.

17. Conference participants were Geno Ballotti, Louis Banks, Robert Bellah, John Brademas, Erik Erikson, Joan Erikson, Paul Freund, Erving Goffman, Stephen Graubard, Phyllis LaFarge, Bernice Neugarten, John Silber, Helen Tartakoff, and Roger Wilkins. See "Planning Conference on the Adult," 18–19 September 1971, Item 1516, Erikson Hrvd. Pprs.

18. "Planning Conference on the Adult," 18–19 September 1971, Item 1516, Erikson Hrvd. Pprs. Also noted by Stephen Graubard. Stephen R. Graubard, interview by author, Cambridge, Mass., 9 October 1995.

19. Erikson acknowledged his tendency toward utopian thinking in, for example, "Planning Conference on the Adult," 18–19 September 1971, Item 1516, Erikson Hrvd. Pprs. See also Erikson, *Insight and Responsibility,* 118.

20. Erikson noted this in his own hand, undated, in margin of transcript. "Planning Conference on the Adult," 18–19 September 1971, Item 1516, Erikson Hrvd. Pprs.

21. Erikson, Gauss Seminars in Criticism, Audiotape 1, Erikson Gauss Lectures.

22. "Albert Einstein, source materials," various dates, for Einstein symposium in March 1979, Item 1602, Erikson Hrvd. Pprs.

23. Erik H. Erikson, "Peter Blos: Reminiscences," in Schlein, ed., *A Way of Looking at Things* 709–712; 711. First published in *Psychosocial Process,* 3, no. 2 (Fall 1974): 4–7.

24. Ibid.

25. Stephen Schlein, interview by author, Lexington, Mass., 18 October 1995.

26. Erikson, "The Syndrome of Identity Diffusion in Adolescents and Young Adults," 166.

27. Ibid.

28. "Sophie Freud Loewenstein questions," 14 September 1983, Item 1626, Erikson Hrvd. Pprs.

29. Erikson, "The Problem of Ego Identity," 65.

30. "Reflections," circa 1983, Item 1631, Erikson Hrvd. Pprs.

31. "Fragments," various dates, Item 1725, Erikson Hrvd. Pprs.

32. Erikson, *Young Man Luther*, 14.

33. Ibid.

34. See Erikson, "The Problem of Ego Identity" and "The Syndrome of Identity Diffusion in Adolescents and Young Adults."

35. David Gutmann, interview by author, Chicago, Ill., 21 August 1995.

36. "Autobiographic statement," undated, Item 1644, Erikson Hrvd. Pprs.

37. Erikson, *Young Man Luther*, 266.

38. Erikson, *Life History and the Historical Moment*, 31.

39. Ibid.

40. "Gandhi's Truth" [Author's manuscript with revisions], undated, Item 1505, Erikson Hrvd. Pprs.

41. See Erikson, *Toys and Reasons*, 121–175.

42. Erikson to Mead, 13 September 1957, container B-4, Mead Papers. Also, in an early draft of *Young Man Luther*, in a sentence fragment that was later omitted, Erikson wondered if he had become a Lutheran. In original typescript (of *Young Man Luther*) for printer, with printer's marks, 10 July 1958, Erikson Institute papers.

43. Erikson, *Insight and Responsibility*, 22–23.

44. Hellmut Wohl, interview by author, Stockbridge, Mass., 12 February 1996.

45. "Reflections on Dr. Borg's life cycle; Miscellaneous notes," undated, Item 1711, Erikson Hrvd. Pprs.

46. *Cassell's German Dictionary, Concise Edition*, s.v. *Vorstellung*.

47. Hellmut Wohl, interview by author, Stockbridge, Mass., 12 February 1996.

48. Ibid.

49. "Memorandum on Adulthood," for the "Planning Conference on the Adult," September 1971, Item 1515, Erikson Hrvd. Pprs.

50. Ibid.

51. Mead to Erikson, 23 June 1939, Container B-4, Mead Papers.

52. Ibid.

53. Ibid.

54. Ibid.

55. "Further autobiographic remarks," August 1977, Item 1581, Erikson Hrvd. Pprs.

56. Ibid.

57. Writing to his son Jon, Erikson said that in his study in Cotuit he had a "view of the ocean." Erikson to Jon Erikson, 31 October 1966, Item 857, Erikson Hrvd. Pprs.

58. Hellmut Wohl, interview by author, Stockbridge, Mass., 12 February 1996.

59. "Notes, Harvard Alumni," 1977, Item 1589, Erikson Hrvd. Pprs.

60. Ibid.

61. Hellmut Wohl, interview by author, Stockbridge, Mass., 12 February 1996.

Chapter 4: Prejudiced Adult

1. Dexter Gate, Harvard University.

2. Erik H. Erikson, *Life History and the Historical Moment*, 175.

3. Erik H. Erikson, *Identity: Youth and Crisis* (New York: Norton, 1968), 41.

4. Ibid.

5. Erikson, *Gandhi's Truth,* 135.

6. "Mikey, fragen" (conversations with Mikey), May, June 1929, Item 1476, Erikson Hrvd. Pprs.

7. Milton Rokeach, *The Nature of Human Values* (New York: Free Press, 1973).

8. "Psychoanalysis and the future of enlightenment" is the original German title. The article was published in English in 1935 as Erik H. Erikson, "Psychoanalysis and the future of education," *Psychoanalytic Quarterly* 4 (1935): 50–68.

9. Erikson, "Observations on Sioux Education," p. 131. See also "Introductory Remarks Made at the Indian Health Service Mental Health Training Conference" [Typescript with revisions], 23 May 1974, Item 1542, Erikson Hrvd. Pprs, in which Erikson said that "marginal truths . . . become the precursors of prejudice."

10. Erik H. Erikson, "Psychoanalysis and Ongoing History: Problems of Identity, Hatred and Nonviolence," in Schlein, ed., *A Way of Looking at Things,* 481–496, 489. First published in the *American Journal of Psychiatry* 122 (1965); 241–250.

11. Erikson, "Observations on Sioux Education," 133.

12. Ibid., 121.

13. Remarks on the 'Wider Identity'" [Typescript with revisions], undated, Item 1714, Erikson Hrvd. Pprs.

14. Erikson said that these two German words were the basis of his term *pseudo-species* in "Reflections on ethos and war," circa 1984, Item 1635, Erikson Hrvd. Pprs. There and elsewhere, he credited Konrad Lorenz for its first use in the context of humans.

15. This address is titled "Insight and Freedom," 6 August 1968, Item 1499, Erikson Hrvd. Pprs. An edited version appears in Erikson, *Life History and the Historical Moment,* under the title "Freedom and Nonviolence," 169–189.

16. "Developmental Considerations" [Typescript with revisions], 4 November 1984, Item 1633, Erikson Hrvd. Pprs.

17. This definition of Erikson's is the one he used most frequently; in Erikson, *Gandhi's Truth,* p. 431. In his 1968 Cape Town "Insight and Freedom" address, the wording was nearly the same except that he inserted the words "a sense of" before the word "immortality" in the Cape Town original. See "Insight and Freedom," 6 August 1968, Item 1499, Erikson Hrvd. Pprs.

18. Erikson, "Freedom and Nonviolence," in *Life History and the Historical Moment,* 176–177.

19. "Pigs, rats, and snakes" are in "Reflections on Ethos and War" [Typescript with revisions], circa 1984, Item 1635, Erikson Hrvd. Pprs. "Forbidding boundaries" is in Erikson, "Pseudospeciation in the Nuclear Age," *Political Psychology* 6, no. 2 (1985): 213– 217; 217.

20. "Developmental Considerations" 4 November 1984, Item 1633, Erikson Hrvd. Pprs.

21. Erikson, "The Ontogeny of Ritualization in Man," 342.

22. "Letter to Cal (no surname)" [Typescript; in lieu of attending meetings in Palm Springs], 23 March 1972, Item 1520, Erikson Hrvd. Pprs.

23. Erikson, "The Ontogeny of Ritualization in Man," 346.

24. Ibid.

25. "The Freud-Jung correspondence; selected issues," circa 15 November 1978, Item 1597, Erikson Hrvd. Pprs. In Greek legend, Laius was the father of Oedipus. The oracle warned Laius not to have a child, for he would have a son who would kill him. Laius disobeyed and had a son. Laius wounded and bound

his son's ankles, branded him, and left him on a mountain to die. The son survived, was raised by others, and named Oedipus, "he of the swollen feet." When an adult, Oedipus, not recognizing his natural father when they met by chance, killed him in rage when Laius provoked him.

26. "Psychoanalysis and Ongoing History; a letter," October 1962, Item 1491, Erikson Hrvd. Pprs.

27. In several sources, Erikson rebuked others for attempting to reify that which has no concrete form. He criticized Anna Freud in particular. See, for example, "White house diary," 12 October 1965, Item 1495, Erikson Hrvd. Pprs. See also "Letter to Cal (no surname)," 23 March 1972, Item 1520, Erikson Hrvd. Pprs, and Erikson, 1975, "'Identity Crisis' in Autobiographic Perspective," 17–47.

28. W. G. Johnson, "Religion, Racism, and Self-Image: The Significance of Beliefs," *Religious Education* 68, no. 5 (1973): 620–630; 621.

29. "Play and Actuality" [Typescript with author's annotations and revisions], 18 April 1970, Item 1511, Erikson Hrvd. Pprs.

30. In an early draft of his 1942 article "Hitler's Imagery and German Youth," Erikson wrote about Hitler: "Some day it may be his worst fate and punishment that with all his hysterical gifts he cannot become insane or commit suicide when it would be most appropriate to do so."

Undated, container M-32, Mead Papers.

31. Erikson, *Gandhi's Truth,* 432.

32. "Introductory Remarks Made at the Indian Health Service Mental Health Training Conference" [Typescript with revisions], 23 May 1974, Item 1542, Erikson Hrvd. Pprs. See also Erikson and Newton, *In Search of Common Ground,* p. 54, in which Erikson said: "I must say that immigrants like myself came to this country without any childhood-conditioned awareness of skin color—a fact which made us believe at first that Americans must be on the way to overcoming this historical childhood disease." He did not mean that racism typically occurs in childhood, for he wrote that "children . . . do not accept difference in skin color as necessarily relevant if such difference has not been given connotations by traditional prejudice." In Erikson, "On the Sense of Inner Identity," footnote, p. 130.

33. Ibid.

34. Ibid., 437.

35. Erikson, *Life History and the Historical Moment,* 47.

36. All quoted material in paragraph is from "Lifecycle and Community" [unpublished manuscript], undated, Item 95M-2, Erikson Hrvd. Pprs.

37. Ibid.

38. All quoted material in paragraph is from "Lifecycle and Community" [Unpublished manuscript], undated, Item 95M-2, Erikson Hrvd. Pprs.

39. Ibid.

40. "Developmental Considerations," 4 November, 1984, Item 1633, Erikson Hrvd. Pprs.

41. "Lifecycle and Community" [Unpublished manuscript], undated, Item 95M-2, Erikson Hrvd. Pprs.

42. Sigmund Freud, *The Future of an Illusion,* trans. James Strachey (1927; reprint, New York: Norton, 1961), 14.

43. See Erikson, *Insight and Responsibility,* 149.

44. Erikson, "The Golden Rule and the Cycle of Life," 417.

45. Ibid., 414.

46. Ibid.

47. Ibid.

48. Ibid., 415.

49. See, for example, Erikson, *Childhood and Society,* 1950, 114 and 127. See also Erikson, *Childhood and Society,* 2d ed. (New York: Norton, 1963), 128.

50. Erikson, "The Ontogeny of Ritualization in Man," 338–339.

51. Ibid., 343.

52. Ibid.

53. Ibid.

54. "Godkin Lectures" [Manuscript drafts and revisions], April 1972, Item 1524, Erikson Hrvd. Pprs.

55. Erikson, *Identity: Youth and Crisis,* 298.

56. Erikson, *Childhood and Society,* 1950, 114.

57. Erikson, "Pseudospeciation in the Nuclear Age," 214.

58. Erikson, *Toys and Reasons,* 79.

59. Ibid.

60. Erikson, *Youth: Identity and Crisis,* 241.

61. Erikson, "The Ontogeny of Ritualization in Man," 343.

62. "Miscellaneous Papers and Notes," various dates, Item 95M-2, Erikson Hrvd. Pprs.

63. Erikson, "The Galilean Sayings and the Sense of 'I,'" 331.

64. Erikson, "The Golden Rule and the Cycle of Life," 417.

65. "Play and Actuality" [Typescript with author's annotations and revisions], 18 April 1970, Item 1511, Erikson Hrvd. Pprs.

66. Erik H. Erikson, "Reflections on Dr. Borg's Life Cycle," *Daedalus* 105, no. 2 (Spring 1976): 1–28.

67. See, for example, Hetty Zock, *A Psychology of Ultimate Concern* (Atlanta, Ga.: Rodopi Press, 1990); and J. Eugene Wright, *Erikson: Identity and Religion* (New York: Seabury Press, 1982).

68. In addition to those *isms,* Erikson also used the terms *elitism, formalism, totalism,* and *idolism,* among others. In all, his writings include nearly 70 words to which he added *ism.* See also, for example, 1982, 32–33, in which he related eight of the nine *isms* he identified with the eight life stages in that variation of his grid, In *The Life Circle Completed.*

69. Erikson, "The Golden Rule and the Cycle of Life," 416.

70. Ibid.

71. Erikson, "The Galilean Sayings and the Sense of 'I,'" 339–340.

72. Ibid.

73. "Identity, Hate, and Non-violence" [Typescript with annotations], undated, Item 1678, Erikson Hrvd. Pprs.

74. Erikson, *Gandhi's Truth,* 135.

75. Erikson, "The Galilean Sayings and the Sense of 'I,'" 357.

76. Erik H. Erikson, *Dimensions of a New Identity* (New York: Norton, 1974), 92.

77. Stephen Jay Gould, "A Biological Comment on Erik Erikson's Notion of Pseudospeciation" [Typescript with Erikson's annotations], 1984, Item 1796, Erikson Hrvd. Pprs.

78. "Developmental Considerations," 4 November 1984, Item 1633, Erikson Hrvd. Pprs.

79. "Remarks on the 'Wider Identity'" [Typescript with revisions], undated, Item 1714, Erikson Hrvd. Pprs.

80. For Erikson's published references to geese, see Erikson, *Insight and Responsibility,* 130; for wolves and lions, see Erikson, *Life History and the Historical Moment,* 148; for stags see, for example, Erikson, *Gandhi's Truth,* 435; for penguins, see Erikson, *Toys and Reasons,* 79.

81. "Gauss Seminars in Criticism. Princeton University: miscellaneous papers," 1969, Item 1506, Erikson Hrvd. Pprs.

82. Ibid.
83. Erik H. Erikson, "Psychoanalysis and Ongoing History: Problems of Identity, Hatred and Nonviolence," in Schlein, ed., *A Way of Looking at Things*, 486.
84. "Introductory Remarks to the Presentation of the 1975 McAlpin Medal for the National Association of Mental Health given to Alexander Hamilton Leighton" [Typescript with author's annotations], 1975, Item 1553, Erikson Hrvd. Pprs.
85. Erikson, *Toys and Reasons*, 79.
86. Erikson, "Freedom and Nonviolence," 188.
87. Ibid.
88. See Sigmund Freud, "Why War?" from *Collected Papers*, authorized translation under the supervision of Joan Riviere, vol. 5. (New York: Basic Books, 1959). See also Einstein's letter to Freud, pp. 104–105, in *Ideas and Opinions by Albert Einstein*, ed., Carl Seelig, and trans. Sonja Bargmann (New York: Random House, 1954).
89. Erikson, "Psychoanalysis and Ongoing History," 485.
90. Said by Erikson, in Erikson and Newton, *In Search of Common Ground*, 56.
91. Erikson, *Identity: Youth and Crisis*, 299.
92. "Response to Kai T. Erikson (on pseudospeciation)" [Transcript with annotations], circa 1982, Item 1623, Erikson Hrvd. Pprs.
93. Erikson, *Identity: Youth and Crisis*, 299.
94. "Systematic and often unconscious" is in ibid. "Murderous mass pseudologia" is in Erikson, *Identity: Youth and Crisis*, 299.
95. Erikson, *Gandhi's Truth*, 438.
96. Erikson, *Identity: Youth and Crisis*, 299.
97. Ibid.
98. "Miscellaneous Papers and Notes," various dates, Item 95M-2, Erikson Hrvd. Pprs.
99. Erikson, *Gandhi's Truth*, 431.
100. "Play and Actuality" [Typescript with author's annotations and revisions], 18 April 1970, Item 1511, Erikson Hrvd. Pprs.
101. Erikson, *Gandhi's Truth*, 435.
102. Erikson, "The Golden Rule and the Cycle of Life," 421.
103. Erikson, *Gandhi's Truth*, 435.
104. Ibid.
105. "Lifecycle and Community" [Unpublished manuscript], undated, Item 95M-2, Erikson Hrvd. Pprs.
106. Ibid.
107. Erikson, "Memorandum on Adulthood," September 1971, Item 1515, Erikson Hrvd. Pprs.
108. In Erikson, *Childhood and Society*, 1960, 281; see footnote 2, in which Erikson cited Sigmund Freud, "Ansprache an die Mitglieder des Vereins B'nai B'rith (1926)," *Gesammelte Werke*, vol. 16 (London: Imago, 1941).
109. Erikson, "The Problem of Ego Identity," 56–57.
110. Sigmund Freud, *The Future of an Illusion*, trans. James Strachey (1927; reprint, New York: Norton, 1961), 16.
111. Oswald Spengler, *The Decline of the West* (1918; reprint, New York: Knopf, 1922; one-volume ed., 1932).
112. Erikson, *Childhood and Society*, 1950, 311. See also Erikson, "Hitler's Imagery and German Youth," in which Erikson cited Spengler, 487.
113. Spengler, *The Decline of the West*, 189.
114. Ibid.

115. Ibid., 206.
116. Ibid., 243.
117. Ibid., 237.
118. Margaret Mead to Erik Erikson, 23 May 1939, Container B-4, Mead Papers.
119. Heinrich Zimmer, *Philosophies of India* (New York: Meridian Books, 1956).
120. Erikson, *Gandhi's Truth*, 75.
121. Zimmer quoted by Erikson, *Gandhi's Truth*, 76.
122. Erikson in Erikson and Newton, *In Search of Common Ground*, 128.
123. Erikson, *Identity: Youth and Crisis*, 43.
124. Ibid., 42.
125. Erikson in Erikson and Newton, *In Search of Common Ground*, 85–86.
126. See, for example, Erikson, "Observations on Sioux Education"; Erikson, "Hitler's Imagery and German Youth"; and Erikson, "Observations on the Yurok: Childhood and World Image."
127. Mead to Erikson, 19 May 1954, container B-4, Mead Papers.
128. "Dear Friends" [Letter sent to Al Emrich for Aspen Conference], 9 August 1976, Item 1558, Erikson Hrvd. Pprs. See also Erikson, *Toys and Reasons*, 59.
129. Ibid.
130. "Fragments, unsorted," various dates, Item 1725, Erikson Hrvd. Pprs.
131. Ibid.
132. Aging" [Typescript], undated, Item 1562, Erikson Hrvd. Pprs.
133. Ibid.
134. Erikson, "The Ontogeny of Ritualization in Man," 342.
135. "Rejectivity," and "negative identity" is ibid. "Does not care to be like or to care for" is from "Memorandum on Pseudo-speciation" [Typescript with annotations], undated, Item 1691, Erikson Hrvd. Pprs.
136. "Psychoanalysis and Ongoing History; a letter," October 1962, Item 1491, Erikson Hrvd. Pprs. See Erich Fromm, *May Man Prevail? An Inquiry into the Facts and Fictions of Foreign Policy* (Garden City, NY: Doubleday, 1961).
137. "Psychoanalysis and Ongoing History; a letter," October 1962, Item 1491, Erikson Hrvd. Pprs.
138. Reflections on Adulthood" [Draft of article published as "Reflections on Dr. Borg's Life Cycle"], Spring 1976, Item 1565, Erikson Hrvd. Pprs.
139. "Developmental Considerations," 4 November 1984, Item 1633, Erikson Hrvd. Pprs.
140. Erikson, "Pseudospeciation in the Nuclear Age," 213.
141. Ibid., 214.
142. Erikson, *Young Man Luther*, 193.

Chapter 5: Moral-Ethical, Spiritual Adult

1. Erik H. Erikson, "On the Potential of Women," in Schlein, ed., *A Way of Looking at Things* 660–669; 666. First published as "Concluding Remarks" in *Women and the Scientific Professions*, ed. Jacquelyn A. Mattfeld and Carol G. Van Aken, (Cambridge, MA: MIT Press, 1965), 232-245
2. Erikson to Curfman, 30 December 1976, Item 811, Erikson Hrvd. Pprs.
3. "Miscellaneous Papers and Notes," various dates, Item 95M-2, Erikson Hrvd. Pprs.
4. Erikson, *Insight and Responsibility*, 225–226.
5. "Psychoanalysis and Ethics—Avowed and Unavowed." Concluding pres-

entation to a symposium of the American Academy of Arts and Sciences and the American Psychoanalytic Association on ethics, moral values and psychological interventions, 1 March 1974, Item 1539, Erikson Hrvd. Pprs.

6. "Our most ethical and most moralistic sides tend to make deals with each other" is ibid. "Superego making deals with the id to develop sadism through morality" is from "Erik Erikson on Play, vision, and deception" [Transcript], 25 August 1973, Item 1534, Erikson Hrvd. Pprs. Ibid.

7. Erikson, *Insight and Responsibility*, 227.

8. "Miscellaneous Papers and Notes," various dates, Item 95M-2, Erikson Hrvd. Pprs.

9. Ibid.

10. Erikson, *Young Man Luther*, 140.

11. "Letter for Bob Shaw on Program in a Transformational Context for Therapy," 20 March 1981, Item 1616, Erikson Hrvd. Pprs.

12. Erikson, *Dimensions of a New Identity*, 90.

13. Peter Blos Discussion" [Typescript with author's revisions], circa 1978, Item 1600, Erikson Hrvd. Pprs.

14. Erikson, "The Golden Rule and the Cycle of Life," 415.

15. Ibid., 422.

16. "Miscellaneous Papers and Notes," various dates, Item 95M-2, Erikson Hrvd. Pprs.

17. Ibid.

18. *The Analects of Confucius*, trans. Arthur Waley (London: Allen & Unwin, 1938), 88.

19. Erikson, *Insight and Responsibility*, 222.

20. See, for example, ibid., 239. See also Erikson, *Gandhi's Truth*, 342.

21. Erikson, "Reflections on Dr. Borg's Life Cycle," 16.

22. Erikson, *Insight and Responsibility*, 100.

23. Erikson, *Dimensions of a New Identity*, 123.

24. Ibid.

25. "Miscellaneous Papers and Notes," various dates, Item 95M-2, Erikson Hrvd. Pprs.

26. See, for example, Erikson, *Insight and Responsibility*, 223.

27. Erikson, *Dimensions of a New Identity*, 124.

28. "Psychoanalysis and Ethics—Avowed and Unavowed," 1 March 1974, Item 1539, Erikson Hrvd. Pprs.

29. "Miscellaneous Papers and Notes," various dates, Item 95M-2, Erikson Hrvd. Pprs.

30. Ibid.

31. "Reflections on Ethos and War" [Typescript with revisions], circa 1984, Item 1635, Erikson Hrvd. Pprs.

32. His search for the "religious genius" through studying Luther and Gandhi is from "Lecture [at Santa Barbara Erikson Symposium]," 19 February 1972, Item 1519, Erikson Hrvd. Pprs. For his search for ethical truth in relativity, see Erikson, *Dimensions of a New Identity*, 103.

33. Erikson, "The Golden Rule and the Cycle of Life," 415.

34. Ibid., 428, and Erikson, *Insight and Responsibility*, 220 and 243.

35. For "hidden God," see Erikson, *Young Man Luther*, 125. For "lurking on the periphery of space and time," see p. 213.

36. Ibid., 264.

37. "Lifecycle and Community" (unpublished manuscript), undated, Item 95M-2, Erikson Hrvd. Pprs.

38. "Miscellaneous Papers and Notes," various dates, Item 95M-2, Erikson Hrvd. Pprs.

39. Ibid.

40. Erikson, "The Galilean Sayings and the Sense of 'I,'" 329.

41. Ibid., 330.

42. "Epilogue" [for Mt. Zion book], undated, Item 1670, Erikson Hrvd. Pprs.

43. "Godkin Lectures" [Manuscript drafts and revisions], April 1972, Item 1524, Erikson Hrvd. Pprs.

44. See, for example, ibid. See also Erikson, *Young Man Luther*, 183.

45. Erikson, "The Galilean Sayings and the Sense of 'I,'" 344–345.

46. Ibid., 345.

47. "Miscellaneous Papers and Notes," various dates, Item 95M-2, Erikson Hrvd. Pprs.

48. Erikson, *Young Man Luther*, 141.

49. "Case History and Life History" [Unpublished manuscript], undated, Item 95M-2, Erikson Hrvd. Pprs.

50. "Godkin Lectures: The Child's Toys and the Old Man's Reasons" [Author's typescript with revisions], April 1972, Item 1523, Erikson Hrvd. Pprs.

51. "Godkin Lectures: Play, Vision, and Deception" [Author's typescript], April 1972, Item 1521, Erikson Hrvd. Pprs.

52. "Miscellaneous Papers and Notes," various dates, Item 95M-2, Erikson Hrvd. Pprs.

53. Erikson, *Young Man Luther*, 124.

54. In "White House diary," 12 October 1965, Item 1495, Erikson Hrvd. Pprs. Also, "Letter to Cal (no surname)," 23 March 1972, Item 1520, Erikson Hrvd. Pprs.; and Erikson, 1975, "'Identity Crisis' in Autobiographic Perspective," 17–47.

55. "Miscellaneous Papers and Notes," various dates, Item 95M-2, Erikson Hrvd. Pprs.

56. Erikson, *Gandhi's Truth*, 34.

57. "Spiritual meaninglessness" is in "Psychoanalysis and Ongoing History; a letter," October 1962, Item 1491, Erikson Hrvd. Pprs. Accentuation of nonbeing by the sense of depleted time, space, and strength is in "Miscellaneous Papers and Notes," various dates, Item 95M-2, Erikson Hrvd. Pprs.

58. Erikson, "Reflections on Dr. Borg's Life Cycle," 5.

59. Erikson, *Gandhi's Truth*, 41.

60. See, for example, Erikson, "Reflections on Dr. Borg's Life Cycle."

61. "Miscellaneous Papers and Notes," various dates, Item 95M-2, Erikson Hrvd. Pprs.

62. Erikson to Curfman, 30 December 1976, Item 811, Erikson Hrvd. Pprs.

63. Erikson used approximately 30 terms for God. In his published writings, the terms he used most frequently were: "Ultimate Other" (see "Reflections on Dr. Borg's Life Cycle," 11, "The Galilean Sayings and the Sense of 'I,'" 330, and "Reflections on the Last Stage—and the First," 160); "God" (see "The Galilean Sayings and the Sense of 'I,'" 353, and *Young Man Luther*, 125, 182–183, and 264), "Absolute Being" (see *Gandhi's Truth*, 411); "supreme counterplayer" (see *Toys and Reasons*, 50); "Super-Identity" (see *Young Man Luther*, 181); "Maker" and "Fabricator" (see *Dimensions of a New Identity* 78); "True Identity . . . True Reality" (see *Young Man Luther*, 76); "Higher Identity" (see *Luther*, 177); "Prime Planner and Builder" (see *Luther*, 184); and "God-head" (see *Luther*, 264). "Great Spirit" is in "Introductory Remarks Made at the Indian Health Service Mental Health Training Conference" [Typescript with revisions], 23 May 1974, Item 1542, Erikson Hrvd. Pprs. "Final Other" and "Numen" are in "The Galilean Sayings and the Sense of 'I'" [Author's typescript with revisions], April 1981, Item 1617, Erikson Hrvd. Pprs. "Divine Thou" and

"Grand Ultimate" are in "Lifecycle and Community" [Unpublished manuscript], undated, Item 95M-2, Erikson Hrvd. Pprs.

64. "Miscellaneous Papers and Notes," various, dates, Item 95M-2, Erikson Hrvd. Pprs.

65. "Play and Actuality" [Typescript with author's annotations and revisions], 18 April 1970, Item 1511, Erikson Hrvd. Pprs.

66. Erikson, "The Galilean Sayings and the Sense of 'I,'" 324.

67. "Psychoanalysis and Ethics—Avowed and Unavowed," 1 March 1974, Item 1539, Erikson Hrvd. Pprs.

68. Erikson, *Life History and the Historical Moment*, 31.

69. Erik H. Erikson, "Psychoanalysis and Ethics—Avowed or Unavowed," *International Review of Psychoanalysis* 3: 409–415; 411.

70. Ibid.

71. Erikson, "The Golden Rule and the Cycle of Life," 426.

72. Erikson, "Psychoanalysis and Ethics—Avowed or Unavowed," 411.

73. Erikson, "The Golden Rule and the Cycle of Life," 427.

74. "Lifecycle and Community" [Unpublished manuscript], undated, Item 95M-2, Erikson Hrvd. Pprs.

75. "Miscellaneous Papers and Notes," various dates, Item 95M-2, Erikson Hrvd. Pprs.

76. See, for example, Paul Roazen, *Erik H. Erikson: The Power and Limits of a Vision* (New York: Free Press, 1976).

77. See, for example, Robert Coles, *Erik H. Erikson: The Growth of His Work* (Boston, Mass.: Little, Brown, 1970); James W. Fowler, Karl E. Nipkow, and Friedrich Schweitzer, eds., *Stages of Faith and Religious Development: Implications for Church, Education, and Society* (New York: Crossroad, 1991); Robert J. Lifton, *The Protean Self* (New York: Basic Books, 1993).

78. "Introductory Remarks Made at the Indian Health Service Mental Health Training Conference" [Typescript with revisions], 23 May 1974, Item 1542, Erikson Hrvd. Pprs.

79. Erik H. Erikson, Gauss Seminars in Criticism, Audiotape 1, Erikson Gauss Lectures.

80. See Erikson, "The Galilean Sayings and the Sense of 'I.'"

81. "Miscellaneous Papers and Notes," various dates, Item 95M-2, Erikson Hrvd. Pprs.

82. Erikson to Curfman, "Is Erikson a Christian?" [Answer to question], 30 December 1976, Item 811, Erikson Hrvd. Pprs.

83. Ibid.

84. In his notes, Erikson said that the female protagonist Marianne in Ingmar Bergman's film *Wild Strawberries* had led him to change the Golden Rule. To him, Marianne embodied generativity. She did not refrain from aiding her own and others' development even when doing so created temporary interpersonal difficulties. In "Reflections on Adulthood" [Draft of article published as "Reflections on Dr. Borg's Life Cycle," Spring 1976, Item 1565, Erikson Hrvd. Pprs.] See Erikson, "Reflections on Dr. Borg's Life Cycle."

85. Joan M. Erikson, interview by author, Harwich, Mass., 11 October, 1995; see Erikson to Curfman, "Is Erikson a Christian?" [Answer to question], 30 December 1976, Item 811, Erikson Hrvd. Pprs.

86. Ibid.

87. Ibid.

88. "Planning Conference on the Adult," 18–19 September 1971, Item 1516, Erikson Hrvd. Pprs.

89. Erikson Institute Papers, Item 1358.

90. "Albert Einstein" [Research materials and notes used for work on Ein-

stein], circa 1979, Item 1601, Erikson Hrvd. Pprs. See Einstein, "A Symposium," Part 2, 44–49, in *Ideas and Opinions by Albert Einstein*, 46.

91. Erik H. Erikson to Peter Blos, 4 November 1974, Item 739, Erikson Hrvd. Pprs.

92. For "Western form of meditation" see Erik H. Erikson, "Reflections on Historical Change: A Foreword." In *Children and Parents in a Changing World*, vol. 5, of *The Child and His Family: Yearbook of the International Association for Child Psychiatry and Allied Professions*, ed., James Anthony and Colette Chiland, (New York: Wiley, 1978), xi–xxi, xx. Expectations that therapists would create substitute faith structures and rituals for patients is in "Introductory Remarks Made at the Indian Health Service Mental Health Training Conference" [Typescript with revisions], 23 May 1974, Item 1542, Erikson Hrvd. Pprs.

93. Erikson, "On the Sense of Inner Identity," 127.

94. "Mikey, fragen" [Conversations with Mikey], May, June 1929, Item 1476, Erikson Hrvd. Pprs.

95. Erikson, *Identity: Youth and Crisis*, 10.

96. "Lifecycle and Community" [Unpublished manuscript], undated, Item 95M-2, Erikson Hrvd. Pprs.

97. Ibid.

98. Carol H. Hoare, "Ethical Self, Spiritual Self: Wisdom and Integrity in the Writings of Erik H. Erikson," in *Creativity, Spirituality, and Transcendence: Paths to Integrity and Wisdom in the Mature Self*, ed., Melvin E. Miller and Susanne R. Cook-Greuter, (Stamford, Conn.: Ablex, 2000); 75–98.

99. Joan M. Erikson, interview by author, Harwich, Mass., 11 October 1995.

100. Erikson, *Young Man Luther*, 41.

101. Erikson, *Gandhi's Truth*, 36.

102. Erikson, *Insight and Responsibility*, 155.

103. "Lifecycle and Community" [Unpublished manuscript], undated, Item 95M-2, Erikson Hrvd. Pprs.

104. Ibid.

105. Erikson, *Dimensions of A New Identity*, 47–48.

106. Erikson, "The Galilean Sayings and the Sense of 'I,'" 346.

107. Ibid., 345–346.

108. Ibid., 360.

109. "A negation of superstition, an imaginary result of its elimination" is from "The Galilean Sayings and the Sense of 'I'" [Author's typescript with revisions], April 1981, Item 1617, Erikson Hrvd. Pprs. See Albert Einstein, "Is There a Jewish Point of View?," in *Ideas and Opinions by Albert Einstein*, 186. "Moralism" and "pietism" are from "Miscellaneous Papers and Notes," various dates, Item 95M-2, Erikson Hrvd. Pprs.

110. "Miscellaneous Papers and Notes," various dates, Item 95M-2, Erikson Hrvd. Pprs.

111. Ibid.

112. Erikson Institute, Item 1358.

113. See Erikson, *Dimensions of a New Identity*.

114. "Virginal" is in Erikson Institute Papers, item 1358. "Purged" of "additions," especially those of "the priests," is in "Miscellaneous Papers and Notes," various dates, Item 95M-2, Erikson Hrvd. Pprs.

115. Erikson, *Young Man Luther*, 188.

116 Ibid., 242.

117. Ibid., 226.

118. Ibid., 187.

119. "Miscellaneous Papers and Notes," various dates, Item 95M-2, Erikson Hrvd. Pprs.

120. See Erikson, *Toys and Reasons*, 36, in which Erikson wrote that Oedipus's pierced feet meant that, when grown, he would be prevented from performing "the sinful initiatives predicted by the Oracle."

121. Erikson, *Insight and Responsibility*, 153.

122. Ibid.

123. Erikson, *Young Man Luther*, 60 and 265.

124. Erikson Institute Papers, Item 1358.

125. Erikson, *Young Man Luther*, 209–210.

126. See Erikson, *Insight and Responsibility*, 91.

127. Ibid., 155.

128. Erikson Institute Papers, Item 1357.

129. Erikson, *Young Man Luther*, 264.

130. Ibid., 265.

131. "Miscellaneous Papers and Notes," various dates, Item 95M-2, Erikson Hrvd. Pprs.

132. See Erikson, "The Galilean Sayings and the Sense of 'I,'" 350, 360.

133. Ibid., 343.

134. See ibid., 336.

135. See Erikson, *Insight and Responsibility*, 115.

136. Ibid.

137. Erikson, *Gandhi's Truth*, 34.

138. Ibid., 87.

139. Ibid.

140. Ibid., 164.

141. Ibid., 165.

142. "Psychoanalysis and Ongoing History; a letter," October 1962, Item 1491, Erikson Hrvd. Pprs.

143. "Play and Actuality" [Typescript with author's annotations and revisions], 18 April 1970, Item 1511, Erikson Hrvd. Pprs.

144. Erikson, *Insight and Responsibility*, 165.

145. Ibid.

146. "The Galilean Sayings and the Sense of 'I'" [Author's typescript with revisions], April 1981, Item 1617, Erikson Hrvd. Pprs.

147. "Psychoanalysis and Ethics—Avowed and Unavowed," 1 March 1974, Item 1539, Erikson Hrvd. Pprs.

148. "Miscellaneous Papers and Notes," various dates, Item 95M-2, Erikson Hrvd. Pprs.

149. Ibid.

150. Erikson, *Life History and the Historical Moment*, 173.

151. Erikson, *Gandhi's Truth*, 412.

152. "Mikey, fragen" [Conversations with Mikey], May, June 1929, item 1476, Erikson Hrvd. Pprs.

153. Evans, *Dialogue with Erik Erikson*, 96.

154. "Miscellaneous Papers and Notes," various dates, Item 95M-2, Erikson Hrvd. Pprs.

155. Erikson, *Insight and Responsibility*, 167.

156. See, for example, Erikson, *Young Man Luther*, 159.

157. Erik H. Erikson to Zvi Luri, 1956, Item 1100, Erikson Hrvd. Pprs.

158. Erikson, *Young Man Luther*, 209.

159. Erikson, *Insight and Responsibility*, 415.

160. See Erikson, *Dimensions of a New Identity*, 104.

161. "Spirituality, its Nature and the Discipline which Studies it" [Berkeley Seminar], undated, Item 1717, Erikson Hrvd. Pprs.

162. Erik H. Erikson, "Godkin Lectures" [manuscript drafts and revisions], April 1972, Item 1524, Erikson Hrvd. Pprs.

163. Ibid.

164. "To Take or Not to Take an Oath," spring 1972, Item 1529, Erikson Hrvd. Pprs.

165. "Miscellaneous Papers and Notes," various dates, Item 95M-2, Erikson Hrvd. Pprs.

166. Erikson, "The Galilean Sayings and the Sense of 'I,'" 323.

167. Erikson, *Insight and Responsibility*, 112.

168. Erikson, *Young Man Luther*, 214.

169. "[Reminiscences] Remarks, Peter Blos Lecture, Jewish Board of Guardians," 7 December 1971, Item 1517, Erikson Hrvd. Pprs.

170. Ibid.

171. Erikson, *Young Man Luther*, 214.

172. Ibid.

173. Erikson, "Reflections on Dr. Borg's Life Cycle," 18.

174. "Remarks on the 'Wider Identity'" [Typescript with revisions], undated, Item 1714, Erikson Hrvd. Pprs.

175. See Erikson, *Gandhi's Truth*, 225.

176. Erikson, *Dimensions of a New Identity*, 58.

177. Erikson, *Young Man Luther*, 73.

178. Lecture on "Evidence and Inference," given in 1957 at the Massachusetts Institute of Technology. In Erikson, *Insight and Responsibility*, 70.

179. "Georgy Kepes," 1970, Item 1513, Erikson Hrvd. Pprs.

180. "Remarks on the 'Wider Identity'" [Typescript with revisions], undated, Item 1714, Erikson Hrvd. Pprs.

181. "Miscellaneous Papers and Notes," various dates, Item 95M-2, Erikson Hrvd. Pprs.

182. "Lifecycle and Community" [Unpublished manuscript], undated, Item 95M-2, Erikson Hrvd. Pprs.

183. See *Tao Te Ching*, trans. Victor H. Mair (New York: Bantam Books, 1990).

184. Erikson, "The Galilean Sayings and the Sense of 'I,'" 327.

185. *Arthur Schopenhauer—Essays and Aphorisms*, trans. R. J. Hollingdale (New York: Penguin Books, 1970), 133. Erikson referenced Schopenhauer in "Epilogue" [for Mt. Zion book], undated, Item 1670, Erikson Hrvd. Pprs.

186. See Erikson, *Dimensions of a New Identity*, 49.

187. "Letter to Cal (no surname)" [Typescript; in lieu of attending meetings in Palm Springs], 23 March 1972, Item 1520, Erikson Hrvd. Pprs.

188. Erikson, *Insight and Responsibility*, 96.

189. "Miscellaneous Papers and Notes," various dates, Item 95M-2, Erikson Hrvd. Pprs.

190. "Psychoanalysis and Ongoing History; a letter," October 1962, Item 1491, Erikson Hrvd. Pprs.

191. "Miscellaneous Papers and Notes," various dates, Item 95M-2, Erikson Hrvd. Pprs.

192. Erikson, *Insight and Responsibility*, 113.

193. Ibid., 140.

194. Ibid., 142.

195. Ibid., 139.

196. See Erikson, "Psychoanalysis and Ethics—Avowed or Unavowed," 411.

Note that Erikson worked in the period before neuropsychiatry isolated the biochemical basis of a number of mental disorders.

197. Miscellaneous Papers and Notes," various dates, Item 95M-2, Erikson Hrvd. Pprs.

198. Erikson, *Gandhi's Truth*, 249.

199. Erikson, "Reflections on Dr. Borg's Life Cycle," 13.

200. Miscellaneous Papers and Notes," various dates, Item 95M-2, Erikson Hrvd. Pprs.

201. "Godkin Lectures: Play, Vision, and Deception" [Author's typescript], April 1972, Item 1521, Erikson Hrvd. Pprs.

202. Ibid.

203. Ibid.

204. Erikson, "The Galilean Sayings and the Sense of 'I,'" 346.

205. Miscellaneous Papers and Notes," various dates, Item 95M-2, Erikson Hrvd. Pprs.

206. Erikson, "The Galilean Sayings and the Sense of 'I,'" 346.

207. Erikson, *Gandhi's Truth*, 100 and 128.

208. "Fragments, unsorted," various dates, Item 1725, Erikson Hrvd. Pprs.

209. Erikson, *Insight and Responsibility*, 220.

210. Ibid., 243.

211. "Miscellaneous Papers and Notes," various dates, Item 95M-2, Erikson Hrvd. Pprs.

212. Erikson borrowed this notion from his friend, Helmutt Wohl. Noted in "Lecture [at Santa Barbara Erikson Symposium]," 19 February 1972, Item 1519, Erikson Hrvd. Pprs.

213. Erikson, *Young Man Luther*, 216.

214. Erikson, "The Galilean Sayings and the Sense of 'I,'" 347.

215. Erikson, *Gandhi's Truth*, 169.

216. Ibid., 348.

217. Erikson Institute, Item 1358.

Chapter 6: Playing, Childlike Adult

1. "Dear Friends" [Letter sent to Al Emrich for Aspen Conference], 9 August 1976, Item 1558, Erikson Hrvd. Pprs.

2. The concept of resisting children is in "Notes on Adulthood," undated, Item 1696, Erikson Hrvd. Pprs. "Stereotype" children is in "Honor thy Children" [A benefit poetry reading], 25 April 1980, Item 1612, Erikson Hrvd. Pprs.

3. Erikson, *Toys and Reasons*, 55.

4. Erik H. Erikson and Huey P. Newton, *In Search of Common Ground* (New York: Norton, 1973), 52.

5. Interviewed by Sharon Waxman, this is the way Schulz said he would like to be remembered. The phrase is E. B. White's description of James Thurber's writing. See *Washington Post*, 22 October 1996, D1–D2.

6. In the total body of Erikson's writings as they appear in Schlein's bibliography, children, their needs, and child's play nearly rival identity in emphasis. Of 120 total publications, 24 address children specifically (including his book *Childhood and Society*, 1950, 1963), and 17 publications address identity (including youth and identity in *Identity, Youth, and Crisis*, 1968; identity-intimacy in *Young Man Luther*, 1957, and identity-generativity in *Gandhi's Truth*, 1969).

7. Erikson, *Childhood and Society*, 1950, 1963.

8. For the "Godkin Lectures" at Harvard University, 1972.

9. Erikson, *Toys and Reasons*, 1977.

10. For childlike wonder, see Erik H. Erikson,"Psychoanalytic Reflections on Einstein's Centenary," in *Albert Einstein: Historical and Cultural Perspectives*, ed. Gerald Holton and Yehuda Elkana. (Princeton, N.J.: Princeton University Press, 1980), 151–173. For the relationship between healthy adult ego evolution and childlike faith see Erikson, "The Galilean Sayings and the Sense of 'I'."

11. For example, notions on play appear in Erikson's books *Young Man Luther, Gandhi's Truth,* and *Life History and the Historical Moment,* and in his article "Reflections on Dr. Borg's Life Cycle."

12. Erikson, *Young Man Luther,* 152.

13. "Godkin Lectures: Play, Vision, and Deception" [Author's typescript], April 1972, Item 1521, Erikson Hrvd. Pprs.

14. Ibid.

15. "Miscellaneous Papers and Notes," various dates, Item 95M-2, Erikson Hrvd. Pprs.

16. "Godkin Seminar" [Transcripts of discussions; author's typescript with annotations], April 1972, Item 1527, Erikson Hrvd. Pprs. See also Erik H. Erikson, "Studies in the Interpretation of Play: Clinical Observations of Play Disruption in Young Children," in Schlein, ed., *A Way of Looking at Things,* 139–236. First published in *Genetic Psychology Monographs* 22 (1940): 557–671.

17. "University College Lectures" [Lectures for London; author's typescript], 28 February 1977, Item 1571, Erikson Hrvd. Pprs.

18. "Psychoanalytic Reflections on Einstein's Life and Work, Personal" [Author's typescript], undated but may be associated with trip to Jerusalem in 1979, Item 1605, Erikson Hrvd. Pprs.

19. Erik H. Erikson, "The Dream Specimen of Psychoanalysis," in *Psychoanalytic Psychiatry and Psychology: Clinical and Theoretical Papers.* The Austen Riggs Center, I eds. Robert P. Knight and Cyrus R. Friedman (New York: International Universities Press, 1954), 131–70. See pp. 149–150. First published in the *Journal of the American Psychoanalytic Association,* 2 (1954), 5–56.

20. "Lifecycle and Community" [Unpublished manuscript], undated, Item 95M-2, Erikson Hrvd. Pprs.

21. "Mikey, fragen" [Conversations with Mikey], May, June 1929, Item 1476, Erikson Hrvd. Pprs.

22. "Miscellaneous Papers and Notes," various dates, Item 95M-2, Erikson Hrvd. Pprs.

23. Ibid.

24. Ibid.

25. Ibid.

26. Ibid.

27. Ibid.

28. Erikson, *Insight and Responsibility,* 227.

29. "Planning Conference on the Adult," 18–19 September 1971, Item 1516, Erikson Hrvd. Pprs.

30. Erikson, *Toys and Reasons,* 34.

31. "Loyola Symposium" [Notes], April 1970, Item 1510, Erikson Hrvd. Pprs.

32. "Planning Conference on the Adult" 18–19 September 1971, Item 1516, Erikson Hrvd. Pprs.

33. "Habitually unresponsive adult" and "inimical other" are in "Godkin Lectures: Play, Vision, and Deception" [Author's typescript], April 1972, Item 1521, Erikson Hrvd. Pprs. "The unresponsive eye becomes an evil one" is in "Godkin Lectures: The Child's Toys and the Old Man's Reasons" [Author's typescript with revisions], April 1972, Item 1523, Erikson Hrvd. Pprs.

34. "Insight and Freedom," 6 August 1968, Item 1499, Erikson Hrvd. Pprs.

35. "Association for Mental Health" [Notes], undated, Item 1641, Erikson Hrvd. Pprs.

36. Erikson, *Young Man Luther*, 119.

37. Erikson, *Toys and Reasons*, 50.

38. "Godkin Lectures: Spheres of Play" [Lecture outline and notes], April 1972, Item 1522, Erikson Hrvd. Pprs.

39. "Erik Erikson on Play, vision, and deception" [Transcript], 25 August 1973, Item 1534, Erikson Hrvd. Pprs.

40. "An impulsive need to coerce by violent means, and a dark impulse to negate others" is in "University College Lectures" [Lectures for London; Author's typescript], 28 February 1977, Item 1571, Erikson Hrvd. Pprs. The exclusion of play from work is in "Comments on the Symposium on Dynamic Psychology and Education: Contributions from a Modern Psychoanalytic Perspective" [Typescript with author's annotations], 20 April 1976, Item 1557, Erikson Hrvd. Pprs.

41. "University College Lectures," 28 February 1977, Item 1571, Erikson Hrvd. Pprs.

42. From "Association for Mental Health" [Notes], undated, Item 1641, Erikson Hrvd. Pprs; also in "Godkin Lectures: The Child's Toys and the Old Man's Reasons" [Author's typescript with revisions], April 1972, Item 1523, Erikson Hrvd. Pprs.

43. "Godkin Lectures: Spheres of Play" [Author's manuscript], April 1972, Item 1522, Erikson Hrvd. Pprs.

44. Erikson, *Childhood and Society*, 1963, 150.

45. Erikson, "Reflections on Dr. Borg's Life Cycle."

46. "Reflections on Adulthood" [Draft of article published as "Reflections on Dr. Borg's Life Cycle"], Spring 1976, Item 1565, Erikson Hrvd. Pprs.

47. Erikson, *Toys and Reasons*, 121.

48. "Play and Actuality" [Typescript with author's annotations and revisions], 18 April 1970, Item 1511, Erikson Hrvd. Pprs. Also "Lecture [at Santa Barbara Erikson Symposium]," 19 February 1972, Item 1519, Erikson Hrvd. Pprs.

49. Ibid.

50. See Erikson, "The Syndrome of Identity Diffusion in Adolescents and Young Adults," pp. 133–167, in *Discussions on Child Development* ed., J. M. Tanner and Barbel Inhelder, Proceedings of the Third Meeting of the Child Study Group, World Health Organization, vol. 3. (New York: International Universities Press, 1958).

51. The Loyola Symposium took place in 1970 and the Godkin Lectures in 1972.

52. "Operations" is in "Godkin Lectures: Play, Vision, and Deception" [Author's typescript], April 1972, Item 1521, Erikson Hrvd. Pprs. "Hypothetical propositions" appears in Erikson, *Identity: Youth and Crisis*, 245. "Constructing" and "re-inventing" appears in Erikson, *Toys and Reasons*, 34.

53. "New identity element" is in Erikson, *Toys and Reasons*, 44. "Experience . . . might lead" is from "Play and Actuality" [Typescript with author's annotations and revisions], 18 April 1970, Item 1511, Erikson Hrvd. Pprs.

54. Erikson, *Toys and Reasons*, 100.

55. "Godkin Lectures: Play, Vision, and Deception" [Author's typescript], April 1972, Item 1521, Erikson Hrvd. Pprs.

56. Erik H. Erikson, "Godkin Lectures" [Manuscript drafts and revisions], April 1972, Item 1524, Erikson Hrvd. Pprs. See also "Godkin Lectures: Play, Vision, and Deception" [Author's typescript], April 1972, Item 1521, Erikson Hrvd. Pprs.

57. "National Academy of Education" [Notes], undated, Item 1693, Erikson Hrvd. Pprs.

58. "Godkin Lectures: Play, Vision, and Deception" [Author's typescript], April 1972, Item 1521, Erikson Hrvd. Pprs.

59. Erik H. Erikson, "Godkin Lectures" [Manuscript drafts and revisions], April 1972, Item 1524, Erikson Hrvd. Pprs.

60. Erikson, *Childhood and Society*, 1963, 220.

61. Ibid.

62. Erik H. Erikson, "Sex Differences in the Play Configurations of Preadolescents," *American Journal of Orthopsychiatry* 21 (1951): 667–692.

63. Erikson, *Toys and Reasons*, 78.

64. Erik H. Erikson, "University College Lectures," 28 February 1977, Item 1571, Erikson Hrvd. Pprs. See Johan Huizinga, *Homo Ludens: A Study of the Play-Element in Culture* (Boston, Mass.: Beacon Press, 1950).

65. "Temporary world" and "new identity elements" are in Erik H. Erikson, "University College Lectures," 28 February 1977, Item 1571, Erikson Hrvd. Pprs. "Territoriality" is in "Godkin Seminar" [Transcripts of discussions; author's typescript with annotations], April 1972, Item 1527, Erikson Hrvd. Pprs. Representation of toy objects is in "Lifecycle and Community" [Unpublished manuscript], undated, Item 95M-2, Erikson Hrvd. Pprs.

66. Erik H. Erikson, "The Ontogeny of Ritualization in Man," in *Philosophical Transactions of the Royal Society of London*, Series B (1966), 251, 337–349, 772.

67. "On Student Unrest," 10–11 May 1969, Item 1501, Erikson Hrvd. Pprs. For the child's loss of self in creativity see "Play and Actuality" [Typescript with author's annotations and revisions], 18 April 1970, Item 1511, Erikson Hrvd. Pprs.

68. "Play and Actuality" [Typescript with author's annotations and revisions], 18 April 1970, Item 1511, Erikson Hrvd. Pprs.

69. "Loyola University symposium, notes," April 1970, Item 1510, Erikson Hrvd. Pprs.

70. Ibid.

71. "Lifecycle and Community" [Unpublished manuscript], undated, Item 95M-2, Erikson Hrvd. Pprs.

72. Erik H. Erikson, "The Ontogeny of Ritualization in Man," in *Philosophical Transactions of the Royal Society of London*, Series B (1966), 251, 337–349, 772.

73. Erikson, *Toys and Reasons*, 103.

74. Ibid., 70.

75. "Godkin Lectures: The Child's Toys and the Old Man's Reasons" [Author's typescript with revisions], April 1972, Item 1523, Erikson Hrvd. Pprs.

76. Erikson, *Gandhi's Truth*, 122.

77. *The Laws of Plato*, trans. A. E. Taylor (London: Dent & Sons, 1934), Book II, 653, 30.

78. "Play—Miscellaneous Notes" [Typescript], undated, Item 1702, Erikson Hrvd. Pprs.

79. "Godkin Lectures" [Manuscript drafts and revisions], April 1972, Item 1524, Erikson Hrvd. Pprs.

80. "Loyola University symposium, notes," April 1970, Item 1510, Erikson Hrvd. Pprs.

81. "Godkin Lectures: Spheres of Play" [Author's manuscript], April 1972, Item 1522, Erikson Hrvd. Pprs.

82. "Erik Erikson on Play, vision, and deception" [Transcript], 25 August 1973, Item 1534, Erikson Hrvd. Pprs.

83. "Godkin Lectures: Spheres of Play" [Author's manuscript], April 1972, Item 1522, Erikson Hrvd. Pprs.

84. Ibid.

85. "Lecture [at Santa Barbara Erikson Symposium]," 19 February 1972, Item 1519, Erikson Hrvd. Pprs.

86. See Walter Lippmann, *Public Opinion* (1922; reprint, New York: Free Press, 1965).

87. Erikson, *Toys and Reasons*, 27. See the original in Lippmann, *Public Opinion*, 11.

88. "Godkin Lectures: Play, Vision, and Deception" [Author's typescript], April 1972, Item 1521, Erikson Hrvd. Pprs.

89. "Homestead" Letter, Erikson to Robert Wallerstein, 30 September 1974, Item 1543, Erikson Hrvd. Pprs.

90. Erik H. Erikson, Joan M. Erikson, and Helen Q. Kivnick, *Vital Involvement in Old Age* (New York: Norton, 1986).

91. Erik H. Erikson, "Godkin Lectures" [Manuscript drafts and revisions], April 1972, Item 1524, Erikson Hrvd. Pprs. See also "Godkin Lectures: The Child's Toys and the Old Man's Reasons" [Author's typescript with revisions], Item 1523, Erikson Hrvd. Pprs.

92. "Godkin Lectures: Play, Vision, and Deception" [Author's typescript], April 1972, Item 1521, Erikson Hrvd. Pprs.

93. "Comments on the Symposium on Dynamic Psychology and Education: Contributions from a Modern Psychoanalytic Perspective" [Typescript with author's annotations], 20 April 1976, Item 1557, Erikson Hrvd. Pprs.

94. "Godkin Lectures: Play, Vision, and Deception" [Author's typescript], April 1972, Item 1521, Erikson Hrvd. Pprs.

95. Ibid. See also "Godkin Seminar" [Transcripts of discussions; author's typescript with annotations], April 1972, Item 1527, Erikson Hrvd. Pprs.

96. See Erikson, *Gandhi's Truth*.

97. "Godkin Seminar" [Transcripts of discussions; author's typescript with annotations], April 1972, Item 1527, Erikson Hrvd. Pprs.

98. "Biographical Note, Excerpt" [Author's typescript with annotations], undated, Item 1528, Erikson Hrvd. Pprs.

99. "Godkin Lectures: Play, Vision, and Deception" [Author's typescript], April 1972, Item 1521, Erikson Hrvd. Pprs.

100. "Lifecycle and Community" [Unpublished manuscript], undated, Item 95M-2, Erikson Hrvd. Pprs.

101. "Play and Actuality" [Typescript with author's annotations and revisions], 18 April 1970, Item 1511, Erikson Hrvd. Pprs.

102. "Godkin Lectures: Play, Vision, and Deception" [Author's typescript], April 1972, Item 1521, Erikson Hrvd. Pprs.

103. "University College Lectures," 28 February 1977, Item 1571, Erikson Hrvd. Pprs.

104. Ibid.

105. Erikson, *Toys and Reasons*, 106.

106. "Godkin Lectures: Play, Vision, and Deception" [Author's typescript], April 1972, Item 1521, Erikson Hrvd. Pprs.

107. "Abstract of First Vikram Sarabhai Memorial Lecture" [Typescript], February 1977, Item 1572, Erikson Hrvd. Pprs.

108. "University College Lectures," 28 February 1977, Item 1571, Erikson Hrvd. Pprs.

109. "Godkin Lectures: Play, Vision, and Deception" [Author's typescript], April 1972, Item 1521, Erikson Hrvd. Pprs.

110. "Psychoanalytic Reflections on Einstein's Centenary" in *Albert Ein-*

stein: Historical and Cultural Perspectives, ed. Gerald Holton and Yehuda Elkana (Princeton, N.J.: Princeton University Press, 1980), 151–173.

111. "Godkin Lectures: The Child's Toys and the Old Man's Reasons" [Author's typescript with revisions], April 1972, Item 1523, Erikson Hrvd. Pprs.

112. "Lecture [at Santa Barbara Erikson Symposium]," 19 February 1972, Item 1519, Erikson Hrvd. Pprs.

113. See "Psychoanalytic Reflections on Einstein's Centenary, first draft" [Author's manuscript with revisions], March 1979, Item 1603, Erikson Hrvd. Pprs., in which is found Joseph Wheelwright's comment to Erikson: "Yes, for both you and your friend Albert, the tension of opposites has been central in your creativity (Sorry—generativity!). To contain them you have had to forego the luxury of belonging."

114. For *begriffen*, see *Toys and Reasons*, 140. For *uebersicht*, an "overview (or) free scanning of a wide area," see "Play and Actuality" [Typescript with author's annotations and revisions], 18 April 1970, Item 1511, Erikson Hrvd. Pprs.

115. Erikson, *Toys and Reasons*, 141.

116. See Erikson, in Schlein, ed., *A Way of Looking at Things*.

117. For "intuitive 'beholding,'" see "Psychoanalytic Reflections on Einstein's Centenary" in Holton and Elkana, eds., *Albert Einstein: Historical and Cultural Perspectives*, 154. For *begreiflichkeit* and "leap(s) of intuition" see "Smithsonian [Address on Albert Einstein]," May 1979, Item 1606, Erikson Hrvd. Pprs.

118. Erikson, *Toys and Reasons*, 141–142.

119. For "swirling" forms see Erikson, *Toys and Reasons*, 141. For the concept of forms that swim see "Smithsonian Address on Albert Einstein," May 1979, Item 1606, Erikson Hrvd. Pprs.

120. Erik H. Erikson, "Psychoanalytic Reflections on Einstein's Centenary," in Holton and Elkana, eds., *Albert Einstein: Historical and Cultural Perspectives*, 151–173.

121. "Miscellaneous Papers and Notes," various dates, Item 95M-2, Erikson Hrvd. Pprs.

122. "Smithsonian Address on Albert Einstein," May 1979, Item 1606, Erikson Hrvd. Pprs.

123. Ibid.

124. Ibid.

125. Ibid.

126. Ibid.

127. William Blake, *Augeries of Innocence; The Pickering Manuscript*, lines 91–92. See, for example, *William Blake: The Complete Poems*, ed. Alicia Ostriker, (New York: Penguin Books, 1977), 506.

128. "Lifecycle and Community" [Unpublished manuscript], undated, Item 95M-2, Erikson Hrvd. Pprs.

129. Erikson, *Toys and Reasons*, 112.

130. Erikson, "The Galilean Sayings and the Sense of 'I'"; and Erikson, "Psychoanalytic Reflections on Einstein's Centenary," in Holton and Elkana, eds., *Albert Einstein: Historical and Cultural Perspectives*, 151–173.

131. See Erik H. Erikson, "Psychoanalysis and the Future of Education," in Schlein, ed., *A Way of Looking at Things*, 14–30.

132. Erikson, *Toys and Reasons*, 54.

133. Erikson, *Toys and Reasons*, 143.

134. Erikson, *Insight and Responsibility*, 45.

135. "Miscellaneous Papers and Notes," various dates, Item 95M-2, Erikson Hrvd. Pprs.

136. Erikson, "The Syndrome of Identity Diffusion in Adolescents and Young Adults." For maintaining childhood strengths into adulthood, see p. 164. Also in "Homestead" Letter, Erikson to Robert Wallerstein, 30 September 1974, Item 1543, Erikson Hrvd. Pprs.

137. Erikson, "The Syndrome of Identity Diffusion in Adolescents and Young Adults," 164.

138. Erikson, *Young Man Luther*, 266.

139. For "joy of self expression," see Erikson, *Toys and Reasons*, 42. For enthusiasm, see Erikson, *Gandhi's Truth*, 90. For "inviolacy of spirit," see ibid., 100.

140. "Play and Actuality" [Typescript with author's annotations and revisions], 18 April 1970, Item 1511, Erikson Hrvd. Pprs.

141. "Godkin Lectures: The Child's Toys and the Old Man's Reasons" [Author's typescript with revisions], April 1972, Item 1523, Erikson Hrvd. Pprs.

142. Erikson, *Young Man Luther*, 258.

143. "Uncorrupted core" is in Erikson, *Young Man Luther*, 178. "'Innocent eye' and ear" is in Erikson, "The Galilean Sayings and the Sense of 'I'," 341.

144. "Miscellaneous Papers and Notes," various dates, Item 95M-2, Erikson Hrvd. Pprs.

145. Erikson, *Insight and Responsibility*, 45.

146. "Insight and Freedom" 6 August 1968, Item 1499, Erikson Hrvd. Pprs.

147. Erikson, *Toys and Reasons*, 18.

148. This insight is from interview notes related to the *Vital Involvement* study found in "Miscellaneous Papers and Notes," various dates, Item 95M-2, Erikson Hrvd. Pprs. See also Erikson, *Gandhi's Truth*, 26.

149. Erikson, *Toys and Reasons*, 18.

150. "Play and Actuality" [Typescript with author's annotations and revisions], 18 April 1970, Item 1511, Erikson Hrvd. Pprs.

151. "Godkin Seminar" [Transcripts of discussions; author's typescript with annotations], April 1972, Item 1527, Erikson Hrvd. Pprs.

152. "Pretend to be free and natural" is from "Play and Actuality" [Typescript with author's annotations and revisions], 18 April 1970, Item 1511, Erikson Hrvd. Pprs. "Play free and equal" is from "Erik Erikson on Play, vision, and deception," [Transcript], 25 August 1973, Item 1534, Erikson Hrvd. Pprs.

153. Ibid.

154. Erikson, *Toys and Reasons*, 161.

155. "Play and Actuality" [Typescript with author's annotations and revisions], 18 April 1970, Item 1511, Erikson Hrvd. Pprs.

156. Erikson and Newton, *In Search of Common Ground*, 128.

157. Ibid., 51–52.

158. "Erik Erikson on Play, vision, and deception" [Transcript], 25 August 1973, Item 1534, Erikson Hrvd. Pprs.

159. Erikson, *Toys and Reasons*, 101–102.

160. "Harvard University: Lecture II, 139, William James," undated, Item 1676, Erikson Hrvd. Pprs.

161. Erikson, *Toys and Reasons*, 102.

162. Erikson, "Psychoanalytic Reflections on Einstein's Centenary" in *Albert Einstein: Historical and Cultural Perspectives*, 160.

163. Joan Mowat Erikson, *Saint Francis et his Four Ladies* (New York: Norton, 1970). Erikson said that Joan Erikson was writing her book on St. Francis

when he was writing his book on Gandhi. He said that "her contemporaneous work on St. Francis helped greatly to clarify the gay kind of sainthood also found in Gandhi." In Erikson, *Gandhi's Truth*, 14.

164. "Honor thy Children" [A benefit poetry reading], 25 April 1980, Item 1612, Erikson Hrvd. Pprs.

165. Ibid.

166. "Miscellaneous Papers and Notes," various dates, Item 95M-2, Erikson Hrvd. Pprs.

167. Lao Tze, *Treatise on Response and Retribution*, ed., Paul Carus, trans. D.T. Suzuki and Paul Carus (1906; reprint, Chicago, IL: Open Court, 1973).

168. "Miscellaneous Papers and Notes," various dates, Item 95M-2, Erikson Hrvd. Pprs.

169. Erikson, *Young Man Luther*, 261–262.

170. *The Analects of Confucius*.

171. "Miscellaneous Papers and Notes," various dates, Item 95M-2, Erikson Hrvd. Pprs.

172. Erikson, "Autobiographic Notes on the Identity Crisis," Holton, ed., *The Twentieth Century Sciences*, 26.

173. "Miscellaneous Papers and Notes," various dates, Item 95M-2, Erikson Hrvd. Pprs.

174. "Lifecycle and Community" [Unpublished manuscript], undated, Item 95M-2, Erikson Hrvd. Pprs.

175. "Miscellaneous Papers and Notes," various dates, Item 95M-2, Erikson Hrvd. Pprs.

176. "Miscellaneous Papers and Notes," various dates, Item 95M-2, Erikson Hrvd. Pprs.

177. Erikson, *In Search of Common Ground*, 85.

178. "Erikson, *Young Man Luther*, 247.

179. "Case History and Life History" [Unpublished manuscript], undated, Item 95M-2, Erikson Hrvd. Pprs.

180. Erikson, "The Galilean Sayings and the Sense of 'I'," 360.

181. "Play and Actuality" [Typescript with author's annotations and revisions], 18 April 1970, Item 1511, Erikson Hrvd. Pprs.

182. William Blake, *Augeries of Innocence; The Pickering Manuscript*, lines 85–90. See, for example, *William Blake: The Complete Poems*, (New York: Penguin Books, 1977), 506.

183. Erikson, *Toys and Reasons*, 115–116.

184. Godkin Lectures: The Child's Toys and the Old Man's Reasons" [Author's typescript with revisions], April 1972, Item 1523, Erikson Hrvd. Pprs.

185. "Play and Actuality" [Typescript with author's annotations and revisions], 18 April 1970, Item 1511, Erikson Hrvd. Pprs.

186. Erik and Joan Erikson, together with Helen Kivnick, worked together on the "Vital Involvement" study. That study was published in Joan M. Erikson, Erik H. Erikson, and Helen Kivnick, *Vital Involvement in Old Age* (New York: Norton, 1986).

187. "Miscellaneous Papers and Notes," various dates, Item 95M-2, Erikson Hrvd. Pprs.

188. Erikson, "The Ontogeny of Ritualization in Man," 338.

189. "Play and Actuality" [Typescript with author's annotations and revisions], 18 April 1970, Item 1511, Erikson Hrvd. Pprs.

190. "Case History and Life History" [Unpublished manuscript], undated, Item 95M-2, Erikson Hrvd. Pprs.

191. "Miscellaneous Papers and Notes," various dates, Item 95M-2, Erikson Hrvd. Pprs.

Chapter 7: Historically and Culturally Relative Adult

1. Erikson, *Gandhi's Truth,* 180.
2. "Erik Erikson on Play, vision, and deception" [transcript], 25 August 1973, Item 1534, Erikson Hrvd. Pprs.
3. "Anything goes" is from "Jefferson Lectures: Dimensions of a New Identity" [Notes and source materials], undated, circa 1973, Item 1533, Erikson Hrvd. Pprs. "Nihilism" is from Erikson, "Hitler's Imagery and German Youth," 488.
4. "Chatauqua Lecture Notes," undated, Item 1655, Erikson Hrvd. Pprs.
5. "Rationalization" is from Erikson, *Life History and the Historical Moment,* 260. "Opportunism" is from "Gandhi's Truth" [Author's manuscript with revisions], undated, Item 1505, Erikson Hrvd. Pprs.
6. "Chatauqua Lecture Notes," undated, Item 1655, Erikson Hrvd. Pprs. The concept of "historical relativity vs. era-centrism" is mine.
7. The notion of geographic, anatomic parallelism is similar to Kroeber's. See, for example, Alfred A. Kroeber, "The Yurok," chaps. 1–4, in *Handbook of the Indians of California,* Bureau of American Ethnology, Bulletin 78 (Washington, D.C.: Government Printing Office, 1925), 1–97.
8. Erikson, "Observations on the Yurok: Childhood and World Image," 273.
9. Expanding "frontier" is from "Jefferson Lectures: Dimensions of a New Identity" [Notes and source materials], undated, circa 1973, Item 1533, Erikson Hrvd. Pprs. "Waves of immigrants" is from Erikson, "Hitler's Imagery and German Youth," 483.
10. "Ranger" and "self-made" man are in "Memorandum on Adulthood," for the "Planning Conference on the Adult," September 1971, Item 1515, Erikson Hrvd. Pprs. "Newness . . . invigorating . . . (and) obsessive" are from Erik H. Erikson, *Dimensions of a New Identity,* 79.
11. "Jefferson Lectures: Dimensions of a New Identity" [Notes and source materials], undated, circa 1973, Item 1533, Erikson Hrvd. Pprs.
12. Erikson, "Hitler's Imagery and German Youth," 483.
13. Ibid.
14. Erik H. Erikson, *The Life Cycle Completed* (New York: Norton, 1982), 18.
15. The wording on the "cultural relativity of symptoms" is from a statement from Commission VIII (1974) of the American Psychoanalytic Association with which Erikson agreed. For the context and for Erikson's use of the term "deficient," see "Homestead" Letter, Erikson to Robert Wallerstein, 30 September 1974, Item 1543, Erikson Hrvd. Pprs.
16. Erikson, *The Life Cycle Completed,* 26.
17. Ibid., 36.
18. Erikson, "Observations on the Yurok: Childhood and World Image," 297.
19. Erikson, *Dimensions of a New Identity,* 59.
20. "Introductory Remarks Made at the Indian Health Service Mental Health Training Conference" [Typescript with revisions], 23 May 1974, Item 1542, Erikson Hrvd. Pprs.
21. Ibid.
22. Erikson and Newton, *In Search of Common Ground,* 106.
23. Erikson, "Hitler's Imagery," 486.
24. Erikson, "Observations on the Yurok: Childhood and World Image," 297.
25. Erikson, *Life History and the Historical Moment,* 101.
26. Erikson, "Observations on the Yurok: Childhood and World Image," 283.

27. Ibid., 290.

28. Ibid., 284.

29. "Crow Indians: Observation Notes on Children," circa 1969–1970, Item 1732, Erikson Hrvd. Pprs.

30. Erikson, "Observations on Sioux Education," 152–153.

31. Ibid., 153.

32. "Every-family-for-itself culture" and "isolated places for childhood" are from Erikson, "Observations on the Yurok: Childhood and World Image," 299. "Prisons" is from Erikson, "Observations on Sioux Education," 146.

33. Erikson, "Observations on Sioux Education," 152–153.

34. Erikson, "Observations on the Yurok: Childhood and World Image," 298.

35. Ibid., 299.

36. Ibid., 292.

37. "Crow Indians: Observation Notes on Children," circa 1969–1970, Item 1732, Erikson Hrvd. Pprs.

38. Erikson, "Observations on Sioux Education," 145.

39. Erikson, Life History and the Historical Moment, 108.

40. Erikson, Gandhi's Truth, 38–39.

41. Erikson, Young Man Luther, 60.

42. Erikson, "Observations on Sioux Education," 123.

43. Ibid., 131.

44. "University College Lectures," 28 February 1977, Item 1571, Erikson Hrvd. Pprs.

45. Erikson, Gandhi's Truth, 412.

46. Erikson, Life History and the Historical Moment, 144.

47. Ibid.

48. Ibid., 145.

49. Erikson, "The Golden Rule and the Cycle of Life," 422.

50. "Lifecycle and Community" [Unpublished manuscript], undated, Item 95M-2, Erikson Hrvd. Pprs.

51. Erikson, "Observations on the Yurok: Childhood and World Image," 259.

52. Ibid.

53. "Conceptual synthesis of the inner and outer environment" is ibid. "Part of a communal one" is from "Reflections on Ethos and War" [Typescript with revisions], circa 1984, Item 1635, Erikson Hrvd. Pprs.

54. "Report to Vikram: Further Reflections on the Life Cycle," February 1977, Item 1573, Erikson Hrvd. Pprs.

55. Erikson, "Observations on Sioux Education," 103.

56. Ibid., 106.

57. Ibid., 110.

58. Ibid., 114.

59. Ibid., 154.

60. Ibid., 111.

61. Ibid.

62. Ibid., 106.

63. Ibid., 115.

64. Erikson, Childhood and Society, 1950, 26.

65. Ibid., 37.

66. Erikson, Young Man Luther, 16.

67. "Psychoanalysis and Ongoing History; a letter," October 1962, Item 1491, Erikson Hrvd. Pprs.

68. "Case History and Life History" [Unpublished manuscript], undated, Item 95M-2, Erikson Hrvd. Pprs.

69. Erikson, *Young Man Luther*, 18. See R. G. Collingwood, *The Idea of History* (Oxford: Clarendon Press, 1946).

70. "The Freud-Jung correspondence; selected issues," circa 15 November 1978, Item 1597, Erikson Hrvd. Pprs.

71. "Reflections on Historical Change: A Foreword," [Transcript with revisions; for *Yearbook of the International Association for Child Psychiatry and Allied Professions*, vol. 5, *Children and Parents in a Changing World*], undated, Item 1712, Erikson Hrvd. Pprs.

72. Erikson, *Life History and the Historical Moment*, 248–249.

73. Erikson, *Gandhi's Truth*, 55.

74. "Reflections on Historical Change: A Foreword," [Transcript with revisions; for *Yearbook of the International Association for Child Psychiatry and Allied Professions*, vol. 5, *Children and Parents in a Changing World*], undated, Item 1712, Erikson Hrvd. Pprs.

75. "Jefferson Lectures" [Author's typescript], 1–2 May 1973, Item 1531, Erikson Hrvd. Pprs.

76. From Erikson, *Life History and the Historical Moment*. "Main currents" is p. 81. "Mood" and "moral climate" are 255. ""Lineage" is 145.

77. "Psychoanalysis and Ongoing History; a letter," October 1962, Item 1491, Erikson Hrvd. Pprs.

78. Erikson, *Dimensions of a New Identity*, 15.

79. "Psychoanalysis and Ongoing History; a letter," October 1962, Item 1491, Erikson Hrvd. Pprs.

80. "Introductory Remarks Made at the Indian Health Service Mental Health Training Conference" [Typescript with revisions], 23 May 1974, Item 1542, Erikson Hrvd. Pprs.

81. Erikson, "Observations on the Yurok: Childhood and World Image," 276–277.

82. "Pre-history" is in "Report to Vikram: Further Reflections on the Life Cycle" [Typescript with revisions], February 1977, Item 1574, Erikson Hrvd. Pprs. "Childhood of mankind" is from "Mikey, fragen [Conversations with Mikey]," May, June 1929, Item 1476, Erikson Hrvd. Pprs.

83. Erikson, "Observations on the Yurok: Childhood and World Image," 277.

84. Erikson, *Young Man Luther*. "Comradeship" is p. 260. The concept of not being alone in the universe is p. 87.

85. "Notes on Lifecycle and Worldview: Letter to MIT" [Transcript with revisions], 15 November 1976, Item 1560, Erikson Hrvd. Pprs.

86. Erikson, "Observations on the Yurok: Childhood and World Image," 271.

87. Erikson, *The Life Cycle Completed*, 51.

88. Erikson, "Observations on the Yurok: Childhood and World Image," 276.

89. Erik H. Erikson, "Reflections on Historical Change: A Foreword." In *Children and Parents in a Changing World*, vol. 5, *The Child and His Family: Yearbook of the International Association for Child Psychiatry and Allied Professions*, ed. James Anthony and Colette Chiland (New York: Wiley, 1978), xi–xxi; xiv.

90. "Memorandum on Adulthood," for the "Planning Conference on the Adult," September 1971, Item 1515, Erikson Hrvd. Pprs.

91. "On Student Unrest," 10–11 May 1969, Item 1501, Erikson Hrvd. Pprs.

92. "Aging," [Typescript], undated, Item 1562, Erikson Hrvd. Pprs.

93. Erikson "The Syndrome of Identity Diffusion in Adolescents and Young Adults," 182.

254 Notes to Pages 165–171

94. "Peter Blos Discussion" [Typescript with author's revisions], circa 1978, Item 1600, Erikson Hrvd. Pprs.

95. "Letter to Cal (no surname)" [Typescript; in lieu of attending meetings in Palm Springs], 23 March 1972, Item 1520, Erikson Hrvd. Pprs.

96. Erikson, "Hitler's Imagery and German Youth," 479.

97. Erikson, *Insight and Responsibility*, 202.

98. "Planning Conference on the Adult," 18–19 September 1971, Item 1516, Erikson Hrvd. Pprs.

99. "Schizoid characters" and "mechanized" era are in Erikson, *Life History and the Historical Moment*, 252. "Plastic" is in "Erik Erikson on Play, vision, and deception" [transcript], 25 August 1973, Item 1534, Erikson Hrvd. Pprs.

100. Erikson, *Life History and the Historical Moment*, 252.

101. "Case History and Life History" [Unpublished manuscript], undated, Item 95M-2, Erikson Hrvd. Pprs.

102. "Introductory Remarks to the Presentation of the 1975 McAlpin Medal for the National Association of Mental Health given to Alexander Hamilton Leighton" [Typescript with author's annotations], 1975, Item 1553, Erikson Hrvd. Pprs.

103. "Gandhi's Truth" [Author's manuscript with revisions], undated, Item 1505, Erikson Hrvd. Pprs.

104. Erikson, *Gandhi's Truth*, 294.

105. "*Inverted revolt* against the values of the existing order" is in Erikson, *Life History and the Historical Moment*," 252. "Inactivated" and "inner conflicts" is in "Jefferson Lectures: Dimensions of a New Identity" [Notes and source materials], undated, circa 1973, Item 1533, Erikson Hrvd. Pprs.

106. "Lecture [at Santa Barbara Erikson Symposium]," 19 February 1972, Item 1519, Erikson Hrvd. Pprs.

107. "Wellfleet 1974 [Miscellaneous Notes]," Item 1549, Erikson Hrvd. Pprs.

108. Sigmund Freud, *Civilization and Its Discontents*, trans. James Strachey (1930; reprint, New York: Norton, 1961), 106–107.

109. Erikson, *In Search of Common Ground*, 119.

110. "Common Themes in the Lives of Uncommon Men" undated, Item 1660, Erikson Hrvd. Pprs.

111. "Themes from Kierkegaard's Early Life" [Typescript with revisions], circa 1977, Item 1594, Erikson Hrvd. Pprs.

112. "Miscellaneous Papers and Notes," various dates, Item 95M-2, Erikson Hrvd. Pprs.

113. "National Academy of Education" [Notes], undated, Item 1693, Erikson Hrvd. Pprs.

114. "Lifecycle and Community" [Unpublished manuscript], undated, Item 95M-2, Erikson Hrvd. Pprs.

115. Erikson, *Life History and the Historical Moment*, 148.

116. "Miscellaneous Papers and Notes," various dates, Item 95M-2, Erikson Hrvd. Pprs.

117. Mead to Erikson, 19 May 1954, Container B-4, Mead Papers.

118. "Psychoanalysis and Ongoing History; a letter," October 1962, Item 1491, Erikson Hrvd. Pprs.

Chapter 8: Insightful Adult

1. Erikson, *Insight and Responsibility*, 10.
2. Ibid.

3. "Psychoanalysis and Ethics—Avowed and Unavowed," 1 March 1974, Item 1539, Erikson Hrvd. Pprs.

4. "On the Generational Cycle and Miscellaneous Papers" [Typescript with author's revisions], 29 July–3 August 1979, Item 1607, Erikson Hrvd. Pprs.

5. "Systematic self-analysis" is from Erikson, *Life History and the Historical Moment*, 96. "Systematic self-awareness" is from "Afterthoughts" [Author's manuscript], 1976, Item 1561, Erikson Hrvd. Pprs.

6. Erikson, *Life History and the Historical Moment*, 173.

7. Erikson, *Insight and Responsibility*, 49.

8. "Sudden synthesis" is from Erikson, *Gandhi's Truth*, 412. "The 'aha' experience . . . not an entirely logical step but a sensory and sense step" is from "Miscellaneous Papers and Notes," various dates, Item 95M-2, Erikson Hrvd. Pprs. "Revelation, that is, a sudden inner flooding with light" is from Erikson, *Young Man Luther*, 205.

9. Erikson, *Gandhi's Truth*, 55.

10. Erikson, "Freedom and Nonviolence," 172.

11. Ibid., 174.

12. Ibid., 179.

13. Ibid., 182.

14. Ibid., 185.

15. Erikson, *Identity: Youth and Crisis*, 281.

16. Ibid., 294.

17. "Inner and Outer Space: Reflections on Womanhood" [Author's manuscript with annotations], undated, Item 1494, Erikson Hrvd. Pprs.

18. Erikson, *Identity: Youth and Crisis*, 262.

19. Erikson, "Freedom and Nonviolence," 183.

20. "Miscellaneous Papers and Notes," various dates, Item 95M-2, Erikson Hrvd. Pprs.

21. Erikson, *Insight and Responsibility*, 53. See also same source, p. 104.

22. See Erikson, "The Syndrome of Identity Diffusion in Adolescents and Young Adults," 144.

23. Ibid.

24. Erikson, *Insight and Responsibility*, 73.

25. For "vacuum of impressions" see Erikson, *Young Man Luther*, 131. For "indoctrination" and "thought reform," see same source, 134.

26. Ibid., 192.

27. "National Academy of Education," [Notes], undated, Item 1693, Erikson Hrvd. Pprs.

28. "Smithsonian [Address on Albert Einstein]," May 1979, Item 1606, Erikson Hrvd. Pprs.

29. "Worldviews," undated, circa 1976, Item 1570, Erikson Hrvd. Pprs.

30. Evans, *Dialogue with Erik Erikson*, 89.

31. Erikson, *Insight and Responsibility*.

32. Ibid., frontispiece.

33. "Insight and Freedom," 6 August 1968, Item 1499, Erikson Hrvd. Pprs.

34. "Miscellaneous Papers and Notes," various dates, Item 95M-2, Erikson Hrvd. Pprs.

35. Søren Kierkegaard, "Either/Or: A Fragment of Life," trans. David F. Swenson, Lillian Marvin Swenson, and Walter Lowrie, in *A Kierkegaard Anthology*, ed., Robert Bretall, (Princeton, N.J.: Princeton University Press, 1946), 19–108, 97.

36. "The ethical consolidation of adulthood is based on insight" is from "Insight and Freedom," 6 August 1968, Item 1499, Erikson Hrvd. Pprs. "Blind obedience" is from Erikson, *Gandhi's Truth*, 251.

37. Erikson, *Gandhi's Truth*, 251.
38. "Peter Blos Discussion" [Typescript with author's revisions], circa 1978, Item 1600, Erikson Hrvd. Pprs.
39. Erikson, *Gandhi's Truth*, 251.
40. "Miscellaneous Papers and Notes," various dates, Item 95M-2, Erikson Hrvd. Pprs.
41. Ibid.
42. Ibid.
43. Erikson, "Autobiographic Notes on the Identity Crisis," *Daedalus*, 745.
44. Erikson, *Life History and the Historical Moment*, 31.
45. Søren Kierkegaard, "The Sickness unto Death," trans. Alastair Hannay (New York: Penguin Books, 1989), 99. [First edition published in Danish as *Syndommen til Doden*, Copenhagen, 1849.]
46. Søren Kierkegaard, "The Journals," trans. David F. Swenson, Lillian Marvin Swenson, and Walter Lowrie, in Bretall, ed., *A Kierkegaard Anthology*, 1–18; 5.
47. Erikson, "The Problem of Ego Identity," 66.
48. "Insight and Freedom," 6 August 1968, Item 1499, Erikson Hrvd. Pprs.
49. Erikson, "Reflections on Dr. Borg's Life Cycle," 1–31; 24.
50. Søren Kierkegaard, "Works of Love," trans. David F. Swenson, Lillian Marvin Swenson, and Walter Lowrie, in Bretall, ed., *A Kierkegaard Anthology*, 281–323; 281.
51. Ibid.
52. Erikson, *Gandhi's Truth*, 10.
53. See, for example, "The Possibility and Actuality of Despair," in Søren Kierkegaard, "The Sickness unto Death," 44–47.
54. Søren Kierkegaard, "Stages on Life's Way: Studies by Sundry Persons," trans. David F. Swenson, Lillian Marvin Swenson, and Walter Lowrie, in Bretall, ed., *A Kierkegaard Anthology*, 172–189.
55. Kierkegaard, "Either/Or: A Fragment of Life," 107.
56. Erikson, *Childhood and Society*, 1963, 91.
57. Erik H. Erikson and Joan M. Erikson, "On Generativity and Identity: From a Conversation with Erik and Joan Erikson," 252.
58. See, for example, Erikson, *Insight and Responsibility*.
59. Ibid., 44.
60. "Miscellaneous Papers and Notes," various dates, Item 95M-2, Erikson Hrvd. Pprs.
61. Erikson, "Hitler's Imagery and German Youth," 487.
62. Ibid.
63. "Miscellaneous Papers and Notes," various dates, Item 95M-2, Erikson Hrvd. Pprs.
64. Ibid.
65. "Jefferson Lectures" [Typescript with author's revisions], 1–2 May 1973, Item 1530, Erikson Hrvd. Pprs.
66. Erikson, *Gandhi's Truth*, 375.
67. "Psychoanalysis and Ethics—Avowed and Unavowed," 1 March 1974, Item 1539, Erikson Hrvd. Pprs.
68. Ibid.
69. Erikson, *Life History and the Historical Moment*, 254.
70. "Lecture [at Santa Barbara Erikson Symposium]," 19 February 1972, Item 1519, Erikson Hrvd. Pprs.
71. Ibid.

Chapter 9: Wise Adult

1. "The Galilean Sayings and the Sense of 'I'" [Author's typescript with revisions], Item 1617, Erikson Hrvd. Pprs.
2. Erik H. Erikson, "Reflections on the Last Stage—and the First," 160.
3. Ibid.
4. "Godkin Papers" [Author's typescript with revisions], April 1972, Item 1524, Erikson Hrvd. Pprs.
5. Erikson, *The Life Cycle Completed*, 65.
6. "Miscellaneous Papers and Notes," various dates, Item 95M-2, Erikson Hrvd. Pprs.
7. Erikson, *Childhood and Society*, 1950, 232.
8. "Gandhi's Truth" [Author's manuscript with revisions], undated, Item 1505, Erikson Hrvd. Pprs.
9. Erikson, *Childhood and Society*, 1950, 231.
10. "Lifecycle and Community" [Unpublished manuscript], undated, Item 95M-2, Erikson Hrvd. Pprs.
11. Erik H. Erikson and Joan M. Erikson, "Reflections on Aging, an Introduction," in *Aging and the Elderly: Humanistic Perspectives in Gerontology*, ed. S. Spicker, K. Woodward, and D. Van Tassel (Atlantic Highlands, N.J.: Humanities Press, 1978), 1–8; 2.
12. "Play and Actuality" [Loyola University, Author's typescript with revisions], 18 April 1970, Item 1511, Erikson Hrvd. Pprs.
13. In his 70s, Erikson changed the negative pole of "stagnation" to "rejectivity."
14. "Fragments, unsorted," various dates, Item 1725, Erikson Hrvd. Pprs.
15. Erikson, *Young Man Luther*, 265.
16. Personal communication from Erik Erikson to David Gutmann. See David L. Gutmann, "Towards a Dynamic Geropsychology," in *Interface of Psychoanalysis and Psychology*, ed. James W. Barron, Morris N. Eagle, and David L. Wolitzky (Washington, D.C.: American Psychological Association, 1992), 284–296; 287.
17. "Tangibly" is from Erikson, *Young Man Luther*, 124. "Burdening" is from "Jefferson Lectures," [Author's typescript], 1–2 May 1973, Item 1531, Erikson Hrvd. Pprs.
18. Erikson, *Gandhi's Truth*, 248.
19. "The Leverage of Truth" [Author's manuscript], 28 July [undated as to year], Item 1686, Erikson Hrvd. Pprs.
20. Erikson, *Gandhi's Truth*, 244.
21. "Gauss Seminars in Criticism" [miscellaneous papers], 1969, Item 1506, Erikson Hrvd. Pprs.
22. Erikson, *Insight and Responsibility*, 128.
23. Ibid.
24. Ibid., 231.
25. Erik H. Erikson, "Eight Ages of Man," *International Journal of Psychiatry* 2, no. 3 (1966), 281–300; 291.
26. See Erikson, *Insight and Responsibility*, 129.
27. Ibid., 128.
28. Ibid., 134.
29. David Gutmann, interview by author, Chicago, Ill., 21 August 1995.
30. "Planning Conference on the Adult" [Transcript], 18–19 September 1971, Item 1516, Erikson Hrvd. Pprs.
31. Erik H. Erikson, "Reflections on Dr. Borg's Life Cycle."

32. "Dr. Borg's Lifecycle: A Revisitation" [Author's Manuscript], circa 1984, Item 1634, Erikson Hrvd. Pprs.

33. Erikson, "The Syndrome of Identity Diffusion in Adolescents and Young Adults," 187.

34. "So far in man's total development, adulthood and maturity have rarely been synonymous" is in Erikson, *Young Man Luther*, 109. "We-ness" and "asceticism" is in "Miscellaneous Papers and Notes," various dates, Item 95M-2, Erikson Hrvd. Pprs.

35. Erikson, *Childhood and Society*, 1950, 231.

36. Erikson, *Insight and Responsibility*, 134.

37. Erik H. Erikson, *Childhood and Society*, 1963, 267.

38. In a personal communication, Gutmann suggested that Erikson became more diffuse in this and other respects because of criticism by feminists.

39. Erikson and Erikson, "Introduction: Reflections on Aging," 11.

40. Erik H. Erikson and Joan M. Erikson, "On Generativity and Identity: From a Conversation with Erik and Joan Erikson," *Harvard Educational Review* 51, no. 2 (May 1981): 249–269; 269.

41. Ibid.

42. Erik H. Erikson, *Identity and the Life Cycle* (1959; reprint, New York: Norton, 1980), 97.

43. Erikson, "Reflections on Dr. Borg's Life Cycle," 16.

44. Erikson, *Identity and the Life Cycle*, 138.

45. Ibid. See also Erikson, *Childhood and Society*, 1963, 267.

46. Ibid, 97.

47. Ibid., 138.

48. Ibid.

49. Erik H. Erikson, "On the Generational Cycle: An Address," *International Journal of Psycho-Analysis* 61, no. 2 (1980), 213–223, 218.

50. Erikson, *The Life Cycle Completed*, 69.

51. "Miscellaneous Papers and Notes," various dates, Item 95M-2, Erikson Hrvd. Pprs.

52. Erikson, *The Life Cycle Completed*, 65.

53. Ibid., 65–66.

54. Erikson, *Young Man Luther*, 260.

55. Erikson and Erikson, "Introduction: Reflections on Aging," 162.

56. "Lifecycle and Community," undated, Item 95M-2, Erikson Hrvd. Pprs.

57. Erikson and Erikson, "Introduction: Reflections on Aging," 156–157.

58. "Tedium vitae" is from "Dear Friends" [Letter sent to Al Emrich in lieu of attending Aspen Conference], 9 August 1976, Item 1558, Erikson Hrvd. Pprs. "Multiple disintegration" is from "Miscellaneous Papers and Notes," various dates, Item 95M-2, Erikson Hrvd. Pprs.

59. Erikson, *Young Man Luther*, 243.

60. Erikson, *Identity: Youth and Crisis*, 141.

61. Erikson, "Reflections on Dr. Borg's Life Cycle," 26.

62. Erikson, "Reflections on the Last Stage—and the First," 159.

63. "Liberated wonder" is in Erikson and Erikson, "Reflections on Aging, an Introduction," 8; "time 'to play with'" is in same source, 5.

64. "Miscellaneous Papers and Notes," various dates, Item 95M-2, Erikson Hrvd. Pprs.

65. Erikson, "Reflections on the Last Stage—and the First," 160.

66. Erikson, "Reflections on Dr. Borg's Life Cycle," 13.

67. "Lifecycle and Community" undated, Item 95M-2, Erikson Hrvd. Pprs.

68. Erikson, *The Life Cycle Completed*, 79.

69. Erikson, *Young Man Luther*, 243.

70. Erikson, *The Life Cycle Completed*, 63.

71. "Doctor Borg's Lifecycle: A Revisitation" [Author's manuscript], circa 1984, Item 1634, Erikson Hrvd. Pprs.

72. "The Last Line and the Diagonal," undated, Item 1683, Erikson Hrvd. Pprs.

73. "Wellfleet 1974 [Miscellaneous Notes]," 1974, Item 1549, Erikson Hrvd. Pprs.

74. "Pettiness" is in "On the Generational Cycle and Miscellaneous Papers," 29 July–3 August 1979, Item 1607, Erikson Hrvd. Pprs. "Pretenses" is in "Toys and Reasons" [Author's typescript with revisions], 1975, Item 1555, Erikson Hrvd. Pprs. "Dogmatism" is in "Miscellaneous Papers and Notes," various dates, Item 95M-2, Erikson Hrvd. Pprs.

75. Memorandum on Adulthood," September 1971, Item 1515, Erikson Hrvd. Pprs.

76. "Sapientism" is in "Toys and Reasons" [Author's typescript with revisions], 1975, Item 1555, Erikson Hrvd. Pprs. "Coercive orthodoxy" is in "Miscellaneous Papers and Notes," various dates, Item 95M-2, Erikson Hrvd. Pprs.

77. See Erikson, "Reflections on Dr. Borg's Life Cycle." "Autocracy," "possessiveness," and "misery" appear on p. 16, and "ossification" on p. 25.

78. "Planning Conference on the Adult," 18–19 September 1971, Item 1516, Erikson Hrvd. Pprs.

79. In this case, Erikson used "dictionaries in 12 languages." From "Report to Vikram: Seminar Notes for Lectures," February 1977, Item 1578, Erikson Hrvd. Pprs.

80. The *Oxford English Dictionary*, Compact Edition, s.v. *wis*, *vise*, and *videre*.

81. Ibid., s.v. *dom*.

82. *Cassell's German Dictionary*, Concise Edition, s.v. *Weise* and *Weisheit*.

83. "Insight and Freedom," 6 August 1968, Item 1499, Erikson Hrvd. Pprs.

84. Erikson, *Insight and Responsibility*, 132.

85. *The Analects of Confucius*, 88.

86. Erikson and Erikson, "Introduction: Reflections on Aging," 4.

87. Expressed in "Godkin Lectures: Play, Vision, and Deception" [Author's typescript], April 1972, Item 1521, Erikson Hrvd. Pprs.

88. "Psychoanalysis and Ongoing History; a letter," October 1962, Item 1491, Erikson Hrvd. Pprs.

89. Ibid.

90. Ibid.

91. "[Reminiscences] Remarks, Peter Blos Lecture, Jewish Board of Guardians," 7 December 1971, Item 1517, Erikson Hrvd. Pprs.

92. "To Take or Not to Take an Oath," spring 1972, Item 1529, Erikson Hrvd. Pprs.

93. Erikson, *Insight and Responsibility*, 22.

94. Erikson, *Young Man Luther*, 232.

95. Erikson, *Life History and the Historical Moment*, 109.

96. For example, in "Godkin Lectures: Play, Vision, and Deception" [Author's typescript], April 1972, Item 1521, Erikson Hrvd. Pprs.

97. Erik H. Erikson, "The Human Life Cycle," in Schlein, ed., *A Way of Looking at Things*, 595–610, 595. First published in the *International Encyclopedia of the Social Sciences* (New York: Crowell-Collier, 1968), 260–265.

Chapter 10: Acclaim and Criticism for Erikson's Theory
and his Concepts of the Adult

1. Evans, *Dialogue*, 107.
2. Sigmund Freud, *Psychopathology of Everyday Life*, trans. A. A. Brill (1901; reprint New York: Mentor Books 1960).
3. Erikson, *Young Man Luther*, 117.
4. Evans, *Dialogue*. Also, *Professor Erik Erikson*. Parts 1 and 2, prod. R.I. Evans, 100 min., Penn State Audio-Visual Services, 1966, videocassettes. See also Erikson in *Gandhi's Truth*, in which he said: "as I, a Freudian, should know" (p. 64).
5. Erikson, *Life History and the Historical Moment*, 33–34. Also, Gauss Seminars in Criticism, Erikson Gauss Lectures.
6. In a number of places Erikson said that he had translated Freud's writings himself. Further, Erikson's annotations are found in his personal copies of Freud's complete writings in the German edition, books that were donated to Houghton Library, Harvard University, by Joan Erikson after her husband's death.
7. Gauss Seminars in Criticism, Audiotape 1, Erikson Gauss Lectures.
8. Arnold A. Rogow, *The Psychiatrists* (New York: Putnam, 1970), 109.
9. Lewis A. Coser, *Refugee Scholars in America: Their Impact and Their Experiences* (New Haven: Yale University Press, 1984), 53.
10. Nathan G. Hale, Jr., "From Berggasse XIX to Central Park West: The Americanization of Psychoanalysis, 1919–1940," *Journal of the History of the Behavioral Sciences* 14 (1978): 299–315; 305.
11. Smelser, Neil J., *The Social Edges of Psychoanalysis* (Berkeley, Calif.: University of California Press, 1998), 111.
12. Robert J. Lifton, "Entering History: Erik Erikson's New Psychological Landscape," in *Ideas and Identities: The Life and Work of Erik Erikson*, eds. R.S. Wallerstein and L. Goldberger (Madison, Conn: International Universities Press, 1998), 99–114; 113.
13. Paul Roazen, "Erik H. Erikson's America: The Political Implications of Ego Psychology," *Journal of the History of the Behavioral Sciences* 16 (1980): 333–341; 334.
14. Robert S. Wallerstein, "Erikson's Concept of Ego Identity Reconsidered," *Journal of the American Psychoanalytic Association* 46, no. 1 (1998): 229–247.
15. Lawrence J. Friedman, "Erik H. Erikson's Critical Themes and Voices: The Task of Synthesis," in Wallerstein and Goldberger, eds., *Ideas and Identities*, 353–377; 353.
16. Mark Novak, "Biography After the End of Metaphysics: A Critique of Epigenetic Evolution," *International Journal of Aging and Human Development* 22, no. 3 (1985–1986): 189– 204; Elizabeth Hall, "A Conversation with Erik Erikson," *Psychology Today* 17 (June 1983): 22–30.
17. Paul Roazen, "Psychology and Politics: The Case of Erik H. Erikson," *The Human Context* 7 (1975): 579–584; 580.
18. See Lawrence J. Friedman, *Identity's Architect* (New York: Scribner, 1999); see also Robert Coles, *Erik H. Erikson: The Growth of His Work* (Boston, Mass.: Little, Brown, 1970).
19. Ibid.
20. For "pioneer" see R. L. Schnell, "Contributions to Psychohistory: IV. Individual Experience in Historiography and Psychoanalysis: Significance of Erik Erikson and Robert Coles," *Psychological Reports*, 46, no. 2 (1980): 591–612; 600; and Heinz Lichtenstein, *The Dilemma of Human Identity* (New York:

Aronson, 1983), 128. For "transformer" see Lewis D. Wurgaft, "Erik Erikson: From Luther to Gandhi," *Psychoanalytic Review* 63, no. 2 (Summer 1976), 209–233; 232; Peter Homans, "Introduction," in *Childhood and Selfhood: Essays on Tradition, Religion, and Modernity in the Psychology of Erik H. Erikson,* ed. Peter Homans, (Lewisburg, Pa: Bucknell University Press, 1978), 13–53, 32; and Gerald Holton, "Introduction," in Holton, ed., *The Twentieth-Century Sciences,* vii–xix; vi. For "guru" see Alan L. Chaikin, review of *Life History and the Historical Moment* by Erik H. Erikson [unknown source; found as in "Clippings and Reviews of *Life History and the Historical Moment* circa 1975, Item 1552, Erikson Hrvd. Pprs]. For "innovator" see David Gutmann, "Erik Erikson's America," *Commentary* 58, no. 3 (September 1974): 60–64. Steven Weiland, "Erik H. Erikson on America: *Childhood and Society* and National Identity," in *Intellectual Craftsmen: Ways and Works in American Scholarship, 1935–1990,* ed. Steven Weiland (New Brunswick, N.J.: Transaction Publishers, 1991), 41–66; 62. For "revisionist" see Paul Roazen, *Erik H. Erikson: The Power and Limits of a Vision* (New York: Free Press, 1976), 64; Robert F. Massey, "Erik Erikson: Neo-Adlerian," *Individual Psychology Journal of Adlerian Theory, Research and Practice* 42, no. 1, (1986) 65–91; 66. For "extender" see Robert Holt, review of *Childhood and Society* by Erik H. Erikson, *Journal of Personality,* 21, no. 1 (September 1952), 149–153, 153; Patrick H. Hutton, "The Psychohistory of Erik Erikson from the Perspective of Collective Mentalities," *Psychohistory Review* 12, no. 1 (Fall 1983), 18–25; 20 and Peter Homans, "The Significance of Erikson's Psychology for Modern Understandings of Religion," in Homans, *Childhood and Selfhood,* 231–263; 236. For "refiner" see Steven Weiland, "Jefferson and Erikson, Politics and the Life Cycle," *Biography* 9 (Fall 1986), 290–305; 291. For "genius," see Robert S. Wallerstein, "Erik H. Erikson, 1902–1994: Setting the Context," in Wallerstein and Goldberger, ed. *Ideas and Identities,* 1–31; 11. For "imaginative reach" see Robert Jay Lifton, "Entering History," 100.

21. For Erikson's contributions of a new viewpoint, see Paul Roazen, *Erik H. Erikson: The Power and Limits of a Vision;* for creating a "yawning gap," see Daniel Yankelovich and William Barrett, *Ego and Instinct: The Psychoanalytic View of Human Nature—Revised* (New York: Random House, 1970), 121.

22. In the literature, reviewers who consider Erikson a Freudian "loyalist" or "centrist" are approximately one third the number of those who see him as a Freudian revisionist or as a trans- or post-Freudian. For his movement beyond the doctrinaire, see Roazen, "Erik H. Erikson's America"; for his role as a synthesizer and integrator, see Neil S. Smelser, "Erik Erikson as Social Scientist," in Wallerstein and Goldberger, eds. *Ideas and Identities;* Stephen Seligman and Rebecca S. Shanok, "Erikson, Our Contemporary: His Anticipation of an Intersubjective Perspective," in Wallerstein and Goldberger, eds., *Ideas and Identities,* 325–351; and Lewis D. Wurgaft, "Erik Erikson: From Luther to Gandhi," *Psychoanalytic Review* 63, no. 2 (Summer 1976): 209–233.

23. For his nonreductionistic stance, see Michael R. Levenson and Cheryl A. Crumpler, "Three Models of Adult Development," *Human Development* 39 (1996): 135–149; Lewis Lipsitz and Herbert M. Kritzer, "Unconventional Approaches to Conflict Resolution: Erikson and Sharp on Nonviolence," *Journal of Conflict Resolution* 19, no. 4 (December 1975): 713–733; and Joel Kovel, "Erik Erikson's Psychohistory," *Social Policy* 24 (March–April 1974), 60–64. For Erikson's role in distinguishing between anxiety and the normal difficulties of life, see Yankelovich and Barrett, *Ego and Instinct.*

24. For his "independent vision," see Seligman and Shanok, "Erikson, Our Contemporary," 325; for his domination of the field and "field's limitations," see Jerome C. Wakefield, "Immortality and the Externalization of the Self: Plato's

Unrecognized Theory of Generativity," in *Generativity and Adult Development,* ed. Dan P. McAdams and Ed de St. Aubin (Washington, D.C.: American Psychological Association, 1998), 133–174; 134.

25. Steven Weiland, "Jefferson and Erikson, Politics and the Life Cycle," *Biography* 9 (Fall 1986), 290–305.

26. David Elkind, "Erik Erikson's Eight Ages of Man," *The New York Times Magazine,* 5 April 1970, sec. 6.

27. See Don S. Browning, *Generative Man: Psychoanalytic Perspectives* (Philadelphia, Pa.: Westminster Press, 1973).

28. Lipsitz and Kritzer, "Unconventional Approaches to Conflict Resolution."

29. Levinson, *The Seasons of a Man's Life;* George E. Vaillant, *Adaptation to Life* (Boston, Mass.: Little, Brown, 1977); George E. Vaillant, *The Wisdom of the Ego* (Cambridge, Mass.: Harvard University Press, 1993); George E. Vaillant and Eva Milofsky, "Natural History of Male Psychological Health: IX. Empirical Evidence for Erikson's Model of the Life Cycle," *American Journal of Psychiatry* 137, no. 11 (November 1980): 1348–1359; and Roger L. Gould, "The Phases of Adult Life: A Study in Developmental Psychology," *American Journal of Psychiatry* 129 (1972): 521–531; Roger L. Gould, *Transformations: Growth and Change in Adult Life* (New York: Simon and Schuster, 1978).

30. For stages of wisdom, see Vivian Clayton, "Erikson's Theory of Human Development as It Applies to the Aged: Wisdom as Contradictive Cognition," *Human Development* 18 (1975): 119–128. For transcendent stages of old age, see Robert C. Peck, "Psychological Developments in the Second Half of Life," in *Middle Age and Aging: A Reader in Social Psychology,* ed. Bernice L. Neugarten (Chicago, Ill.: University of Chicago Press, 1968), 88–92. For substages of intimacy, see George W. Goethals and Dennis S. Klos, *Experiencing Youth* (Boston, Mass.: Little, Brown, 1976). For stages of ego development, see Jane Loevinger, *Ego Development* (San Francisco: Jossey-Bass, 1976). For stages of identity development, see James E. Marcia, "Development and Validation of Ego Identity Statuses," *Journal of Personality and Social Psychology* 3 (1966): 551–558.

31. For stages of faith, see *Stages of Faith and Religious Development: Implications for Church, Education, and Society* ed. James W. Fowler, Karl E. Nipkow, and Friedrich Schweitzer (New York: Crossroad, 1991). For variations on Erikson's concept of generativity, see John Kotre, *Outliving the Self: Generativity and the Interpretation of Lives* (Baltimore, Md.: Johns Hopkins University Press, 1984), and Browning, *Generative Man.*

32. Carol Gilligan, *In a Different Voice* (Cambridge, Mass.: Harvard University Press, 1982).

33. Edmund Bourne, "The State of Research on Ego Identity: A Review and Appraisal. Part I." *Journal of Youth and Adolescence* 7, no. 3 (1978): 223–251.

34. Yankelovich and Barrett, *Ego and Instinct.*

35. Schlein, interview by author. See, for example, Seligman and Shanok, "Erikson, Our Contemporary" and Heinz Lichtenstein, *The Dilemma of Human Identity* (New York: Aronson, 1983).

36. Friedman, "Erik H. Erikson's Critical Themes and Voices."

37. Robert M. Crunden, "Freud, Erikson, and the Historian: A Bibliographical Survey," *Canadian Review of American Studies* 4, no. 1 (Spring, 1973): 48–64.

38. See Friedman, "Erik H. Erikson's Critical Themes and Voices"; Paul Roazen, "Erik H. Erikson as a Teacher," *Michigan Quarterly Review* 31, no. 1 (Winter, 1992): 19–33.

39. For Erikson's disinterest in systematizing his thought, see Rebecca S. Shanok, "Towards an Inclusive Adult Developmental Theory: Epigenesis Reconsidered," in *The Course of Life, Vol. 6, Late Adulthood* ed. George H. Pollock

and Stanley I. Greenspan (Madison, Conn.: International Universities Press, 1993), 243–259. For Erikson's disenchantment with psychoanalytic theory in general, see Friedman, "Erik H. Erikson's Critical Themes and Voices."

40. Marcia Cavell, "Erik Erikson and the Temporal Mind," in Wallerstein and Goldberger, eds., *Ideas and Identities,* 33–47, 33.

41. Erik H. Erikson, "The Problem of Ego Identity," *Journal of the American Psychoanalytic Association,* 4 (1956): 56–121; Erik H. Erikson, "Reflections on the Dissent of Contemporary Youth," *Daedalus* 97, no. 1 (Winter 1970): 154–176.

42. Wurgaft also noted the differences in Erikson's uses of analytic distinctions in *Young Man Luther* compared with *Gandhi's Truth.* See Lewis D. Wurgaft, "Erik Erikson: From Luther to Gandhi," *Psychoanalytic Review* 63, no. 2 (Summer 1976), 209–233.

43. John Bowlby, *Attachment,* Vol I. of *Attachment and Loss* (New York: Basic Books: 1969); Mary D. Ainsworth, "Attachment and Dependency: A Comparison," in *Attachment and Dependency* ed. J. L. Gewirtz (Washington, D.C.: Winston, 1972); Jaques, "Death and the Mid-life Crisis."

44. See Howard A. Bacal and Kenneth M. Newman, *Theories of Object Relations: Bridges to Self Psychology* (New York: Columbia University Press, 1990); Heinz Kohut, *The Analysis of the Self: A Systematic Approach to the Psychoanalytic Treatment of Narcissistic Personality Disorders* (New York: International Universities Press, 1971); Heinz Kohut, *The Restoration of the Self* (New York: International Universities Press, 1977); Heinz Kohut, *How Does Analysis Cure?* (Chicago, Ill: University of Chicago Press, 1984).

45. Lichtenstein, *The Dilemma of Human Identity*; A. H. Modell, *Object Love and Reality: An Introduction to a Psychoanalytic Theory of Object Relations* (New York: International Universities Press, 1968).

46. Wallerstein, "Erikson's Concept of Ego Identity Reconsidered."

47. See Arnold H. Modell, *Object Love and Reality: An Introduction to a Psychoanalytic Theory of Object Relations.* (New York: International Universities Press, 1968); Arnold H. Modell, *Psychoanalysis in a New Context* (New York: International Universities Press, 1984); Arnold H. Modell, *Other Times, Other Realities: Toward a Theory of Psychoanalytic Treatment* (Cambridge, Mass.. Harvard University Press, 1990); Arnold H. Modell, *The Private Self* (Cambridge, Mass.: Harvard University Press, 1993).

48. Robert S. Wallerstein, "Erik H. Erikson, 1902–1994: Setting the Context," in Wallerstein and Goldberger, eds., *Ideas and Identities,* 1–31; 21.

49. See Elkind, "Erik Erikson's Eight Ages of Man."

50. Ibid.

51. See George E. Vaillant, *Ego Mechanisms of Defense* (Washington, D.C.: American Psychiatric Association Press, 1992).

52. For "suspicion," see Margaret Brenman-Gibson, *Clifford Odets: American Playwright* (New York: Atheneum, 1981), xiii. For "limbo," see Wallerstein, "Setting the Context," 21.

53. Ess White, Jr., interview by author, Stockbridge, Mass., 23 August 1994.

54. For "painterly prose," see Seligman and Shanok, "Erikson, Our Contemporary," 340.

55. See, for example, Roazen, *Erik H. Erikson: The Power and Limits of a Vision*; Novak, "Biography After the End of Metaphysics."

56. Yankelovich and Barrett, *Ego and Instinct,* 141.

57. See, for example, Robert F. Massey, "Erik Erikson: Neo-Adlerian," *Individual Psychology Journal of Adlerian Theory, Research and Practice* 42, no. 1, (1986), 65–91; *Explorations in Psychohistory: The Wellfleet Papers,* ed. Robert J. Lifton (New York: Simon and Schuster, 1974); Phyllis Tyson and Robert L.

Tyson, *Psychoanalytic Theories of Development: An Integration* (New Haven, Conn.: Yale University Press, 1990).

58. See, for example, Seligman and Shanok, "Erikson, Our Contemporary."

59. See, e.g., Yankelovich and Barrett, *Ego and Instinct.*

60. Ibid., 434.

61. See, for example, Ed de St. Aubin, "Truth Against the World: A Psychobiographical Exploration of Generativity in the Life of Frank Lloyd Wright," in *Generativity and Adult Development,* ed. Dan P. McAdams and Ed De St. Aubin, 391–427.

62. See, for example, Roazen, *The Power and Limits of a Vision*; Smelser, "Erik Erikson as Social Scientist."

63. Robert J. Lifton, *The Protean Self* (New York: Basic Books, 1993).

64. See Erikson, *Toys and Reasons.*

65. See, for example, Harry J. S. Guntrip, *Psychoanalytic Theory, Therapy, and the Self* (New York: Basic Books, 1971); Robert Simmermon and Karen M. Schwartz, "Adult Development and Psychotherapy: Bridging the Gap Between Theory and Practice," *Psychotherapy* 23, no. 3 (Fall 1986), 405–410; and Coles, *Erik H. Erikson: The Growth of His Work.*

66. David Lipset, "The Missing Identity Crisis," *The New Leader,* 21 July 1975, 25–26; Robert Coles, *The Mind's Fate: A Psychiatrist Looks at His Profession,* 2d ed. (Boston, Mass.: Little, Brown, 1995). See the introduction.

67. Coles, *The Mind's Fate,* introduction to the second edition, xiv.

68. John Snarey, "Ego Development and the Ethical Voices of Justice and Care: An Eriksonian Interpretation," in *Personality Development: Theoretical, Empirical, and Clinical Investigations of Loevinger's Conception of Ego Development,* ed. P. Michiel Westenberg, Augusto Blasi, and Lawrence D. Cohn, (Mahwah, N.J.: Erlbaum, 1998), 163–180; 164.

69. See also Guntrip, *Psychoanalytic Theory, Therapy, and the Self,* 86.

70. See also John J. Fitzpatrick, "Erik H. Erikson and Psychohistory," *Bulletin of the Menninger Clinic* 40, no. 4 (July 1976), 295–314.

71. Erikson, "The Syndrome of Identity Diffusion in Adolescents and Young Adults."

72. Waud H. Kracke, "A Psychoanalyst in the Field: Erikson's Contributions to Anthropology," in Homans, ed., *Childhood and Selfhood,* 147–188; 151.

73. Yankelovich and Barrett, *Ego and Instinct,* 323–324.

74. David Gutmann, interview by author, Chicago, Ill., 21 August 1995. See also David Gutmann, "Erik Erikson's America," 60–64; and Kovel, "Erik Erikson's Psychohistory."

75. No author given, "Erik Erikson: The Quest for Identity," *Newsweek,* 21 December 1970, 84–89; 86.

76. See Kotre, *Outliving the Self*; Seligman and Shanok, "Subjectivity, Complexity and the Social World."

77. See Hutton, "The Psychohistory of Erik Erikson from the Perspective of Collective Mentalities"; Kotre, *Outliving the Self*; Weiland, "Intellectual Craftsmen."

78. Sylvia Brody, review of *Childhood and Society* by Erik H. Erikson [unknown source; found in "Clippings and Reviews of *Childhood and Society,*" circa 1950–1951, Item 1481, Erikson Hrvd. Pprs.

79. Writing to Margaret Mead about his book on Martin Luther, Erikson said "I got a lot off my chest, more than I knew was on it." Erikson to Mead, 13 September 1957, Container B-4, Mead Papers.

80. Erikson Institute, Item 1358.

81. Erikson, *Young Man Luther,* 94.

82. Ibid., 128.

83. Ibid., 131.

84. Erikson Institute, Item 1358.

85. "We can only sketch," Erikson, *Young Man Luther,* 222; "we can only outline what we are reasonably competent to perceive," ibid., 225.

86. "Utterly undogmatic religious person," Erikson, *Gandhi's Truth,* 110; "straight and yet not stiff; shy and yet not withdrawn . . . willful and yet not stubborn," ibid., 113; "in his presence *one could not tell a lie,*" ibid., 63.

87. "Delighted to be arrested" and "he never felt happy in making life harder for others," ibid., 388.

88. "To have been almost anxiously eager to know," ibid., 405; "a teased government . . . becomes brutal until it learns to respond parsimoniously to a new weapon," ibid., 210.

89. See, for example, Heinrich Bornkamm, "Luther and His Father: Observations on Erik H. Erikson's *Young Man Luther: A Study in Psychoanalysis and History,*" in Homans, ed., *Childhood and Selfhood,* 59–88.

90. Coles, *Erik H. Erikson: The Growth of His Work,* 162.

91. Evans, *Dialogue with Erik Erikson,* 30.

92. Hall, "A Conversation with Erik Erikson," 27.

93. See, for example, Roazen, "Erik Erikson as a Teacher."

94. See, for example, Mary Austin Doherty, "Sexual Bias in Personality Theory," in *Counseling Women,* ed. L. W. Harmon, J. M. Birk, L. E. Fitzgerald, and M. F. Tanney, (Monterey, Calif.: BrooksCole, 1978) 94–105; Wallerstein, "Setting the Context"; John Snarey and Peter Y. Clark, "A Generative Drama: Scenes From a Father-Son Relationship," in McAdams and de St. Aubin, ed., *Generativity and Adult Development,* 45–74; Vaillant, *The Wisdom of the Ego;* and Elkind, "Erik Erikson's Eight Ages of Man."

95. See, for example, Yankelovich and Barrett, *Ego and Instinct;* Novak, "Biography After the End of Metaphysics"; Wallerstein, "Erik H. Erikson, 1902–1994: Setting the Context;" Vaillant, *The Wisdom of the Ego;* Seligman and Shanok, "Erikson, Our Contemporary"; Elizabeth Douvan, "Erik Erikson: Critical Times, Critical Theory," *Child Psychiatry and Human Development* 28, no. 1 (Fall 1997): 15–21; Dana L. Farnsworth, review of *Life History and the Historical Moment* by Erik H. Erikson, *American Journal of Psychiatry* 132 (October 1975): 1089–1090; Elkind, "Erik Erikson's Eight Ages of Man"; Patrick H. Hutton, "The Psychohistory of Erik Erikson from the Perspective of Collective Mentalities," *Psychohistory Review* 12, no. 1 (Fall 1983): 18–25; and Geoffrey Garwick, review of *Life History and the Historical Moment* by Erik H. Erikson, *Minnesota Daily,* 17 June 1975. [page unknown; found in item 1552].

96. See, for example, Yankelovich and Barrett, *Ego and Instinct;* Browning, *Generative Man;* Seligman and Shanok, "Erikson, Our Contemporary"; and Levenson and Crumpler, "Three Models of Adult Development."

97. Seligman and Shanok, "Erikson, Our Contemporary," 329.

98. See, for example, Edmund Bourne, "The State of Research on Ego Identity: A Review and Appraisal. Part 2. *Journal of Youth and Adolescence* 7, no. 4 (1978): 371–392; Richard D. Logan, "A Reconceptualization of Erikson's Theory: The Repetition of Existential and Instrumental Themes," *Human Development* 29 (1986), 125–136; and Seligman and Shanok, "Erikson, Our Contemporary."

99. Gutmann, "Erik Erikson's America"; Wurgaft, "Erik Erikson: From Luther to Gandhi"; Roazen, *The Power and Limits of a Vision;* Carol E. Franz and Kathleen M. White, "Individuation and Attachment in Personality Development: Extending Erikson's Theory," *Journal of Personality* 53 (June 1985): 224–256; Lipsitz and Kritzer, "Unconventional Approaches to Conflict Resolu-

tion"; Edith Jacobson, *The Self and the Object World* (New York: International Universities Press, 1964).

100. See, for example, Crunden, "Freud, Erikson, and the Historian"; Peter Homans, "Introduction," in Homans, ed., *Childhood and Selfhood*, 13–54; Fitzpatrick, "Erik H. Erikson and Psychohistory."

101. Sudhir Kakar, review of *Gandhi's Truth* by Erik H. Erikson, *Journal of Interdisciplinary History* 1, no. 1 (Autumn 1970): 187–194; 194.

102. See, for example, Steven Weiland, "Erik H. Erikson on America: *Childhood and Society* and National Identity," in *Intellectual Craftsmen: Ways and Works in American Scholarship, 1935–1990*, ed. S. Weiland (New Brunswick, N.J.: Transaction, 1991), 41–66.

103. See, for example, Coles, *Erik H. Erikson: The Growth of His Work*; Kakar, review of *Gandhi's Truth*.

104. See Erikson, *Toys and Reasons*; Browning, *Generative Man*.

105. Erikson to Curfman, 30 December 1976, Item 811, Erikson Hrvd. Pprs.

106. Yankelovich and Barrett, *Ego and Instinct*.

107. Erikson, *Young Man Luther*, 183.

108. Zock, *A Psychology of Ultimate Concern*, 207.

109. See Erikson, *Young Man Luther*, 10.

110. Erik H. Erikson, "Peter Blos: Reminiscences," in Schlein, ed., *A Way of Looking at Things*, 709–712; 710. First published in *Psychosocial Process* 3, no. 2 (Fall 1974): 4–7.

111. For "prescribing" see Wright, *Erikson: Identity and Religion*, 212. For "ethicist" see Don Browning, "Erikson and the Search for a Normative Image of Man," in *Childhood and Selfhood*; Browning, *Generative Man*, 12, and Homans, ed., 264–292; 265. For "moralizing" see Kovel, "Erik Erikson's Psychohistory," 60; Frederick Crews, review of *Life History and the Historical Moment* by Erik H. Erikson, *The New York Review*, of Books, 16 October 1975, 9–15, 10; and Marshall Berman, review of *Life History and the Historical Moment* by Erik Erikson, *The New York Times Book Review* 30 March 1975, Sec. 7. For "preaching," see Roazen, "Psychology and Politics," 585; Roazen, *The Power and Limits of a Vision*, 171; Kovel, "Erik Erikson's Psychohistory," 62; and William G. Domhoff, "Two Luthers: The Traditional and the Heretical in Freudian Psychology," *Psychoanalytic Review* 57, no. 1 (July, 1970), 15–17, 25. For "haranguing" see Kovel, "Erik Erikson's Psychohistory," 60.

112. Erik H. Erikson, "Reality and Actuality," *Journal of the American Psychoanalytic Association* 10 (1962), 451–473; 472.

113. Erikson, "Lifecycle and Community" [unpublished manuscript], undated, Item 95M-2, Erikson Hrvd. Pprs.

114. Erikson, *Dimensions of a New Identity*, 32.

115. Ibid., 41.

116. Frederick Crews, review of *Life History and the Historical Moment*.

117. Gutmann, "Erik Erikson's America," 60.

118. Ibid.

119. Ibid.

120. See David L. Gutmann, "Towards a Dynamic Geropsychology," in *Interface of Psychoanalysis and Psychology*, ed. James W. Barron, Morris N. Eagle, and David L. Wolitzky (Washington, D.C.: American Psychological Association, 1992), 284–296.

121. "Reflections on Dr. Borg's life cycle; Miscellaneous notes," undated, Item 1711, Erikson Hrvd. Pprs.

122. Coles, *Erik H. Erikson: The Growth of His Work*.

123. Kovel, "Erik Erikson's Psychohistory," 60.

124. Erikson, *Young Man Luther*, 153.

125. Gutmann, "Erik Erikson's America," 61.

126. Any efforts to clarify and explain are, necessarily, distillations. This book is a case in point even though every effort was made to avoid reducing Erikson's concepts.

127. Peter Blos to Erikson, 15 January 1978, Item 60, Erikson Hrvd. Pprs.

128. For elaborations of this point, see Zock, *A Psychology of Ultimate Concern*, and Lifton, *Explorations in Psychohistory.*

129. See Smelser, *The Social Edges of Psychoanalysis*, and Cracca, "A Psychoanalyst in the Field."

130. See Kotre, *Outliving the Self.*

131. Matilda White Riley, "Aging, Social Change, and the Power of Ideas," *Daedalus* 107, no. 4 (1978): 39–52.

132. Erikson, *Young Man Luther,* 22.

133. For Erikson's philosophical writing, see Roazen, *The Power and Limits of a Vision*, and Wright, *Erikson: Identity and Religion.*

134. For Erikson as a phenomenologist, see Rosemary Dianage, "Truly Leaping," review of *Toys and Reasons* by Erik Erikson, *Times Literary Supplement*, 24 February 1978; Berman, review of *Life History and the Historical Moment.*

135. Yankelovich and Barrett, *Ego and Instinct.*

136. Steven Weiland, "Psychoanalysis without Words: Erik H. Erikson's American Apprenticeship," *Michigan Quarterly Review* 31 (Winter 1992):, 1–18.

137. J. S. Nevi, "An Indian Psychiatrist Examines Erikson's View of Gandhi," *Roche Reports: Frontiers of Psychiatry* [unknown date and pages; found in item 1504]; Coles, *Erik H. Erikson: The Growth of His Work.*

138. Marshall Edelson, *Hypothesis and Evidence in Psychoanalysis* (Chicago, Ill: University of Chicago Press, 1984), 34.

139. See, for example, P. Cushman, "Why the Self Is Empty: Toward a Historically Situated Psychology," *American Psychologist* 45 (1990): 599–611; I. Z. Hoffman, "The Patient as Interpreter of the Analyst's Experience," *Contemporary Psychoanalysis* 19 (1983): 389–422; R. Stolorow and G. Atwood. *Contexts of Being* (Hillsdale, N.J.: Analytic Press, 1992); and Seligman and Shanok, "Subjectivity, Complexity and the Social World."

140. Kakar, review of *Gandhi's Truth.*

141. Edelson, *Hypothesis and Evidence in Psychoanalysis*, xiii.

142. R. L. Schnell, "Contributions to Psychohistory: IV. Individual Experience in Historiography and Psychoanalysis: Significance of Erik Erikson and Robert Coles," *Psychological Reports* 46, no. 2 (1980): 591–612; 594.

143. For "success ideology" see Vaillant, *The Wisdom of the Ego*, 174. For "romanticization" see Roazen, *The Power and Limits of a Vision*, 127.

144. Roazen, *The Power and Limits of a Vision,* 49.

145. Roazen, "Psychology and Politics," 582.

146. Erik H. Erikson and Joan M. Erikson, "On Generativity and Identity: From a Conversation with Erik and Joan Erikson," *Harvard Educational Review* 51, no. 2 (May 1981): 249–269; 259.

147. Stephen Schlein, "Editor's Preface," in *A Way of Looking at Things*, xix–xxvi; xxv.

148. Roazen, *The Power and Limits of a Vision*, 171.

149. Peter Heller, interview by author, Williamsville, New York, 13 December 1994.

150. Hale, "From Berggasse XIX to Central Park West."

151. B. R. Slugoski and G. P. Ginsburg, "Ego Identity and Explanatory Speech," in *Texts of Identity*, ed. John Shotter and Kenneth J. Gergen (Newbury Park, CA: Sage Publications, 1989), 36–55, 38.

152. Maria W. Piers and Carla Berry, review of *Life History and the Historical Moment* by Erik H. Erikson, *Chicago Sun Times* [date and page unknown; copy found in item 1552].

153. "Planning Conference on the Adult," 18–19 September 1971, Item 1516, Erikson Hrvd. Pprs.

154. Crews, review of *Life History and the Historical Moment*, p. 13.

155. Frank E. Manuel and Fritzie P. Manuel, *Utopian Thought in the Western World* (Cambridge, Mass.: Harvard University Press, 1979). The authors allude to Erikson in writing about stages and utopianism but do not name him as such. For the association of utopian thought with the "nostalgic mode," see p. 5. See Erikson, *Childhood and Society*, 1950, in which he wrote of the "nostalgia for familiar images undamaged by change" (p. 220).

156. Hoare, "Ethical Self, Spiritual Self: Wisdom and Integrity in the Writings of Erik H. Erikson."

157. For "edifying" see Coles, *Erik H. Erikson: The Growth of His Work*, xvi. For "testament to moral courage" see Walter H. Capps, "Erik Erikson's Contribution Toward Understanding Religion," in Wallerstein and Goldberger, eds., *Ideas and Identities*, 67–78; 76.

158. Erikson, *Identity: Youth and Crisis*.

159. See the directory to the Erikson Papers, The Houghton Library of Harvard University, 1987. The composition section, Section VI, runs from Item 1476 through Item 1744.

160. Many empirical studies designed to replicate Erikson's findings about gender differences have not borne out his findings.

161. Gilligan, *In a Different Voice*. See also Nancy Chadorow, *The Reproduction of Mothering* (Berkeley, Calif: University of California Press, 1978).

162. Evans, *Dialogue with Erik Erikson*, 43.

163. For "male-dominated heritage" see Wright, *Erikson: Identity and Religion*, xv. For his role not as "anti-feminist" but as an "advocate" of a "more 'feminized' world," see Piers and Berry, review of *Life History and the Historical Moment*.

164. Erikson, *Gandhi's Truth*, 252.

165. Erikson, *Identity: Youth and Crisis*, 262.

166. "To Take or Not to Take an Oath," spring 1972, Item 1529, Erikson Hrvd. Pprs.

167. "Further Thoughts on Freud–Jung," undated, Item 1675, Erikson Hrvd. Pprs.

168. Erikson, *Insight and Responsibility*, 106.

169. "White House Remarks made at staff dinner discussing whether universities with disorders should be punished with a withdrawal of funds," 11 June 1969, Item 1502, Erikson Hrvd. Pprs.

170. Erikson to Margaret Mead, 16 July 1959, Item 1130, Erikson Hrvd. Pprs.

171. "Inner and outer space: Reflections on womanhood," undated, Item 1494, Erikson Hrvd. Pprs. The article was published in *Daedalus*, 2 (Spring, 1964): 582–606.

172. Erikson to Kurt von Fritz, 20 December 1976, Item 1347, Erikson Hrvd. Pprs.

173. Ibid.

Index